FROMMER'S

FAMILY TRAVEL GUIDE

LOS ANGELES WITH KIDS

W9-CMH-482

by Carey Simon and
Charlene Marmer Solomon

PRENTICE HALL TRAVEL

NEW YORK • LONDON • TORONTO • SYDNEY • TOKYO • SINGAPORE

This book is dedicated to Janey, who didn't have to go anywhere on an airplane this time, and to Danny, who just had to listen.

—C.S.

To Alan, Andrew, and Elizabeth and all the adventures we have yet to share.

—C.M.S.

FROMMER BOOKS

Published by Prentice Hall General Reference
A division of Simon & Schuster Inc.
15 Columbus Circle
New York, NY 10023

ISBN 0-13-333337-X
ISSN 1058-496X

Design by Robert Bull Design
Maps by Geografix Inc. of New York

Manufactured in the United States of America

FROMMER'S LOS ANGELES WITH KIDS '92-'93

Editor-in-Chief: Marilyn Wood
Senior Editors: Judith de Rubini, Pamela Marshall, Amit Shah
Editors: Alice Fellows, Paige Hughes, Theodore Stavrou
Assistant Editors: Suzanne Arkin, Peter Katucki, Lisa Renaud, Ellen Zucker
Managing Editor: Leanne Coupe

CONTENTS

LIST OF MAPS

ACKNOWLEDGMENTS

This book was a natural outgrowth of our *Frommer's California with Kids*. We were excited to have the chance to write a book that would focus on one particular area of the state, affording us the opportunity to include lots of interesting new things appropriate to all age groups.

Writing books like this one, and our new *Frommer's San Francisco with Kids*, takes the assistance and support of lots of people.

My personal thanks again go to Helen Hawekotte and Joe Stewart, and to Magdalena Diaz Velasquez, without whom I could never finish any writing project. I am also delighted I could once again work with such a talented writing partner. **—C.S.**

Thank you to Sam Greengard and Shirley Solomon for being such good friends, and to Terry Paule and Michelle Cutrow for understanding a writer's temperament. To Carey: Here's to years of family travel.**—C.M.S.**

OUR THANKS GO TO: Among the scores of people who supported our efforts on this book, we would especially like to thank Marilyn Wood and Judith de Rubini at Prentice Hall. Special thanks go also to Margaret Basalone, Jody Welborn, and Pooky Garthoff.

We won't forget the continuing assistance of Fred Sater of the California Office of Tourism, and the support of Gary Sherwin of the Los Angeles Convention and Visitors Bureau. Thanks, too, to the many other helpful people in the convention and visitors bureaus in Southern California, including Elaine Cali and Barbara McClelland (Anaheim), Laurie Smith (Palm Springs), and Tami Bissell (Long Beach).

INVITATION TO THE READERS

In researching this book, we have come across many wonderful establishments, the best of which we have included here. We are sure that many of you will also come across family-friendly hotels, inns, restaurants, guesthouses, shops, and attractions. Please don't keep them to yourself. Share your experiences, especially if you want to comment on places that have been included in this edition that have changed for the worse. You can address your letters to:

Carey Simon & Charlene Marmer Solomon
Frommer's Los Angeles with Kids '92–'93
c/o Prentice Hall Press
Travel Books
15 Columbus Circle
New York, NY 10023

A DISCLAIMER

Readers are advised that prices fluctuate in the course of time and travel information changes under the impact of the varied and volatile factors that affect the travel industry. Neither the authors nor the publisher can be held responsible for the experiences of readers while traveling. Readers are invited to write to the publisher with ideas, comments, and suggestions for future editions.

SAFETY ADVISORY

Whenever you're traveling in an unfamiliar city or country, stay alert. Be aware of your immediate surroundings. Wear a moneybelt and keep a close eye on your possessions. Be particularly careful with cameras, purses, and wallets, all favorite targets of thieves and pickpockets.

PLANNING A FAMILY TRIP TO LOS ANGELES

Los Angeles has lots of kid appeal. Just tell your kids you're planning a trip to Los Angeles and watch their eyes grow huge with excitement. The older ones might first think of movie stars and rock bands. The little ones will want to see Mickey Mouse right away. But there's more to a trip to L.A. than glitter and glamour and larger-than-life cartoon characters. There's the opportunity to play tag with ocean waves or take a dip in a hotel pool on a warm California night. The desert is nearby, ripe for exploring, and downhill skiing is only a couple of hours away. Outdoor adventures abound, from hiking to the top of a ridge for a look at the never-ending Pacific Ocean to renting a convertible and "cruising" Rodeo Drive with the top down—in December. You can take the family to a wealth of museums and still have time to attend a TV taping.

Yes, Los Angeles has kid appeal—but it has adult appeal too.

1. TOURIST INFORMATION

Before you leave, we suggest that you write the **Greater Los Angeles Convention and Visitors Bureau,** 515 South Figueroa Street, 11th Floor, Los Angeles, CA 90071, to ask for maps and brochures.

Once you arrive, you'll want to contact the **Los Angeles Visitors Information Center,** 695 South Figueroa Street, between Wilshire Boulevard and 7th Street, Los Angeles (tel. 213/689-8822), open Monday through Saturday from 8am to 5pm. There is also another **information center** in Hollywood at the Janes House, Janes House Square, 6541 Hollywood Boulevard, near Vine Street (tel. 213/461-4213), open Monday through Saturday from 9am to 5pm.

The Visitors Bureau and the information centers will help make your visit a memorable experience. They've had lots of practice: Last year alone, over 60 million visitors came to the Greater Los Angeles area. The tourist bureau staff know that the sprawling metropolis can at first seem impossible to master; you'll find them very helpful.

WHAT THINGS COST IN LOS ANGELES	U.S. $
Taxi from the airport to downtown L.A.	22.00–27.00
Shuttle bus from the airport to downtown L.A.	11.00
Local telephone call	.20
Double room at the Four Seasons (very expensive)	250.00
Double room at the Sheraton Universal (expensive)	170.00
Double room at the Holiday Inn Westwood (moderate)	130.00
Double room at the Travelodge (budget)	65.00
Lunch for one adult at the Cheesecake Factory (moderate)	10.00
Lunch for one child at the Cheesecake Factory (moderate)	4.50
Lunch for one adult at Carney's (budget)	3.50
Lunch for one child at Carney's (budget)	2.50
Dinner for one adult at Lawry's (expensive)	30.00
Dinner for one child at Lawry's (expensive)	13.00
Dinner for one adult at Hard Rock Café (moderate)	12.00
Dinner for one child at Hard Rock Café (moderate)	3.00
Dinner for one adult at Ed Debevic's (budget)	7.00
Dinner for one child at Ed Debevic's (budget)	3.50
Taco	1.25
Coca-Cola	1.25
Ice-cream cone	1.50
Roll of ASA 100 Kodacolor film, 36 exposures	5.50
Admission to Universal Studios Hollywood	
Adult	22.00
Child	16.50
Movie ticket	
Adult	6.50
Child	3.25
Theater ticket (orchestra seat at the Music Center)	30.00–50.00

2. WHEN TO GO

THE CLIMATE The Los Angeles climate is wonderful year round. True, people talk about smog, and it is a consideration when you want to do something active, but more important is the pleasure and ease of a reliably pleasant 70° to 85° Fahrenheit day with low humidity. Angelenos do take it for granted and rain does throw them into a tizzy. Even night and morning low clouds (common in the late spring and early summer) are met with grumbles. If you're coming strictly for sun worshipping, you should know that May and June bring hazy, foggy mornings, and it's not until afternoon that the sun breaks through. L.A.'s real summer is July through September. But few activities will need to be canceled or postponed because of weather.

KIDS' FAVORITE EVENTS

JANUARY

⊙ *THE INTERNATIONAL CHILDREN'S FILM FESTIVAL* Little Meryl Streeps and burgeoning Steven Spielbergs—ages 4 and up—can watch everything from short films to full-length features from around the world.
   Where: Barnsdall Art Park's Gallery Theatre in Hollywood. *When:* January. *How:* Call 213/485-4474 for further information on this year's screening schedule. Tickets and parking are free.

⊙ *OSHOGATSU* The Japanese New Year Celebration introduces children of all ages to traditional Japanese foods, ceremonies, and art.
   Where: Japanese American Cultural & Community Center, downtown Los Angeles. *When:* The first weekend in January. *How:* Call 213/628-2725 for details.

⊙ *TOURNAMENT OF ROSES PARADE* The year begins with the startling colors and exotic perfumes of millions of flowers used to make the floats for this world-renowned event. Families camp out for curbside viewing or reserve seats in the grandstand nearly a year in advance. Alternatively, come by to see the floats after the parade. (See Section 1, "Pasadena," in Chapter 9 for more details.)
   Where: Pasadena. *When:* January 1. *How:* Phone 818/449-ROSE year round for information on the parade and reserving grandstand seats.

FEBRUARY

☐ **Chinese New Year,** downtown Los Angeles's Chinatown. The Golden Dragon Parade is a particularly popular event. Call 213/617-0396 for this year's date.

MARCH

⊙ *AMERICAN INDIAN FESTIVAL & MARKET* The festival has entertained and educated families for almost 20 years. In addition to showcasing Native American arts and crafts and traditional foods, there are dance performances and a children's program that usually includes storytelling and films.

Where: Los Angeles Natural History Museum, in Exposition Park. *When:* March. *How:* Call 213/744-3314 for this year's dates and details. Festival tickets are included in the price of admission to the museum: $3 for adults, $1.50 for children 12 to 17 and seniors, 75¢ for kids 5 to 12; under 5, free.

APRIL

✪ *RENAISSANCE PLEASURE FAIRE* This reenactment of a centuries-old English rural faire is loved by children of all ages. Actors parade through the crowd in authentic costumes speaking the queen's English of yore. Authentic food, games, fire-eaters, jousting, and much, much more make it a good full-day activity.
Where: Glen Ellen Regional Park in San Bernardino, about 1 hour from downtown Los Angeles. *When:* Weekends, April to June. *How:* Call toll free 800/52FAIRE for details about dates and tickets. Tickets are available by phone or at the gate.

✪ *BLESSING OF THE ANIMALS* This traditional event acknowledges the loyal affection that animals have for their owners. Children of all ages enjoy watching the parade of animals—dressed in bonnets, jackets, and other finery—as they make their way to be blessed by the local Catholic bishop.
Where: Olvera Street, downtown Los Angeles. *When:* The day before Easter. *How:* Phone 213/628-7833 for this year's date.

MAY

✪ *VERY SPECIAL ARTS FESTIVAL* Disabled children and young adults are recognized for their very special talents in this festival featuring workshops in all artistic disciplines, performances by and for disabled students, a parade, puppet shows, art exhibits, celebrity and cartoon-character appearances, and media theater.
Where: Los Angeles Music Center's outdoor plaza, downtown. *When:* May. *How:* Call 213/972-7285 for specific details. Admission is free.

✪ *CHILDREN'S DAY* This traditional 2-day event celebrates kids with a mini-marathon (for ages 4 to 12), Japanese dancing, magic shows, the Asian Pacific arts and crafts fair, and other events.
Where: Little Tokyo, downtown Los Angeles. *When:* Beginning of May. *How:* Call 213/628-2725 for further information.

☐ **Cinco de Mayo** (May 5). Mexico's Independence Day is celebrated at various locations throughout Los Angeles for about a week. The *Los Angeles Times* carries daily listings of events.

JUNE

✪ *ANNUAL GRAND NATIONAL IRISH FAIR AND MUSIC FESTIVAL* Leprechauns, a medieval village, bagpipes, and Irish

wolfhounds are just some of the surprises on hand. Numerous stages offer continuous Gaelic music, song, dance, jugglers, and more.
   Where: *The Equestrian Center in Griffith Park.* ***When:*** *June.* ***How:*** *Phone 213/395-8322 for information. Admission costs $12 for adults, $4 for teens 13 to 18, and $7 for students with ID and seniors.*

☐ **Los Angeles Jewish Festival,** West Los Angeles. A 1-day event. Telephone 213/938-2531 for this year's date and location.

JULY

✪ ***HOLLYWOOD BOWL SUMMER FESTIVAL*** *All summer, the sounds of jazz, pop, and classical music from the world's greatest performers fills the air around the outdoor stage of the Hollywood Bowl, one of Southern California's most famous events. Some performances are particularly appropriate for children, including the July 4 concert. Also check the* **Open House at the Bowl,** *the Bowl's children's arts festival, with daytime performances and workshops geared to kids over 5.*
   Where: *Hollywood.* ***When:*** *July through mid-September.* ***How:*** *For information about the regular Bowl season, call 213/850-2000; for information about the children's festival, call 213/850-2077.*

AUGUST

✪ ***CHILDREN'S FESTIVAL OF THE ARTS*** *For one weekend day this hands-on workshop festival encourages children to try making shadow puppets, flip-book construction, chalk drawing, and other art forms they might never have experienced.*
   Where: *Barnsdall Art Park in Hollywood.* ***When:*** *One weekend day in August.* ***How:*** *Call 213/485-4474 for information. Supplies and admission are free.*

✪ ***NISEI WEEK FESTIVAL*** *Little Tokyo comes alive with this 1-week celebration of Japanese-American heritage. Dragon dancers, floats, bands, a 2-day carnival, and musical concerts are sure to delight children of all ages.*
   Where: *Japanese American Cultural & Community Center Plaza in Little Tokyo.* ***When:*** *August.* ***How:*** *Phone 213/687-7193 for information.*

☐ **African Marketplace & Cultural Faire,** Rancho Cienega Park. This is considered the largest display of Africana anywhere with arts, crafts, food, and music. Admission is free. Call 213/734-1164 for information.
☐ **International Surf Festival,** in the South Bay. Early August. Sandcastle-building and lifeguard competitions are featured at this weekend event. Call 213/546-8843 for location and dates.

SEPTEMBER

☐ **Annual Korean Parade & Festival,** for 2 weeks at various locations in Los

Angeles. One of the most all-encompassing festivals in town, featuring 40 different events for children, seniors, adults, and even babies. All events are free. Call 213/730-1495.

✪ *LOS ANGELES COUNTY FAIR* *The largest county fair in the world, its 12 acres of carnival grounds, entertainment, and exhibits fascinate all age groups.*

Where: Los Angeles County Fair and Exposition Center in Pomona, approximately 30 miles east of Los Angeles. When: From September through the beginning of October. How: Call 714/623-3111 for details. Weekday and weekend admission charges vary.

OCTOBER

☐ **Annual Los Angeles Bach Festival,** First Congregational Church, 540 South Commonwealth Street, Los Angeles. In this feast of large and small concerts, the best for the kiddies are the free noontime concerts. Call 213/385-1345 for details.

✪ *INTERNATIONAL FESTIVAL OF MASKS* *Hundreds of people line Wilshire Boulevard in the Mid-Wilshire area to watch the parade of masks representing numerous cultural groups throughout the city. Many children participate in the parade. Afterward, exhibits, performances, food stands, and family activities take place in nearby Hancock Park, adjacent to the La Brea Tar Pits.*

Where: Wilshire Boulevard near Fairfax. When: Usually around Halloween. How: For further information and this year's date, call 213/628-2725.

DECEMBER

✪ *MEXICAN HERITAGE FESTIVAL* *Everyone gets involved in the Mexican tradition of Nacimiento: the building of the Nativity scene in the home, in which each family member is assigned a portion of the work. This festival includes music, entertainment, piñata-making for the children, and the traditional art of* papel picado *(paper construction).*

Where: The Southwest Museum, in Highland Park. When: December. How: Phone 213/221-2164 for details and dates. Admission is free.

☐ **Hollywood Christmas Parade,** Hollywood Boulevard. For date and times, call 213/469-2337 or 213/461-4213.

☐ **Las Posadas,** at Olvera Street, Plaza de la Raza, and other city locations. Highlight of this Christmas pageant is the candlelight procession reenacting Mary and Joseph's search for lodgings. For details, call 213/628-7833.

☐ **Marina del Rey Christmas Boat Parade,** in the marina. A typically Southern Californian way of celebrating the holidays. Call 213/822-9344 or 213/821-0555 for this year's date.

3. WHAT TO PACK

FOR YOU   Winters in Los Angeles rarely get below 60°F during the day, but winter nights have been known to drop as low as 40°F (rarely). Bring jackets for winter evenings, sweaters for winter days. Rain is rare in Los Angeles, but bring a raincoat just in case.

Summer days range from warm to hot; August, September, and sometimes even October are the hottest months. Summer clothes are all you'll need. Although some restaurants require a coat and tie for men, most places do not.

FOR THE KIDS   Do you ever feel like you have to be a wizard to pack for your family trip? Yes, it takes some magic, but it can be done! Before we pack, we first decide whether we're going to use coin-operated laundries or hotel cleaning services, or whether we're going to bring all the soiled laundry home. We basically try to take as little as we can, and then we think again to see if we can cut back. This requires planning—actually laying out clothes a few days ahead and making lists. We start planning about a week in advance, make a list for each child, and then ask the kids to start thinking about what they'll want to take. We encourage them to bring along only what they can carry, so that we're not bogged down with their backpacks and extra luggage.

Of course, kids get dirty, wet, and messy, and we've learned that we need an extra outfit per day for each of our kids over the age of 3 (excluding teens). For tots, we pack at least three outfits, or plan which ones we'll hand-wash.

4. HEALTH & OTHER PRECAUTIONS

HEALTH   Be sure to pack all the **medications** your children may need, and have your doctors' phone numbers. (Even if it's long distance, call your physician if you have a serious problem.) If you're going to be flying, be sure that any signs of congestion or a cold are seen by your doctor before departure. He or she can tell you what to do to prevent inner ear injury. You might also ask about nasal sprays and oral decongestants for your kids for takeoffs and landings.

Be prepared for **motion sickness.** Kids who never get motion sickness in a car can get it on a boat, in a stuffy airplane, or on a train. Those of you who have tried to get a pill down the throat of an uncooperative child will appreciate liquid Dramamine, which you can give to kids over 2 (we mixed it with soda before getting on the boat from Catalina). Ask your pediatrician about other remedies.

You'll want a **first-aid kit.** A small, basic kit is available at most pharmacies. For a more comprehensive kit, contact the American Red Cross (tel. 201/568-8787) and ask how to obtain a Top Gun EMS Kit, which is endorsed by the Red Cross. It comes in a compact easy-to-pack size, but is filled with all you'll need in most emergencies.

SAFETY   There are a few general safety precautions that should be discussed ahead of time, and one that especially applies to the Los Angeles area.

  If You Become Separated   When visiting crowded sightseeing attractions, dress your kids in bright-colored clothing so it will be easy for you to keep an eye on them. Also, talk with them about what they should do if you become separated. Theme-park employees are all schooled to handle the problem of lost children, so tell your kids it's safe to walk up to any park employee and report they are lost. At most theme parks, special name tags can be obtained to aid identification should a child become separated from his or her party.

Fire Every time you check into a new hotel room, it's a good idea to consider what you would do if there was a fire. Where are the exits? Which adult is responsible for which children? Be sure you don't try to leave by elevator. Feel the door to the stairwells before pushing it open. If it's hot, don't attempt to open the door—the fire could be traveling through that stairwell.

Earthquakes Earthquakes do occur here. They are usually quite small, and you may never know one even happened. But if a more significant quake should occur, remember the following: If you are inside a building, *don't run outside*. Keep away from windows and other large glass items. Get under a sturdy piece of furniture, such as a desk or dining table, or stand under a doorway. Never use the elevator to get out, only the stairwells, and don't try to get out if the building is still shaking.

Should you be in your car when a quake hits, pull over and stop—but not under power lines or near trees. Don't stop on a bridge or overpass, and don't get out of the car.

If you're out walking, get into the open, but stay clear of trees, power lines, signs, and the sides of buildings.

OTHER PRECAUTIONS On a less threatening note, we always have all **reservation confirmations** sent to us in writing. Whenever possible, it's best to have something written to show in the event of a problem.

If you are planning to register your kids for a **children's program** at a hotel or in the day-care or ski schools we describe, be sure to find out if you need to make your reservations for those programs in advance. You don't want to make big plans that include children's programs only to get there and find out that your kids can't get in.

5. GETTING THE KIDS INTERESTED

Assuming that you've included the children in your decision to vacation in Los Angeles, and that you've decided how long you're going to stay, it's time to get the kids involved again.

SPECIAL PROJECTS

Take them with you to get travel brochures and maps. Once you have a map, plot out your route with a yellow marking pen, circling points of interest and milestones. On the trip, when we pass those points (or a few minutes before), we talk about them. This not only gives children the sense of accomplishing the miles, but also tends to make them take a more active interest in the landmarks of the trip. This works best for automobile trips, of course, but you can also do it on an airplane if you have a cooperative flight attendant who will indicate the points of interest during your journey.

Get empty notebooks so the kids can keep a journal of their trip. (This may also be the time to buy them that camera they've been wanting.)

RECOMMENDED BOOKS FOR KIDS

California in Words and Pictures, by Dennis Fradin (Chicago: Childrens Press, 1977). Ages 5 and up.

California Indians: An Educational Coloring Book, by Spizzirri (Rapid City, S.D: Spizziri Publishing). (Call Spizzirri Publishing at 800/325–9819 to see if it's still in print and to obtain the publication.)

California Coloring Guide, by Seth Seablom (Seattle: Seablom Design Books, 1979).

California Alphabet Book, by Susan Torrence (Santa Barbara, Calif.: Torrence Publications, 1987).

California Missions: An Educational Coloring Book, by Spizzirri (Rapid City, S.D.: Spizzirri Publishing, 1985).

Song of the Swallows, by Leo Politi (New York: Scribner's, 1949). Ages 5 and up. Caldecott winner. Also by Leo Politi about Los Angeles: *Mieko* (San Carlos, Calif.: Golden Gate Junior Books, 1969), *Moy Moy* (New York: Scribner's, 1960), *The Nicest Gift* (New York: Scribner's, 1973), *Three Stalks of Corn* (New York: Scribner's, 1976), *Picolo's Prank* (New York: Scribner's, 1965).

La Brea Story, by Gretchen Sibley (Los Angeles; Los Angeles County Museum of Natural History, 1968). Ages 10 and up.

Yamino Kwiti: The Story of Indian Life in the Los Angeles Area, by Donna Preble (Berkeley Calif.; Heyday Books, reprinted 1983). Ages 10-12.

Broderick, by Edward Ormondroyd (Berkeley, Calif.: Parnassus Press, 1969). Ages 5-8.

Island of the Blue Dolphins, by Scott O'Dell (Boston: Houghton Mifflin, 1960). Ages 10 and up. Newbery Award.

Confessions of a Prime Time Kid, by Mark Jonathon Harris (New York: Lothrop, Lee & Shepard, 1985). Ages 10-12.

6. GETTING THERE

TRANSPORTATION

BY PLANE

AIRPORTS The major airport in Los Angeles is **Los Angeles International Airport (LAX),** which serves some 80 major airlines and is the third-largest airport in the world in terms of passenger traffic. Depending on your travel plans, you may prefer to fly into other, smaller regional airports. **Burbank-Glendale-Pasadena Airport** (tel. 818/840-8847), **Long Beach Municipal Airport** (tel. 213/421-8293), and **Ontario International Airport** (tel. 714/983-8282) are possibilities that are often more convenient than LAX. If you're planning to start your trip in Orange County, you might consider landing at **Orange County–John Wayne Airport** (tel. 714/252-5006) in Santa Ana.

AIRLINES Many national and international carriers have service between Los Angeles and San Francisco. Don't rule out these carriers if you're traveling between these two cities because they sometimes offer better fares. In addition, **Alaska Air** (tel. toll free 800/426-0333) has convenient service from Long Beach Airport to San Francisco and Oakland, or from LAX to San Francisco, weekends only. **American Airlines** (tel. toll free 800/433-7300) services many of the smaller airports such as Fresno, Monterey, Palm Springs, Redding, San Jose, and San Luis Obispo, as well as the Bay Area (San Francisco/Oakland) and Southern California (LAX, Burbank, Ontario, Long Beach, Orange County–John Wayne, and San Diego) airports; **America West** (tel. toll free 800/247-5692) has over 100 daily flights between nine major airports; **USAir** (formerly PSA) services many small cities, such as Burbank, Concord, Fresno, Long Beach, Monterey, Ontario, and Orange County–John Wayne, as well as the major airports in the state. (Call information to find your local toll-free 800 number.)

Typical fares. If you've flown recently, you know there is no such thing as a "typical" or "normal" fare. For every flight there are usually several fares available under three main categories: first class, coach, and discount. While visitors to L.A. benefit from a wide choice of flights, they may grow dizzy deciphering the ever-changing fare structure. Generally, midweek fares ticketed a month or more in advance are the lowest. Holidays are often subject to blackout restrictions, as in "no bargains spoken here." Watch for newspaper ads announcing special promotions. They pop up unexpectedly throughout the year and can save you big bucks. If you don't qualify for a promotional or other reduced fare, you could end up paying substantially more for your ticket. To get the most for your travel dollar, plan well in advance and do a bit of comparison shopping by calling the airlines or consulting an accredited travel agent.

BY CAR

The major north-south route, I-5, is a heavily traveled freeway that bisects both Los Angeles proper and the entire metropolitan area. From the north this inland route approaches through the San Joaquin Valley, crosses the Tehachapi Mountains and enters the city as the Golden State Freeway; from the south at San Diego it follows the coast to Capistrano Beach, turns inland, then, as the Santa Ana Freeway, passes through Anaheim and sweeps into central Los Angeles. Route I-405 (San Diego Freeway) joins I-5 at San Fernando and south of the town of Irvine; a good alternate route, it avoids the busy downtown Los Angeles area, although it is typically as heavily traveled as the central route.

From the north two other controlled-access routes, Calif. 99 and U.S. 101, roughly parallel I-5 on the east and the west, respectively. Calif. 99 crosses the San Joaquin Valley and merges with I-5 a few miles south of Bakersfield. U.S. 101 is a 204-mile scenic stretch from its northern terminus at San Luis Obispo. Almost continuously in sight of the coastal ranges, U.S. 101 follows the Salinas River Valley, runs along the

**FROMMER'S SMART FAMILY TRAVELER:
AIRFARES**

VALUE-CONSCIOUS TRAVELERS SHOULD TAKE ADVANTAGE OF
THE FOLLOWING:

1. Shop all the airlines that fly to your destination.
2. Always ask for the lowest fare, not just a discount fare. Ask about special
   family fares.
3. Keep calling the airline of your choice—availability of cheap seats changes
   daily. Airlines would rather sell a seat at a discount than have it fly empty. As
   the departure date nears, additional low-cost seats may become available.
4. Ask about frequent-flier programs that give you bonuses and free flights
   when you use an airline regularly.
5. Ask airlines about their family tour packages. Land arrangements are often
   cheaper when booked with an air ticket.
6. Be flexible with your times and days of departure—the best prices are often
   offered midweek.

coastline through Santa Barbara and terminates at I-5 in the center of Los Angeles. SR
1, which traverses the rugged coast, is slower and more dangerous when fog sets in or
rain increases the possibility of slides. Outstanding coastal views make it the most
scenic north-south route.

Route I-15 links Las Vegas and San Diego. Passing east of Los Angeles, it provides
access to the area via freeway connections at San Bernardino and Riverside.

Direct access from the east is via I-10, which enters Los Angeles as the San
Bernardino Freeway and ends at Santa Monica. Indirect access from points east is
provided by I-40, a fast route across the desert that ends at I-15 in Barstow.

BY TRAIN

The train is an exciting way to travel. **Amtrak,** with its terminal at 800 North
Alameda Street, Los Angeles (tel. 213/624-0171, or toll free 800/USA-RAIL), is the
way to go. Amtrak's *Coast Starlight,* originating in Los Angeles, runs the length of
California, Oregon, and Washington. The *San Diegan* and the *San Joaquin* travel
throughout the state.

If you're coming from out-of-state, you'll find that Amtrak offers transportation to
Los Angeles from many cities. The *Southwest Chief* offers service between Los
Angeles and Chicago via Albuquerque. The *Desert Wind* services Los Angeles,
Denver, and Chicago. The *Sunset Limited* services Los Angeles and New Orleans via
San Antonio. And if you're coming from the Northeast, the *Cardinal* runs from New
York to Chicago, where you would connect with the *Southwest Chief.*

Some of the trains have complete dining cars with full-service restaurants; others
have snack bars. Some have bedrooms with sleeping berths; others have family
bedrooms—rooms that are the full width of the train, with windows on both
sides.

When you consider train travel, ask about family fares and package tours. They
make it considerably more affordable.

BY BUS

The major transcontinental bus line that services Los Angeles is **Greyhound/ Trailways Bus Lines** (tel. 213/620-1200).

KEEPING THE KIDS ENTERTAINED

People have different opinions about the number of toys you should take on a trip. We bring some new toys and some old favorites. The kids each get their own backpack (or small toy box in the backseat of the car) in which they pack the toys and books they especially want. We stash new toys in our suitcases or bags and dole them out when the kids tire of what they've brought. When the trip is a long one, we actually wrap the new toys and distribute them to the kids at key moments—timed to hold their interest. We alternate creative-type toys, such as crayons, with toys and games that require some concentration and thinking. We always include toys that *we* enjoy playing with, too, since we'll be doing lots of that. Most toy stores have a large variety of travel games and toys.

Once your child is old enough to enjoy cassette-tape stories and songs, you've found a real treasure. These kept Andrew occupied for hours at a time, long enough to endure very long car trips.

Be sure to leave the messy, noisy toys and projects at home. Games with little pieces and puzzles can also give you grief. Our least favorite words on a cross-country flight were, "Oh, I dropped some again!" Picture yourself picking up little game pieces in a crowded, baggage-filled row of airline seats. There are better toys and better ways to meet your neighbors.

Here are some ideas of things to take along: packages of stickers and sticker books, magnetic drawing and alphabet boards, magnetic games, hand puppets, write-and-wipe boards, Colorforms, coloring books and crayons that don't melt, tracing paper and designs to trace, and self-inking stamps and paper. For older kids, you might want to bring small cars, decks of cards, blank notebooks, and a cassette recorder with earphones. (Check the size of the earphones before you purchase the recorder; after surprising then 4-year-old Jane with a recorder on the plane, we spent the next hour trying to make the earphones fit her small head.) Hand-held video games are, of course, the newest craze, and you probably won't have to remind your child to bring his or hers along. We often make up a crafts box with lots of goodies that the kids can use to create artistic treasures. On car trips, you can bring song books and music cassettes. (If you are renting a car, check ahead as to whether there's a tape deck.)

More and more companies are putting out items created especially for traveling kids: activity books; books of games especially for car, train, or plane travel; travel packs made up of age-appropriate diversions; audio tapes that describe travel games; and more. Check with your favorite toy store and bookstore for the latest items.

SPECIAL TIPS FOR AIRPLANE TRIPS   Flying is always an adventure, but unfortunately you can't predict whether it's going to be a good or a bad one.

The kids, especially young ones, get very antsy when confined to a small area. Unlike in a car, you can't stop when you want to let the kids run around. Also, some young children may become frightened on the airplane.

To ward off negative experiences, before the trip we talk with our young children about what will happen. If your children are flying for the first time, some people think it helps if you take them to an airport to look at the planes before your trip. A favorite blanket or stuffed animal will help too.

Once on board, remember that cabin temperature can vary. Bring extra clothes for each child (always a change of clothes) and have them wear layered, loose, comfortable clothing.

Waiting in airports can be the torment of many a parent. Although we try to time our arrival so that we won't be too early but also won't have to run for the plane, you can never predict when that plane will leave late. If our flight is delayed, we take the kids for walks, try to find video arcades, and look for other kids their age in the waiting area for them to play with. When all else fails, we attempt to find a corner area where we can spread out and play on the floor (ugh!).

Whatever you do, don't leave the terminal. We were once assured by airline officials that we had a 3-hour delay, so we took a long walk. When we returned (an hour ahead of time), the plane had departed. The airline officials said they had paged and paged, and all passengers who didn't return to the flight had to rebook.

Many airline personnel suggest bringing your young child's car seat if you've purchased a separate seat for him or her. It helps to protect and, in some cases, to keep the child where you want him or her. Also, your child may be more likely to sit for a longer period of time in a familiar car seat than in a large seat with a lap belt. If the plane isn't full, sometimes the airline staff will try to make sure there's an empty seat next to you for the car seat (if you didn't purchase a ticket for the child).

Always bring a carry-on bag with snacks and beverages. The kids may not always be able to wait for the scheduled airline meals, and you don't even know if they will actually eat the airline food. (Goodness knows, many adults don't!) We pack a full goodie bag, complete with fresh fruit, bread, raisins, crackers and cheese, pretzels, and lots of individual boxes of juice. Kids get very thirsty on flights. We also include several flexible straws, and for little ones, drinking cups with lids.

Finally, airlines allow you to board in advance if you have children. This is wonderful if you're carrying tons of things or have more than one child to settle. If you feel your child needs to expend that last bit of energy before the flight, ask the flight attendant if one adult can board with all the paraphernalia while the other one stays with the child until the last minutes of boarding.

SPECIAL TIPS FOR CAR TRAVEL   Traveling in a car with children is unlike any other experience, one you have to undergo to understand. Remember that you'll all be enclosed in a very small space for an extended period of time. Good humor, plenty to do, and lots of food and drink are the order of the day.

The main rule is to stop every few hours to break up the monotony and allow the kids time to get out and move around. Also, instead of stopping at a restaurant to eat, you can stop at a lovely park or where you know there's a special attraction.

Seating arrangements are important. One parent might sit in the backseat with the kids to ward off trouble. It's especially helpful if one child is having a hard time, or if the group of kids tends to bicker or get rowdy when you're on the road. It's better than constantly turning around and leaning over the front seat, and it also protects you from running the risk of being ticketed for not wearing a seatbelt (a California law).

Also, be sure to bring along an adequate supply of pacifiers, bottles, and snacks. Pack enough pillows and blankets for everyone.

To prevent cranky kids, anticipate where the sun will be on their faces. If you can't keep them out of the sun, use a visor. Kids get really uncomfortable with the sun in their eyes, and they can complain unmercifully if they're hot and sweaty. Driving through the California desert can be a grueling experience. Without our knowing it until later, one of our children actually got a sunburn from it. You can get a dark cellophanelike material that sticks to the window and can be moved around depending where the sun is.

To combat motion sickness, experts suggest lemon drops, lemon cookies, peppermint, foods high in carbohydrates, and salt-covered foods such as crackers or pretzels, which cut down the production of what causes nausea. Again, ask your pediatrician for advice. Also remember not to let the kids read while the car is in motion.

The question "When will we get there?" signals the time to take out the prerouted map we suggested you make (see "Special Projects" in Section 5, "Getting the Kids Interested," above). The activity can be as simple as calculating where you'll stop for gas and roadside stretches.

Another game especially well suited for automobile travel (and for kids over 6) is the geography game, in which one player names a place (country, city, region, etc.) and the next player has to come up with a place whose name begins with the last letter of the previous place name.

Other fun ways to pass the time involve using license plates of passing vehicles. Young kids can look for the alphabet in sequence. Older children can try to spell words or find all the states of the United States. Very little children can look for colors of passing cars.

And an all-time favorite is to sing songs together.

SPECIAL TIPS FOR TRAIN TRAVEL   Although not the luxurious form of transportation it used to be, train travel is still one way to see the scenery without constantly stopping for gas, restaurants, and hotels. Kids can move around, play easier than in a car, and often learn a great deal about this mode of transportation. When you make your reservations, ask about family bedrooms, offered on some Amtrak trains. Short trips, such as those from Los Angeles to San Diego or Santa Barbara, can be fun experiences for children, and the journey itself can be the adventure.

CHAPTER 2

GETTING TO KNOW LOS ANGELES

1. **ORIENTATION**
- **NEIGHBORHOODS IN BRIEF**
2. **GETTING AROUND**
- **FAST FACTS: LOS ANGELES**

Los Angeles is many things to many people. To some it represents movie stars; to others, the land of Mickey Mouse. But at some point almost everyone who thinks of Los Angeles thinks of freeways—never-ending, curving, crowded gray paths cutting through all parts of this sprawling metropolis. But don't be afraid: The city of Los Angeles and its freeways are **easy** to learn. Well, maybe not **easy** but **possible.**

---

1. ORIENTATION

ARRIVING

BY PLANE   Your choice of ground transportation depends on the airport you use and your destination.

From Los Angeles International Airport (LAX)   From LAX, ground transportation is available via bus, shuttle, taxi, limousine, or rental car. Also, check ahead about courtesy van service available from some hotels. In each baggage-claim area at LAX there is an information board listing transportation services plus a direct information telephone line.

Taxi service can be very expensive, so be sure you know how much the tab will run before you tell the driver to go ahead. The average taxi fare between LAX and downtown Los Angeles is about $27; from LAX to Beverly Hills, about $25. Confirm the cost first, however.

Door-to-door airport service is available 24 hours a day from **Prime Time Shuttle** (tel. 818/901-9901) and **SuperShuttle** (tel. 213/417-8427, 818/244-2700, or 714/973-1100). Make reservations early.

From the other regional airports   When you arrive you'll find signs indicating the different transportation services available: private shuttle services, taxis, and public bus service.

CALIFORNIA

Sacramento ★

Los Angeles ●

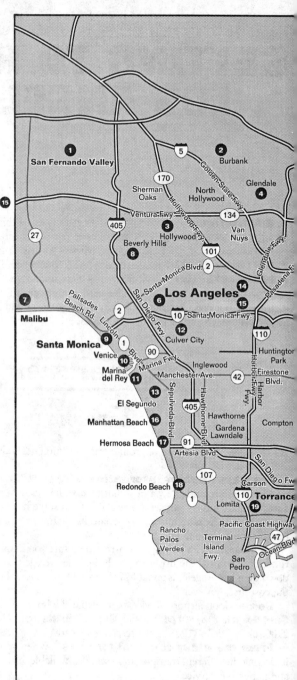

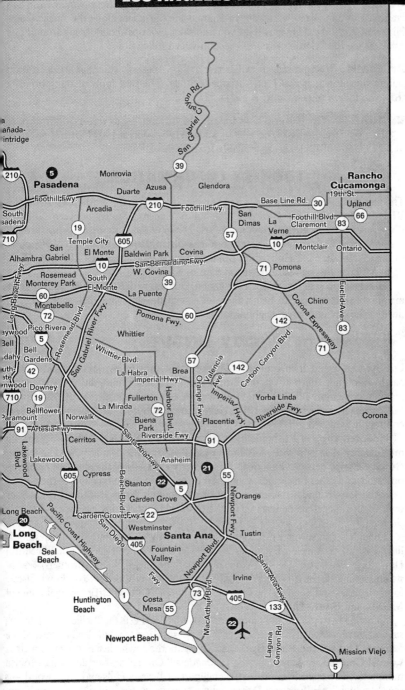

LOS ANGELES AREA ORIENTATION

BY CAR   Many families choose to drive to L.A., especially those coming from San Francisco or San Diego who want to enjoy the scenic route along the Pacific Coast Highway. A good road map will get you into town. For tips about driving around Los Angeles, see the "Getting Around" section which follows.

BY TRAIN   Train passengers will arrive at Los Angeles's stunning art deco train station downtown, at 800 North Alameda Street. The best form of transportation from the station to your hotel is a taxi.

BY BUS   Two **Greyhound Bus terminals** are available to visitors: downtown at 208 East 6th Street (tel. 213/629-8400), and in Hollywood at 1409 North Vine Street (tel. 213/466-6381). Taxis are available from both stations.

TOURIST INFORMATION

The first thing you'll want to do when you get to town, is contact the **Los Angeles Visitors Information Center,** 695 South Figueroa Street, between Wilshire Boulevard and 7th Street, Los Angeles (tel. 213/689-8822), open Monday through Saturday from 8am to 5pm. There's another **information center** in Hollywood at the Janes House, 6541 Hollywood Boulevard, near Vine Street (tel. 213/461-4213), open Monday through Saturday from 9am to 5pm.

The helpful staff at these information centers will help make your visit a memorable experience. To help visitors deal with the sprawling metropolis, they've divided the city into large neighborhoods.

CITY LAYOUT

Los Angeles is an incongruous collection of communities, joined like a crazy patchwork quilt. Each town or district has been sewn onto the ever-expanding blanket, none more notably than **Hollywood,** eight miles northwest of "downtown L.A.," which was annexed in 1910. New areas in suburbia, as they emerged, were continuously tacked on.

However, there were holdouts, such as monied **Beverly Hills**—a separate municipality that is a virtual island inside Los Angeles. Similarly, the mile-long **Sunset Strip,** between Hollywood and Beverly Hills—long the refuge of nightclub operators and other businesses wanting to escape the restraining hand of the City of Los Angeles—is under the jurisdiction of the county. **West Hollywood** holds its own as Los Angeles's newest separate city, hosting marvelous eateries and trendy shops.

Though some towns or cities are independently incorporated, their destiny is linked with Los Angeles. Examples include the sheep ranch that became "Beautiful Downtown **Burbank**" (NBC-TV, major aircraft industries, Warner Brothers), **Pasadena** (setting of the New Year's Tournament of Roses and the Rose Bowl Classic football game, and home of the Pasadena Playhouse), **Culver City** (original home of MGM), and **Santa Monica** (known for its beaches).

Sprawled between sea and mountains, Los Angeles meets the Pacific at settlements such as **Venice,** while in the east it encompasses treeless foothills leading toward the **Mojave Desert** and **Palm Springs.** There are those who live in the hills, such as **Laurel Canyon,** and there are the "flatlanders." On the crest of the Santa Monica mountain chain from the north—forming part of Beverly Hills and Hollywood—is the "sky-high" **Mulholland Drive,** where tourists go for a bird's-eye view. From here one can see a flatland called the **San Fernando Valley,** between the Hollywood Hills and the Mojave Desert mountains. Once all orange groves, it is now both residential and commercial. There are those who say that it—not Hollywood—is the movie and TV capital of the world, because of the location of such studios as **Universal City.**

The more commercial areas of Los Angeles have remained in the flatlands, including **Wilshire Boulevard** running from downtown to the sea. The highest point in Los Angeles is Mount Hollywood. **Sunset** and **Hollywood boulevards** run along the foot of the mountains.

MAIN ARTERIES AND STREETS   The **major east-west streets** in "town" are Wilshire Boulevard, Sunset Boulevard, Pico Boulevard, and Olympic Boulevard. The **major north-south streets** are Lincoln Boulevard, Sepulveda Boulevard, La Cienega Boulevard, La Brea Avenue, and Vermont Avenue.

Santa Monica Boulevard is one of the more confusing thoroughfares: At one point it runs parallel to Wilshire Boulevard, then crosses it in Beverly Hills. Also, there's a short portion of street running parallel to Santa Monica Boulevard beginning at Rexford Drive in Beverly Hills and continuing west to Sepulveda Boulevard in West Los Angeles. Its street signs call it Santa Monica Boulevard, but it's usually referred to as "Little Santa Monica."

In the San Fernando Valley, **Ventura Boulevard** is the main east-west thoroughfare.

FINDING AN ADDRESS   When you're in downtown Los Angeles, addresses are fairly easy to find. For instance, 711 Figueroa Street is at 7th Street and Figueroa. But probably the best way to find an address is to call the establishment you want to reach and ask how to get there. Make sure to tell them where you are and whether you will be driving or traveling by public transportation. Ask if the place is accessible by freeway, and if so, how; ask for major cross streets, and find out if the street address is north or south, east or west. Also, the Thomas Bros. Popular Street Atlas is an excellent street guide.

NEIGHBORHOODS IN BRIEF

Downtown   This is the central part of the city, including the area surrounding the Civic Center, east Wilshire, **Little Tokyo,** and **Chinatown.**

Hollywood   Most people now think Hollywood is a state of mind, but there still is such an area, long known as the world's glamour and film capital. It's a place everyone seems to need to make a pilgrimage to.

West Hollywood, Mid-Wilshire, Fairfax, and Melrose Area This section of town is loosely bordered by Doheny Boulevard to the west, La Brea Avenue to the east, Santa Monica Boulevard to the north, and Wilshire Boulevard to the south. It's a section of town burgeoning with top boutiques, unusual shops, and many ethnic restaurants, and combines an older European population with artists, designers, and other trend-setters.

Westside   This section, comprised of Beverly Hills, Century City, West L.A., and Westwood, is alive with shopping, restaurants, and delightful places for the family. **Beverly Hills** still draws thousands of people to its golden streets, while **Century City** pulsates with the energy of everyday business combined with professional theater, cinema, and shopping. **Westwood** is the fun, youthful village of first-run movie theaters, clothing shops for the college set, and good, informal restaurants.

   The Coastal Region   This area includes **Santa Monica, Venice, Marina del Rey,** and the **airport.** Beautiful beaches are everywhere, and the Marina and Santa Monica Pier are fun places to explore with the kids. This is the part of town where the family can get out and roller skate, ride bikes, and simply enjoy what Los Angeles is lucky enough to have.
   The San Fernando Valley   Both **Universal City** and **Burbank** are part of the San Fernando Valley. Although Johnny Carson has traditionally made fun of this part of town, it is where many films are now being produced.

2. GETTING AROUND

BY PUBLIC TRANSPORTATION

There's no subway, but there is a widespread bus network covering the entire region, as well as downtown minivans and the Fairfax Trolley.

BY BUS   The Southern California Rapid Transit District (RTD) can give you information about bus routes. They offer frequent service to major area sightseeing venues, including those in Anaheim. Bus service is 24 hours per day, every day of the year. Fares vary depending on the distance traveled, and exact change is required; children under 6 ride free. Transfers are available from the driver. For information, call 213/626-4455 from 5:30am to 11pm.

DASH   The Downtown Area Short Hop (DASH) is a shuttle service that makes getting around downtown Los Angeles much easier. There are two routes, which include many downtown points of interest such as the Music Center, the Museum of Contemporary Art, Olvera Street, and Chinatown. Minivans run every 6 to 10 minutes at 15-minute intervals from 6:30am to 6:30pm Monday through Friday and from 10am to 5pm on Saturday. The one-way fare is 25¢ and exact change is required. Call toll free 800/252-7433 for routes and stops.

BY TROLLEY   For 25¢ one way, you can take the Fairfax Trolley to several local destinations in the Fairfax and Melrose areas. The trolley runs Monday through Saturday from 9am to 6pm, except on holidays. Call toll free 800/252-7433 for route information and boarding locations.

BY CAR

As we said earlier, Los Angeles is synonymous with **freeways.** Fortunately, you don't have to be an expert on the freeway system to find your way around: If you have a good map (the Thomas Bros. L.A. Guide is tops), you can get anywhere. And don't be shy—you can ask for directions.
   Freeway driving can be a pleasant or a harrowing experience. Be sure you allow plenty of time to get to your destination. Know where you're going, and if you get

confused, it's a good idea to exit the freeway and stop to read your map rather than drive uncertainly on the freeway.

If you can avoid the freeways during the two rush hours, from 6 to 9am and 4 to 7pm, you're better off. We often keep water or juice for the kids inside the car (not in the trunk) as there have been many times when the freeway has been jammed, turning a 10-minute jaunt into a 25-minute ordeal with thirsty, uncomfortable children.

If you need assistance, the **Automobile Club of Southern California** (tel. 213/741-3111) is extremely helpful to its members, providing emergency service, travel advice, and other services. AAA members in other states are automatically covered here.

For information about **road conditions,** call the California Transportation Department (CALTRANS) (tel. 213/620-3270). Or for frequent **traffic reports** you can listen to KFWB (980 AM) or KNX (1070 AM).

DRIVING RULES Before you get behind the wheel, familiarize yourself with California's driving regulations since some of them differ from rules in other parts of the country.

California law requires *everyone* in a car to wear a seatbelt. In addition, children 40 pounds and less, or 4 years old and under, must be strapped in an approved car seat, so be sure to bring one with you (if you plan to rent a car, be sure that the agency has a car seat available for you).

In Los Angeles you can make a right turn on a red light, unless indicated otherwise. You can also make a left turn on a red light from one one-way street onto another one-way street.

In California, pedestrians *always* have the right-of-way.

If speed limits aren't posted, the maximum speed is 25 m.p.h. on surface streets and 55 m.p.h. on freeways.

RENTAL CARS All major car-rental companies are located in Los Angeles, including **Avis Rent-A-Car** (tel. 213/645-1044, or toll free 800/331-1212), **Budget Rent-A-Car** (tel. 213/645-4500, or toll free 800/527-0700), **Dollar Rent-A-Car** (tel. 213/645-9333, or toll free 800/800-4000), **Hertz Rent-A-Car** (tel. 213/646-4861, or toll free 800/654-3131), and **Thrifty Rent-A-Car** (tel. 213/645-1880, or toll free 800/367-2277). Most have counters at the airports as well as offices throughout the Greater Los Angeles area.

Should you want to look "the part"—sell a screenplay or get your daughter into commercials—check out the Rolls Royces, Ferraris, and other exotic automobiles at **Budget Rent-A-Car, Beverly Hills Car Collection,** 9815 Wilshire Boulevard, Beverly Hills (tel. 213/274-9173, or toll free 800/527-0700).

BY TAXI

You won't find taxis cruising the streets of Los Angeles. There are regular taxi stops at the airport, train, and bus terminals, but elsewhere you must call for a cab or have one summoned by the doorman at your hotel or restaurant. Fares start at $1.90, then increase by $1.40 per mile thereafter. Be sure to confirm the cost before you get into the cab. You might try these taxi companies: **United Independent Cab Co.** (tel. 213/558-8294), **Beverly Hills Cab Co.** (tel. 213/273-6611), or **Yellow Cab Co.** (tel. 213/413-7890).

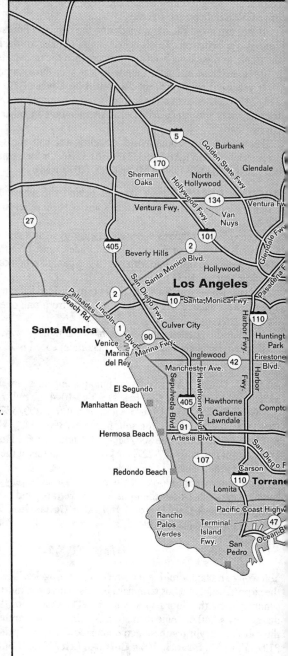

(2) Glendale Fwy.
(5) Golden State Fwy.
(5) Santa Ana Fwy.
(10) Santa Monica Fwy.
(10) San Bernardino Fwy.
(22) Garden Grove Fwy.
(47) Terminal Island Fwy.
(55) Newport Fwy.
(57) Orange Fwy.
(60) Pomona Fwy.
(90) Marina Fwy.
(91) Redondo Beach Fwy.
(91) Artesia Fwy.
(101) Riverside Fwy.
(101) Ventura Fwy.
(101) Hollywood Fwy.
(110) Pasadena Fwy.
(110) Harbor Fwy.
(134) Ventura Fwy.
(170) Hollywood Fwy.
(210) Foothill Fwy.
(405) San Diego Fwy.
(605) San Gabriel River Fwy.
(710) Long Beach Fwy.

LOS ANGELES FREEWAY SYSTEM

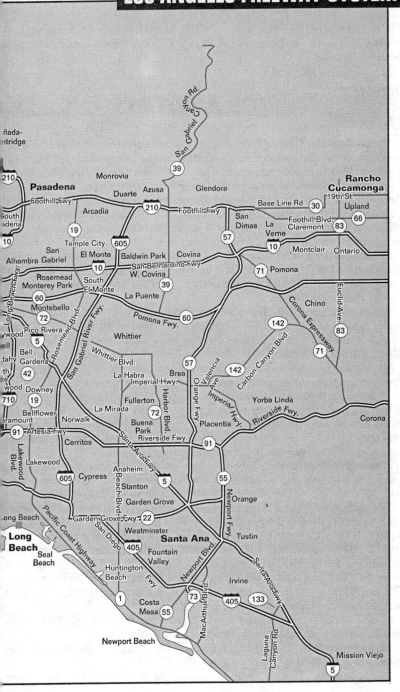

BY METRO RAIL

The recently opened Blue Line service of RTD's Metro Rail connects downtown Los Angeles with downtown Long Beach. Call 213/972-6000 for route information and boarding locations.

 LOS ANGELES

Area Codes   Currently, Los Angeles and its surrounding areas use the **213** area code. For the San Fernando Valley, it's **818,** and for Orange County, **714.** As of February 1992 that will change somewhat. Downtown Los Angeles, Hollywood, Montebello, and some other surrounding areas will continue to use 213, but the Los Angeles International Airport area and the western, southern, coastal, and eastern portions of the county, including West Los Angeles, San Pedro, and Whittier, will use the new **310** area code. Don't worry—if you dial the wrong area code, an operator will come on the line and give you the correct one.

Baby-sitters   Check first with your hotel concierge for recommended sitters. You should ask if they are bonded and licensed, what the hourly rate is (be sure to specify how many kids you have), and whether or not you have to provide meals and pay for their transportation.

Another alternative is the **Baby Sitters Guild** (tel. 818/441-4293), which comes highly recommended; it has been in business since 1948 and is licensed by the state. The company by the same name in Los Angeles is not affiliated with the original Guild. **Sitters Unlimited** (tel. toll free 800/339-1287 in Los Angeles, or 800/328-1191 outside Los Angeles) is franchised coast-to-coast. In California they have locations in Orange County, the South Bay, Newport Beach, and Long Beach.

Business Hours   **Stores** are usually open Monday through Saturday from 10am to 6pm; shopping-center stores stay open longer, and usually have Sunday hours. **Banks** are generally open Monday through Thursday from 9am to 4pm, and stay open later on Friday; a few banks are open on Saturday morning. **Markets** are open until at least 9pm; Hughes Markets stay open 24 hours.

Dentists/Doctors   For both dentists and doctors, check with your hotel; some may even have one on call. Or call the **Los Angeles Dental Society** (tel. 213/380-7669) or the **Los Angeles Medical Society** (tel. 213/483-6122).

Drugstores   These pharmacies have extended hours: **Horton & Converse,** with locations at 11600 Wilshire Boulevard, West Los Angeles (tel. 213/478-0801), open daily from 8:30am to 2am, and at 9201 Sunset Boulevard, West Hollywood (tel. 213/272-0488), open daily from 9am to 10pm; **Thrifty Drugs Store,** with locations at 300 North Canon Drive, Beverly Hills (tel. 213/273-7293), open daily from 9am to 10pm, and at 4633 Santa Monica Boulevard, West Hollywood (tel. 213/666-6126), open Monday through Friday from 9am to 9pm, on Saturday from 9am to 6pm, and on Sunday from 10am to 6pm.

There is one 24-hour pharmacy in Van Nuys (the San Fernando Valley)—**Horton & Converse,** 6625 Van Nuys Boulevard (tel. 818/782-6251).

Emergencies   Dial **911** for fire, police, and paramedics. **Poison information** is at 213/484-5151.

Eyeglasses   Contact these companies for a location near you: **Lens**

Crafters (tel. toll free 800/522-LENS), **Pearle Vision** (tel. toll free 800/YES-EYES), or **Pearle Vision Express** (tel. 213/542-0206) for fast service on glasses. Most optical shops will make easy repairs for you while you wait.

Hairdressers/Barbers   Most large hotels have salons on the premises, or they will recommend someone. The following salons specialize in children's haircuts and styling: **Tipperary,** 9422 Dayton Way (tel. 213/274-0294), **Kiddie Cuts,** 245 South Robertson Boulevard (tel. 213/659-4790), or **Yellow Balloon,** 2009 Westwood Boulevard (tel. 213/475-1241). You can also call **Supercuts** (tel. toll free 800/225-6565) for the nearest location.

Hospitals   These hospitals have 24-hour emergency rooms: **Cedars-Sinai Medical Center,** 8700 Beverly Boulevard, Los Angeles (tel. 213/855-5000, or 213/855-6517 for the emergency room); **Queen of Angeles Medical Center,** 1300 North Vermont Avenue, Los Angeles (tel. 213/413-3000, or 213/413-4896 for the emergency room); and **Glendale Adventist Medical Center,** 1509 Wilson Terrace, Glendale (tel. 818/409-8000, or 818/409-8202 for the emergency room).

Liquor Laws   California's legal drinking age is 21. Liquor cannot be consumed or purchased in public establishments between the hours of 2am and 6am daily.

Laundry/Dry Cleaning   Any one of the major hotels can take care of these services for you, but allow two days to do the job.

Luggage Repair   Shoe- and purse-repair shops can often make minor luggage repairs. You'll find repair services in the **Westside Pavilion,** 10800 W. Pico Blvd.; **The Beverly Connection,** 100 N. La Cienega Blvd., Los Angeles; and in the **Century City Shopping Center & Marketplace,** 10250 Santa Monica Blvd., Century City. Check the *Yellow Pages* under "Luggage Repairing" if your needs are more complicated.

Newspapers and Magazines   The *Los Angeles Times* and the *Daily News* are the local newspapers, delivered mornings or available at newsstands or in coin-operated newspaper bins. *Los Angeles* magazine is a monthly magazine. The *LA Weekly* and *The Reader* are available free at most shops and restaurants on Melrose Avenue; *LA Parent* (focusing on services for toddlers to preteens) and *Noise* (for teenagers) are monthly and are available free in children's stores and some bookstores.

Police   In an emergency, dial 911; for other matters, phone 213/485-2121 in Los Angeles or 213/550-4951 in Beverly Hills.

Post Office   The downtown post office is at 900 North Alameda Street (tel. 213/617-4641), open Monday through Friday from 8am to 9pm and on Saturday and Sunday from 8am to 4pm. In Beverly Hills there is a post office at 469 North Crescent Drive (tel. 213/247-3400), open Monday through Friday from 8:30am to 5pm. The postage machines are usually accessible even when the offices are closed. The airport post office, at 5800 West Century Boulevard (tel. 213/337-8840 for the main lobby, 213/337-8846 for the Express Mail office), is open Monday through Friday from 7:30am to midnight (call for weekend hours) and open 24 hours daily for Express Mail service.

Safety   Like any big city, Los Angeles has its share of crime. The best thing to remember is to lock valuables in a hotel safe-deposit box, stay off deserted streets at night, and ask how far your destination is before you venture off on foot. Don't walk through parks in the evening, and make sure your car is locked.

Taxes   In Los Angeles, the **sales tax** on merchandise and restaurant food is

8.25%. The **accommodations tax** on your hotel bill is 12.50%, in addition to other taxes.

Telephones Pacific Bell coin-operated phone calls are 20¢; many places you call in the Los Angeles area will have a toll charge (the operator will inform you of the charge). Credit-card calls can be made from most phones. Sometimes you'll see a pay telephone with a company name other than Pacific Bell. Calls from these privately owned phones usually require a deposit of 25¢.

Television Stations The broadcast channels in Los Angeles are Channel 2, KCBS (CBS); Channel 4, KNBC (NBC); Channel 5, KTLA (local); Channel 7, KABC (ABC); Channel 9, KCAL (independent); Channel 11, KTTV (Fox); Channel 13, KCOP (local); and Channel 28, KCET (PBS).

If you have cable TV in your hotel room or condominium, check for the Disney Channel, Nickelodeon, and USA for children's programming.

Time Los Angeles is on Pacific time, which is 3 hours earlier than the U.S. East Coast.

Useful Telephone Numbers You may find some of the following numbers helpful during your stay: **Alcoholics Anonymous** (tel. 213/387-8316), **Mexico Tourist Information** (tel. 213/203-8191), **Overeaters Anonymous** (tel. 213/657-6252), **Time** (tel. 213/853-1212), **Traveler's Aid InfoLine** (tel. 213/686-0950 24 hours), and **Western Union** (tel. toll free 800/325-6000).

In addition, the **disabled** can call the Westside Center for Independent Living (tel. 213/390-3611) and **senior citizens** can contact the Los Angeles Department of Aging (tel. 213/485-4402).

Weather For a recorded weather forecast, phone 213/554-1212.

CHAPTER 3

FOR FOREIGN VISITORS

1. PREPARING FOR YOUR U.S. TRIP

2. GETTING TO & AROUND THE U.S.

- **FAST FACTS: THE FOREIGN VISITOR**

- **THE AMERICAN SYSTEM OF MEASUREMENTS**

The United States, like any foreign country, can be confusing at times, especially if you aren't totally at ease with the language or familiar with the customs. The purpose of this chapter is to offer practical information to help the foreign visitor have as easy a stay as possible. There is also helpful information in "Fast Facts: Los Angeles" in Chapter 2.

1. PREPARING FOR YOUR U.S. TRIP

ENTRY REQUIREMENTS

NECESSARY DOCUMENTS Canadian nationals need only proof of Canadian residence to visit the United States. Citizens of the United Kingdom and Japan need only a current passport; a visa is not necessary. Citizens of other countries, including Australia and New Zealand, usually need two documents: a valid passport with an expiration date at least 6 months later than the scheduled end of their U.S. visit, plus a visa available at no charge from a U.S. embassy or consulate.

To get a tourist or business visa to enter the United States, contact the nearest American embassy or consulate in your country. If there is none, you will have to apply in person in a country where there is a U.S. embassy or consulate. Present your passport, a passport-size photo of yourself, and a completed application, which is available through the embassy or consulate.

You may be asked to provide information about how you plan to finance your trip or show a letter of invitation from a friend with whom you plan to stay. Those applying for a business visa may be asked to show evidence that they will not receive a salary in the United States.

Be sure to check the length of time allotted you on the visa; usually it's 6 months. If you want to stay longer, you may file for an extension of the visa with the Immigration and Naturalization Service once you are in the United States. If permission to stay is granted, a new visa is not required unless you leave the country and want to reenter.

MEDICAL REQUIREMENTS You won't need any **inoculations** unless you are arriving from, or have stopped off recently in, a country that is experiencing an outbreak of cholera, yellow fever, or another contagious dangerous disease.

If you have a medical condition requiring you to take **prescription drugs** (or use a syringe), be sure to bring along a valid prescription signed by your doctor.

TRAVEL INSURANCE

Travel insurance and assistance can get you out of a bind or a scrape (literally), but it's not a requirement to visit the United States. Coverage can include loss of stolen baggage, illness or injury, and last-minute or midtrip cancellation due to illness or emergency (a special consideration when traveling with children). Travel insurance and assistance policies are sold through insurance companies, automobile clubs, travel agencies, and at airports.

2. GETTING TO & AROUND THE U.S.

GETTING TO THE U.S. In addition to the domestic American airlines listed in Section 6, "Getting There," Chapter 1, several international carriers, including Air Canada (tel. toll free 800/776-3000), British Airways (tel. toll free 800/247-9297), Japan Airlines (tel. toll free 800/525-3663), and SAS (tel. toll free 800/221-2350), also serve Los Angeles International Airport. For the best rates, compare fares and be flexible with the dates and times of travel.

GETTING AROUND THE U.S. Some large airlines (for example, American Airlines, TWA, Northwest, and Delta) offer travelers on their transatlantic or transpacific flights special discount tickets under the name **Visit USA,** allowing travel between any U.S. destinations at minimum rates. They are not on sale in the United States and must be purchased abroad in conjunction with your international ticket. See your travel agent or airline ticket office for full details, including terms and conditions.

European visitors can also buy a **USA Railpass,** good for unlimited train travel on Amtrak. The pass is available through some airlines and travel agents, including Thomas Cook in Great Britain and Cuoni on the continent. Various itinerary options are available for $299 and up. Amtrak officials suggest that you make route reservations as soon as possible, as many trains are often sold out.

With a foreign passport and airline ticket, you can also buy the passes at Amtrak offices in Seattle, San Francisco, Los Angeles, Chicago, New York, Miami, Boston, and Washington, D.C. For further information, contact the Amtrak Distribution Center, P.O. Box 7700, 1549 West Glen Lake Avenue, Itasca, IL 60143 (tel. toll free 800/USA-RAIL in the U.S.).

 THE FOREIGN VISITOR

In addition to the details we've presented below, you'll find the information given in "Fast Facts: Los Angeles" in Chapter 2 to be helpful.

Accommodations Hotels and motels, in many different price ranges, and with a variety of services and amenities, are the most usual accommodations in the United States, although short-term condominium rentals (fully furnished) are quite popular and are the equivalent of renting a flat in Europe. Home and apartment exchanges are also available, as are bed-and-breakfast establishments. Ranch, farm, and family camps are yet other alternatives. And don't forget tent and RV (recreational vehicle, or carvan) camping.

Automobile Associations   If you are a member of a motor club in your home country, you may be eligible for reciprocal services with the American Automobile Association (AAA); it's affiliated with 19 foreign countries, mostly in Europe. If you are eligible, when you need assistance the **Automobile Club of Southern California** (tel. 213/741-3111) can be extremely helpful, providing emergency service, travel advice, and other services.

Business Hours   In Los Angeles, most **banks** are open Monday through Thursday from 9am to 4pm, with later hours on Friday, and a few have Saturday hours as well. **Bars** can be open all day, but they must stop serving liquor daily between the hours of 2 and 6am. **Office hours** are generally Monday through Friday from 9am to 5pm. Most **markets** are open until at least 9pm, and there is usually at least one 24-hour market in a major city; in Los Angeles, 7-Eleven stores, a nationwide chain offering limited groceries, sundries, and beverages, are open 24 hours daily, as are Hughes Markets. Downtown **shops** are open Monday through Saturday from 10am to 6pm. Stores in shopping malls tend to have later hours, and are usually open on Sunday. Call ahead.

Climate   The California climate varies from north to south and inland. Within driving distance of Los Angeles you'll find hot deserts, cool mountains, and foggy seaside towns. San Francisco rarely gets unbearably hot, and Los Angeles rarely gets cold. Coastal towns can change from one moment—or turn—to the next, from sunny and balmy to foggy and misty. San Diego claims perfect weather in the 70s (Fahrenheit) year round.

Consulates   Among the foreign nations with consulates in Los Angeles are the following: **Australia,** 611 North Larchmont Boulevard, Hancock Park (tel. 213/469-4300); **Canada,** 300 South Grand Avenue, Los Angeles (tel. 213/687-7432); **France,** 8350 Wilshire Boulevard, Beverly Hills (tel. 213/479-4426); **Japan,** 250 East 1st Street, Los Angeles (tel. 213/624-8305); **Mexico,** 125 Paseo del La Plaza, Los Angeles (tel. 213/351-6800); **New Zealand,** 10960 Wilshire Boulevard, West Los Angeles (tel. 213/477-8241); and the **United Kingdom,** 3701 Wilshire Boulevard, Suite 312, Los Angeles (tel. 213/385-7381).

Currency and Exchange   The **Los Angeles Currency Exchange** is located at the Los Angeles International Airport in the Tom Bradley International Terminal (tel. 213/646-9346). There you can exchange over 100 currencies and cash traveler's checks; there are six other locations at the airport. Some branches of the **Bank of America** (tel. 213/568-8066) exchange currency; call for information. The **Thomas Cook Currency Exchange** has locations downtown at the Hilton Hotel, 900 Wilshire Boulevard (tel. 213/624-4221, or toll free 800/426-0456); in Beverly Hills at 452 North Bedford Drive (tel. 213/274-9176); and in West Hollywood in the Bank of Los Angeles building, 8901 Santa Monica Boulevard (tel. 213/659-6092).

Customs and Immigration   You may not bring foodstuffs or plants into the United States. Each adult foreign traveler may import no more than $10,000 in cash and $1,000 in gifts. If you enter the country by way of any of the major cities—New York, Los Angeles, San Francisco, Miami, or Dallas—be prepared for long lines to clear Customs.

Drinking Laws   The legal drinking age in California is **21.** Liquor cannot be consumed or purchased in public establishments between the hours of 2 and 6am daily.

Electricity   The electricity in the United States is 110–120 volts, 60 cycles, compared with 220 volts, 50 cycles, in most of Europe. The plugs are flat. It's best to purchase a converter before arriving in the U.S.

Emergencies   Dial **911** for fire, police, or paramedics. In Los Angeles, **poison information** is at 213/484-5151. Three hospitals have 24-hour emergency rooms: **Cedars-Sinai Medical Center,** 8700 Beverly Boulevard, Los Angeles (tel. 213/855-5000, or 213/855-6517 for the emergency room); **Queen of Angeles Medical Center,** 1300 North Vermont Avenue, Los Angeles (tel. 213/413-3000, or 213/413-4896 for the emergency room); and the **Glendale Adventist Medical Center,** 1509 Wilson Terrace, Glendale (tel. 818/409-8000, or 818/409-8202 for the emergency room).

Gasoline   Many California gas stations have self-serve islands, in which you pay first and pump your own gas; you'll pay less than at the full-service islands. One U.S. gallon equals 3.75 liters; 1.2 U.S. gallons equals 1 Imperial gallon.

Holidays   Banks, post offices, government offices, and many stores, restaurants, and museums are closed on the following legal national holidays: January 1 (New Year's Day), third Monday in January (Martin Luther King, Jr., Day), third Monday in February (President's Day), last Monday in May (Memorial Day), July 4 (Independence Day), first Monday in September (Labor Day), second Monday in October (Columbus Day), November 11 (Veteran's Day), last Thursday in November (Thanksgiving Day), and December 25 (Christmas Day).

Information   The helpful **Los Angeles Visitors Information Center** is at 695 South Figueroa Street, between Wilshire Boulevard and 7th Street, Los Angeles (tel. 213/689-8822), open Monday through Saturday from 8am to 5pm. There's another **information center** in Hollywood at the Janes House, 6541 Hollywood Boulevard, near Vine Street (tel. 213/461-4213), open Monday through Saturday from 9am to 5pm. Each location has a multilingual staff to help you make room reservations and give transportation advice, as well as to help plan travel itineraries.

Legal Aid   Should you require legal assistance while visiting, the **Legal Aid Foundation of Los Angeles** (tel. 213/487-3320) will refer you to an appropriate office based on your need.

Mail   Your mail can be sent to you via General Delivery (Poste Restante) through the downtown **U.S. Post Office,** Terminal Annex, 900 North Alameda Street, Los Angeles, CA 90051 (tel. 213/617-4641); it's open Monday through Friday from 8am to 9pm and on Saturday and Sunday from 8am to 4pm. In Beverly Hills there is a post office at 469 North Crescent Drive (tel. 213/247-3400), open Monday through Friday from 8:30am to 5pm. The airport post office, at 5800 West Century Boulevard (tel. 213/337-8840), is open Monday through Friday from 7:30am to midnight (call for weekend hours).

Postage machines are usually accessible even when the post offices are closed. First-class domestic **postage** is 29¢, and a postcard costs 19¢. Airmail charges vary according to country of destination. The international rate is 50¢ for the first half ounce, and 45¢ for every half ounce thereafter.

Medical Emergencies   See "Emergencies," above.

Newspapers and Magazines   The *Wall Street Journal, USA Today, The New York Times,* and the *Christian Science Monitor* are the most popular national newspapers. Each city has its own local newspaper, and some cities have more than one. Our national weeklies include *Time, Newsweek,* and *U.S. News & World Report.* Most large cities have their own city magazine, but it is usually published monthly. See "Fast Facts: Los Angeles" in Chapter 2 for local publications. Foreign newspapers and magazines can be found at the larger newsstands and at airports and some bookstores.

Radio and Television   The four national television networks are the American Broadcasting Company (ABC), the Columbia Broadcasting System (CBS), the National Broadcasting Company (NBC), and the Fox Network. The Public Broadcasting System (PBS) and Cable News Network (CNN) are also seen nationwide. Cable channels, which include movie, news, sports, and children's programming, are available in many hotels in California. NPR is National Public Radio. For the television channels available in Los Angeles, see "Fast Facts: Los Angeles" in Chapter 2; in addition, there are a variety of radio stations—from all-news stations to specialized musical tastes—on both AM and FM frequencies.

Safety   In general the United States is a safe country. But like anywhere else, it has its safety problems, many of which are found in the larger cities. Simply be aware of your surroundings, don't carry your passport with you (have the hotel clerk lock it in a safe), and keep an eye on your valuables. Stay away from deserted areas at night, and don't walk through parks in the evening. See "Fast Facts: Los Angeles" in Chapter 2 for more information.

Taxes   There is no national sales tax (although there are federal excise taxes on alcoholic beverages, gasoline, and interstate and international telephone calls); sales taxes are set by the individual states and municipalities. In California, you'll be charged sales tax on clothing and most other purchases, and tax on food in a restaurant; the combined state/city sales tax in Los Angeles is 8.25%. The "bed" tax, or tax on hotel rooms, also varies with the city; in Los Angeles it's 12.50%.

Telephone   Telephone service in the United States is provided by private companies. Pacific Bell is the company that provides local telephone service in the Los Angeles region. The Greater Los Angeles area is so large that it is currently divided into three **area codes:** 213 for Los Angeles and the surrounding sections, 818 for the San Fernando Valley, and 714 for Orange County. In February 1992, however, the 213 area code will apply only to downtown Los Angeles, Hollywood, Montebello, and a few other sections, while a new 310 area code will be created for Los Angeles International Airport and the western, southern, coastal, and eastern portions of the county, including West Los Angeles, San Pedro, and Whittier. Don't worry—if you dial the wrong area code a recorded message will come on the line to give you the correct code.

A **local call** made at a public pay phone owned by Pacific Bell costs 20¢ for the first 3 minutes, although the minimum charge to call some more distant sections will be higher (the operator will inform you of the charge). Local calls made at a pay phone owned by a company other than Pacific Bell (that is, a privately owned phone) usually have a minimum charge of 25¢. Instructions for using a pay phone are usually printed on the front of the phone. Generally, to place a local call at a pay phone, lift the receiver and listen for the dial tone (a constant midrange tone; if you don't hear the dial tone, the telephone is broken and you should use another phone). When you hear the dial tone, insert your coins (note that the phones do not give change) and dial the area code (if you're phoning a number in the same area code you're calling from, omit dialing the area code) and the seven-digit number; if you hear a high-pitched buzzing sound, the line is busy and you should try again later. When time expires, an operator will announce how much must be deposited to continue the call.

To reach **directory assistance,** dial 411 locally or the area code and 555-1212 nationally.

To place an **international call,** check with your hotel operator for instructions; from a pay telephone, call the international operator by dialing 00 ("double zero").

Telex and Fax   Telex and fax services are available at most large hotels, or from numerous facilities in town; look in the *Yellow Pages* under "Mail Receiving Service."

Time   All of California is in the Pacific time zone, which is 3 hours behind the U.S. East Coast and 8 hours behind Greenwich mean time (when it's 5pm in London, it's noon in New York and 9am in Los Angeles). The United States goes on daylight saving time from the first Sunday in April until 2am on the last Sunday in October.

Tipping   A gratuity of $1 per day left for the maid is especially appreciated. Hotel porters and airport skycaps usually get 75¢ to $1 per bag. Taxi drivers normally get 15%. Most California restaurants do *not* add the tip to the bill, unless it is for a large party and by prearrangement; 15% is the standard tip, 20% for excellent service. If your valet parking was complimentary, the driver who brings you your car should get $1.

Toilets   Unlike some European cities, you won't find many public toilets available on city streets. You will find them in hotel lobbies, shopping centers, museums and libraries, some parking lots, and most public parks and beaches.

Yellow Pages   The *Yellow Pages* is the yellow telephone directory you'll usually find in your hotel room or attached to a pay telephone. It lists businesses, restaurants, services, and industries alphabetically by category. It also has maps, ZIP (postal) Codes, post offices, and even theater and stadium seating charts.

THE AMERICAN SYSTEM OF MEASUREMENTS

LENGTH

1 inch (in.)			=	2.54cm		
1 foot (ft.)	=	12 in.	=	30.48cm	=	.305m
1 yard (yd.)	=	3 ft.			=	.915m
1 mile	=	5,280 ft.			=	1.609km

To convert miles to kilometers, multiply the number of miles by 1.61 (example: 50 mi. × 1.61 = 80.5km). Also use to convert speeds from miles per hour (m.p.h.) to kilometers per hour (kmph).

To convert kilometers to miles, multiply the number of kilometers by .62 (example: 25km × .62 = 15.5 mi.). Also use to convert kmph to m.p.h.

CAPACITY

1 fluid ounce (fl. oz.)			=	.03 liters		
1 pint	=	16 fl. oz.	=	.47 liters		
1 quart	=	2 pints	=	.94 liters		
1 gallon (gal.)	=	4 quarts	=	3.79 liters	=	.83 Imperial gal.

To convert U.S. gallons to liters, multiply the number of gallons by 3.79 (example: 12 gal. × 3.79 = 45.48 liters).

To convert liters to U.S. gallons, multiply the number of liters by .26 (example: 50 liters × .26 = 13 U.S. gal.).

To convert U.S. gallons to Imperial gallons, multiply the number of U.S. gallons by .83 (example: 12 U.S. gal. × .83 = 9.95 Imperial gal.).

To convert Imperial gallons to U.S. gallons, multiply the number of Imperial gallons by 1.2 (example: 8 Imperial gal. × 1.2 = 9.6 U.S. gal.).

WEIGHT

1 ounce (oz.)			=	28.35g		
1 pound (lb.)	=	16 oz.	=	453.6g	=	.45kg
1 ton			=	2,000 lb.	=	907kg = .91 metric tons

To convert pounds to kilograms, multiply the number of pounds by .45 (example: 90 lb. × .45 = 40.5kg).

To convert kilograms to pounds, multiply the number of kilograms by 2.2 (example: 75kg × 2.2 = 165 lb.).

AREA

1 acre			=	.41ha		
1 square mile	=	640 acres	=	259ha	=	2.6km²

To convert acres to hectares, multiply the number of acres by .41 (example: 40 acres × .41 = 16.4ha).

To convert hectares to acres, multiply the number of hectares by 2.47 (example: 20ha × 2.47 = 49.4 acres).

To convert square miles to square kilometers, multiply the number of square miles by 2.6 (example: 80 square miles × 2.6 = 208km²)

To convert square kilometers to square miles, multiply the number of square kilometers by .39 (example: 150km² × .39 = 58.5 square miles).

TEMPERATURE

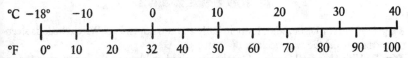

To convert degrees Fahrenheit to degrees Celsius, subtract 32 from °F, multiply by 5, then divide by 9 (example: 85°F – 32 × 5/9 = 29.4°C).

To convert degrees Celsius to degrees Fahrenheit, multiply °C by 9, divide by 5, and add 32 (example: 20°C × 9/5 + 32 = 68°F).

WHAT KIDS LIKE TO SEE & DO

Los Angeles is many things to many people. It's a place so well suited to children that you almost don't have to think about where to take them—you just take them. The wide-open spaces and the good weather make it easy and simple to do almost anything with kids.

SUGGESTED ITINERARIES

Everybody's children are different: Some are early risers and only make it until 3pm, at which point they turn into people you'd rather not know. Other kids can go all day and into the evening—only to fall apart at dinner. Then there are those rare ones you see fast asleep on dad's shoulder, quiet, angelic, sleeping right on until morning, allowing parents to make it back to the hotel with time to read a good book. We don't know your kids or their ages. So the itineraries that follow can be customized to fit your children's ages and needs.

IF YOU HAVE 2 DAYS

Day 1: Head for Disneyland. It opens early and stays open late. Watch the kids sleep in the car on the way back to the hotel.

Day 2: Visit Universal Studios. Or take your tired children to the beach, stop for an early dinner at Carlos and Pepe's or Gladstone's. When your day is over, head right for the airport. Then watch your children sleep on the plane.

IF YOU HAVE 3 DAYS

Day 1: Spend the day as suggested in the above itinerary.

Day 2: Go to the beach, walk on the Santa Monica Pier, have dinner in Westwood Village, and take in a movie.

Day 3: Spend 5 hours at Universal Studios, then head for the pool in your hotel.

IF YOU HAVE 5 DAYS

Days 1 and 2: Try to spend 2 days in Disneyland, staying overnight at one of the local Anaheim hotels (many of which have packages that include passes to Disneyland). Younger children may only need 1 day in Disneyland, mainly to see Fantasyland.

Day 3: Spend a relaxing day at one of the area beaches and have dinner overlooking the Pacific. Or spend the afternoon in Exposition Park, taking a picnic lunch from a local deli.

Day 4: Plan to spend 5 hours at Universal Studios, then relax in the hotel pool or have an early dinner and a stroll in Beverly Hills or on Melrose Avenue. Make this the evening to see a TV taping.

Day 5: Visit the County Museum of Art; most children won't make it longer than 1 hour, so then head next door for about an hour to visit the La Brea Tar Pits. Stop nearby for lunch, then visit Olvera Street in downtown Los Angeles, and nearby Chinatown. Stay for a festive Mexican dinner or a special Chinese banquet.

IF YOU HAVE 7 DAYS

Days 1 and 2: It's Disneyland again. Consider leaving the park early the first day and playing a round of miniature golf at Golf-'N-Stuff Miniature Golf Course across from Disneyland. You may want to stay 3 days and include Knott's Berry Farm in your itinerary.

Days 3 and 4: Assuming everyone is worn out, consider leaving Anaheim for a weekend in Palm Springs (about 2 hours away); or try 2 days in Newport Beach or Dana Point (both within an hour's driving time). If you choose to return to L.A. from Disneyland instead, spend at least 1 day at the beach. The next day, have a late breakfast at Nate 'N Al's in Beverly Hills, and meander down Rodeo Drive. Spend the afternoon at a TV taping at CBS.

Day 5: Spend the morning at Universal Studios, then pass the afternoon at Griffith Park, not far away. There you can visit the Gene Autry Museum, the Zoo, or take the kids on the pony rides. Alternatively, make this the afternoon to visit Hollywood and see the Hollywood Walk of Fame. If the kids are still standing, have dinner at Johnny Rockets followed by a stroll down Rodeo Drive.

Day 6: If this is a weekend day, visit the Los Angeles Children's Museum in the morning, and spend the late afternoon on Olvera Street. Plan dinner at one of Olvera Street's restaurants, or stop at El Cholo, a 15-minute drive away (be sure to make reservations). If it's summer, get tickets for the Hollywood Bowl.

Day 7: Hop a boat for Catalina and spend the entire day exploring the island. Have dinner on the *Queen Mary* in Long Beach or at Ports O' Call in San Pedro, depending on where you embarked.

RAINY-DAY SUGGESTIONS

They say it never rains in southern California, but if you experience a little dampness or fog during your stay—or if you prefer an indoor activity—here are a few things you can see or do indoors. You'll find specific information in Section 2, "More Attractions," below.

- Visit one of the numerous museums in the area.
- Go ice skating (each rink listed rents adults' and children's skates).
- Visit a shopping mall.
- Sit in on a TV taping.
- Attend a library story hour.
- Go to a puppet show downtown.
- Take the kids to the movies.

---

1. KIDS' TOP 10 ATTRACTIONS

DISNEYLAND, 1313 Harbor Blvd., Anaheim. Tel. 714/999-4565 or 213/626-8605 ext. 4565.

⭐ This is the granddaddy of all the theme parks. Disneyland is still a world of magic and wonderment—even when compared with the dozens of other parks that have sprung up in recent years. Many of us remember Disneyland in its infancy, when orange groves and walnut trees surrounded the park, when you could see the Matterhorn from miles away, when the Jungle Cruise ride was state-of-the-art fun. Disneyland has matured (from 18 attractions to more than 60), but it still maintains the Disney hallmarks that make it special. For us, the Disney magic is as much the friendliness and helpfulness of the people who work there as the rides. The streets and walkways are so clean that you never think twice about sitting on the curb to watch a parade.

And of course Disneyland is the place where fantasy is elevated to a classic art form, where the outside world seems less real than the heightened reality inside the park. One family tells the tale of visiting Santa Fe, New Mexico, only to have the youngsters exclaim that it looked just like Frontierland.

Situated on 80 acres (there's another 100 acres just for parking), Disneyland originated the theme-land concept. Today there are seven theme areas. They radiate out from a central hub at the end of Main Street, U.S.A.

Main Street, U.S.A., the entry to the park, is modeled on small-town turn-of-the-century America, and offers many intriguing one-of-a-kind shops. This is also where you can rent strollers, grab a storage locker (for that extra change of clothes, sweaters, etc.), and have the children meet you if they get separated from you. For parents of infants, the Baby Center is an area where you can change diapers (although many rest rooms throughout the park have these facilities), prepare formula, and warm bottles.

The theme of **Adventureland** is the exotic regions of Asia, Africa, and the South Pacific. You'll find the Jungle Cruise ride, Swiss Family Robinson Treehouse, and the Enchanted Tiki Room. The show gives them a chance to sit and rest in a cool spot, but it may be a bit long for antsy toddlers. (We have noticed that some very

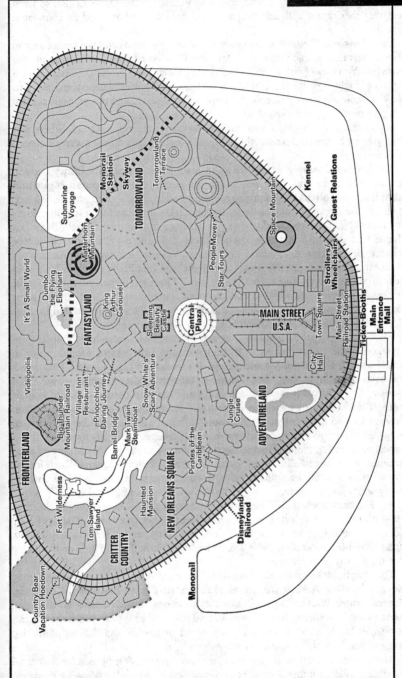

DISNEYLAND

Monorail

Submarine Voyage

It's A Small World

Monorail Station

Skyway

TOMORROWLAND

Tomorrowland Terrace

Matterhorn Mountain

Dumbo the Flying Elephant

FANTASYLAND

King Arthur Carousel

Sleeping Beauty Castle

Videopolis

Space Mountain

Kennel

Guest Relations

PeopleMover

Star Tours

Central Plaza

MAIN STREET U.S.A.

Strollers/ Wheelchairs

FRONTIERLAND

Big Thunder Mountain Railroad

Village Inn Restaurant

Pinocchio's Daring Journey

Barrel Bridge

Mark Twain Steamboat

Snow White's Scary Adventure

Town Square

Main Street Railroad Station

City Hall

Ticket Booths

Main Entrance Mall

Fort Wilderness

Tom Sawyer Island

Haunted Mansion

Pirates of the Caribbean

NEW ORLEANS SQUARE

Jungle Cruise

ADVENTURELAND

CRITTER COUNTRY

Country Bear Vacation Hoedown

Disneyland Railroad

Monorail

young ones are afraid of the mechanical wild animals on the Jungle Cruise, so warn them that they're not real, and prepare them for the gunshots fired by your safari leader.)

New Orleans Square is the home of pirates and ghosts and is a quaint area in which to rest and people-watch. Park favorites **Pirates of the Caribbean** and the **Haunted Mansion** (with its 999 ghosts) are located here. Note: Children under 6 might be frightened by these rides. In Pirates of the Caribbean, there are two lose-your-stomach water descents and some loud gunshots, and the Mansion is filled with ghostly cries and darkened rooms.

If you can time it right, a meal at Blue Bayou Restaurant is a treat. Where else could you eat by the cool moonlight to the sound of crickets during a warm southern California day?

The **Critter Country** theme area is the down-home backwoods. Disney's newest attraction—and the one that's well worth the wait in line—is **Splash Mountain** (get in line while others are waiting to see the parades). This water-slide ride is based on the movie *Song of the South,* in which delightful characters give you a lively rendition of "Zip-A-Dee-Doo-Dah" as you zip along in your boat. The thrill ride has a flume that drops 52 feet and has more than 100 AudioAnimatronic characters, including Br'er Rabbit, Br'er Bear, and Br'er Fox. We loved it as much as Pirates of the Caribbean and Star Tours. (We don't take 4-year-old Elizabeth on Splash Mountain because she's uneasy about the water slide. However, other parents do take preschoolers. Again, each child reacts differently.) Popular with the littlest ones is the Country Bear Playhouse, where they can sing along with the animated stuffed animals. Older children enjoy Davy Crockett's Explorer Canoes.

For a trip back to the days of the pioneers and the Old West, when shoot-'em-ups happened at the town square and riverboats coursed the waters, meander over to **Frontierland. Big Thunder Mountain Railroad** is a huge hit with kids over 7 (and even brave little ones). **Big Thunder Ranch,** a 2-acre replica of an 1880s homestead, is a hit with the smallest children. There is a petting barnyard here (it closes at dusk) and a walk-through model of an antique pioneer log cabin. **Tom Sawyer Island** is the original "run-around and play area" for children with lots of energy. Even parents enjoy it. It has caves, a rope bridge, and balancing rocks. If you happen to be in Frontierland in the morning, don't miss the Mickey Mouse–shaped pancakes at the River Belle Terrace overlooking New Orleans Square. Watch for the newest extravaganza, **Imagination,** a dazzling choreographed show of favorite Disney songs and characters.

Ah, **Fantasyland.** If ever there was a land of fairytales—where dreams do come true—it's this one. The little ones' eyes grow huge as they spot Sleeping Beauty Castle and cross the bridge to where Pinocchio, Mr. Toad, and Peter Pan are waiting. Larger-than-life Cinderellas, Snow Whites, and Seven Dwarfs greet little ones with big hugs on the castle drawbridge.

The storybook kingdom has more than 17 attractions. The gentle, nonfrightening rides are the **King Arthur Carousel, Dumbo the Flying Elephant, Casey Jr. Circus Train, Motor Boat Cruise, Storybook Land Canal Boats,** and **Fantasyland Autopia. It's a Small World** may well be the favorite of the under-6 set—small boats cruise through a wonderland of singing and dancing dolls that serenade you with that namesake catchy tune.

Many of the adventure rides (often in the spooky dark) may be best for children 4 and older (children under 7 must be accompanied by an adult): **Alice in Wonderland, Peter Pan's Flight, Snow White's Scary Adventures,** and **Mr. Toad's**

Wild Ride may frighten very young children. **Pinocchio's Daring Journey** isn't very daring and children of almost any age love to point out all the characters they recognize.

The one problem with rides in Fantasyland is that they are low capacity, so lines move slowly. If you can't avoid the crowds, it may be best if one adult wanders with the kids while the other one waits in line.

But Fantasyland isn't relegated exclusively to tiny tots. This is also the home of the **Matterhorn Bobsleds,** a thrilling ride through the snow-capped park landmark, the Matterhorn. While the older kids and teens love this, don't subject your little tykes to it. Although it is open-air and not darkened, the bobsleds move very quickly, encountering the Abominable Snowman along the way.

And the ultimate teen party has to be Videopolis (open from 8pm until closing on Saturday and holidays, and in the summer). This futuristic dance area with continuous music has 90 television monitors going at once, two 12- by 16-foot projection screens, and a roving camera. Simultaneously, you might have 30 monitors with a music video, 30 with a Charlie Chaplin silent film, and 30 with dancers from the dance floor.

The dynamic, vibrant world of **Tomorrowland** features **Space Mountain, Rocket Jets, Submarine Voyage, Captain EO** (the 3-D movie featuring Michael Jackson), and **Star Tours.** These are among the most popular attractions in the park. Note: Although Captain EO is one of our all-time favorite attractions, the sound is so loud that it scares some toddlers. Instead, we take the toddlers to Skyway to Fantasyland. A trip on the **Disneyland Monorail** is always a thrill.

Tips on How to "Do" the Park: Disneyland's off-season is mid-September through mid-June, except for holiday periods such as Thanksgiving, Christmas, and spring break. Off-season is the best time to come. But, obviously, most visitors come during the peak times. No matter what season you plan to be there, Saturday is the busiest day. Surprise, surprise—during the summer, Friday and Sunday are less crowded (although not by much). Weekdays are the lightest during the rest of the year.

Peak hours are noon to 5pm. Many people leave after sunset, and in the summer another large group leaves after the first Electrical Parade and fireworks (about 9pm). If you have older kids who can stay up late, you can go on rides while everyone else is watching the first parade and then catch the second parade at 11pm.

For the most popular attractions, such as Star Tours, Captain EO, Space Mountain, the Matterhorn, Splash Mountain, Big Thunder Mountain, Haunted Mansion, and Pirates of the Caribbean, try to do them as early as possible. This goes for many of the low-capacity rides in Fantasyland as well. If you're lucky enough to have more than 1 day at Disneyland, you might consider doing what many veteran Disneyland visitors do. Get to the park early! When it gets extremely crowded, get your hand stamped and leave the park until late afternoon. You can return in time for dinner—and thinner crowds.

If you're coming in the summer, you can purchase your tickets in advance and arrive at 8am (when the park opens) to get a head start on the crowds. If you can't do that, park officials suggest that you get there at 7:30am because the ticket lines can be long.

As soon as you get your *Disneyland Souvenir Guide,* take a little time to plan your day so that you don't waste time backtracking. If you've never been to the park before, you can write for the guide ahead of time to decide which attractions you want to see most. Address your request to Disneyland Guest Relations, P.O. Box 3232, Anaheim, CA 92803; or pick up a copy of *The Unofficial Guide to Disneyland* (Prentice Hall Press, 1991) at your local bookstore.

Lost Children: Young strays can be retrieved from the "Lost Children Station," located next to Central First Aid, near Main Street. Or you can go to City Hall, where the staff will contact the "Lost Children Station" for you.

Baby Needs: Baby food is available in the Market House on Main Street, which also stocks medium-size diapers, and at the Gerber Changing Room. Diapers are also available at the Emporium on Main Street at the women's counter, in Tomorrowland at Star Traders (at the camera counter), and at the Hat Shop in New Orleans Square.

Healthier Foods: If you're like many people we know, one of the banes of a theme park is the junk food. Disneyland offers alternatives—even at the fast-food service lines. Check the back pages of the *Disneyland Souvenir Guide* for a complete listing.

Admission: Adults pay $35.50 for a 1-day pass, $46 for a 2-day pass, and $66.50 for a 3-day pass; children 3–11, $20.50 for a 1-day pass, $36.75 for a 2-day pass, and $53.25 for a 3-day pass; children under 3, free.

Open: Mid-June to Aug, daily 8am–1am (closes earlier a few nights); early June and late Aug to Labor Day, daily but the hours vary; Sept to May, Mon–Fri 10am–6pm, Sat–Sun 9am–midnight. There are special hours during holidays—it's best to check hours beforehand. **Parking:** Own parking lot; fee $4. **Directions:** From Los Angeles, take the Harbor Boulevard exit off the Santa Ana Freeway (I-5); Disneyland is about 27 miles south of Los Angeles.

KNOTT'S BERRY FARM, 8039 Beach Blvd., Buena Park. Tel. 714/220-5200 or 714/827-1776.

⭐ Don't expect glamour and glitter when you visit Knott's Berry Farm. Knott's is still a pretty down-to-earth theme park. It has its own charm, mostly because of its small size (it can be visited in 1 day) and the rustic Old West theme that prevails over even the most modern sections. Knott's began as a real farm, and owner Walter Knott cultivated the first boysenberries here. Mrs. Knott (Cordelia) began selling her boysenberry pies and chicken dinners to make money during the Depression. Her famous dinners and pies are still a roaring success at the Chicken Dinner Restaurant in the Marketplace.

If you have young children, you'll probably want to start with **Camp Snoopy,** where they'll meet up with Lucy, Snoopy, and Charlie Brown. In Camp Snoopy there are more than 6 acres of rides tailor-made for youngsters. In fact, some of the "toddler-appropriate" rides are extremely short and very gentle. The staff takes longer than necessary to get kids ready for a ride (even with short lines), so be prepared. Beary Tales Playhouse was undoubtedly our 4-year-old's favorite Camp Snoopy activity. She reported that going through the bears' tree house was scary and fun at the same time. In front of some of the bear scenes along the way are narrow semi-enclosed "trails" for the toddlers to crawl through. They are dark and can be claustrophobic—each time we've been there we've watched one or two youngsters needing to be pulled out by their parents midway along the trail.

Next along the road, **Fiesta Village** is where you'll find Montezooma's Revenge. Sure to cause excitement in preteens and teens, this roller coaster goes not only in a loop, but backward too! Brave souls can move on to the **Roaring '20s,** home of the sky tower, a parachute jump that deposits you 20 stories down at free-fall speed. Not for the faint of heart.

Calmer experiences can be found in **Ghost Town,** an authentic 1880s Old West gold-rush town and the original section of the amusement park. Kids love the ride on the authentic stagecoach. Be prepared for long lines. The steam engine fascinates children of all ages. Even if they don't take the ride, kids love to stand close to this monstrous iron horse and just see how it's put together.

The next star in Knott's world is the **Kingdom of the Dinosaurs.** We can honestly say that the "monsters" are extremely realistic and were quite frightening to Janey when she was 4 (and to her mother). But by age 5 she couldn't wait to go back. In this age of dinosaurmania, it's a perfect thrill ride for ages 7 and up. As you exit this ride, you'll come to a huge arcade of games with something for every age group.

Newest to the park is the **Wild Water Wilderness Area,** which features an exhilarating ride down the longest artificial white-water rapids.

Altogether there are over 165 rides at Knott's, so there will be something to appeal to every age in your group.

Baby Needs: Near the exit of Beary Tales in Camp Snoopy is a baby station with changing tables and a microwave for heating bottles. There's another one in the Marketplace at the First Aid Station. Stroller rentals are available here.

Admission: $21 adults and children 12 and older, $17 children 3–11, $15 for the handicapped, expectant mothers, and seniors 60 and over; free for children 3 and under. Holidays often mean special rates, so call first. Off-season there's sometimes a "Kids Are Free" promotion, during which time one child is admitted free per paid adult; call for details.

Open: In summer (Memorial Day to Labor Day), Sun–Fri 9am–midnight, Sat 9am–1am; winter, Mon–Fri 10am–6pm, Sat 10am–10pm, Sun 10am–7pm. Call for holiday hours. **Closed:** Christmas Day. **Directions:** From Los Angeles, take the Santa Ana Freeway (I-5) south to Calif. 39 (the Knott's Berry Farm exit is noted on the freeway); then just follow the signs (which are very small).

UNIVERSAL STUDIOS HOLLYWOOD, 100 Universal City Plaza, Universal City. Tel. 818/777-1000.

This, the world's largest—and busiest—motion-picture and television studio, is quintessential Hollywood. The tour thrills nearly everyone over the age of 4. If this is your first visit, plan to spend at least 5 to 7 hours.

The **Guided Tram Tour** is a 2½-hour open-air tram excursion through the front and back lots of Universal. Not only do you get backstage knowledge about the making of movies and television shows, but visitors are also treated to an array of special-effects creations as you travel through the 420-acre back lot of more than 500 outdoor sets, such as *The Sting, Psycho,* and "Murder, She Wrote."

Visitors are "introduced" to the enormous 30-foot, 30,000-pound King Kong (the world's largest animated figure) and the 24-foot killer shark from *Jaws.* In *Earthquake,* The Big One, the ground sinks beneath you, the walls come crumbling down, and everything in sight is ripped apart by mother nature's awesome fury. Experience the parting of the Red Sea and special effects from *ET* and the *Back to the Future* trilogy.

This adventurous tour is certainly worth the time, but it's difficult to predict how your youngsters will react to some of the special effects. The enormous King Kong may be frightening to toddlers, although some very young kids love it; others might get scared by the *Jaws* shark. The spinning Ice Cave is another special effect that alarms some young children, but most children over the age of 5 or 6 delight in almost all of them. There are bathroom breaks along the way, and if you find that your child is having too much trouble, the tram can be stopped at any time and standby vans will take you back to the central area.

The **Entertainment Center** is the unguided portion of the tour that offers live amphitheater shows. All shows are 15 to 30 minutes in length and are timed so that you can see one after another (but on crowded days you may have to line up early).

Universal Tours is also known for its **stunt shows,** and *The Miami Vice Action Spectacular,* a live-action show with dynamic special effects. Young children love the *Animal Actors Stage,* where trainers show how they get animals to act, and the *American Tale Show* and Fievel's Playland.

Definitely for older children is *The Adventures of Conan: A Sword and Sorcery Spectacular.* The special effects are beautifully created, but it's a very intense, loud show.

"Trekies" will go for *The Star Trek Adventure,* a 30-minute show that allows guests to participate in a production of "Star Trek," using actual sets, special effects, music, and costumes from the original shows. A 7-minute feature, using the guests, is produced and shown to the audience.

At **Streets of the World** you'll see the actual movie sets that were used in some of the all-time great movies. There's Baker Street from Sherlock Holmes' London, for instance, and Mel's Diner from *American Graffiti.* Cartoon and famous Hollywood personalities stroll around the park, greet guests, and sign autographs.

A museum of memorabilia and film clips dedicated to Lucille Ball, **A Tribute to Lucy,** is extremely popular with kids and adults alike. And the new $36-million **E.T. Adventure** ride takes you flying by bicycle, with E.T. leading the way.

Outdoor eating areas abound and offer a choice of Italian, Mexican, and American goodies. If you want regular restaurant fare and would prefer to eat indoors, see Section 3, "Kid-Rated Restaurants," in Chapter 7 for details.

In the summer, be sure to bring plenty of sunscreen, sun visors, and little hats for the kids. In the winter, bring warm jackets and layer clothes (it may be only 60° but the wind on the hill really picks up). Approximately 70 of the attractions are outdoors, so you'll want to be comfortable.

Admission: $22 adults, $16.50 children 3–11 and seniors, free for children under 3. Admission entitles you to the 2-hour Tram tour and all the shows and attractions in the Entertainment Center.

Open: Summer (June through August) and holidays year round, daily 8am–5pm; the rest of the year, daily 9:30am–3:30pm. **Closed:** Thanksgiving and Christmas days. **Parking:** $4 cars, $5 RVs. **Directions:** Take the Hollywood Freeway (U.S. 101) to either Universal Center or the Lankershim Boulevard exit.

GEORGE C. PAGE MUSEUM OF LA BREA DISCOVERIES, 5801 Wilshire Blvd., Mid-Wilshire District. Tel. 213/857-6311 or 213/936-2230.

Known by most locals as the La Brea Tar Pits, this museum has one of the largest deposits of Ice Age mammals and birds in the world. The pits were found by the first overland explorers in 1769, who saw bubbling pools of asphalt. The first American to own the land, Henry Hancock, started quarrying the area but thought that the bones he found were just from cows and other local animals. Later, however, paleontologists realized these were the remains of Ice Age animals that had become trapped in the tar over the last 40,000 years. In 1912 George Allen Hancock, Henry's son, gave the Los

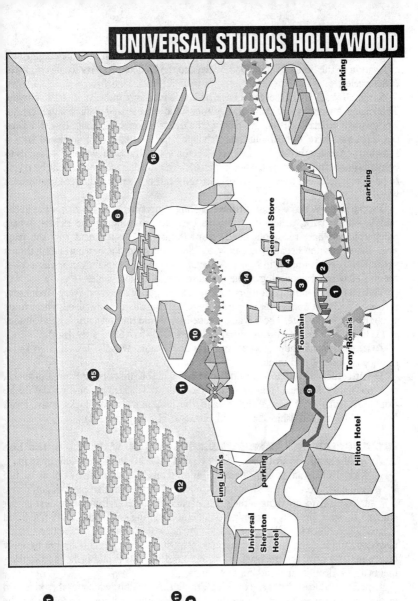

UNIVERSAL STUDIOS HOLLYWOOD

Entertainment Center ⑭
Entrance and Ticket Booth ①
First Aid Station ⑩
Guest Relations ③
Informational Booth ②
Set Streets ⑮
Starway Escalator ⑨
Studio Backlot ⑧
Studio Center ⑬
Studio Front Lot ⑫
Studio Tram Ride Entrance ⑪
TV Audience Ticket Booth ④
Studio Tram Ride ⑯

Angeles Museum of Natural History the rights and jurisdiction over the digging and excavation of the bones, and in 1918 he deeded the 23-acre property to the county of Los Angeles.

Some 60 years later George C. Page built this museum and gave it to the county. The Page is a working museum, and visitors stand mesmerized as they watch careful workers behind glass sorting and dusting the delicate bones and fragments. Kids can see displays where optical illusions "change" the skeleton of a mammal into a ferocious saber-toothed tiger. Another skeleton—the "La Brea Woman"—seems to come to life before their eyes. They experience the stickiness of the asphalt by trying to pull large poles out of it, and see—close up—just how large an imperial mammoth was.

Even today you'll see ponds of the bubbling material. There is a major dig in the middle of the park, called Pit 91. This excavation is one of the richest, where paleontologists have recovered hundreds of thousands of specimens over the years since the excavation began. You can watch them work from a viewing station (hours vary). This place is unique in North America. Two movies explain various aspects of the museum and paleontology. The museum is stroller-accessible.

Tours: Free 1-hour park tours for the general public are given every Wednesday through Sunday at 1pm (weather permitting). Call for the meeting place. These tours go to the excavation site. There is also a general museum tour on Saturday and Sunday at 11:30am and 2pm. Call for special tours (tel. 213/857-6306 after 1pm).

Admission: $3 adults, $1.50 students and seniors over 62, 75¢ children 5–12, free for children 4 and under.

Open: Tues–Sun 10am–5pm. **Directions:** If you are coming from a distance, take the Santa Monica Freeway (I-10) and exit at Fairfax; go north to Wilshire Boulevard, turn right onto Wilshire and the museum is two blocks away. From Beverly Hills, take Wilshire Boulevard east, two blocks past Fairfax.

LOS ANGELES CHILDREN'S MUSEUM, 310 N. Main St., in the Los Angeles Mall, downtown. Tel. 213/687-8800 for 24-hour information.

Kids always want to come back to this museum. The interactive exhibits are fun and educational at the same time. Children love the fact that parents don't have to say no to anything—they can participate in everything. Our first-grader enjoyed dressing up in a fireman's costume and playing with giant foam-filled and Velcro-edged blocks, acting as a television anchorwoman on a videotape of a nightly newscast, and making music on jug-band instruments. Our preschooler got to apply facepaints and drive the once-active city bus, and she was proud of her accomplishments at the drop-in arts-and-crafts sessions.

Especially educational is the ongoing Ethnic L.A. exhibit, which teaches kids—in an interactive way—about various Los Angeles ethnic cultures. On one visit the Japanese-American culture was featured and our first-grader was taught how to make elaborate Japanese paper dolls. Another permanent exhibit, the Louis B. Mayer Performance Space, provides a stage for mimes, actors, and storytellers. Theatrical games and music and dance workshops are also featured.

The museum is geared to kids from 2 to 12, but adults will thoroughly enjoy the experience. The building is not stroller-accessible, but is accessible to the disabled. Fast food is available Monday through Saturday downstairs in the Mall.

Admission: $4 adults and children, free for youngsters under 2.

Open: June–Aug, Mon–Fri 11:30am–5pm, Sat–Sun 10am–5pm; Sept–May

Wed–Thurs 2–4pm, Sat–Sun 10am–5pm. Call about special holiday hours. **Parking:** Park in the L.A. Mall garage (the entrance is on Los Angeles Street) on weekdays, at Municipal Lot 7 on weekends (on the corner of Temple Street and San Pedro Street), at Union Station on Alameda Street, or in the Olvera Street lots (two blocks north); some street parking is available on weekends. **Directions:** Get there on the Hollywood Freeway (U.S. 101); the museum is next to the freeway on Main Street, one block north of Los Angeles City Hall.

EXPOSITION PARK, bounded by Exposition Boulevard, Martin Luther King, Jr., Boulevard, Menlo Avenue, and Figueroa Street.

Exposition Park is a culturally and recreationally rich area. The site of the Los Angeles Memorial Coliseum, the Los Angeles Memorial Sports Arena, the Rose Garden, the California Museum of Science and Industry, the Museum of Natural History, and the California Afro-American Museum, it is a place you'll want to spend quite a bit of time. (For details on these three museums, see "Museums" in Section 2, "More Attractions," below.)

If you don't want to pack a lunch, there is a McDonald's—with an exhibit—next to the main building of the Museum of Science and Industry.

Directions: Take the Santa Monica Freeway (I-10) to the Harbor Freeway (I-110) south and follow the exit signs to the museums.

GRIFFITH OBSERVATORY AND PLANETARIUM, 2800 E. Observatory Rd., north of Hollywood. Tel. 213/664-1181, or 213/664-1191 for recorded information.

The observatory and planetarium are a highlight of any trip to Los Angeles. Fascinating and educational at the same time, the **planetarium theater** with its 75-foot domed ceiling re-creates the skies, taking kids and adults on journeys through space. Serious stargazers and awe-struck children alike watch as the enormous domed ceiling is transformed from nothing to astral heavens with thousands of stars. The narrator takes you on voyages through these stars to different planets and eras.

This is best for children over 5 (unless yours are exceptional). While children 5 and over delight as the room gets dark (complete with a sunset over the mountains) and the "sky" becomes jet-black, setting the stage for the evening stars and a lesson in astronomy, younger ones tend to get scared by the darkness.

The 2-year-old with us couldn't quite decide whether or not she liked it. She'd be content for a while, and then, when the music rose or the sky changed in a dramatic way, she'd start to cry and one of us would have to stand with her near the exit, where there was more light. There is a special performance for children under 5 on Saturday and Sunday at 1:30pm (they're not admitted to the other performances) when the shows are a little shorter and a little more general. We found the major difference to be that young children are in abundance so we didn't have to worry so much about disturbing other people who may be serious about their astronomy education.

The shows generally last 1 hour, and several different presentations are offered during the year.

The **Hall of Science** at the planetarium has displays as well as interactive exhibits about physical science, astronomy, and geology. The Foucault Pendulum is one of the most fascinating exhibits you're likely to see. You watch as the earth's rotation causes the pendulum to knock down little pegs as it swings. There's also a solar telescope,

6-foot globes of the earth and moon, and a working seismograph. (Watch the kids jump in an effort to get the needle to register.) There's also a large telescope you can use on clear evenings from sunset to 9:45pm when the hall is open.

Don't miss the bookstore, one of the best for astronomical slides, book starfinders, and souvenirs.

The **Laserium, The Laser Show** (tel. 818/997-3624) is presented at the Observatory. This fantastic light-and-music extravaganza is a favorite of teens and adults who like bold, pulsating music. The performer projects laser imagery on the domed planetarium ceiling (five stories high at the top) to accompany and accentuate the musical beat. Performances are done to rock, new age, and classical music; call ahead for the schedule. This isn't an event for little ones. In fact, children under 5 aren't admitted.

Admission: Hall of Science, free. Planetarium shows, $3.50 adults, $2.50 children 5–15 and seniors, free for children under 5 (only admitted to the children's show Sat–Sun at 1:30pm or other special shows). Laserium, $6 adults, $5 children 5–12 (children under 5 not admitted).

Open: Hall of Science, summer, daily 12:30–10pm; winter, Tues–Fri 2–10pm, Sat–Sun 12:30–10pm. Planetarium shows, summer, Mon–Fri at 1:30, 3, and 7:30pm, Sat–Sun at 1:30 (young children's show), 3, 4:30, and 7:30pm; winter, Tues–Fri at 3 and 7:30pm, Sat–Sun at 1:30 (young children's show), 3, 4:30, and 7:30pm. Laserium shows, Tues–Thurs at 6 and 8:45pm, Fri–Sat at 6, 8:45, and 9:45pm, Sun at 6:30pm. Be sure to get to the Laserium well ahead of time because it's often crowded. **Parking:** Parking lot; no charge. **Directions:** Take either the Hollywood Freeway (U.S. 101) to the Vermont Avenue exit, or the Golden State Freeway (I-5) to the Los Feliz exit and drive west to Vermont Avenue; the observatory is located at the north end of Vermont Avenue.

LOS ANGELES ZOO, 5333 Zoo Dr., Griffith Park, north of Hollywood. Tel. 213/666-4090.

The Los Angeles Zoo has over 2,000 different mammals, birds, and reptiles of about 500 different species. Sitting on 113 acres, the zoo is organized "zoogeographically." This means that the animals are divided into the areas resembling those in which they live in the wild (the five continents). With a zoo this large (and hilly), it's a good idea first to sit down with the zoo map and chart out what you want to see. During the summer, get an early start because the zoo tends to get hot and smoggy. Plan to spend at least half a day here, probably more with older children.

The zoo is not to be outdone by all the theme parks and attractions surrounding it. It, too, has special shows. There is *The World of Birds, Animals and You,* and *Wild in the City.* It's a good idea to plan around these events when mapping out your day. On the weekends year round, and daily during the summer, you can hear the keepers talk about their animals—orangutans, gorillas, rhinoceroses, hippos, giraffes, and tigers. The kids love this part! Don't miss the elephant and camel rides.

The children's zoo, **Adventure Island,** opened in May 1989. The focus is on the wildlife of the southwestern U.S.—the shorelines, caves, deserts, meadows, mountains, haciendas, barnyards, and nurseries. The Pepsi Zoorific Theater is the site for *Wild in the City,* an imaginative re-creation of a night hike through Griffith Park with the fauna and flora encountered along the way. Throughout Adventure Island interactive devices allow curious visitors to see through the eyes of a prairie dog, compare their sense of smell to a bear's, try on a pair of horns, hatch a variety of eggs, and much more. The cave of nocturnal animals is quite popular.

Admission: $6 adults, $2.75 children 2–12, $5 seniors, free for children under 2. Stroller rental is $2.

Open: Summer, daily 10am–6pm; winter, daily 10am–5pm. **Closed:** Christmas Day. **Directions:** Take the Golden State Freeway (I-5) north to the junction with the Ventura Freeway (U.S. 101); the zoo is at the junction of the two freeways.

SIX FLAGS MAGIC MOUNTAIN, 26101 Magic Mountain Pkwy., Valencia. Tel. 818/367-2271 or 805/255-4100.

Magic Mountain's 260 acres offers family fun for every age. Always popular with thrill-seeking teens and preteens who delight in the stupendous roller coasters and water adventures, Magic Mountain has added several attractions to entertain the younger set. There are 100 rides in all, plus live shows, a dance club, a petting zoo, and a year-round crafts village.

Magic Mountain is best known for its electrifying **roller-coaster rides.** Viper, the world's tallest and fastest steel looping roller coaster, is the newest. Its highest point is 188 feet above the ground, and it plunges down a 55° drop. Ninja—the black belt of roller coasters—is the fastest suspended roller coaster. Traveling at speeds up to 55 m.p.h. on a half-mile route through the surrounding forest, this roller coaster is suspended from an overhead track. There's nothing underneath riders as they go through steep drops and side-to-side swings of up to 110°. Colossus is the gargantuan double-track wooden roller coaster that is invariably rated in the top 10 in America. Revolution was the world's first coaster with a 360° vertical loop, and has the distinction of being one of the world's largest steel coasters. New to the park is Psyclone, a wooden roller coaster and a replica of Coney Island's legendary Cyclone. The sounds of creaking wood are sure to get you!

Magic Mountain was one of the first amusement parks to have **water-flume rides.** Log Jammer takes its riders in hollowed-out logs through a winding, twisting voyage that plunges through the water. In Jet Stream, riders in speedboats plummet down a 52-foot drop. Tidal Wave is a ride that takes 20-passenger boats on a plunge over a 50-foot waterfall.

Younger children enjoy **Bugs Bunny World,** a 6-acre area especially designed for little kids. Little squeals of excitement can be heard from the Wile E. Coyote Roller Coaster, a scaled-down version of the bigger item. After the young ones have had their share of rides, you'll want to meander to **Wile E. Coyote Critter Canyon** with its 55 different kinds of animals, including miniature horses.

When we need a break, we hightail it over to **Spillikin Handcrafter's Junction,** an 1800s-style crafts village where we find some shade and just relax.

Show highlights change from year to year. Try to catch the U.S. High-Dive Team stunt show for a real thrill. The Foghorn Leghorn Wild Animal Show is bound to delight kids as young as 3. We always like the Dolphin and Sea Lion Show. And don't miss out on the puppet theaters.

Tips for Doing the Park: Arrive early in the day. If you have very young kids, you might want to bring some juice. Many a time we've been hard-pressed to find a vending machine or snack bar that has anything other than soft drinks and milk. But if your kids are like ours, they'll want to try all the goodies and sweets they see, so expect to be reaching in your pocket often. Valencia can be quite warm on summer days. Be sure to bring sunscreen, hats, and a change of clothes (there are lots of water rides) if you'll be visiting during the summer. Rental strollers and coin lockers are available. You can find diapers at the Pamper Baby Care Center, located near Bugs Bunny World.

Admission: $23 adults, $11 seniors and children under 4 feet tall, free for children under 3—including unlimited use of all rides, shows, and attractions.

Open: Memorial Day–Labor Day, daily from 10am; the rest of the year, Sat–Sun and school hols. from 10am. Call ahead for specific dates and closing times. **Parking:** $4. **Directions:** Take the Magic Mountain Parkway exit off the Golden State Freeway (I-5) about 25 minutes north of Hollywood.

THE BEACHES

One of Southern California's biggest claims to fame is its glorious beaches. Kids of all ages love them, even in the winter. See Section 4, "Letting off Steam" below, for specifics on the individual beaches. Unless indicated otherwise, all parking lots charge a fee, usually $4 to $5. In some cases you can find street parking as well.

2. MORE ATTRACTIONS

MUSEUMS

BARNSDALL ART PARK, 4800 Hollywood Blvd., near Vermont Ave., Hollywood. Tel. 213/485-4474.

The Barnsdall Art Park houses the **Los Angeles Municipal Art Gallery** and the **Junior Art Gallery,** just a few yards away, where there's always something of interest on display. If you're around on a Sunday (except in June), you're invited to Sunday Open Sunday, Barnsdall's Junior Arts Center free family art workshops, with sessions open to all age groups (most Sundays from 2 to 4pm).

Admission: Municipal Art Gallery, $1 adults, free for children under 13; Junior Arts Gallery, free.

Open: Both galleries, Tues–Sun 12:30–5pm.

CRAFT AND FOLK ART MUSEUM, 6067 Wilshire Blvd., 4th Floor, May Company Building, Mid-Wilshire District. Tel. 213/937-5544.

This small museum pays tribute to the ethnic diversity of Los Angeles and southern California and has rotating exhibits of traditional folk arts and international crafts. Its gift shop is a museum in itself, displaying textiles, masks, ceramics, jewelry, books, and contemporary crafts. The gift shop is found at 5800 Wilshire Boulevard (tel. 213/937-9099) and is open Tuesday through Saturday from 10am to 5pm and on Sunday from 11am to 5pm.

If you're in town at the end of October, call for information about the amazing International Festival of Masks sponsored by the museum. The museum also hosts monthly family programs held on Sunday evenings from 5:30 to 7:30pm. It might be an evening of storytelling, art, or folk music. Craft classes are also available from time to time.

Note: The museum is currently located on Wilshire Boulevard at the corner of

Fairfax Avenue, but in the next 2 to 3 years it will be moving along Wilshire to a new location at the corner of Curson Avenue.

Admission: Free.

Open: Tues–Sat 10am–5pm, Sun 11am–5pm.

CALIFORNIA AFRO-AMERICAN MUSEUM, 600 State Dr., in Exposition Park, downtown. Tel. 213/744-7432.

This small museum is one of the few that focuses on the talents and contributions of African Americans in such fields as the arts, humanities, sciences, and sports. The atrium-court sculpture garden is a place where children can feel comfortable speaking in normal tones and wandering around the sculptures of African-American artists. Special very involving hands-on workshops are held throughout the year. Call for details.

Admission: Free.

Open: Daily 10am–5pm. **Directions:** Take the Santa Monica Freeway (I-10) to the Harbor Freeway (I-110) south and follow the exit signs to the museums.

CALIFORNIA MUSEUM OF SCIENCE AND INDUSTRY, 700 State Dr., in Exposition Park, downtown. Tel. 213/744-7400.

Most people don't know that the California Museum of Science and Industry is the second-largest science/technology museum compound in the United States. (The largest is the Smithsonian Institution in Washington, D.C.) But you won't be surprised by that fact once you see the complex of buildings. This is a lively place where kids will want to spend time learning and experimenting.

The museum, with its many exhibit halls, gives new meaning to the word "interactive." Here kids and adults can "talk" with the exhibits, go inside them, move them around, even create with them. And there are so many different kinds of exhibits that each family member is sure to find something that strikes a responsive chord.

As you wander through Exposition Park, you'll see an F-104 Starfighter plane suspended on the outside of one structure. This is the **Aerospace Building.** School-age children just love this place because they can almost touch many of the aircraft and satellites suspended in the air. You can see the *Gemini II* spacecraft and replicas of *Explorer 1, Sputnik 1, Pioneer 1,* and *Pioneer 5* satellites and the *Viking* spacecraft, the Mars lander. In addition to satellites and spacecraft, it has many full-size and model airplanes, including the 1911 Wright brothers Model B aircraft, an air force T-38, and a Northrop F-20 Tigershark.

At the interactive exhibits, the children can maneuver a model rocket, and can pull levers and push buttons to experience such concepts as lift and thrust.

The Aerospace Building has a wonderful gift store that has many unique items for children and adults interested in astronomy, aircraft, and space paraphernalia.

The **Science Wing and Industry Hall,** also known as the **Ahmanson Building,** is the main exhibit building of the compound. It's ironic that this building, which housed the realistic earthquake exhibit, is now closed indefinitely for earthquake reinforcement! Check when you're in the park to see if it has reopened. The McDonald's fast-food restaurant it houses is still open.

Another delight is the **Technology Hall** with its popular, not-to-be-missed displays—Mathematica, the Bicycle Company, and Invisible Forces/Electricity and Magnesium.

CALIFORNIA

Sacramento ★

Los Angeles ●

Barnsdall Art Park **26**
Descanso Gardens **23**
Disneyland **22**
Exposition Park **16**
Gene Autry Western Heritage
    Museum **11**
George C. Page Museum of
    La Brea Discoveries **15**
Griffith Observatory and
    Planetarium **14**
Griffith Park **13**
J. Paul Getty Museum **2**
Kidspace **24**
Knott's Berry Farm **21**
Los Angeles County Museum
    of Art **18**
Los Angeles Zoo **12**
Manhattan Beach State Park **7**
Medieval Times **20**
Movieland Wax Museum **19**
Museum of Contemporary Art **17**
Museum of Flying **27**
Raging Waters **29**
Redondo Beach Pier and King
    Harbor **8**
Redondo Beach State Park **9**
Redondo Sport Fishing Pier **10**
Santa Monica Pier **6**
Santa Monica State Beach **5**
Seaside Lagoon **9A**
Six Flags Magic Mountain **25**
Topanga State Park **1**
Universal Studios Hollywood **28**
Warner Bros. Studio VIP Tour **10**
Will Rogers State Beach **4**
Will Rogers State Historic Park **3**

LOS ANGELES AREA ATTRACTIONS

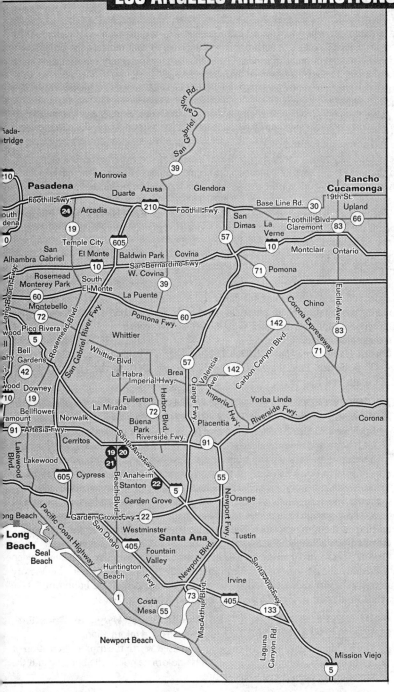

The **Kinsey Hall of Health** is unique in that you can actually get a medical self-checkup. Check yourself for breathing, pulse, heart rate, and nutritional habits, and a computer will give you a health profile. But the highlight of the hall is the neon-lit "Diner," complete with bar stools and menus that indicate the protein, fat, and carbohydrate content of foods. The menus are for imaginary restaurants such as "Hamburger Heaven" (featuring hamburgers and apple pie). You are "served" nutritional information by an outrageous waitress, who interacts with you through a touch-screen video terminal.

Don't leave Exposition Park without visiting the **IMAX Theater** (tel. 213/744-2014 for information). On a huge screen you'll see live-action movies that almost make you feel as though you're experiencing the real thing. The sound system (developed by Lucasfilm Ltd., which created *Star Wars*) intensifies the experience. It's incredible, and the movies are usually educational to boot. Young children, although welcome, may not do well—the sound effects are quite loud and can be overwhelming to a 3-year-old.

The first of its kind, the **Mark Taper Hall of Economics and Finance** explains the basic rules of economics and finance in language all of us can understand. Of the 60 exhibits, more than 30 are controlled by interactive computers so you can participate. You might be surprised, but our kids enjoy this hall thoroughly. (Be sure they're old enough to read and have a concept of money, though.) Dramatic simulations make it entertaining to learn about the laws of supply and demand, inflation, and many other economic concepts. As an example, you get to try your hand at making money running an umbrella stand and selling umbrellas for $3 each. How will a typhoon affect their price? What about sunny weather?

Admission: Free.

Open: Daily 10am–5pm. **Closed:** New Year's, Thanksgiving, and Christmas days. **Directions:** Take the Santa Monica Freeway (I-10) to the Harbor Freeway (I-110) south and follow the exit signs to the museums.

GENE AUTRY WESTERN HERITAGE MUSEUM, 4700 Zoo Dr., in Griffith Park, north of Hollywood Tel. 213/667-2000.

 Fairly new to Los Angeles, the Gene Autry Museum captures the spirit of the Old West and communicates it to children instantly. Murals, movies, and interactive exhibits tell the story of the West in a way that few other museums have been able to do so far. One of the world's most comprehensive repositories of American western history, its collections include firearms, common tools, clothing, toys, games, and furnishings of many of the famous, and not-so-famous, people of that era. Allow enough time to meander through the entire space, wander outside, and spend time in the museum store. Kids and grownups will delight in this museum.

Admission: $5.50 adults, $4 students and seniors, $2.50 children 2–12.

Open: Tues–Sun 10am–5pm. **Directions:** From downtown, take the Golden State Freeway (I-5) north, or the Ventura Freeway (Calif. 134) east to the Victory Boulevard exit, turn right, and follow the signs to the museum; from Hollywood, take Los Feliz Boulevard to Zoo Drive, turn left, and follow the signs.

J. PAUL GETTY MUSEUM, 17985 Pacific Coast Hwy., at Coastline, Malibu. Tel. 213/458-2003 for reservations and information.

The building that houses the museum is in itself worth the trip. A re-creation of an Italian villa, complete with fountains and ornate pools, the building and the surrounding complex are very impressive.

The Getty has an unusual attitude toward children. Kids are encouraged to look closely. Parents of young children are not admonished if their kids make noise, but instead are invited to take a break with the kids in the lovely gardens.

Gallery teachers recommend a number of exhibits for children, including the Decorative Arts Collection, paintings from the 12th century to the early 20th century, and the Antiquities Collection (artifacts from ancient life). Their attitude is that children are never too young to start appreciating fine art. Children will enjoy the experience if their parents don't expect too much of them.

The Getty hosts an excellent and extensive series of programs expressly for families each month. Small groups of children with their parents delve into one aspect of art that is presented in the museum, for example, mythology, cover portraiture, or animals on puzzling pots. You must sign up in advance.

Admission: Free, but *no walk-in traffic is allowed*. If you plan to come by car and park, you must make a (free) parking reservation 7–10 days in advance (by mail or by telephone)—you cannot park on the streets near the museum. If you don't get a parking permit, you may enter the museum grounds only by bicycle, motorcycle, taxi, or RTD bus no. 434 (get a museum pass from the driver).

Open: Tues–Sun 10am–5pm. **Directions:** Take the Santa Monica Freeway (I-10) west to the Pacific Coast Highway (Calif. 1) north, and continue 5 miles north.

KIDSPACE, 390 S. El Molino Ave., Pasadena. Tel. 818/449-9143.

This is a small participatory museum geared to spark the curiosity of children ages 2 to 12. Kids will feel comfortable in this small, casual museum, which has a number of permanent exhibits as well as special programs throughout the year. Plan to spend a couple of hours here.

The Television Studio and Disc Jockey Booth is a permanent exhibit that gives kids the chance to play at performing in the glamorous broadcast world. Kids feel uninhibited enough to just start dancing to the music coming from the booth, and they take turns recording their own messages. Human Habitrail allows curious kids to study a live ant colony, and then pretend to be ants in the carpeted Ant Wall. Grown-Up Tools gives kids the opportunity to learn about adult occupations by trying on authentic uniforms and using real equipment from various trades and professions. There are clothes for dress-up and mirrors for preening. The little—and big—kids love the face-painting bar.

There's a small giftshop, and vending machines and picnic tables are outside.

Admission: $3.25, free for children under 2.

Open: Oct–June, Wed 2–5pm, Sat–Sun 12:30–5pm. Call for special summer hours and to find out about special workshops, programs, and performances.

Parking: Street parking available.

LOS ANGELES COUNTY MUSEUM OF ART, 5905 Wilshire Blvd., Mid-Wilshire District. Tel. 213/857-6000.

To get the most out of the day, we usually go to one of the museum galleries, have a snack or lunch, let the kids romp in the adjacent Hancock Park (or watch the mimes and musicians), and then spend another hour at the Page Museum, also in the park.

Opened in 1965 with three buildings, the Los Angeles County Museum of Art has almost doubled in size. Today it's the largest art museum in the West. The original structure is the **Ahmanson Building,** housing the permanent art collection that

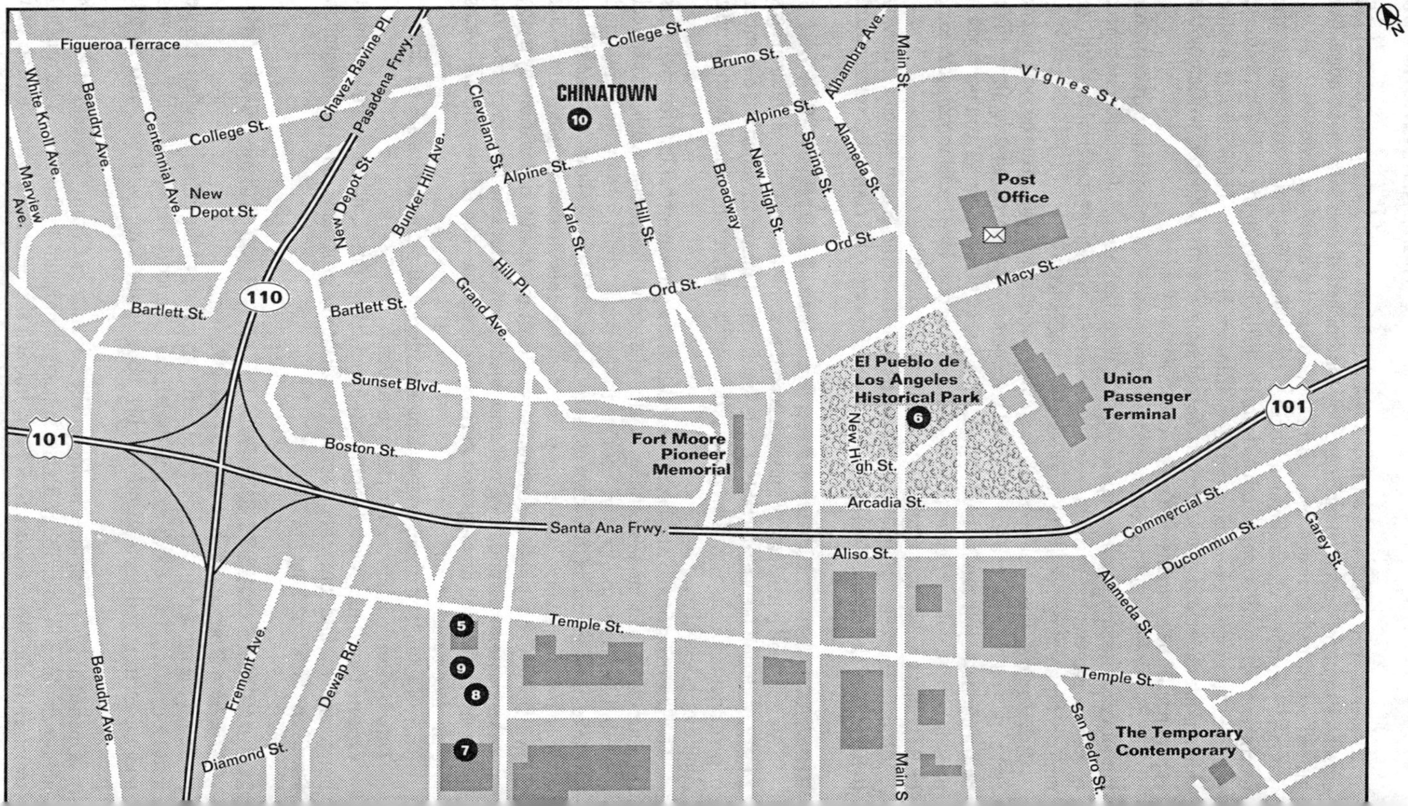
CHINATOWN
10
Post Office
Union Passenger Terminal
El Pueblo de Los Angeles Historical Park
6
Fort Moore Pioneer Memorial
The Temporary Contemporary
5
9
8
7
101
110
Santa Ana Frwy.
Pasadena Frwy.
Figueroa Terrace
White Knoll Ave.
Beaudry Ave.
Centennial Ave.
Marview Ave.
New Depot St.
College St.
Chavez Ravine Pl.
Bartlett St.
Cleveland St.
Bunker Hill Ave.
Alpine St.
Yale St.
Hill St.
Hill Pl.
Grand Ave.
Bruno St.
Broadway
New High St.
Spring St.
Alhambra Ave.
Alameda St.
Main St.
Vignes St.
Ord St.
Macy St.
Sunset Blvd.
Boston St.
Arcadia St.
Aliso St.
Commercial St.
Ducommun St.
Garey St.
Temple St.
San Pedro St.
Fremont Ave.
Dewap Rd.
Diamond St.

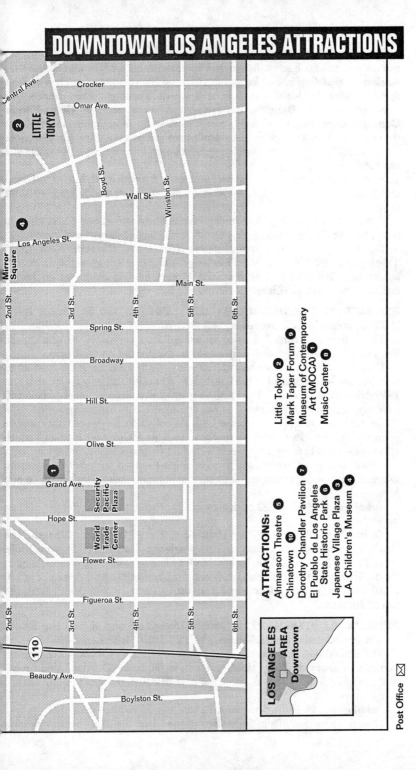

DOWNTOWN LOS ANGELES ATTRACTIONS

ATTRACTIONS:

Ahmanson Theatre ⑤
Chinatown ⑩
Dorothy Chandler Pavilion ⑦
El Pueblo de Los Angeles
State Historic Park ⑥
Japanese Village Plaza ③
L.A. Children's Museum ④

Little Tokyo ②
Mark Taper Forum ⑨
Museum of Contemporary
Art (MOCA) ①
Music Center ⑧

LOS ANGELES AREA
Downtown

Post Office ⊠

includes American and European paintings and sculpture, decorative arts, costumes and textiles, and Far Eastern, Indian, and Southeast Asian art. The new **Robert O. Anderson Building** is the place for modern and contemporary art. The **Pavilion for Japanese Art** has screens and scrolls as well as paintings. The **Frances and Armand Hammer Building** has special exhibitions, and the **Times-Mirror Central Court** is a cool, partially covered plaza with a most unusual fountain that the children adore. The new outdoor **sculpture garden** is a lovely place to stroll.

If you don't want to bring lunch or go elsewhere, there are two cafés where you can lunch or snack.

Family programs are offered the last Sunday of the month for children 5 to 12 and their parents. There are programs for younger children as well. Call 213/857-6108 for details.

Admission: $5 adults, $3.50 students with ID and seniors over 62, $1 children 6-17, free for children under 6; free for all on the second Tues of each month.

Open: Tues–Fri 10am–5pm, Sat–Sun 10am–6pm. **Closed:** New Year's, Thanksgiving, and Christmas Days. **Parking:** Available at meters on the street or in nearby lots. **Directions:** Take the Santa Monica Freeway (I-10) west to Fairfax Avenue; drive north to Wilshire Boulevard and turn right.

MUSEUM OF CONTEMPORARY ART [MOCA], 250 S. Grand Ave., California Plaza, downtown. Tel. 213/62-MOCA-2.

This collection is actually housed in two buildings, the second of which is the **Temporary Contemporary,** a mile away at 152 North Central Avenue.

If you want to show arts-oriented kids what's really new, this is the museum to visit. MOCA, which opened in 1983, is dedicated to exhibiting only art created from 1940 through the present. Today, MOCA's permanent collection numbers about 650 paintings, sculptures, prints, photographs, drawings, and mixed-media works.

MOCA wants kids to see and experience the collection. To this end, they provide visitors with a booklet entitled "Together at MOCA: A Guide for Families," which offers tips on how to enjoy the museum with children. It is published in five languages.

This is challenging artwork, and it's a rather quiet and subdued adult environment. Older kids, infants in carriers, and sophisticated little art connoisseurs tend to do best here.

Admission: $4 adults, $2 students with ID or seniors over 65, free for children under 12.

Open: Tues–Wed and Fri–Sun 11am–6pm, Thurs 11am–8pm. **Closed:** New Year's, Thanksgiving, and Christmas Days. **Parking:** The two buildings are 1 mile apart. For the MOCA, park beneath California Plaza or at the nearby Music Center; for the Temporary Contemporary, park near 1st Street and Central Avenue or at 140 North San Pedro Place. **Directions:** Take the Pasadena Freeway (I-110) north and exit at 4th Street.

MUSEUM OF FLYING, 2772 Donald Douglas Loop N., at the Santa Monica Airport, Santa Monica. Tel. 213/392-8822.

The exhibits here celebrate the history and achievement of aviation. The museum houses an amazing display of vintage aircraft, including the Douglas World Cruiser (the first to circle the globe, in 1924), the P-51 Mustang, the Spitfire Mark IX, and many others.

Admission: $4 adults, $3 seniors, $2 students, $1 children under 12.

Open: Thurs–Sun 10am–5pm. **Directions:** Take the Santa Monica Freeway

(I-10) west and exit at Bundy Drive south; turn right onto Ocean Park Boulevard and then left onto 28th Street.

MUSEUM OF NATURAL HISTORY, 900 Exposition Blvd., in Exposition Park, downtown. Tel. 213/744-3466 or 213/744-3414.

⭐ The museum's permanent collections include a megamouth shark, the second one ever found, and an exhibit entitled "Chaparral: A Story of Life from Fire," from which you are taught the importance of chaparral through a fascinating multimedia display. Dinosaurs, nearly every child's favorite thing "ever," are well represented here, as are "younger" North American and African mammals. An **American History Gallery** and **Gem and Mineral Hall** will appeal to youngsters above toddler age. But don't leave the little ones at home, because one of the best things about the museum is the **Ralph M. Parsons Discovery Center,** a multisensory space for children ages 2 and up.

Finally there is a place where children can touch, examine, smell, and manipulate the things that are so often behind glass in a museum. Once in the Discovery Center, our kids can't wait to check out a "discovery box." Different boxes offer different educational activities, such as challenging a child to identify sounds made with assorted objects with eyes closed, or allowing a youngster to create a turtle from skeletal bones. Our children also love to try on the costumes from around the world, then touch the taxidermied wild animals, which suddenly look so gentle. This is one of the few places that children can actually touch fossils or the teeth of a full-size polar bear. They get to listen to the ocean through seashells, use a magnifying glass for a better look at butterflies, and make crayon rubbings of fossils that are embedded in a rocklike wall.

An indoor-outdoor cafeteria in the museum is open during museum hours.

Admission: $3 adults, $1.50 children 12–17 and seniors, 75¢ children 5–12, free for children under 5; free for everyone the first Tues of every month. Admission to the Discovery Center is free with museum admission.

Open: Permanent exhibits, Tues–Sun 10am–5pm; Discovery Center, Tues–Sun 11am–3pm. **Parking:** Park on the street or in the lot off Menlo Avenue (bring quarters). During Coliseum events, parking is $10. For parking information call 213/744-3414. **Directions:** Take the Santa Monica Freeway (I-10) to the Harbor Freeway (I-110) south and follow the exit signs to the museums.

THE SOUTHWEST MUSEUM, 234 Museum Dr., at Marmion Way, Highland Park. Tel. 213/221-2164, or 213/221-2163 for recorded information.

Los Angeles's oldest museum is devoted to the study of Native American cultures from Alaska to South America. It has one of the finest collections of Indian art in the country.

Children who have studied Native Americans in school love the romance that surrounds the stories they hear. At the museum they get to see many of the things they've read about, such as a real tepee, baskets, pottery, and jewelry made by various tribes, and items used for carrying and clothing babies and small children many years ago.

If you plan to be in town a while, check with the museum to see if any of the special family programs is coming up. Past events have included Navajo storytelling by a real Navajo woman, paper cutting and piñata making during a Mexican Traditions festival, and a craft workshop on making a simple Native American toy.

Although the Southwest Museum is not near many other attractions and does take some time to get to, it's a special little museum for those interested in the arts and artifacts of the Americas. It's not far from Pasadena and Lawry's California Center.

Admission: $4 adults, $2 students and seniors, $1 juniors 7–18, free for children 6 and under.

Open: Tues–Sun 11am–5pm. **Directions:** Take the Pasadena Freeway (I-110) north, exit at Avenue 43, and follow the signs to the museum.

STUDIO TOURS & TV AUDIENCE TICKETS

One of the reasons people come to Southern California is to see the stars. And one way to do it is by attending an audience-participation TV show, some of which allow children. Another way is by taking a studio tour.

ABC-TV TICKETS, 4151 Prospect Ave., Hollywood. Tel. 213/557-4396.
Tickets are available for this network's taped shows by either showing up in person or sending in for tickets with a self-addressed stamped envelope as far in advance as possible (to the address above, ZIP Code 90027). You can pick up tickets 1 week in advance of a show. The minimum age is 16. Tickets are free.

AUDIENCES UNLIMITED, Fox Television Center, 5746 Sunset Blvd., Hollywood. Tel. 818/506-0067.
Tickets for many different network shows and specials, including Fox-TV tickets, are available through Audiences Unlimited. Tickets are on a first-come/first-served basis, and are available 6 days in advance of showtime. You can pick up tickets at the Fox Television Center, on the Van Ness side of the street, off the Hollywood Freeway (U.S. 101) at the Sunset Boulevard exit. The office is open Monday through Friday from 8:30am to 6pm.

To order tickets by mail for future shows, send a self-addressed, stamped envelope to Audiences Unlimited, 100 Universal City Plaza, Bldg. 153, Universal City, CA 91608. Expect a 2- to 3-week response. All tickets are free.

CBS-TV, 7800 Beverly Blvd., Los Angeles. Tel. 213/852-2458.
CBS tickets are available on the morning of the show, so you don't need to write for them. If you do write, you must do so 8 weeks in advance. Call for show taping schedules. Minimum age is 14. Tickets are free. **Directions:** Take the Santa Monica Freeway (I-10) east, exit at Fairfax Avenue north; the building is located on the corner of Fairfax Avenue and Beverly Boulevard. From Beverly Hills drive east on Beverly Boulevard to Fairfax Avenue.

KCET-TV, 4401 Sunset Blvd., Hollywood, CA 90027. Tel. 213/667-9242.
KCET is Los Angeles's public television station. You can take a technical tour that lasts 1½ hours and includes a visit to production areas and a look at lighting, cameras, stages, technical operations, and the master control room. Guides tell you about the history of the lot, which is the old Allied Artists studio, but you won't see shows being filmed. For this tour, children must be a minimum of 11 years old. Write for your reservations 1 week in advance. There is no charge for the tour, which is offered on Tuesday and Thursday, usually at 10am. The station is on Sunset Boulevard a half block east of Hillhurst Avenue.

NBC STUDIOS, 3000 W. Alameda Ave., Burbank. Tel. 818/840-3537.

You can join the audience for an NBC television show. Age minimums vary by show: For game shows the minimum age is usually 10 or 12; "The Tonight Show" has an age minimum of 16. NBC handles the audiences for such shows as "Classic Concentration" and for specials. Shows tape at various times and days. You can write or call for schedules.

Here's how to get tickets for shows: If you live within a 150-mile radius of Burbank, contact NBC Tickets, 3000 West Alameda Avenue, Burbank, CA 91523 (tel. 818/840-3537). Include the name of the show you want to see, the number of tickets, and the preferred date, if any; include a self-addressed, stamped envelope. The ticket limit for "The Tonight Show" is four. If you're outside the 150-mile radius, you'll receive a "Guest Letter" that can be exchanged at the NBC Ticket Counter on the day of the show. Write well in advance for these, because only a certain number of tickets are held for out-of-towners. Show up early on the day you requested for the best ticket selection; "The Tonight Show" tickets are available only on the day of the show at the Ticket Counter. *Remember:* Holding a ticket does not guarantee admission to a show—it only guarantees you a place in line. Be sure to arrive early for seating because seats are given on a first-come/first-served basis. If you aren't fussy about what show you see, there are a limited number of tickets available on the day each show is taped, but this is taking a chance.

The NBC Ticket Counter is at the corner of Olive Street and Alameda Street in Burbank. It's open Monday through Friday from 8am to 5pm, on Saturday from 10am to 4pm, and on Sunday from 10am to 2pm. Tickets to all NBC shows are complimentary, and parking is free.

The NBC Studio Tour was cancelled indefinitely some time back; inquire when you arrive to see if it has been reinstated.

PARAMOUNT STUDIOS, 860 N. Gower St., Hollywood. Tel. 213/956-5575.

Paramount offers free tickets for tapings of "A Different World," "Cheers," "Dear John," "In Living Color," and "Fresh Prince of Bel Air." You must arrive early on the day of the taping—tickets can't be ordered in advance. The Visitors Center opens at 8am. Line up really early for "Cheers" and "Arsenio Hall," the two shows hardest to get tickets for. Kids must be 16 or older to attend most tapings. The ticket office is on North Gower Street between Santa Monica Boulevard and Melrose Avenue, near Vine Street. It's open Monday through Friday from 8am to 4pm.

Paramount has recently started a walking tour that covers the historic and current aspects of this celebrated studio. You see the back lot, sound stages, and props from many of its well-known shows. It's a 2-hour tour, best for teens on up, although the minimum age for the tour is 10. Tours are offered Monday through Friday at 11am and 2pm. Sign up for the tour at the ticket office half an hour to an hour before departure time. Tickets are $10 per person, adult or child.

THE WARNER BROS. VIP TOUR, 4000 Warner Blvd., Burbank. Tel. 818/954-1744.

This is a technical/educational behind-the-scenes look at video tapings, television programs, and movies in production, geared to serious production buffs. Tours are limited to 15 people, and children under 10 are not permitted. You never know what you're going to see when you sign up—tours depend on daily production schedules and the whims of various directors. You might see something in production from Warner Bros. or an independent production company. In addition to watching filmmaking in progress, you'll see where sets are made and visit sound studios where sound effects are created and where music is recorded for shows.

Tours are offered two times a day (sometimes four in the summer), Monday through Friday—there are no tours on weekends or holidays. Tickets are by reservation only. It's best to call a week in advance, but reservations can be arranged up to 60 days ahead. You can also make reservations to eat in the Blue Room, the studio commissary (available only to those who take the morning tour). You must make your dining reservations at the time you make the tour reservations. Tickets for the tour are $22 per person, adult or child. The ticket office is at Hollywood Way and Olive Street, Gate 4, in Burbank.

AND MORE . . .

FARMERS MARKET, at 3rd St. and Fairfax Ave., Mid-Wilshire. Tel. 213/933-9211.

It's hard to believe that this corner was once a vacant field on the edge of Los Angeles. But that was the case in 1934 when 18 farmers set up their stalls to try to make a living during the Depression. Today the Farmers Market is made up of more than 150 individually owned businesses.

You can take the children here and walk through the various food stalls and stores. Locals love to eat in the open-air dining area, where you can choose from all types of ethnic food for breakfast, lunch, or early dinner from more than 25 kitchens. It's also a good spot just to stop and have a sundae or other afternoon treat. If you go in the morning, don't miss Bob's Coffee & Donuts, Stall 450 (tel. 213/933-8929), for possibly the best doughnuts in town.

Visitors go crazy over the fresh fruit and vegetables displayed in the stands. This is also a popular place to get gift-wrapped packages of dried fruits and nuts. Many visitors send oranges, grapefruit, and other seasonal fruit back to their homes from here. There's even a good-sized supermarket, Alexander's, Stall 150 (tel. 213/936-2596), for diapers and other necessary items to take back to the hotel.

Open: Summer, Mon–Sat 9am–7pm, Sun 10am–6pm; winter, Mon–Sat 9am–6:30pm, Sun 10am–6pm.

MEDIEVAL TIMES, 7662 Beach Blvd., Buena Park, Orange County. Tel. 714/521-4740, or toll free 800/826-5358, 800/438-9911 in California.

As kids, many of us daydreamed about castles and kings, knights and chivalry. Perhaps your children do, too. Medieval Times takes you back to 11th-century Europe. You are the guests—the nobility—at the castle of the Count of Perelada and his countess, where you partake in a four-course feast and watch the tournament of knights.

Each guest, young and old alike, is given a colored paper crown as he or she enters the castle. The colors of your crown are the colors of the knight you are to cheer on to victory during the games. The Hall of Arms contains authentic medieval artifacts and lots of souvenir vendors. Hold on to your wallets, though, because souvenir vendors and picture-taking minstrels hail you on a regular basis. One of them will even research your family's coat-of-arms and motto (for an extra fee) and present you with a sketch of it.

The kids really get into the spirit of it, skipping happily through the grand halls wearing their crowns and waving their colored banners in anticipation of the show. The real production is inside the 1,000-seat main arena, where you and the kids sit at long tables surrounding the open central arena. Serfs and wenches in medieval attire serve you soup, chicken, ribs, and potatoes—all of which you must eat with your fingers as they did in the 11th century (or you'll be thrown in the dungeon). As you eat, the show goes on.

Trumpeters herald the entrance of the knights of the realm, and the show begins. During the 2-hour performance, the knights parade on horseback, show how their Arabian stallions were trained, joust, and compete in games on horseback. There is even swordplay.

Although you can take children as young as 4 here, the show requires a considerable attention span to really enjoy it.

Admission: Evening performances, $28.95–$32.95 adults, $18.95–$19.95 children 12 and under. Major credit cards accepted.

Open: Shows given Mon–Thurs at 7:30pm; Fri at 6:15 and 9pm; Sat at 4, 6:30, and 9:15pm; Sun at 1, 4:45, and 7:30pm. Additional performances during the summer. Reservations are required (make them as far in advance as possible, since Medieval Times is a very popular year-round attraction). **Parking:** Available in the lot. **Directions:** Take the Santa Ana Freeway (I-5) south to the Beach Boulevard exit; it's between La Palma Avenue and Orangethorpe Avenue across the street from the Movieland Wax Museum.

MOVIELAND WAX MUSEUM, 7711 Beach Blvd., Buena Park, Orange County. Tel. 714/522-1155.

Possibly one of the best wax museums in the country, Movieland is a place that movie buffs shouldn't miss. We wonder just how many of the movie stars children recognize (there are more than 240), but even 6-year-olds appreciate the craft that goes into creating these life-size replicas of celebrities in their most famous roles. The exhibits are staged with realistic props and authentic costumes that re-create famous movie and television scenes.

Although your children may not have seen *Dr. Zhivago* or *Gone with the Wind,* they'll surely appreciate the bridge of the "Star Trek" Starship *Enterprise* manned by Captain Kirk, Mr. Spock, and the rest of the crew. You can be sure they'll marvel as you join Superman in the walk-through Fortress of Solitude from a scene from the movie. And of course there's Michael Jackson (complete with background vocal), Mr. T., and Sylvester Stallone as Rocky. Much to our delight, the Chamber of Horrors is set off by itself and can easily be avoided. In addition to lots of movie-star memorabilia, you can spend time watching old-fashioned motion-picture machines (mutoscopes and biographs). These are a real treat and also give our video-generation kids a chance to see some of the development of the medium.

Allow about 1 to 2 hours for the self-guided tour. It's completely stroller-accessible.

Admission: $11.95 adults, $9.55 seniors, $6.95 children 4–11, free for children under 4.

Open: Summer, daily 9am–10pm; winter, daily 10am–8pm (the box office closes 1 hour before the museum closes). **Directions:** Take the Santa Ana Freeway (I-5) south to the Beach Boulevard exit; it's between La Palma Avenue and Orangethorpe Avenue.

3. FOR KIDS WITH SPECIAL INTERESTS

If you're looking for something specific to your kids' special interests, you may find the outline below helpful. Unless otherwise noted, full details on all the following attractions are found in this chapter.

Airplanes/Space
Aerospace Building in Exposition Park
Museum of Flying
Spruce Goose (see Section 2, "Long Beach," in Chapter 9)

Art
California Afro-American Museum
Craft and Folk Art Museum
Huntington Museum (see Section 1, "Pasadena," in Chapter 9)
J. Paul Getty Museum
Junior Art Gallery in Barnsdall Art Park
Los Angeles County Museum of Art
Municipal Art Gallery in Barnsdall Art Park
Museum of Contemporary Art
Norton Simon Museum of Art (see Section 1, "Pasadena," in Chapter 9)
Pacific Asia Art Museum

Cowboys and Indians
Gene Autry Western Heritage Museum
Knott's Berry Farm
Southwest Museum

Dinosaurs
California Museum of Natural History
George C. Page Museum of La Brea Discoveries
Knott's Berry Farm

The Heavens
Griffith Observatory and Planetarium

Nature/Recycling
Babes at the Beach
Coldwater Canyon Park—TreePeople
Griffith Park Ranger Visitors Center
Palisades-Malibu YMCA Nursery Walks
Peter Strauss Ranch
Upper Franklin Canyon Ranch

The Ocean
Cabrillo Marine Museum (see Section 3, "San Pedro," in Chapter 9)
Los Angeles Maritime Museum (see Section 3, "San Pedro," in Chapter 9)
Orange County Marine Institute

TV/Movie Making
ABC-TV Tickets
Audiences Unlimited
CBS-TV
KCET-TV
NBC Studios
Paramount Studios
Universal Studios

4. LETTING OFF STEAM

Museums and theme parks can be a lot of fun, but after a while your kids will probably feel confined and get antsy. With its warm climate and loads of sunshine, Los Angeles offers many opportunities to take them outdoors to romp around and generally let off steam. Since you're near the Pacific, we'll begin this section with activities on or near the ocean ("The Beaches," "The Piers," and "Water Sports") and then move on to inland possibilities ("Bicycling and Roller Skating," "Hiking," "Nature Walks," and "Neighborhood Parks"). In the final category, "More Action," we've included a water park, ice-skating rinks, and miniature golf.

THE BEACHES

Some of the best beaches on the West Coast are only a short distance from wherever you're staying in the Los Angeles area. We'll begin with those farthest north, in Malibu, and work our way south along the coast through Santa Monica to Manhattan Beach and Redondo Beach.

MALIBU

World famous Malibu is a haven for movie stars and celebrities. What may not be as widely known are its recreational possibilities for families.

Half the fun is getting there. The drive on the Pacific Coast Highway (Calif. 1) through Malibu is an experience in itself. The 27 miles of shoreline front shimmering emerald seas, while eroded cliffs and chaparral-covered rolling hills border the highway. Tile-roofed Spanish-style villas and homes with enormous picture windows line the beach for miles at a stretch. Then, as you get farther up the coast, Malibu becomes more rural. Homes dot the hillsides of the Santa Monica Mountains, and kennels and boarding stables appear. The best beaches are here. Malibu beaches vary from rocky coves and little pocket beaches to long white sandy stretches.

Getting your bearings on the Pacific Coast Highway isn't difficult at all. Just remember that this part of the Santa Monica Bay coastline runs east and west. So when people say they're going "up" the coast to Malibu, here Malibu is actually west of Santa Monica. The coastline starts to curve north near the Los Angeles–Ventura County line.

During the weekends, and every day in summer, the Pacific Coast Highway (PCH, as it's affectionately known) becomes clogged with beach-going traffic. We suggest that you plan for this and bring things for the kids to do in the car in case you get hopelessly stuck in traffic.

Before you start, you might want to contact the **Malibu Chamber of Commerce,** 23805 Stuart Ranch Road, Suite 100, Malibu, CA 90265 (tel. 213/456-9025).

LEO CARRILLO STATE BEACH, 36000 block of the Pacific Coast Hwy., Malibu. Tel. 818/706-1310.

This 1,600-acre beach and campground 28 miles west (north) of Santa Monica, offers a wonderful day in the sun and salt air. In addition to good swimming and surfing, it has a nature trail, tidepools, and even sea caves. There are rest rooms, lifeguards, firepits, and a parking lot.

NICHOLAS CANYON COUNTY BEACH, on the Pacific Coast Hwy., 1 mile south of Leo Carrillo State Beach. Tel. 213/457-9891.

Nicholas Canyon is delightful, small, and hidden from the road by eroded cliffs that rise out of the sand. It's across from the Malibu Riding and Tennis Club. A parking lot is available above the beach and there are stairs and a ramp going down.

ZUMA BEACH COUNTY PARK, 30000 block of the Pacific Coast Hwy., Malibu. Tel. 213/457-9891.

Zuma, large and sandy, has playground equipment, a snack bar, rest rooms, and lifeguards. San Fernando Valley kids and teens love it. Lots of parking is available.

WESTWARD BEACH, on the Pacific Coast Hwy. southeast of Zuma Beach. Tel. 213/457-9891.

If you continue to walk southeast from Zuma, you'll come to Westward, a long, narrow beach with good swimming, boogie boarding, and surfing. It's a good choice for families. There are lifeguards, rest rooms, and a parking lot.

MALIBU LAGOON STATE BEACH and SURFRIDER BEACH, 23200 block of the Pacific Coast Hwy., Malibu. Tel. 213/456-9497.

Want a beach that's great for little kids as well as for teenagers? These two beaches are perfect for all ages. Picnic tables, rest rooms, and parking are available, and there are lifeguards on duty.

SANTA MONICA

Hugging the coastline of Santa Monica Bay, the city of Santa Monica is excellent for families. It has 13 miles of wide, white-sand beaches with endless year-round activities. See Section 5, "Perfect for Strolling," below, for more Santa Monica activities.

Directions: To get to all these beaches, take the Santa Monica Freeway (I-10) west to the Pacific Coast Highway (Calif. 1), turning north for the first two and south to Peninsula Beach. **Parking:** Unless indicated otherwise, all beaches are free but all beach parking lots charge a fee, usually $4 to $5; in some cases you can find street parking as well.

WILL ROGERS STATE BEACH, off the Pacific Coast Hwy., Santa Monica. Tel. 213/394-3266.

This clean family beach, starting at Chautauqua Boulevard, just north of Santa

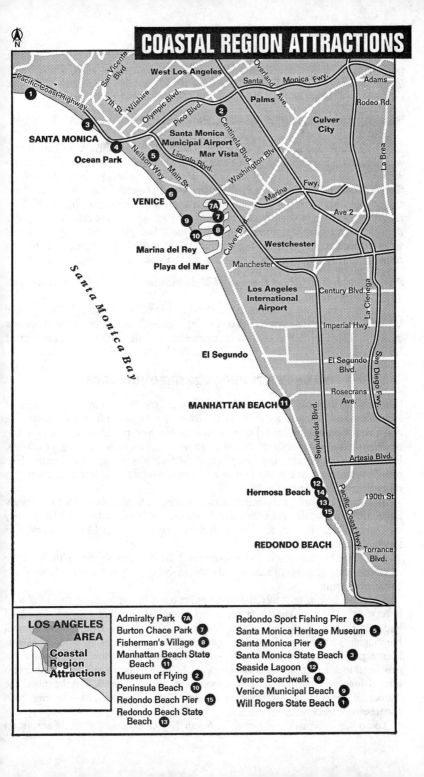

Monica Beach, and running north for 3 miles to Topanga Canyon, is one of our most popular spots. It has two designated surfing areas and a few playgrounds—near lifeguard Towers 8 (near Temescal Canyon), 10, 12, and 14. There are rest rooms, showers, a snack bar, volleyball courts, and lifeguards. Parking is available.

SANTA MONICA STATE BEACH, Palisades Beach Rd. Tel. 213/394-3266.

This 3.3-mile-long stretch of sandy beach below the bluffs of Palisades Park is very wide and offers just about all the facilities you could hope for—and the crowds to go with them as it's a tourist-oriented beach. Most of the activity centers around the **Santa Monica Pier** (see "The Piers," below), which divides the beach into northern and southern sections. (If you want fewer crowds, drive farther north and you'll be rewarded.) You might want to stay north of the pier, where the ocean is much safer than the south side. Just south of the pier you'll find gymnastics equipment and volleyball courts. There are rest rooms and outdoor showers along the beach, with ample snack bars and concessionaires and an abundance of parking.

PENINSULA BEACH, at the end of Washington St. in Marina del Rey. Tel. 213/394-3266.

This is more of an adult beach than a kids' beach, but it's lovely. South of the Venice Fishing Pier is a very nice part. Parking is difficult, which keeps the beach less crowded. There are rest rooms and a smattering of little restaurants at the foot of Washington Street.

MANHATTAN BEACH & REDONDO BEACH

If Malibu is a retreat for the rich and famous, the South Bay beach towns of Manhattan and Redondo are the suburban havens for the upwardly mobile. Charming beachfront cottages, multilevel condominiums, and high-priced apartments line the beaches. On busy weekends the beaches teem with active families carrying ice coolers, Frisbees, and exotic sand toys. Bicyclists pedal their way along the shorefront bike path (recognized as one of the best in southern California), and lean and tan singles roller skate or lounge on the beach.

You can play volleyball, roller skate, bicycle, surf, and swim in these sandy sanctuaries. And while the beaches may be more crowded than those in Malibu, they are less crowded than those of their northern neighbor, Santa Monica. (Parking is tough, though.)

One of the features you'll notice about South Bay beaches is their width. Some are incredibly wide stretches of sand—and unbearably hot on bare feet after the sand has baked in the sun.

Redondo Beach, probably the best-known town in the area, boasts a colorful history. In 1890 well-known entrepreneur Henry Huntington opened the Hotel Redondo on a bluff overlooking the Pacific. In 1907, during a vacation in Hawaii, Huntington saw a young Polynesian man ride the ocean waves on wooden planks. Huntington invited the young man, George Freeth, to do surfing exhibitions at his new hotel as a way to advertise the property. In 1909 a plunge was built, and Freeth trained lifeguards to protect the thousands of weekly bathers. Freeth, called the "father of surfing," is acclaimed as the first American lifeguard—he even won congressional medals for his rescues.

For other information about these South Bay cities, contact the **Manhattan**

Beach Chamber of Commerce, P.O. Box 3007, Manhattan Beach, CA 90266 (tel. 213/545-5313), and the **Redondo Beach Chamber of Commerce,** 1215 N. Catalina Ave., Redondo Beach, CA 90277 (tel. 213/376-6913).

Directions: Take the Santa Monica Freeway (I-10) west to the San Diego Freeway (I-405S) to the Rosecrans Avenue exit and follow Rosecrans west to Manhattan Beach. For Redondo Beach, turn off Rosecrans Avenue onto the Pacific Coast Highway (Calif. 1) and drive south. **Parking:** Except as noted below, the beaches are free but there is a small charge for parking.

MANHATTAN BEACH STATE BEACH, Highland Ave. between 1st St. and 45th St.

Manhattan Beach State Beach is large and has a playground, rest rooms, outdoor showers, and volleyball courts. Parking is difficult, so come early. The South Bay Bicycle Trail runs along the edge of the sand. The adjacent 900-foot **Manhattan Beach Pier,** at the foot of Manhattan Beach Boulevard, is a lovely place to take a stroll; it marks the area where you can find food and sundries.

SEASIDE LAGOON, at the corner of Harbor Dr. and Portofino Way, Redondo Beach. Tel. 213/372-1171, ext. 291.

This large heated saltwater lagoon has a wading area and diving boards, making it a wonderful swimming area for children of all ages. There are lifeguards, a sandy beach, playground equipment, volleyball courts, rest rooms with hot showers, and a snack bar.

Admission: $1.75 adults, 80¢ children.

Open: Memorial Day weekend to early Sept, daily 10am–5:45pm.

REDONDO BEACH STATE BEACH, off Torrance Blvd. and the Pacific Coast Hwy., near the Redondo Beach Pier.

This very wide beach is located below the bluffs. It has lifeguards, rest rooms, and parking. The South Bay Bicycle Trail follows the coast here.

THE PIERS

Over the years a number of recreational and amusement piers have been built projecting out into the ocean, and three of the remaining ones may be of particular interest to families. As with the beaches, we'll discuss the piers as they appear from north to south.

SANTA MONICA PIER, Ocean Ave. at the end of Colorado Ave. Tel. 213/458-8900.

The famous Santa Monica Pier, the oldest pleasure pier on the West Coast, was built in 1908. At that time it was one of several piers in the area built to house amusement parks and fun zones, probably the most popular one being Lawrence Welk's Aragon Ballroom. Today the pier is host to arcades, shops, restaurants, and kiddie rides.

The Fun Zone is a seasonal mini-midway of rides for young children, plus a ferris wheel. Kiddie rides are 75¢; the ferris wheel costs $1.50. Open from Memorial Day to Labor Day, daily from 10am to 9pm; in April and May, on Saturday and Sunday from 10am to 9pm.

The beautiful, historical **carousel,** with its hand-painted wooden horses, is open Memorial Day to Labor Day, Tuesday through Sunday from 10am to 9pm; the rest of the year, on Saturday and Sunday from 10am to 5pm. Rides cost 50¢ for adults, 25¢ for children 12 and under.

Near the pier at **Sea Mist Skate and Bike Rental,** at 1619 Ocean Front Walk, across from the carousel (tel. 213/395-7076), you can rent bikes and roller skates (for details, see "Bicycling and Roller Skating," below).

REDONDO SPORT FISHING PIER, 233 Harbor Dr., Redondo Beach. Tel. 213/372-2111.

As its name indicates, this pier is for fishing. You can fish directly off the pier itself—pier poles rent for $5.50 and live bait is available—or you can go out on a fishing barge moored alongside. The barge is good for children because it doesn't rock much. An hour on the barge costs $15 for adults, $7.50 for children.

Sport-fishing trips are also offered. Half-day fishing trips run $18 for adults and $13 for children under 12; full-day trips cost $45 to $85 for adults, $34 to $85 for kids—including bait, bunk, and parking.

Whale-watching cruises start at the end of December and go through April.

Open: Pier, daily 24 hours. Fishing barge, Memorial Day–Labor Day, daily 6am–midnight; the rest of the year, daily 7am–4:30pm (closed Dec–Easter).

REDONDO BEACH PIER AND KING HARBOR, at the foot of Torrance Blvd., Redondo Beach. Tel. 213/372-1171, ext. 274.

This area offers restaurants, fast-food places, shopping, pier fishing, fish markets, and an amusements zone. The **International Boardwalk,** located just north of the pier, has shops and casual restaurants; it's open 365 days a year. The **Redondo Fun Factory** (tel. 213/379-8510) is a 30,000-square-foot indoor "carnival" with hundreds of video-pinball games and rides.

Open: Pier (not the shops and restaurants), daily 24 hours; Fun Factory, Mon–Thurs 2–10pm, Fri 2pm–midnight, Sat 11am–midnight, Sun 2–10pm.

WATER SPORTS

BOAT RENTALS You can rent a boat at several places up and down the coast. Here are two in Marina del Rey:

Rent-A-Sail, 13719 Fiji Way, Fisherman's Village (tel. 213/822-1868), rents sailboats, powerboats, canoes, and catamarans. Rates range from $14 to $34 per hour (2-hour minimum), depending on the boat. Hours vary, but it's usually open daily from about 10am to sundown.

California Sailing Academy, 14025 Panay Way (tel. 213/821-3433), rents sailboats. Hours vary.

FISHING In addition to fishing at the **Redondo Sport Fishing Pier** (see "The Piers," above), you can also go dock-fishing at **Fisherman's Village,** 13763 Fiji Way, in Marina del Rey.

More extensive sportfishing trips can be arranged at the Redondo Sport Fishing

Pier and at **Marina del Rey Sportfishing**, 13759 Fiji Way, in Marina del Rey (tel. 213/822-3625).

SURFING AND WINDSURFING There are good surfing possibilities at a number of beaches along the coast. If you need equipment for the kids, **Dive 'n Surf**, 504 North Broadway, next to the Sheraton Hotel in Redondo Beach (tel. 213/372-8423), rents boogie boards ($5 per day) and wet suits ($12.50 per day).

To rent equipment and take windsurfing lessons, try **Del Ray Water Sports**, 507 Washington Boulevard, Marina del Rey (tel. 213/305-1101).

BICYCLING & ROLLER SKATING

BIKE TRAILS

The **South Bay Bicycle Trail** is part of a longer trail that's more than 22 miles long (if you take it all the way from Will Rogers Beach in the north to Torrance Beach in the south). The wide path (with markers indicating the direction of traffic) follows the beach, with rest rooms and telephones all along the way. This is probably the most popular bike path in the Los Angeles area, which means that it's best to do it early or late in the day to avoid the crowds. It's even better if you can do it off-season. We find that the kids enjoy it more when there aren't so many other riders stacked up.

While you can drive to any parking area near the beach and pick up the bike path there, you may want to start your ride on the trail at the Bird Sanctuary near the Marina International Hotel at Palawan Way and Admiralty Way in Marina del Rey. There's a county parking lot where you can park for $1 in winter, $5 in summer (bring quarters). Your 2-mile ride to Fisherman's Village will take you across Admiralty Way past the huge pleasure boats in drydock. Beware of a couple of unmarked crossings across busy streets.

We usually start at Fisherman's Village in Marina del Rey and head south. If you choose to do that and go all the way south, you can ride 12 miles from this point. Along the way you can make stops at Manhattan Beach Pier, Hermosa Beach Pier, or Redondo's King Harbor.

From Fisherman's Village you can also ride along the **Ballona Creek Bike Trail**, which winds inland along Ballona Creek from Fisherman's Village all the way to Culver City.

ROLLER SKATING

You can go roller skating almost anywhere along the coast, but perhaps the best skating is in Venice (between Santa Monica and Marina del Rey). There, much of Ocean Front Walk has been designated for bikes, skateboards, and roller skates. In fact, you can ride all the way from the Venice Beach boardwalk north past the Santa Monica Pier.

BICYCLE & ROLLER-SKATE RENTALS

Again, moving from north to south, you can rent bicycles, skates, and other equipment at the following places:

SEA MIST SKATE AND BIKE RENTAL, 1619 Ocean Front Walk, Santa Monica. Tel. 213/395-7076.

Sea Mist, across from the carousel at the Santa Monica Pier, rents kids' and adults' bikes at $5 for the first hour, $3.50 for each additional hour. Tandems rent for $9 for the first hour and $5 for each additional hour. Child carriers and helmets are free. Roller skates, for kids and adults, are $4 for the first hour, $3 for each additional hour.

Open: Memorial Day–Labor Day, Mon–Fri 10am–6pm, Sat–Sun 9am–7pm; the rest of the year, Mon–Fri 10am–4:30pm, Sat–Sun 9am–6pm. **Parking:** Parking lot available.

SPOKES 'N STUFF, 36B Washington Blvd., Venice. Tel. 213/306-3332.

This place rents 10-speeds, children's bikes, bicycles with baby seats, tandems, mountain bikes, and adult tricycles, as well as roller skates. Rates start at $2.50 per hour for bikes and go up to $6; skates cost $4 per hour. They also rent fins, nonmotorized scooters, and boogie boards. Prices are better the longer you rent.

Open: Memorial Day–Labor Day, Mon–Fri 10:30am–6:30pm, Sat–Sun 10am–6:30pm. Call for winter hours.

VENICE PIER BIKE SHOP, 21 Washington Blvd., Venice. Tel. 213/823-1528.

Here you can rent children's bikes as well as 3-, 10-, and 15-speeds, tandems, bikes with baby seats, and helmets. Rates begin at $2.50 per hour.

Open: Memorial Day–Labor Day, Mon–Fri from 10am, Sat–Sun from 9am; call for closing hours and winter hours.

JAMAICA BAY INN BEACH HUT, 4175 Admiralty Way, Marina del Rey. Tel. 213/306-1763.

The Beach Hut rents beach cruisers and 10-speeds at $3.50 for the first hour, $10.50 for 4 hours, $14 for the day (10:30am to 6pm). Mountain bikes are $5.50 for the first hour, $16.50 for 4 hours, $22 for the day. Tandem bikes are $6 for the first hour, $18 for 4 hours, and $24 for the day. Children's bicycles are available, as are baby carriers and helmets.

Open: Memorial Day–Labor Day, daily 10:30am–6pm; the rest of the year, Wed–Sun 10:30am–6pm.

ROBBIE'S BIKE AND SKATE, Washington St. and Pacific Ave., Marina del Rey. Tel. 213/306-3332.

Robbie's has beach cruisers, mountain bikes, children's bikes, 10-speeds, roller blades, and tandems. Rates range from $2.50 to $6.50 per hour, $7.50 to $18.50 for a half-day rental, and $8 to $24 for an all-day rental. Helmets and baby carriers are available.

Open: Memorial Day–Labor Day, daily 9am–7:30pm; the rest of the year, daily 10am–5pm (weather permitting).

SKATEY'S, 102 Washington St., Marina del Rey. Tel. 213/823-7971.

Skatey's, as its name indicates, rents roller skates of all types.
Open: Mon–Fri 10am–6pm, Sat–Sun 9am–6pm.

FUN BUNNS BEACH RENTALS, 1144 Highland Ave., Manhattan Beach. Tel. 213/545-3300.

Three blocks from the beach, Fun Bunns rents adults' and children's bikes, toddler carriers, and roller skates for children and adults. Helmets, knee guards, roller blades, mountain bikes, and wrist guards are available. Bikes rent for $4 to $5 per hour; skates are $4.50.

Open: Daily 10am–dusk.

HERMOSA CYCLERY, 20 13th St., Hermosa Beach. Tel. 213/376-2720.

At Hermosa Cyclery, one block north of Hermosa Pier, children's and adults' bikes are available, and will run you $3 to $10 per hour. Carriers and helmets are free with bike rental. Roller skates for adults and children are also for rent. No reservations are accepted, so in summer and on weekends it's best to get there before 10am.

Open: Memorial Day–Labor Day, daily 8am–8pm; the rest of the year, daily 9am–7pm.

HIKING

For specific hikes in the Santa Monica Mountains, you'll want to contact the **Santa Monica Mountains National Recreation Area Visitor Center,** 30401 Agoura Road, Suite 100, Agoura Hills, CA 91301 (tel. 818/597-9192). The office is open Monday through Saturday from 9am to 5pm. For free maps and detailed printouts of more than 100 parks and beaches in Los Angeles and Ventura counties, call the **Mountain Parks Information Service** (tel. toll free 800/533-PARK).

DESCANSO GARDENS, 1418 Descanso Dr., La Canada–Flintridge, Pasadena. Tel. 818/952-4400.

Whether or not you and the family are garden buffs, you'll all be happy you stopped here while in Pasadena. This makes a peaceful walk in the midst of touring "fast-track" Los Angeles. A picnic (or a stop at a restaurant) and a walk through the gardens will take 2 to 3 hours.

Set on 165 acres in the San Rafael Hills northeast of L.A. (55 acres are open to the public), Descanso is home to the largest-known camellia forest in the world. Above it towers a 30-acre parasol of California oaks. There is also a rare lilac grove, a wide selection of azaleas, and a History of Roses Garden.

There are two ways to experience Descanso. Short walking trails enable you to see the plants close up and invite you to take your time meandering through the area. Alternatively, you can take the 45-minute narrated tram ride with a stop at the Hospitality House where there's an art gallery. Afterward you can visit the Japanese Tea House, set in the tranquility of pools, waterfalls, and azalea beds. Treat the kids to punch and cookies while you sample Japanese tea or a soft drink.

Food service is available at the entrance to the gardens on weekends, or bring a picnic (picnic grounds are adjacent to the parking lot).

Admission: Gardens, $3 adults, $1.50 seniors and students with ID, 75¢ children 5–12, free for children under 5; tram tours, $1.50 adults and children.

Open: Gardens, daily 9am–4:30pm. Tram tours, Tues–Fri at 1, 2, and 3pm; Sat–Sun at 11am and 1, 2, and 3pm. **Parking:** Free. **Directions:** Take the Golden State Freeway (I-5) north, then the Glendale Freeway (Calif. 2) north to the Foothill Freeway (I-210); the gardens are at the junction of the Glendale and Foothill Freeways.

FRANKLIN CANYON RANCH, at Coldwater Canyon and Beverly Dr., Beverly Hills. Tel. 213/271-5013.

Very conveniently located near Beverly Hills, Franklin Canyon Ranch is chaparral-covered canyon trails leading to marvelous views of the city. Picnic areas are available. See "Nature Walks," below, for information on Upper Franklin Canyon.

GRIFFITH PARK RANGER VISITORS CENTER, 4730 Crystal Springs Dr., Los Angeles, CA 90027. Tel. 213/665-5188.

The best way to learn about hiking in this large park is by calling or writing the visitors center to get information about group nature walks led by naturalists and for hiking maps of the park.

The **Fern Canyon Nature Trail** is a good one for children. Trails start to the northwest of the visitors center, but there aren't any trailhead signs. You can hike up about a mile and turn around, and this will give you a chance to see the flora and fauna of the park. Located near the merry-go-round and large grassy areas, this might be a good beginning trail if you're unsure how your children will do on a hike.

Rangers also recommend the **Mount Hollywood Trail.** Start at the back of the Observatory parking lot (2800 East Observatory Road). Take it up to the top of Mount Hollywood (about 3 miles). There's a constant incline for about a quarter of a mile, but nothing a child can't handle. From the top you can see the Hollywood sign, the Observatory, and the entire L.A. basin. On a clear day you can see the ocean and Catalina Island.

Open: Park, daily 24 hours; visitors center, daily 7am–5pm. **Directions:** Take either the Hollywood Freeway (U.S. 101) to the Vermont Avenue exit, or take the Golden State Freeway (I-5) to the Los Feliz exit and drive west to Vermont Avenue.

MALIBU CREEK STATE PARK, south of Mulholland Hwy. in Calabasas. Tel. 818/706-1310.

Here you can choose from more than 30 miles of hiking trails, and a visitor center will assist you. A 2-acre lake, rock pool, volcanic cliffs, and grassy meadows await you. There are picnic areas and some fishing. Take Craggs Road to the spot where TV's "M*A*S*H" was filmed.

Open: Park, daily 24 hours; visitor center, Sat–Sun noon–4pm. **Directions:** Take the Golden State Freeway (I-5), the Hollywood Freeway (U.S. 101), or the San Diego Freeway (I-405) north to the Ventura Freeway (U.S. 101) west, or the Pacific Coast Highway (Calif. 1) north, and exit Las Virgenes Road/Malibu Canyon Road.

PARAMOUNT RANCH, Agoura Hills. Tel. 818/597-9192.

There are picnic areas, hiking trails (including some short trails good for kids), and a western town movie set (which is open to visitors during filming).

Directions: Take the Golden State Freeway (I-5), the Hollywood Freeway (U.S. 101), or the San Diego Freeway (I-405) north to the Ventura Freeway (U.S. 101) west, and exit at Kanan Road in Agoura Hills. Then go south three-quarters of a mile and turn left on Cornell Road and drive 2½ miles to the ranch.

PETER STRAUSS RANCH, 30000 Mulholland Hwy., Agoura. Tel. 818/ 597-9192.

The self-guided nature hikes and trails include an easy-to-moderate ¾-mile loop trail up into chaparral and back through oak trees. Picnic areas are available. Call for information about special children's events, including music festivals and ranger-led hikes.

Directions: Take the Golden State Freeway (I-5), the Hollywood Freeway (U.S.

101), or the San Diego Freeway (I-405) north to the Ventura Freeway (U.S. 101) west, and exit at Kanan Road; go south to Troutdale and turn right onto Mulholland Highway.

TOPANGA STATE PARK, 20825 Entrada Rd., Topanga Canyon. Tel. 213/455-2465 or 818/706-1310.

This wooded area off Topanga Canyon Road has self-guided nature trails and 32 miles of hiking trails.

Open: Apr–Oct, daily 8am–7pm; Nov–Mar, daily 8am–5pm. **Parking:** Available.

WILL ROGERS STATE HISTORIC PARK, 14253 Sunset Blvd., Pacific Palisades. Tel. 213/454-8212.

This is a wonderful place with trails that are easy for kids of all ages. Everyone enjoys the self-guided audio tours of Will Rogers's Ranch House, and there are two enormous fields for picnicking and romping. One is a polo ground where polo matches take place Saturday afternoon and Sunday morning (call for specific hours). The trails offer splendid views of the ocean and city on clear days. There are picnic tables at the top.

Open: Memorial Day–Labor Day, daily 8am–7pm; the rest of the year, daily 8am–6pm. **Admission:** $5 per car; includes parking. **Directions:** From Beverly Hills or downtown L.A., drive west on Sunset Boulevard. Or take the San Diego Freeway (I-405) to the Sunset Boulevard exit. Drive west on Sunset. You'll find the park between Amalfi Drive and Brooktree Road.

NATURE WALKS

BABES AT THE BEACH. Tel. 213/858-3834 for locations.

If you know ahead of time that you'll be in the area, why not make reservations for a naturalist-led walk designed especially for tots? Babes at the Beach is a sensory nature walk scheduled once a month for children 3 months to 6 years and their parents. Sponsored by the William O. Douglas Outdoor Classroom, the group explores the estuary and tidepool habitats. The nature guide leads the group out on the rocks and points out the various marine animals in the intertidal zone—starfish, sea urchins, and anemones. If you're coming in from out of town, be sure to tell the reservationist, who will make an extra effort to fit you in.

Admission: Free, but reserve months in advance: William O. Douglas Outdoor Classroom, P.O. Box 2488, Beverly Hills, CA 90213.

COLDWATER CANYON PARK, on the east side of the intersection of Coldwater Canyon and Mulholland Dr. Tel. 213/273-8733 or 818/753-4600.

TreePeople Park is found here, an organization committed to protecting the environment through recycling and by replenishing the supply of trees. Children are encouraged to learn gardening skills and are taught about conservation. Sunday nature walks include tours of the recycling center, nursery, and organic center, and there's a short guided trail tour of the seedlings taking root and the animal habitats. These nature walks begin at 11am and reservations are required. On Thursday and Saturday, people from the community can help the volunteer gardeners.

Admission: Free.
Open: Park, daily 9am–dusk.

PALISADES-MALIBU YMCA NURSERY WALKS, 821 Via de la Paz, Pacific Palisades. Tel. 213/964-3955.

Another family activity geared toward the very young is sponsored by the Palisades-Malibu YMCA. Trained volunteers lead nature walks for infants, toddlers, and preschoolers (older brothers and sisters are welcome too). Their goal is to foster an appreciation and love for the outdoors so that as they get older, children will have a healthy respect for the environment. The leaders get the children to try to use all the senses—they do a lot of looking, listening, touching, and smelling. Walks are 2 hours long and about half a mile in length; halfway along, they take a break. Walks are conducted at Leo Carrillo State Beach, Malibu Lagoon, Topanga State Park, Will Rogers State Park, Griffith Park, and several other locations. Make reservations 10 days to 2 weeks in advance.

Admission: $5 donation requested.

UPPER FRANKLIN CANYON RANCH, 2600 Franklin Canyon, Beverly Hills. Tel. 213/858-3834.

The **William O. Douglas Outdoor Classroom** offers more than 30 guided walks per month, many of which are geared for families. Walks cover such varied topics as the food chain, ecology, photography, and wildflower exploration. Two to three times a week they offer **Babes in the Woods Walks** for children 3 months to 3 years and their parents, and on the weekends they also offer **Tykes on Hikes** for children 4 to 6 years old and their parents.

On these sensory-oriented nature walks, children smell, touch, look, and listen to nature. Kids sit under the trees and the guide uses puppets to tell stories. The big hit is to feed the ducks. Children touch the soft sycamore leaves, listen to the birds, and look for little mosquito fish in the pond and scoop them up to study them. The program also offers **Adventure Quest,** designed for teens. (Teens walk with their peers while the family goes on another walk.) There's a **Full-Moon Hike** monthly.

Admission: Free, but by reservation only: William O. Douglas Outdoor Classroom, P.O. Box 2488, Beverly Hills, CA 90213.

Directions: The ranch is in the hills above Beverly Hills past where Beverly Drive meets Coldwater Canyon; call for directions.

NEIGHBORHOOD PARKS

With so much land in Los Angeles, neighborhood parks—large and small—are not too difficult to find. Here are a few we find special:

THE "BIGGIE"

GRIFFITH PARK, enter off Los Feliz Boulevard or Zoo Drive, north of Hollywood. Tel. 213/664-1181.

Griffith Park is 4,100 acres of wooded park area tucked into the Hollywood Hills and bordered by three freeways—the Golden State Freeway (I-5) to the east, the Ventura Freeway (Calif. 134) to the north, and the Hollywood Freeway (U.S. 101) to the west. The largest park within the boundaries of any U.S. city, it's over three times as large as San Francisco's Golden Gate Park. Dry foothills, shady little valleys, and wooded areas range in elevation from 384 feet to 1,600 feet above sea level. Its abundant recreational facilities offer something for everyone, including the Griffith Observatory, the Laserium, the Los Angeles Zoo, the Greek Theatre, Travel

Town, and myriad other delights. Don't even bother to try to see a lot of it in a single day because you can't make a dent in it. There are over 53 miles of hiking trails and bridle paths, four golf courses, and two overnight camps. In fact, the park is so large that many Los Angeles locals who visit it regularly are surprised to learn that it has a municipal swimming pool.

The park was given to the city of Los Angeles in 1896 by Col. Griffith J. Griffith, and its natural beauty is largely preserved today. In later years the Greek Theatre and the Griffith Observatory and Planetarium were added.

Visitor Center: The best way to learn about the wealth of attractions in this large park is by calling or writing the **Griffith Park Ranger Visitors Center,** 4730 Crystal Springs Drive, Los Angeles, CA 90027 (tel. 213/665-5188). For information about hiking and nature walks in the park, see "Hiking" and "Nature Walks," above; for information about the Griffith Observatory and Planetarium, see Section 1, "Kids' Top 10 Attractions," above.

The Rides: Young children love spending the day in Griffith Park enjoying the ponies and riding on the miniature train, the carousel, and the Simulator, which gives them an opportunity to show how brave they are. These rides are located on the east side of Crystal Springs Drive (in the park), near Los Feliz Boulevard.

A miniature open-air train, the **Griffith Park & Southern Railroad** (tel. 213/664-6788) runs on a 1¼-mile track through an environment that makes junior riders feel as if they are actually taking a little trip. It runs year round, Monday through Friday from 10am to 5pm and on Saturday and Sunday from 10am "till the crowds leave." Adults are charged $1.50; children under 13, $1.25; those under 19 months, free.

The **Simulator** (tel. 213/664-6788) takes you on a 4½-minute ride that first imitates a ride on a roller coaster and then an airplane ride. Children must be over 2 years old, and those under 5 must ride with an adult. Like the train ride, it's open year round, Monday through Friday from 10am to 5pm and on Saturday and Sunday from 10am "till the crowds leave." All tickets cost $1.25.

The **pony rides** (tel. 213/664-3266) provide something for everyone. Little children ride in a circle on ponies tied to a stationary hookup. Older kids can ride around a separate track on their own. All children must be under 100 pounds to ride the ponies. There are also wagon rides, for those kids not yet too keen about horses, that take the children on a short ride around a track. The pony rides are open daily from 10am to 5pm (closed Monday, except on Monday holidays, from mid-September to mid-May). Pony and wagon rides are $1 per child. (You'll also find a stationary pony ride in Travel Town).

Our young children love to ride the antique **Merry-Go-Round** over and over again. However, it's far enough away from the miniature train that you'll want to drive to it—it's just off Griffith Park Drive, near the main concession stand (tel. 213/665-3051). It's open Memorial Day to Labor Day, Monday through Friday from 11am to 5pm and on Saturday and Sunday from 11am to 7pm; the rest of the year, on Saturday and Sunday from 11am until sunset. Rides are 75¢ for everyone.

Travel Town: On Zoo Drive, near Griffith Park Drive, Travel Town (tel. 213/662-5874) is a small outdoor museum of transportation vehicles. Some of the most interesting sights are the old Hawaiian narrow-gauge sugar train, the 110-ton Union Pacific steam engine, and 14 other locomotives. Youngsters love to look at the old fire engines. They are also introduced to the yellow streetcars that once ran in Los Angeles. There is a miniature steam engine here that goes around a 1-mile track.

Travel Town is open April through October daily from 10am to 5pm; November to March, Monday through Friday from 10am to 4pm and on Saturday and Sunday from 10am to 5pm. Admission to Travel Town is free, but there's a charge for the miniature train ride: $2 for adults and $1.50 for children 2 to 13 (under 2, free).

Other Park Activities: The **Griffith Park Recreation Center** (tel. 213/666-2703) has a **swimming pool** (tel. 213/665-4372) that is open from mid-June through mid-September. Call for hours and fees.

For information about the **tennis courts,** you can call 213/662-7772 for the Riverside Drive courts, 213/664-3521 for the Vermont Avenue courts, and 213/661-5318 for the Griffith Park courts. For reservations, call 213/520-1010.

For information about **golf courses,** call 213/663-2555 for the Wilson/Harding starters office, 213/665-2011 for the Roosevelt course, and 213/663-7758 for the Los Feliz course.

Located at the northeast corner of Griffith Park, just south of Riverside Drive, the **J. P. Horseback Riding Stables,** 914 South Mariposa Street, Burbank (tel. 818/843-9890), offers guide-led horseback rides through Griffith Park. Your family may have a guide of its own or share with other people. The fees are $13 per person for the first hour, $11 for each additional hour; there's an $11 deposit on each horse, and no credit cards are accepted. The minimum age is 6 years old. Horses are available on a first-come, first-served basis. The stables are open daily from 8am to 4pm.

Open: Park, daily 24 hours; Visitors Center, daily 7am–5pm; various rides and attractions have differing operating hours (see above). **Directions:** Take either the Hollywood Freeway (U.S. 101) to the Vermont Avenue exit, or take the Golden State Freeway (I-5) to the Los Feliz exit and drive west to Vermont Avenue.

OTHER NEIGHBORHOOD PARKS

PALISADES PARK, Ocean Ave., Santa Monica.

Perched on the bluffs overlooking the ocean, palm–tree–studded Palisades Park is 26 acres of walkways and lawns. The views are unparalleled, and it's a wonderful place for tykes on trikes. The southern boundary is Colorado Avenue; go north for a mile for an even prettier view of the park. There is metered street parking.

DOUGLAS PARK, 1155 Chelsea Ave., Santa Monica. Tel. 213/458-8311.

This charming little park, between Wilshire Boulevard and 20th Street, is complete with a duck pond, a wading pool (which doubles as a tricycle demolition racetrack when it's dry), and fabulous wooden play structures. The equipment offers amusement for older kids as well as the younger ones. Picnic facilities, barbecue stands, rest rooms, and tennis courts complete the picture.

CHEVIOT HILLS RECREATION AREA, 2551 Motor Ave., West Los Angeles. Tel. 213/837-5186.

This large recreation area, at the corner of Pico Boulevard and Motor Avenue, has playground equipment, basketball courts, baseball diamonds, a pond, a par course (with 18 stations), tennis courts, picnic and barbecue facilities, and a very large municipal swimming pool (tel. 213/836-3365). The recreation center also offers a wide variety of activities.

ROXBURY PARK, 471 S. Roxbury St., at Olympic Blvd., Beverly Hills. Tel. 213/550-4864.

This is one beautiful in-town place to run off some excess energy. Besides paths for walking, a softball field, and bocce ball and basketball courts, there are two large play areas for children in the rear of the park; rest rooms and soda machines are nearby. Near the equipment are picnic tables and barbecue grills. Come early on weekends for a picnic table because Beverly Hills residents get first choice by reserving tables by telephone.

Open: Daily 7am–11pm. **Parking:** There is ample parking weekdays, and fairly easy parking on nonholiday weekends; park in the back of the park if you intend to stay by the playground equipment.

LA CIENEGA PARK, 8400 Gregory Way, Beverly Hills. Tel. 213/550-4864.

This park, on Gregory Way between Olympic Boulevard and La Cienega Boulevard, has brand-new play equipment and tennis courts. There are also picnic tables and a softball field; rest rooms are adequate. Park in the lot across the street.

MORE ACTION

Here we've included some miscellaneous activities: a water theme park, two ice-skating rinks, and a miniature golf course.

RAGING WATERS, 111 Raging Waters Dr., San Dimas. Tel. 714/592-8181 or 714/592-6453.

Located on 44 acres inside the 2,200-acre Frank G. Bonelli Regional Park in San Dimas, Raging Waters makes you feel as if you've entered a beach town designed for the young and daring.

Large sandy areas (where lotion-covered moms and dads watch swimming youngsters) surround enormous sandy-bottomed swimming holes, where school-age kids and preteens enjoy small water slides, water swings, a lily-pad walk, and rope nets above the water. An area called Wavecove is the closest you'll come to bodysurfing in this neck of the woods. Waves as high as 3 feet give even the meekest among us the chance to experience an oceanlike ride.

But this is not a place for the faint of heart. Teens, preteens, and others who believe they're invincible are the ones who probably enjoy it the most. Billing itself as the largest water theme park west of the Mississippi, Raging Waters has four speed slides, ranging from four- to eight-stories tall, with speeds of 25 to 40 m.p.h., four flume rides, and a water rapids. The flumes have more than 400 feet of curves and dips, ending in a refreshing splash-down pool. Raging Rivers is the longest artificial innertube rapids; this quarter-mile waterway has rapids, whirlpools, and waterfalls. For the littlest tots, Little Dipper is a grassy area with pools only a foot deep, fountains, and mini-water slides. Children over 8 aren't even allowed in these pools.

Although there are lifeguards and trained slide operators, we're always super-cautious, especially when there are lots of kids in the water. For the rapids, flumes, and steep slides, the park has its own rules, which should be strictly adhered to. And at this kind of park, more than almost anywhere else, remember the sunscreen and sunblock, since the kids will be in the sun all day.

Dressing rooms and coin-operated lockers are available. Life vests are provided free, and you can rent rafts and innertubes for $5 ($2 is refunded when you return the item). You'll find a variety of food—from Mexican to Italian—at the snack stands. There are also picnic areas.

Admission: $15.50 for anyone taller than 48 inches ($9.50 after 5pm), $8.50 for children 42–48 inches tall and seniors ($6.50 after 5pm), free for children under 42 inches tall. Parking costs $2.

Open: Apr to early Oct; call ahead for specific dates and times as these vary greatly. (Be sure to get there when the park opens for the smallest crowds.) **Parking:** $2. **Directions:** Take the San Bernardino Freeway (I-10) 30 minutes east of downtown Los Angeles (20 minutes north of Anaheim) to its junction with the Foothill Freeway (Calif. 210); exit at Raging Waters Drive.

CULVER CITY SKATING RINK, 4545 Sepulveda Blvd., Culver City. Tel. 213/398-5719.

This makes a good place to take a break on sizzling August days. Skate rentals are available in adults' and children's sizes ($1.75). There are lockers and a snack bar. Weekends can get quite crowded. It's on Sepulveda between Culver Boulevard and Jefferson Boulevard.

Admission: $4.75 adults, $4.25 children 12 and under.

Open: Mon 10am–5pm, Tues–Fri 10am–5pm and 8–10:30pm, Sat 9:45am–1pm and 8–10pm, Sun 8–10pm. Be sure to call ahead—the rink closes to the public when the Los Angeles Kings practice. **Parking:** Free in the lot.

PICKWICK ICE ARENA, 1001 Riverside Dr., Burbank. Tel. 818/846-0032.

As at the Culver City rink, the Pickwick Ice Arena also has skates for children of all ages. Adults' and children's skates rent for $2.

Admission: $4.75 adults, $4.25 juniors 13–18, $3.75 children 12 and under.

Open: Mon–Tues and Fri 1:15–5:30pm, Wed 1:15–5:30pm and 7:45–9:45pm, Sat 8am–10:30pm, Sun 2:30–4:30pm and 8–10pm. **Directions:** Take the Hollywood Freeway (U.S. 101) to the Ventura Freeway (U.S. 101) west; take the Buena Vista exit and turn right on Riverside Drive for three blocks.

SHERMAN OAKS CASTLE MINIATURE GOLF, 4989 Sepulveda Blvd., Sherman Oaks. Tel. 818/990-8101.

This is a miniature golf lover's dream. Three attractively designed golf courses with an abundance of fountains, ponds, and greenery delight children. There are also batting cages, a huge video arcade, and a snack bar.

Admission: $4.75 adults, $3.75 children 13 and under.

Open: Daily 10am–midnight. **Directions:** Take the Santa Monica Freeway (I-10) west to the San Diego Freeway (I-405) north; exit left onto Burbank Boulevard and turn right onto Sepulveda Boulevard. The course is at the corner of Magnolia Street.

5. PERFECT FOR STROLLING

If your young children are like ours, they aren't really up to a formal "walking tour"—they have either too much energy (and want to run loose) or too little (and have to be pushed in a stroller or carried), or they lose interest too rapidly to enjoy the tour. Thus the following are set up as strolls, sort of "guided walks," around some of Los Angeles's more interesting neighborhoods. If you're in one of these areas, these strolls will cover the highlights at a gentle pace. You can pick one (or more) that suit your family's itinerary and interests. We've started with everybody's favorite, the movie capital of Hollywood, and then followed with several downtown neighborhoods (Olvera Street, New Chinatown, and Little Tokyo), moving to some of the more outlying areas (Melrose/Mid-Wilshire, Beverly Hills, and Westwood Village), and concluded with strolls through three oceanfront communities (Santa Monica, Venice Beach, and Marina del Rey).

HOLLYWOOD

Entertainment capital of the world, glitter capital of the world—Hollywood is a state of mind, where dreams come true. You've probably heard all the clichés, and now you want to see the real thing. Well, the Hollywood of your dreams is no more—it's a bit tacky, a little "under the weather," and certainly not the place for an evening stroll with the family. But everyone who comes to Los Angeles must see Hollywood. So put on your blinders, ignore the shabby parts, and take a daytime stroll down legendary Hollywood Boulevard.

Beginning at Hollywood Boulevard and La Brea Avenue and walking east, you'll come to **Mann's Chinese Theater,** 6925 Hollywood Boulevard (tel. 213/464-8111 for movie information), where Mary Pickford and Douglas Fairbanks initiated the footprint ceremony in 1927, the year the theater was built by Sid Grauman. From then on, whenever a movie premièred there, the stars embedded their foot- and handprints in the cement. One of the most ornate movie palaces of the time, the building was decorated with rare Chinese artifacts, authentic temple bells, and pagodas. Kids love to try to match their footprints with those of the stars.

Premiering as the first of many theaters to make up the new Hollywood Cinema District is the **El Capitan Theatre,** 6838 Hollywood Blvd. (tel. 213/467-7674). In 1923 it opened as a legitimate theater, but was subsequently refurbished in 1942. The new Hollywood Paramount, as it was called, covered up the lavish interior of the original theater. Fully restored, it now features first-run films.

One block east is the **Hollywood Wax Museum,** 6767 Hollywood Boulevard (tel. 213/462-8860). If you don't see a live celebrity on your trip, at least you can see your favorites duplicated in wax. The museum is open Sunday through Thursday from 10am to midnight and on Friday and Saturday from 10am to 2am. Admission is $7 for adults, $6 for seniors, $5 for children 6 to 12, free for children under 6.

Right across the street, the Max Factor Building, 1666 Highland Avenue (tel. 213/463-6668), houses a retail store and the **Max Factor Museum,** which opened in 1935. What more perfect place for a beauty museum than Hollywood? Such stars as Judy Garland, Claudette Colbert, Rita Hayworth, and Marlene Dietrich attended the museum's opening. If your girls have just discovered makeup, they'll enjoy seeing how it was used on the stars of the 1920s and 1930s. The museum is open Monday through Saturday from 10am to 4pm; admission is free.

Practically next door on the Hollywood Boulevard side is the **Egyptian Theater,** 6708 Hollywood Boulevard (tel. 213/467-6167), which was built by Sid Grauman in 1922, before he built the Chinese Theater. The Egyptian was actually the first of the spectacular movie palaces, with ornately carved columns and sphinxes flanking the screen. The opening of *Robin Hood,* Hollywood's first movie première, was held here.

Walk across the street about half a block and you'll see the arch identifying the **Janes House,** where you'll find an office of the **Los Angeles Convention and Visitors Bureau** in the Queen Anne Victorian home in the rear, at 6541 Hollywood Boulevard (tel. 213/461-4213). The Janes House, the oldest house on the street, was a one-owner private residence from 1903 until its restoration in 1985. The Janeses made it into a schoolhouse for a time, and educated the children of such motion-picture pioneers as Douglas Fairbanks, Jesse Lasky, and Noah Berry. Now you'll find helpful brochures, maps, and even complimentary tickets to various TV shows. Open Monday through Saturday from 9am to 5pm.

Across the street is **Hollywood Toys & Costumes, Inc.,** 6562 Hollywood Boulevard (tel. 213/465-3119), a treasure trove of children's costumes, wigs, masks, and toys. Backtrack one block west to **Larry Edmund's Book Store,** 6644 Hollywood Boulevard (tel. 213/463-3273), where you'll discover one of the most comprehensive collections of movie- and theater-related books and posters.

If you stand at the corner of Hollywood Boulevard and Vine Street, just a few blocks east, and look north, you'll spot the **Capitol Records Building,** 1750 North Vine Street (tel. 213/462-6252), completed in 1956 in the shape of a stack of 45-rpm records—remember those?—as the first round office building in the country. In the lobby you'll see displays of gold records (open Monday through Friday from 9am to 5:30pm). If you know Morse code, you'll figure out what the flashing light on top of the building spells out. As you're looking up this way, you can't help but see the famous **Hollywood sign,** which has gone through so many transformations since it was put up in 1923 to advertise Hollywoodland, a real-estate development.

Back on Hollywood Boulevard, a little east of Vine, is the **Pantages Theater.** Pop in, if they'll let you, to see the magnificent art deco interior. Currently a legitimate theater, the Pantages was originally built as a movie theater and was host to the Academy Awards from 1949 to 1959.

Hollywood has also given us **Roscoe's House of Chicken and Waffles,** 1514 North Gower Street (tel. 213/466-7453), a Hollywood institution serving nothing but those two dishes; **C. C. Brown's,** 7007 Hollywood Boulevard (tel. 213/464-9726), which, although more than 75 years old, still serves the hot-fudge sundae it first created (and had as one of its waitresses none other than Judy Garland); and **Musso and Frank's,** 6667 Hollywood Boulevard (tel. 213/467-7788), Hollywood's oldest restaurant, where Hollywood's famous writers used to gather, and where important people still stop for a bite to eat.

If you're going to be in town during the winter season, watch for the **Hollywood Christmas Parade,** originally called the Santa Claus Lane Parade in the early 1920s. It has evolved into one of the grandest city parades and is seen on TV all over the world.

While walking down the boulevard, you can't help but notice the pink and charcoal terrazzo stars embedded in the sidewalk on both sides of Hollywood Boulevard between Sycamore Street and Gower Street, and on Vine Street between Sunset Boulevard and Yucca Street. Nearly every month since 1961 the Hollywood Chamber of Commerce has honored a movie star on the **Walk of Fame** with a ceremony dedicating his or her star (call 213/469-8311 for information on the next ceremony).

A short ride in the car will take you to the other sights Hollywood claims as its own, such as **Paramount Studios,** at 5555 Melrose Avenue. This famous studio, in business as Paramount since the 1920s, is still producing movies, making it the longest continuously operating film studio in Los Angeles.

OLVERA STREET [OLD LOS ANGELES]

Even this super-modern metropolis has its historical roots. **El Pueblo de Los Angeles State Historic Park,** bordered by Alameda Street and Arcadia Street, and intersected by Main Street and Los Angeles Street, will give you and the kids a flavor of the Los Angeles of days past.

Nothing remains of the original cluster of earth-and-willow huts built around 1780 that constituted the first incarnation of Los Angeles. However, on the spot of those original huts sits this park, a collection of 27 historic buildings that date from 1818 to 1926. Plan to spend several hours wandering around.

We like to start with the excitement of **Olvera Street,** a colorful Mexican-style marketplace. For kids, this street is definitely the highlight of the tour. In a city with strong Hispanic ties, this area gives children a better awareness of the city's roots. Over 85 gift shops and stalls offer authentic Mexican goods, such as sombreros, piñatas, and leather goods. Children especially like to watch the craftspeople—glassblowers, silversmiths, candle makers, and leather makers—create their wares.

Our kids are always ready to sample the local tasty treats—sugary churros are one such specialty. You probably won't be able to keep your kids away from the other colorful Mexican candies for sale. If you can bargain with them to have lunch first, you'll find a bounty of choices here, from casual food stalls to sidewalk cafés and full-scale restaurants. The most historic choice is **La Golondrina Restaurant** (tel. 213/628-4349), housed in the Pelanconi House. Built in the mid-19th century as a private residence, it was one of the earliest buildings in Los Angeles made of fired brick. The food served here is very traditional Mexican fare.

Olvera Street is often host to special events, so write ahead for exact dates of events to the **Olvera Street Merchants Association,** W-17 Olvera Street, Los Angeles, CA 90012 (tel. 213/687-2525). The Cinco de Mayo (May 1 to 5) and Mexican Independence Day (September 16 to 18) celebrations are especially fun.

Perhaps the most kids-oriented of these events is the **Blessing of the Animals** in mid-April, when local residents dress up their animals, parade them down the street, and have them blessed by the local Catholic bishop. The ceremony dates back to the 16th century when the farmers brought their animals to the church with the hope the blessings would give them fertility and health. Kids of all ages are delighted by the animals, which range from cats in hats, dogs on fancy leashes, cows in bonnets, birds in colorful cages, to even goldfish. Nowadays the blessing is meant to acknowledge the loyal affection that animals have for their human owners.

At the center of Olvera Street is the historic **Sepulveda House,** built in 1887, which houses the park's visitor center. Here, if your kids are historically inclined, an 18-minute film on Los Angeles's past can be viewed at 11am and noon. You can also buy the self-guided walking-tour brochure for 50¢ and see the rest of the historic park on your own. Also sold here are children's books and gifts.

If you prefer **guided tours,** walk to the Docent Office, 130 Paseo de la Plaza, next to the Old Plaza Firehouse at 501 North Los Angeles Street. The free tours last 45 minutes and are conducted Tuesday through Saturday at 10am, 11am, noon, and 1pm. At this office, you can also sign up for 2-hour guided bus tours of the central city, which are given the first and third Wednesdays of the month at 9:45am. Reservations are required (tel. 213/628-1274). The visitor center is open Monday through Friday from 10am to 3pm and on Saturday from 10am to 4:30pm.

Beyond Olvera Street, it takes a parent's knowledge to determine which sights will interest kids. **Firehouse Number 1,** which displays fire-fighting memorabilia from the 19th century, is often a favorite. The **Avila Adobe,** the oldest existing residence in Los Angeles, gives kids a sense of what everyday life was like for wealthy California ranchers in the 1840s. And since kids are often intrigued by statues, you might show them the **Felipe de Neve Statue** (the Spanish governor of California who was responsible for founding El Pueblo del Rio de Nuestra Señora la Reina de Los Angeles in 1781), and the **Fray Junípero Serra Statue** (the Franciscan padre who founded the first 9 of California's 21 missions).

Check to see whether the new **Museum of Chinese American History** has opened. This museum is being built to honor the contributions of Chinese Americans to the area.

The majority of El Pueblo de Los Angeles State Historic Park is stroller-accessible. There are a number of bathrooms, most equipped with changing tables. The park is open daily from 10am to 10pm in summer, till 9pm the rest of the year. Parking is available on Main Street between Hope Street and Arcadia Street at $7.50 for the full day or $1.50 for each 20 minutes.

NEW CHINATOWN

Although not as impressive as Little Tokyo (see below) or Chinatown in San Francisco, New Chinatown is worth the short walk from Olvera Street. Remember, though, that it's a congested, small area. (Old Chinatown originally occupied what is now Union Station.) The section is bounded by North Broadway, North Hill Street, Bernard Street, and Sunset Boulevard. Gin Ling Way leads to the heart of New Chinatown. You can sit for a moment by its ornate **West Gate,** the area's oldest gateway. Herb shops, poultry stores (with birds dressed to order), and stores for tea and seafood surround the area. Make a stop at the **Phoenix Bakery,** 969 North Broadway, if you can get in. Famous for its strawberry whipped-cream cake, Phoenix is one of the oldest, and by far busiest, bakeries in the area.

For information on seasonal festivals and events, contact the **Chinese Chamber of Commerce,** 978 North Broadway, Suite 206, Los Angeles, CA 90012 (tel. 213/617-0396).

LITTLE TOKYO

A walk through Little Tokyo is like stepping through a portal into the Far East. Los Angeles has traditionally had many Japanese residents, and Little Tokyo, located between Alameda Street and Los Angeles Street and 1st Street and 3rd Street, contains traditional Japanese shops and restaurants.

A walk around **Japanese Village Plaza,** on 1st Street and 2nd Street between

San Pedro Street and Central Avenue (tel. 213/620-8861), is a pleasant way to spend an hour. The plaza area features authentic Japanese shops (as well as American ones) in a distinctly Japanese setting. You might want to make a special stop at **Mikawaya Sweet Shop.**

The **New Otani Hotel & Garden,** 120 South Los Angeles Street, at 1st Street (tel. 213/629-1200, or toll free 800/421-8795, 800/273-2294 in California), is the most dazzling building here. The garden walkways are especially beautiful. If you have a chance, go to the rooftop garden for a peaceful few moments.

Of special interest are Nisei Week and Children's Day in Little Tokyo, during which time there are crafts fairs, performances for children, and fun-runs for kids. For specific information about Children's Day, contact the **Japanese-American Cultural and Community Center** (tel. 213/628-2725); for general information and Nisei Week information, call 213/687-7193. For general questions about the area, contact the **Little Tokyo Business Association,** 244 South San Pedro Street, Room 501, Los Angeles, CA 90012 (tel. 213/620-0570).

MELROSE/MID-WILSHIRE

This area, roughly bordered by Wilshire Boulevard to the south, Melrose Avenue to the north, La Cienega Boulevard to the west, and La Brea Avenue to the east, is the location of many of the new boutiques, restaurants, and hotels that have been going up at breakneck speed. **Mid-Wilshire,** home to the L.A. County Museum of Art, the Craft and Folk Art Museum, and the La Brea Tar Pits, was once a very important retail center of town. Today it is beginning its renaissance. The **Fairfax** area, where you'll find the CBS Studios and the Farmers Market (see Section 2, "More Attractions," above), is also home to much of L.A.'s older Eastern European population. Although Fairfax Avenue, between Beverly Boulevard and Melrose Avenue, has been spruced up with new storefronts and a giant mural, it still retains its open-air fish and fruit stands, Hungarian and Israeli restaurants, kosher meat markets, and numerous bakeries. **Melrose Avenue,** an exciting place for a walk with the kids (preteens and teenagers will love this street), has been written up in newspapers all over the country as Los Angeles's trendiest section of town. Non-Equity (99-seat) live-performance theaters, clothing boutiques, casual and chic restaurants, funky stores, and antique shops line the avenue from just east of La Brea, west to La Cienega.

If you're looking for something to do for a short time with very young children, or want to see the area without driving your car around, hop on the **Fairfax Trolley** (tel. 213/666-7990). This cute little green-and-orange trolley with wooden seats and Grandma and Grandpa passengers takes you through the Fairfax District, and by the Pacific Design Center, Farmers Market, and the Beverly Center. Or it goes down Melrose Avenue, where you can get off and shop in the boutiques, or stop in at the Los Angeles County Art Museum. (The stops you make depend on which line you take.) The trolley runs about every 15 minutes Monday through Saturday from 9am to 5pm (no service on Sunday and holidays). Call for pickup points. Fare is 25¢.

BEVERLY HILLS

In the 1880s Beverly Hills was a series of bean fields—lima beans, to be exact. But instead of beans—or underground diamond mines—it was water that made Beverly Hills come alive. Burton E. Green was the man who founded the water company and created the residential community in the early 1900s. The city's growth did not happen all at once, however. Although business tycoons had mansions in the area that now surrounds the Beverly Hills Hotel, few others lived there. It wasn't until the 1920s, when Mary Pickford and Douglas Fairbanks moved in, that Beverly Hills really became a popular place to live for the movie industry crowd.

Today you'll find a Beverly Hills no worse for wear. Household income is one of the highest in the country; property values are astronomical—even in bad times—and mansions are common. Even the high school is famous for its oil wells. The city also has what is possibly the most expensive jogging track in the world, based on land values, located on the parkway that runs parallel to Santa Monica Boulevard. Stars live, work, and dine in Beverly Hills, and are regularly seen here.

The Beverly Hills **Golden Triangle** is the business district bordered by Canon Drive, Santa Monica Boulevard, and Wilshire Boulevard. The streets burst with shops sporting price tags often beyond the reach of the average consumer. But don't let that stop you—there are also shops with "normal" prices, and wonderful sales (see Chapter 5, "Their Shopping List," for names of stores). There are also good family restaurants (see Section 3, "Kid-Rated Restaurants," in Chapter 7). Christmas is a great time to walk the streets of Beverly Hills. You are likely to spot a celebrity popping in at his or her favorite store to stock up on presents, and you can't help but want to peek into the ever-present limousines to see who might be sitting there. At other times you'll find an almost-constant promenade up and down the streets, day or night. In fact, no matter where your family has dinner, **Rodeo Drive** (pronounced Ro-*day*-oh) is a great place to walk it off in the evening. Take the kids and join the rest of the crowd, especially on Saturday night or Sunday afternoon, and window-shop and people-watch to your heart's content.

Possibly the best tour deal in town is found on the two **Beverly Hills Trolleys**, which depart from the corner of Rodeo Drive and Brighton Way, and Dayton Drive and Rodeo Drive. The 35-minute narrated ride travels through the Golden Triangle and past the toney boutiques, popular restaurants, and elegant hotels. You also travel through a bit of the nearby residential area, where the celebrity homes of such notables as Gene Kelly and Carl Reiner are pointed out. Want a bit of trivia to take home? Our guide explained that there are 100 licensed gardeners per square mile in the city of Beverly Hills, and that most of the business licenses in the city are given out to gardeners! Catch a ride for $1, Tuesday through Saturday (except rainy days and holidays), every half hour from 10:30am to 5pm.

There are other sights to see in Beverly Hills. **Greystone Mansion,** 905 Loma Vista Drive (tel. 213/550-4654), is possibly the most extravagant mansion ever built in Beverly Hills. This 55-room mansion, with an adjacent mini-mansion for the grandchildren, was built by oil magnate Edward Doheny, Sr., in 1928. Although the city is restoring the mansion itself, you can stroll through the lush grounds, a part of what was once a 428-acre estate. They're open May through September, daily from 10am to 6pm; October to April, daily from 10am to 5pm. No admission fee.

Although there's no playground equipment, **Will Rogers Memorial Park** (not to be confused with Will Rogers State Historical Park), across the street from the Beverly Hills Hotel, is one of the prettiest parks in which to push a stroller or relax under the gigantic palm trees. (Also see "Neighborhood Parks" in Section 4, "Letting Off Steam," above, for information on two Beverly Hills parks with playground equipment.)

For more information on Beverly Hills, contact the **Beverly Hills Visitors**

Bureau, 239 South Beverly Drive, Beverly Hills, CA 90212 (tel. 213/271-8174, or toll free 800/345-2210).

WESTWOOD VILLAGE

With its beginnings as a college town, home of UCLA, Westwood Village has become one of the hottest communities in Los Angeles. The area termed Westwood (bordered by Pico Boulevard to the south, Sunset Boulevard to the north, Sepulveda Boulevard to the west, and Beverly Hills to the east), was originally called Westwood Hills in 1923, and now has over 5,000 shops and services, several hotels, and more than 500 eating establishments. It has within these boundaries four parks (Cheviot Hills Recreation Center, Palms Park, Westwood Park, and Stoner Recreation Center) and one golf course, and is generally recognized to be the cinema capital of Los Angeles, with its dozens of first-run movie theaters. Not surprisingly, Westwood is a favorite of young teenagers and the college crowd.

One way to see Westwood Village is to take the kids in the late afternoon to window-shop or walk on the UCLA campus, and then have an early dinner. You can do all this before the Village gets too crowded with evening visitors or you might want to take in a matinee.

Caution: The Village is jammed with people—many of them teens—on Friday and Saturday nights. It's alive with activity and a fun place to people-watch, but be careful to hold onto your kids. During these crowded times we never use a stroller; instead, we carry our toddlers. Be prepared for potential street closings (closed to cars) on Friday and Saturday nights in the summer and during holidays and special events. Hours will vary.

This is a particularly popular place for clothing shops and shoe stores for the under-30 set. (See Chapter 5, "Their Shopping List," for some ideas.)

The world-famous **University of California at Los Angeles (UCLA),** 405 Hilgard Avenue (tel. 213/825-4321), is a beautiful hilly campus set between Westwood Village and Bel Air. The school is large—over 400 acres—with more than 30,000 full-time students. If you need information or would like to take a tour, contact the **Community Relations/Visitors Center,** 1417 Ueberroth Bldg., 405 Hilgard Avenue, Los Angeles, CA 90024 (tel. 213/206-8147).

If you prefer simply to wander around, a walk on campus during the quieter weekends is delightful and gives the kids an opportunity to rollick in the open grassy areas while you witness an amazing mix of architectural styles.

Don't miss Royce Hall and "the Quad," the spiritual heart of the campus. From there, wander to the **Franklin D. Murphy Sculpture Garden** (north of Royce Hall, near the University Research Library), where green lawns dotted with trees are home to more than 50 sculptures. Originally conceived as a place to bring art to the outdoors, where students could enjoy it as they studied, visited, and relaxed, the Sculpture Garden is a welcome retreat for families. You'll see lots of kids playing tag, reading, and picnicking with their parents.

If your family likes botanical gardens, you might enjoy a stroll through the **Mildred E. Mathias Botanical Garden** (tel. 213/825-3620), located at the southeastern part of the campus (enter at Le Conte Avenue and Hilgard Avenue). This compact garden features 4,000 species (225 families of plants) and specializes in subtropical and tropical plants that aren't grown in other parts of the U.S. except in greenhouses. It's open Monday through Friday from 8am to 5pm and on Saturday and Sunday from 8am to 4:30pm (closed university holidays). Admission is free.

SANTA MONICA

When you close your eyes, what images do the words "Santa Monica" conjure up? Palm trees lining the boulevards, miles and miles of ocean, children building sand castles, and almost perfect weather. These are the fantasies most people have, and surprisingly, they're reality.

You'll probably want to contact or stop at the **Santa Monica Visitors Information Center,** 1400 Ocean Avenue, Santa Monica, CA 90401 (tel. 213/393-7593), in Palisades Park.

A walk along Santa Monica's **Main Street** is a pleasant way to spend an hour or so. Trendy shops, art galleries, one-of-a-kind novelty stores, and restaurants line Main Street from Pico Boulevard to Rose Avenue, but the main cluster of shops is from Ocean Park Avenue to Pier Avenue.

The **Third Street Promenade** is touted as a "three-block-long festive marketplace," and it offers a wonderful opportunity for you to stroll amid artwork and fountains while the kids romp. There are numerous specialty bookstores and wonderful cafés. Each week there's an outdoor farmers market.

Angel's Attic, 516 Colorado Avenue (tel. 213/394-8331), is a delightful museum in a restored Victorian home. Especially captivating for children from 5 to 95 who love full-size and miniature dollhouses, dolls, and miniatures, the museum also has a collection of stuffed animals and toys. It's a nonprofit museum and contributes to the support of the Brentwood Center for Educational Therapy. Open Thursday through Sunday from 12:30 to 4:30pm.

VENICE BEACH OCEAN FRONT WALK

The key words to remember when visiting Venice Beach's Ocean Front Walk are "experience" and "keep an open mind." Strolling down this boardwalk is truly an experience. On a Sunday afternoon you'll see a cornucopia of L.A.'s most eclectic population. Some are scantily clothed; some have blue hair, some yellow; a few come decked-out in chains; one or two are covered with cloth from head to toe. But there are "normal" people here too, including the archetypal southern California man and woman. It's an inexpensive and fun way to spend a Saturday or Sunday afternoon.

You can take children of any age on this walk, but beware of some raunchy language used in some of the street acts. It's also quite crowded on weekends (the best time to come for prime people-watching), so hold onto those little hands.

Begin your Ocean Front Walk going north, and the first sight you'll see is **Muscle Beach,** where men—and women—with giant muscles lift weights and work out in front of dozens of observers. Jugglers, comedians, artists, musicians, and mimes line the walkway, much of which has been designated for bikes, skateboards, and roller skates (see "Bicycling and Roller Skating" in Section 4, "Letting Off Steam," above, for details on rentals). You have probably never seen the artistic roller skating you'll see here. You can bike or skate all the way from the Venice Beach boardwalk past the Santa Monica Pier.

There are a couple of **children's playgrounds** on the beach, one a half block north of Ocean Front Walk and Paloma Avenue, the other about two blocks north of Venice Boulevard and Ocean Front Walk. We don't recommend Venice Beach as a swimming beach because there are riptides, but for playing and picnicking, the sand is fine.

If you've wanted to find a California **souvenir,** you should be able to find one on Ocean Front Walk—for sale are thousands of T-shirts, hats of every description, sandals, sunglasses, jewelry, clothes, bathing suits, and much more. You might be surprised when you catch a glimpse of the Venice police, who are always patrolling the area—in their shorts.

There are lots of fast-food stands serving up hot dogs, sandwiches, ice cream, frozen yogurt, pizza, hamburgers, and popcorn. Rest your weary feet by having lunch on the beach, or stop by one of three sit-down restaurants: **Sidewalk Café,** 1401 Ocean Front Walk, open for breakfast, lunch, and dinner, with an extensive reasonably priced menu; the **Figtree Café,** 429 Ocean Front Walk, specializing in natural foods and serving breakfast items, salads, fish, pizzas, and many vegetarian specialties; or the **Beachhouse Market & Deli,** 1101 Ocean Front Walk, for well-priced sandwiches.

To get to Venice, take the Santa Monica Freeway (I-10) west to the San Diego Freeway (I-405) south; exit at Venice Boulevard, turn west, and you'll run right into Venice Beach. There's parking on the southeast corner of Venice Boulevard and Pacific Avenue for $5 all day, or find a spot on the street (more difficult on summer weekends). Alternatively, you can take the Pacific Coast Highway (Calif. 1) south to Venice Boulevard.

MARINA DEL REY

Just 5 miles north of Los Angeles International Airport you'll find Marina del Rey, a pocket of blue water, sailboats, and yachts. Although just minutes outside the city, it makes you feel as if you've been transported to a European seaside village.

Marina del Rey is the largest artificial pleasurecraft harbor in the world. Bounded by Lincoln Boulevard, Washington Street, and the Pacific Ocean, the area is home to more than 6,000 boats, myriad shops, pricey condos and apartments, movie theaters, singles bars, and a huge array of restaurants.

Here you can rent boats, cruise the marina, sunbathe, swim, fish, windsurf, roller skate, fly kites, walk, and ride bikes. One of our favorite pastimes is to take breakfast to the **North Jetty** between Via Marina and Pacific Avenue, find a spot, and enjoy our meal while we watch the boats as they pass through the main channel of the marina. For more information, the marina has its own visitor center. Contact the **Marina del Rey Visitors Information Center,** 4701 Admiralty Way, Marina del Rey, CA 90292 (tel. 213/305-9545).

If you're just looking for a nice place to let the kids run around, **Burton Chace Park** is a 9-acre waterfront park at the end of Mindanao Way with picnic areas, a fishing dock, and views of the boats.

Admiralty Park is on Admiralty Way between Palawan Way and Bali Way, near the bird sanctuary.

Serious shopping in the Marina district is best at the **Villa Marina Center,** at Mindanao Way and the Marina Freeway (Calif. 90). Here you'll find 20 restaurants, first-run movie theaters, a Von's supermarket, a Savon/Osco drugstore, a video arcade, and other necessities.

Fisherman's Village, at 13755 Fiji Way (tel. 213/823-5411), looks like a little fishing village, and it's a delightful place to walk and relax with the family for an afternoon. As you stroll along the boardwalk on a sunny weekend day, you'll see hundreds of pleasure boats of all sizes. You, too, can cruise the harbor on a 40-minute tour: **Hornblower Dining Yachts** (tel. 213/301-6000), located right at the village, has boats that leave daily in summer from Memorial Day to Labor Day (Saturday and Sunday only the rest of the year), every hour on the hour from 11am to 5pm. The fare is $7 for adults, $4 for children 2 to 12; children under 2 are free.

In the village there are art, souvenir, and jewelry stores; an import shop; a kite and toy store; and a T-shirt shop all housed in little cottages. Four sit-down restaurants serve Mexican food, pizza and pasta, seafood, and steaks. Outdoor snacks on the boardwalk include cookies, ice cream, hamburgers, candy, sandwiches, and fish and chips. On Sunday, weather permitting, you can hear free live jazz concerts from 2 to 5pm in the center of the village. Most of the shops and restaurants are open Sunday through Thursday from 10am to 9pm and on Friday and Saturday from 10am to 10pm. Parking is free.

CHAPTER 5

THEIR SHOPPING LIST

Los Angeles is one of the country's premier shopping spots. It has always been a city unafraid to make its own fashion statement, from the surfer look to haute couture.

In addition to its own talented designers, Los Angeles has always attracted the most exclusive stores in the world. Almost everyone has heard of elegant Rodeo Drive, and by now the rest of the world also knows about funky Melrose Avenue. It also boasts Westwood Village, which bursts with boutiques for the under-30 set. Brentwood and Santa Monica both have growing cosmopolitan shopping areas. Downtown Los Angeles has its share of stores and shopping centers, including the Seventh Street Market Place at Citicorp Plaza and Broadway Plaza.

The urban shopping centers are chock full of every kind of merchandise imaginable. The three biggest centers—the Beverly Center, Westside Pavilion, and Century City Shopping Center & Marketplace—are like self-contained cities with multiscreen movie theaters, sit-down and fast-food restaurants, and even grocery stores. The centers in the surrounding areas, such as Sherman Oaks Fashion Square, Sherman Oaks Galleria, and the Glendale Galleria, all abound in great shopping and eating places.

For the purposes of this book, we've concentrated on stores with kid appeal— whether your young sophisticates are doing the shopping, or whether you plan to bring home gifts for every imaginable young relative. In some cases these stores are favored by parents, in other cases by the kids themselves. There are those that cater to youngsters and others that have particular teen appeal.

Store Hours   Most stores are open Monday through Saturday from 10am to 6pm. There are exceptions, so you should always call ahead. Shopping centers have longer hours, and are usually open on Sunday as well.

Sales Tax   The sales tax in Los Angeles is 8.25%.

BASEBALL CARDS & COMIC BOOKS

BEVERLY HILLS BASEBALL CARD SHOP, 1137 S. Robertson Blvd., Beverly Hills. Tel. 213/278-4263.

Don't be put off by the Beverly Hills moniker: the Beverly Hills Baseball Card Shop only sounds expensive. It carries a wide range of baseball and other sports cards that children, amateur collectors, and sports buffs alike will enjoy. Open

Tuesday through Thursday from 11am to 6pm, on Friday from 11am to 7pm, on Saturday from 11am to 5pm, and on Sunday from noon to 4pm.

GOLDEN APPLE COMICS, 7711 Melrose Ave., West Hollywood. Tel. 213/658-6047, or 213/651-0455 for a 24-hour hotline.

Plan to spend some time just looking through the fabulous collection of new and "old" comic books, some dating back to the 1950s. There are also collectible editions and books of unusual facts. Open Monday through Wednesday from 11am to 9pm, on Thursday and Friday from 11am to 10pm, on Saturday from 11am to 9pm, and on Sunday from 11am to 7pm.

Other branches are in West Los Angeles (which also carries baseball trading cards) at 8934 West Pico Boulevard (tel. 213/274-2008), and in Northridge at 8958 Reseda Boulevard (tel. 818/993-7804).

HI DE HO, 525 Santa Monica Blvd., Santa Monica. Tel. 213/394-2820.

This comics and fantasy store caters to people of all ages, with the largest selection of popular comics and underground comics in southern California. They also carry fantasy art, books, posters, limited-edition prints, and other graphic arts. Trading-card collectors will find a good selection of baseball cards here. Open Sunday through Thursday from 11am to 7pm and on Friday and Saturday from 11am to 9pm.

There's another location in Venice at 64 Windward Avenue (tel. 213/399-6206).

BOOKS

B. DALTON, 6333 W. 3rd St., in the Farmers Market, Mid-Wilshire. Tel. 213/936-7266.

This nationwide chain carries a wide variety of books for all ages. As an added service, they will special-order any book they don't have in stock. The Beverly Center location has a large section of popular children's titles. Open Monday through Saturday from 9am to 6:30pm and on Sunday from 10am to 5pm. Longer summer hours.

Other locations are in West Hollywood at the Beverly Center, 8500 Beverly Boulevard (tel. 213/657-3011), in the ABC Entertainment Center at 2020 Avenue of the Stars (tel. 213/552-0637), in Westwood Village at 904 Westwood Boulevard (tel. 213/208-7395), and in Santa Monica in Santa Monica Place at 395 Santa Monica Place (tel. 213/451-8419).

BRENTANO'S, in the Century City Shopping Center, 10250 Santa Monica Blvd., Century City. Tel. 213/785-0204.

⭐ This store stocks more publications than any other bookstore chain in the area. They often host author signings, as well as parties to promote new publications. Customer service and special ordering are emphasized here. There's an excellent children's-book section. Open Monday through Thursday from 10am to 9pm, on Friday and Saturday from 10am to 11pm, and on Sunday from 10am to 9pm.

There's also a branch in Sherman Oaks in the Sherman Oaks Fashion Square at 14000 Riverside Drive (tel. 818/788-8661).

CALIFORNIA MAP AND TRAVEL CENTER, 3211 Pico Blvd., Santa Monica. Tel. 213/829-MAPS.

Maps, maps, and more maps here, plus travel guides to every destination you could possibly think of. Electronic translators, travel gadgets/accessories, and foreign dictionaries are also available. Open Monday through Friday from 8:30am to 6pm, on Saturday from 9am to 5pm, and on Sunday from noon to 5pm.

CHILDREN'S BOOK AND MUSIC CENTER, 2500 Santa Monica Blvd., Santa Monica. Tel. 213/829-0215.

This store is tops with local parents. In fact, it claims to carry the largest collection of children's books and records in the country. You can buy just about any kind of cassette or record for kids, and the selection of books is amazing. The staff is extremely knowledgeable. Open Monday through Saturday from 9am to 5:30pm (on Wednesday until 7pm).

CHILDREN'S BOOK WORLD, 10580½ W. Pico Blvd., West Los Angeles. Tel. 213/559-2665.

Don't let the size of this place fool you. CBW carries an extensive selection of books, educational aids, records, and cassettes for infants up to high-schoolers. The staff knows just what is appropriate, and will even help you choose books by phone for mailing. Open Monday through Friday from 10am to 5:30pm and on Saturday from 10am to 5pm.

CROWN BOOKS, 10751 W. Pico Blvd., West Los Angeles. Tel. 213/474-0556.

Crown specializes in discounted books. Each location also has a good selection of magazines and caters to all ages. Open Monday through Saturday from 10am to 9:30pm and on Sunday from 10am to 6pm.

Other locations are in Beverly Hills at 320 North Canon Drive (tel. 213/278-1522), and in Westwood at 10912 Lindbrook Avenue (tel. 213/208-1052).

DISTANT LANDS, A TRAVELER'S BOOKSTORE, 62 S. Raymond Ave., Old Pasadena. Tel. 818/449-3220.

The size of this bookstore belies its selections. In addition to general travel guides, it's a place to find travel videos, maps (foreign, regional, and domestic), and travel books for the armchair traveler. Open Tuesday through Thursday from 10:30am to 7pm, on Friday and Saturday from 10:30am to 9pm, and on Sunday from 11am to 6pm.

DUTTON'S, 11975 San Vicente Blvd., Brentwood. Tel. 213/476-6263.

Loyal fans don't care how far they have to travel to get to Dutton's. It's the book lover's dream store. Browse to your heart's content; get lost in the stacks and stacks of books. Want help? You'll get excellent service. Want to be left alone? It's okay. The children's store (adjacent) is fabulous. Open Monday through Friday from 9:30am to 9pm, on Saturday from 9:30am to 6pm, and on Sunday from 11am to 5pm.

Also in North Hollywood at 5146 Laurel Canyon Boulevard (tel. 818/769-3866).

HAPPILY EVER AFTER CHILDREN'S BOOKSTORE, 2640 Griffith Park Blvd., Los Feliz. Tel. 213/668-1996.

You won't want to leave the warm inviting atmosphere of this children's bookstore, and neither will the kids. You can sit, browse, and even come just for storytelling time (see Section 6, "Story Hours," in Chapter 6). There are books on all subjects, plus a selection of cassettes and videos. Open Monday through Saturday from 10am to 5:30pm and on Sunday from noon to 5pm.

CALIFORNIA

Sacramento ★

Los Angeles ●

The Beverly Center: ①
  The Broadway
  Brooks Stride Rite
  Bullocks
  California Pizza Kitchen
  F.A.O. Schwarz
  The Gap & GapKids
  Hard Rock Café
  Irvine Ranch Market
  Sam Goody's
  Sanrio
  Starkey's Deli
The Beverly Connection: ②
  The Good Guys
  Sports Chalet
  The Wherehouse
Bullocks, Sherman Oaks ③
Century City Shopping Center
  & Marketplace: ④
  Brentano's
  The Broadway
  Bullocks
  Contempo Casuals
  Disney Store
  Footlocker
  The Imaginarium
  Judy's
  The Nature Company
Farmers Market: ⑤
  B. Dalton
Saks Fifth Avenue ⑥
Santa Monica Place: ⑦
  The Broadway
  Footprints
  The Game Keeper
  The Imaginarium
  Robinson's
  See's Candy
  The Very Very Beast
Sherman Oaks Galleria ⑧
Westside Pavilion: ⑨
  The Gap
  Hanna-Barbera
  Judy's
  May Company
  Nordstrom
  Waldenbooks
Westwood Village ⑩

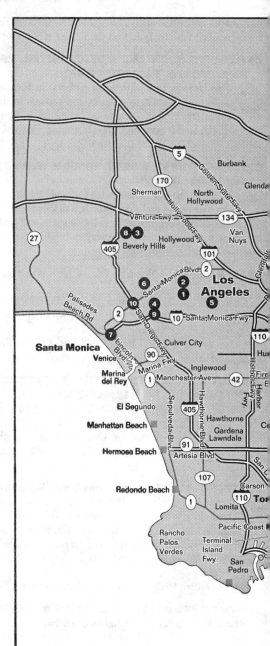

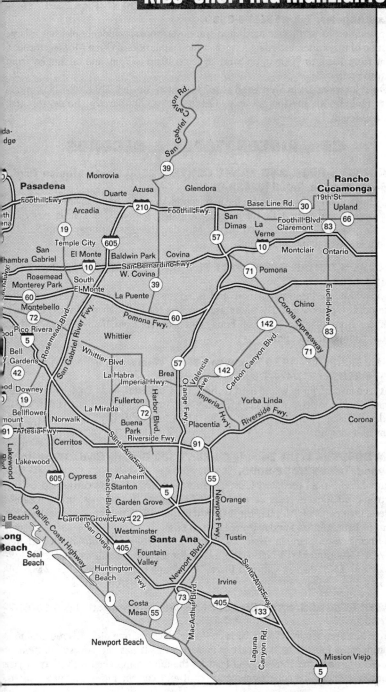

WALDENBOOKS, in the Westside Pavilion, 10800 W. Pico Blvd., West Los Angeles. Tel. 213/474-6550.

In addition to its regular hard- and soft-cover books, Waldenbooks has a large selection of magazines, including foreign fashion publications. Open Monday through Friday from 10am to 9:30pm, on Saturday from 10am to 7pm, and on Sunday from 11am to 6pm.

Other locations are in Westwood at 1073 Broxton Ave. (tel. 213/208-7295), and in West Hollywood in the Beverly Center at 8500 Beverly Boulevard (tel. 213/652-6582).

CDs, VIDEOS, TAPES & RECORDS

CHILDREN'S BOOK AND MUSIC CENTER, 2500 Santa Monica Blvd., Santa Monica. Tel. 213/829-0215.

★ In addition to its wonderful book selection, this store has many records, tapes, videos, and some CDs for infants and older children. The staff is extremely helpful and well informed. Open Monday through Saturday from 9am to 5:30pm (on Wednesday until 7pm).

McCABE'S GUITAR SHOP, 3101 Pico Blvd., Santa Monica. Tel. 213/828-4497.

Kids love the neat percussion and wind instruments here. There are also songbooks. On some Sundays there are concerts for kids. Open Monday through Thursday from 10am to 10pm on Friday and Saturday from 10am to 6pm, and on Sunday from 10am to 5pm.

RHINO RECORDS, 1720 Westwood Blvd., Westwood Village. Tel. 213/474-8685 or 213/474-3786.

A teen favorite for new and used records, CDs, cassettes, and LPs, Rhino Records carries a wide variety of music, including imports and international titles. Open Sunday through Thursday from 10am to 11pm and on Friday and Saturday from 10am to midnight.

SAM GOODY'S, in the Beverly Center, 8500 Beverly Blvd., West Hollywood. Tel. 213/652-5058.

In addition to all the latest CDs, cassettes, and LPs, Goody's carries videos and electronic equipment such as portable CD players, headphones, and miniature cassette players. Open Monday through Friday from 10am to 9pm, on Saturday from 10am to 8pm, and on Sunday from 11am to 6pm.

Other branches are in West Los Angeles at 11876 Wilshire Boulevard (tel. 213/477-7400) and 11201 National Boulevard at Sepulveda Boulevard (tel. 213/479-0599), and downtown in Citicorp Plaza, 735 South Figueroa Street (tel. 213/614-0125).

TOWER RECORDS, 8801 Sunset Blvd., West Hollywood. Tel. 213/657-7300.

If it has been recorded, they carry it. Tower Records, one of L.A.'s most famous institutions, is located at the heart of Sunset Strip. It has the largest selection of domestic music in the country, and features the most comprehensive variety of jazz recordings. There are collections of classical and current music, imports, videos, music-related books, and plenty of children's tapes. International mail-order service is available. Open Sunday through Thursday from 9am to midnight and on Friday and Saturday from 9am to 1am—365 days a year.

Also in Westwood at 1028 Westwood Boulevard (tel. 213/208-3061) and in Sherman Oaks at 14570 Ventura Boulevard (tel. 818/789-0500).

THE WHEREHOUSE, in the Beverly Connection, 100 N. La Cienega Blvd., West Hollywood. Tel. 213/659-0542.

This is a popular choice for CDs, videos, laser videos, records, and cassettes. There's even some computer software. Open Monday through Thursday from 9am to midnight and on Friday and Saturday from 9am to 1am.

There are also branches in West Los Angeles at 1860 Westwood Boulevard (tel. 213/470-7926), in Westwood Village at 1095 Broxton Avenue (tel. 213/824-2255), and in Santa Monica at 3015 Wilshire Boulevard (tel. 213/453-7874) and at 391 Santa Monica Place (tel. 213/394-1060).

DEPARTMENT STORES

THE BROADWAY, in Santa Monica Place, 315 Colorado Ave., Santa Monica. Tel. 213/393-1441.

If you've run out of the kids' socks, or need basic clothing or household items, this is the place to go. It has a good infants' department. Open Monday through Friday from 10am to 9pm, on Saturday from 10am to 7pm, and on Sunday from 11am to 6pm.

Also located in West Hollywood in the Beverly Center at 8500 Beverly Boulevard (tel. 213/854-7200), and in Century City in the Century City Shopping Center at 10250 Santa Monica Boulevard (tel. 213/277-1234).

BULLOCKS, in the Beverly Center, 8500 Beverly Blvd., West Hollywood. Tel. 213/854-6655.

Many of our friends buy their children's clothes here. It also has a good junior department. Brands are a step above basic department-store goods. Open Monday through Saturday from 10am to 9pm and on Sunday from 11am to 7pm.

Other branches are located in Century City in the Century City Shopping Center at 10250 Santa Monica Boulevard (tel. 213/556-1611), in Westwood Village at 10861 Weyburn Avenue (tel. 213/208-4211), and in Sherman Oaks in Fashion Square at 14000 Riverside Drive (tel. 818/788-8350).

NORDSTROM, in the Westside Pavilion, 10830 W. Pico Blvd., West Los Angeles. Tel. 213/470-6155.

Nordstrom is known for its excellent service and its fabulous adult shoe departments. They carry especially nice holiday clothes for adults and children. In addition to traditional items, the stock includes Absorba, Esprit, Adrienne Vittadini, Guess, Generra, and others. Brass Plus is the popular department for teenagers. The children's clothing and shoe departments are great. Open Monday through Friday from 10am to 9:30pm, on Saturday from 10am to 7pm, and on Sunday from 11am to 6pm.

SAKS FIFTH AVENUE, 9600 Wilshire Blvd., Beverly Hills. Tel. 213/275-4211.

The service, in the infant department in particular, is great, especially when it comes to mailing and gift wrapping. Want a leather suit—for a 4-year-old? It'll cost you $400! You'll find it, and lots of special items like it, in the children's department. Open Monday through Saturday from 10am to 6pm (on Thursday until 8:30pm) and on Sunday from noon to 5pm.

ELECTRONICS & VIDEO GAMES

ADRAY'S, 11201 W. Pico Blvd., West Los Angeles. Tel. 213/479-0797.

There's a good selection of video games here, at very reasonable prices. Know what you want ahead of time: This is the place to buy, not shop. Open Monday through Friday from 10am to 8pm and on Saturday and Sunday from 10am to 6pm.

Also in the Mid-Wilshire District at 5575 Wilshire Boulevard (tel. 213/935-8191), and in Van Nuys at 6609 Van Nuys Boulevard (tel. 818/908-1500).

GAME DUDE, 12104 Sherman Way, North Hollywood. Tel. 818/764-2442.

This store buys and sells used video games and systems, including discontinued models, generally at reduced prices. They carry such brands as Nintendo and Sega, with a variety of educational games, like *Sesame Street,* for the kids. They will also ship items domestically. Open Monday through Friday from 9am to 6pm, on Saturday from 9am to 5pm, and on Sunday from 11am to 5pm.

THE GOOD GUYS, in the Beverly Connection, 100 N. La Cienega Blvd., West Hollywood. Tel. 213/659-6500.

The Good Guys claims to beat any advertised price for any model electronic they carry. In addition to audio and video equipment, they sell phones, business machines, and cameras, and stock film, batteries, and miscellaneous photographic accessories. They carry many versions of Nintendo, Sega, and other video games. Open 24 hours daily.

TOYS 'Я' US, 1833 S. La Cienega Blvd., Los Angeles. Tel. 213/558-1831.

Know what you want and shop here because of the good prices—not the service. Most video systems and games are available. Open Monday through Saturday from 9:30am to 9:30pm and on Sunday from 10am to 7pm.

There's another location in Culver City at 11136 Jefferson Boulevard (tel. 213/398-5775).

FASHIONS FOR KIDS

AMERICAN RAG COMPAGNIE YOUTH, 136 S. La Brea Ave., Wilshire District. Tel. 213/965-1404.

This children's-clothing store specializes in "cheap" chic, with lots of funky items for little boys and girls, such as dyed jeans with ruffles, funky boxer shorts, and great hats. Clothes start at $14.95. Open Monday through Saturday from 9:30am to 8pm and on Sunday from 12:30 to 7pm.

BENETTON, 344 N. Rodeo Dr., Beverly Hills. Tel. 213/273-1247.

Benetton, known for its wide selection of sweaters, also carries a stylish collection of items ranging from cotton shorts to knitted dresses in a wide range of interchangeable colors and prints. The Rodeo Drive location has plenty to choose from, including a fairly large section of boys' and girls' clothing. The Beverly Center location is tiny but stocked with the famous Italian knitwear popular with ages 13 and up. In addition to the sweaters, T-shirts, pants, and shorts Benetton is known for, there's a great makeup kit for young ladies, fragrances for both men and women, and a neat travel kit for the guys. Open Monday through Saturday from 10am to 8pm and on Sunday from noon to 7pm.

Also in West Hollywood in the Beverly Center at 8500 Beverly Boulevard (tel. 213/657-1227), in West Los Angeles in the Westside Pavilion at 10800 West Pico Boulevard (tel. 213/470-9857), and in Century City in the Century City Shopping Center at 10250 Santa Monica Boulevard (tel. 213/556-1893).

BOYS WILL BE BOYS, 2530 San Vicente Blvd., Santa Monica. Tel. 213/451-9423.

As the name implies, this children's clothing store is for boys only, sizes 4 to 20, and features a barbershop in addition to its full room of dress wear. To make it easy on mom and dad, they also do normal alterations for free. Open Monday through Friday from 9:30am to 6:30pm, on Saturday from 9:30am to 6pm, and on Sunday from noon to 5pm.

There's another location in Sherman Oaks at 14962 Ventura Boulevard (tel. 818/986-2697).

CAMP BEVERLY HILLS, 9615 Brighton Way, Beverly Hills. Tel. 213/274-8317.

Nowadays, CBH is showing an eclectic grouping of modern, fun casual wear, with a European twist, side by side with unusual accessories and a small selection of "off the wall books"—including a compilation of works by famed poets on dogs. The women's selections are more feminine than they used to be. They still have clothes for the whole family, including a good children's section. Select anything from a typical California T-shirt to a fanciful silk dress. Open Monday through Saturday from 10am to 6:30pm and on Sunday from noon to 5pm.

A CHILD'S ROOM, 199 S. Beverly Dr., Beverly Hills. Tel. 213/273-2199.

This is a great place for that special gift to take back to friends. Gorgeous clothes from Mousefeathers, Babi Mini, 100,000 Watts, and other European labels are featured in sizes for infants to 6X. You'll find the newest in European accessories, including great hats, necklaces, earrings, bracelets, and cute items for the hair. The staff stresses personal service. Open Monday through Saturday from 10am to 5pm, and by appointment.

THE CHOCOLATE GIRAFFE, 516 S. Lake Ave., Pasadena. Tel. 818/796-5437.

Clothing, accessories, books, and toys for boys and girls from newborns to 10 years old are featured here. The emphasis is on European styles. Can't make up your mind? Visit one of the store's fashion shows. There are also clowns and food on some days—call for details. Open Monday through Saturday from 10am to 6pm.

Another location is in Glendale at 121 North Maryland Avenue (tel. 818/243-5437).

CONTEMPO CASUALS, in the Century City Shopping Center, 10250 Santa Monica Blvd., Century City. Tel. 213/277-8630.

Contempo is the perfect place for trendy clothing without the trendy price tag. Geared toward teenagers, it has a large selection of funky accessories, casual wear, and even formal items. Your teen will be able to find everything from stylish T-shirts to that outrageous little Lycra dress for evenings out. Open Monday through Saturday from 10am to 9pm and on Sunday from 11am to 7pm.

Also in West Hollywood in the Beverly Center at 8500 Beverly Boulevard (tel. 213/652-4968), in West Los Angeles in the Westside Pavilion at 10800 West Pico Boulevard (tel. 213/474-1485), and in Westwood at 1081 Westwood Boulevard (tel. 213/208-8503).

COTTON RAINBOW, 156 S. Beverly Dr., Beverly Hills. Tel. 213/859-7328.

Featured here are 100% cotton clothes in fun, colorful designs by designer Kjersti. Every piece is preshrunk and dyed by hand. In addition to "California-casual" dresses, leggings, and T-shirts, you can find socks and other matching accessories for infants to adults. Want to dress alike? Mommy and daughter can pick out matching outfits. Open Monday through Saturday from 10am to 6pm.

Other locations are in Santa Monica at 2408 Wilshire Boulevard (tel. 213/828-1945), and in Sherman Oaks at 14537 Ventura Boulevard (tel. 818/784-7787).

ESPRIT, 8491 Santa Monica Blvd., West Hollywood. Tel. 213/659-7575.

Esprit is synonymous with natural, but they don't sacrifice style. The whole family will be able to select from a large collection of comfortable cottons and denims in innovative prints and styles. Most of the items can be mixed and matched, and they also carry a large selection of accessories. The clothes, including their dressier items, have a certain ease that makes them perfect for traveling. Esprit carries children's to adult sizes. Open Monday through Friday from 10am to 7pm, on Saturday from 10am to 6pm, and on Sunday from 11am to 6pm.

Other Esprit outlets can be found in major department stores throughout Los Angeles.

THE GAP, in the Westside Pavilion, 10800 W. Pico Blvd., West Los Angeles. Tel. 213/470-3300.

American classics, the rage of the L.A. fashion scene, are sold here. Especially attentive salespeople will help you find the Levi's jeans you were always looking for, with the perfect one-pocket white T-shirt to go with it. There is a large selection of basics featuring the Gap private label, including turtlenecks and simple sweaters, for both men and women, from teens to adults. New styles and colors arrive every 6 weeks. Open Monday through Friday from 10am to 9:30pm, on Saturday from 10am to 7pm, and on Sunday from 11am to 6pm.

Other locations are at 7650 Melrose Avenue (tel. 213/653-3847), in Westwood Village at 1000 Westwood Boulevard (tel. 213/208-0660), in the Beverly Center at 8500 Beverly Boulevard in West Hollywood (tel. 213/657-1404), in Beverly Hills at 420 North Beverly Drive (tel. 213/859-2987), and in Sherman Oaks at 15301 Ventura Boulevard (tel. 818/783-9800).

GAPKIDS and BABYGAP (see addresses above).

⭐ To meet the demand created by grownups who live in Gap clothes, the company created these stores for you-know-who. Not only are the styles and colors appealing to boys and girls and their parents, but the stores themselves are scaled down for easier shopping. The unfussy Gap-inspired styles include jeans, jumpers, jackets, T-shirts, sweats, socks, and belts to match. The kids' section dresses sizes 2 to 12; baby sizes are for newborns to 24 months. Gapkids can be found in the Westside Pavilion. Both BabyGap and GapKids can be found in Santa Monica at the corner of Wilshire Boulevard and 20th Street (tel. 213/453-4511), in the Beverly Center, and in Beverly Hills across the street from the adult Gap store.

JUDY'S, in the Century City Shopping Center, 10250 Santa Monica Blvd., Century City. Tel. 213/277-1440.

Judy's offers everything from trendy items for 14-year-olds to *Vogue* knock-offs. It's a great place to pick up fun accessories, including lacy gloves, hats, and earrings at moderate prices. Guys can find the latest styles here, too. The atmosphere seems teen oriented, but there are plenty of items for adults. Open Monday through Friday from 10am to 9pm, on Saturday from 10am to 6pm, and on Sunday from 11am to 6pm.

Other locations are in West Hollywood in the Beverly Center at 8500 Beverly Boulevard (tel. 213/657-2072), in West Los Angeles in the Westside Pavilion at 10800 West Pico Boulevard (tel. 213/470-3788), and in Sherman Oaks in the Sherman Oaks Galleria (tel. 818/986-1078).

LIMITED, TOO, in the Beverly Center, 8500 Beverly Blvd., West Hollywood. Tel. 213/652-3193.

If you're familiar with the Limited's store for adult women, you'll appreciate their newest addition for girls ages 2 to 14. The richly colored European clothes are mostly interchangeable. Cotton ramie sweaters and cotton and Lycra leggings, plus T-shirts, adorable French-style dresses, and skirts can be worn with the simple but "grownup" accessories. The children's version of Forenza and the OBR label are found here. The prices are excellent, and the store often offers two or three of something for one lower price. Open Monday through Friday from 10am to 9pm, on Saturday from 10am to 8pm, and on Sunday from 11am to 6pm.

LITTLE FOLKS, in the Beverly Center, 8500 Beverly Blvd., Beverly Hills. Tel. 213/657-1233.

Ⓢ The stock consists mostly of American brands such as Eve Too!, Amy Byer, and Buster Brown. The wide selection fits boys and girls from infants to size 14. Prices are very reasonable; the clothes are adorable. Open Monday through Friday from 10am to 9pm, on Saturday from 10am to 8pm, and on Sunday from 11am to 6pm.

OILILY, 9520 Brighton Way, Beverly Hills. Tel. 213/859-9145.

Los Angeles has recently received a slice of bright Dutch life straight from the Netherlands. The unique designs in rich, sun-drenched colors somehow work with patterns you'd never thought could make it together. You might recognize some of these clothes on Keshia Knight Pulliam, Bill Cosby's youngest daughter on "The Cosby Show." The clothes are for sizes 0 to 12, boys and girls. They carry shoes, too. Open Monday through Friday from 10am to 6pm, on Saturday from 10am to 7pm, and on Sunday from noon to 5pm.

PIXIE TOWN, 400 N. Beverly Dr., Beverly Hills. Tel. 213/272-6415.

Many Beverly Hills locals shop here. Inside you'll find traditional, imported, and southern California styles in all price ranges for sizes from newborns to preteen girls, and up to size 14 boys. There is a wealth of neat accessories, and a full-service shoe department is upstairs. Open Monday through Saturday from 10am to 5:30pm.

SACKS SFO KIDS, 7018 Melrose Ave. (at La Brea Ave.), Los Angeles. Tel. 213/935-2390.

S Here moms and dads take a break from department-store prices with the large selection of designer children's clothing at 50% to 80% off. There's a wide variety of 100% cotton merchandise and many L.A.-based brands—with new arrivals each week—for newborns to size 14, boys and girls. Open Monday through Saturday from 10am to 7pm and on Sunday from 11am to 6pm.

Other locations are in Santa Monica at 11807 Santa Monica Boulevard (tel. 213/312-0388) and in Burbank at 1421 West Olive Avenue (tel. 818/972-2797).

0 TO 14, 371 N. Beverly Dr., Beverly Hills. Tel. 213/859-0214.

Check out the adorable clothes for children 6 months to 14 years old. In addition to the Baby Guess line, they carry French Chipae and Les Enfants du Vallon, as well as their private label, Gantom. Open Monday through Saturday from 10am to 6:30pm and on Sunday from noon to 5pm.

Other locations are in West Los Angeles in the Westside Pavilion at 10800 West Pico Boulevard (tel. 213/470-6078), in Sherman Oaks at the Sherman Oaks Galleria (tel. 818/783-0214), and in Glendale in the Glendale Galleria at 200 West Broadway (tel. 818/242-0214).

NOVELTY ITEMS

COSTUMES FOR KIDS, 7206½ Melrose Ave., West Hollywood. Tel. 213/936-5437.

Indulge your children's fantasies. Owner Wanda Fudge claims that as far as she knows, this is the only costume store for kids in the whole country. The choices will definitely knock your socks off—these are not your usual boxed ghost costumes and wigs. There are poodle skirts and cheerleader outfits, gorgeous king and queen garments, and everything in between for sizes 2 to 12. You might even run into your favorite movie star shopping for this year's Halloween costume. Open Monday through Friday from 10am to 5pm and on Saturday from 11am to 5pm; in October, open daily with expanded hours.

EVERY PICTURE TELLS A STORY, 836 N. La Brea Ave., Los Angeles. Tel. 213/962-5420.

More than a bookstore, this is actually a gallery of original artwork from a variety of children's books. You'll find pieces from *Babar* and *Tom Thumb* and works by Maurice Sendak. There's also a beautiful selection of illustrated children's books. Open Tuesday through Saturday from 10am to 5pm and on Sunday from noon to 5pm.

HANNA-BARBERA, in the Westside Pavilion, 10800 W. Pico Blvd., West Los Angeles. Tel. 213/470-6649.

As you'd expect, you'll find the licensed products of many of the Hanna-Barbera characters, including the Flintstones and the Jetsons. Besides T-shirts, sweatshirts, watches, and jewelry, there are toys and animation art. Open Monday through Friday from 10am to 9:30pm, on Saturday from 10am to 7pm, and on Sunday from 11am to 6pm.

HOLLYWOOD TOYS & COSTUMES, 6562 Hollywood Blvd., Hollywood. Tel. 213/465-3119.

Just like the hardware stores of yesteryear filled with "stuff" from floor to ceiling, this old-fashioned toy store appeals to those who aren't looking for a slick toy store. Kids have a heyday looking up and down the aisles. It has the best-priced boxed costumes in town, plus all the masks and accessories; there's practically any costume you can imagine in a multitude of sizes, children through adult. Open Monday through Saturday from 9:30am to 7pm and on Sunday from 11am to 6pm.

THE NATURE COMPANY, in the Century City Shopping Center, 10250 Santa Monica Blvd., Century City. Tel. 213/785-0262.

As the name implies, all the merchandise here, from such unusual gift items as potato clocks and inflatable dinosaurs to New Age music, is nature related. It's a great place to browse with the kids, and the outgoing salespeople can help you choose from the many coloring and activities books that will appeal to your budding environmentalist. Open Monday through Friday from 10am to 9pm, on Saturday from 10am to 8pm, and on Sunday from 10am to 7pm.

There's another branch in Beverly Hills at 270 North Beverly Drive (tel. 213/274-9971).

SANRIO, in the Beverly Center, 8500 Beverly Blvd., West Hollywood. Tel. 213/657-7040.

All the Hello Kitty brand merchandise for boys and girls you could possibly imagine in backpacks, lunch boxes, jewelry boxes, pencil cases, wallets, and much more exists in this store. Open Monday through Friday from 10am to 9pm, on Saturday from 10am to 8pm, and on Sunday from 11am to 6pm.

SHOES FOR KIDS

BROOKS STRIDE RITE, in the Beverly Center, 8522 Beverly Blvd., West Hollywood. Tel. 213/657-2200.

Good shoes for kids—girls up to size 3, boys to size 7. They carry their own brand and other popular brands, some European. Open Monday through Saturday from 10am to 9pm and on Sunday from 11am to 6pm.

Other locations are in West Los Angeles in the Westside Pavilion at 10800 West Pico Boulevard (tel. 213/570-7206), in Sherman Oaks in the Fashion Square at 14000 Riverside Drive (tel. 818/501-2982), and in Santa Monica in Santa Monica Place at 395 Santa Monica Place (tel. 213/394-1662) and at 1703 Wilshire Boulevard (tel. 213/315-9898).

CONVERSE FACTORY OUTLET, 423 S. Lincoln Blvd., Venice. Tel. 213/396-0719.

The store carries Converse athletic footwear for men, women, and kids, as well as activewear. Open Monday through Wednesday from 10am to 6pm, Thursday through Saturday from 10am to 7pm, and on Sunday from 11am to 6pm.

FOOTLOCKER, in the Century City Shopping Center, 10250 Santa Monica Blvd., Century City. Tel. 213/556-1498.

For you or the little athlete in your life, there is an assortment of adults' and children's sports and active shoes, including footwear by Nike and Reebok. Open Monday through Friday from 10am to 9pm, on Saturday from 10am to 6pm, and on Sunday from 11am to 6pm.

Other locations are in West Hollywood in the Beverly Center at 8500 Beverly Boulevard (tel. 213/652-5749), and in West Los Angeles in the Westside Pavilion at 10800 West Pico Boulevard (tel. 213/470-2911).

FOOTPRINTS, 388 Santa Monica Place, Santa Monica. Tel. 213/394-6377.

Here you'll find a good selection of children's shoes. The friendly owner is gentle with kids and doesn't push you to buy the most expensive shoes. Open Monday through Friday from 10am to 9pm, on Saturday from 10am to 6pm, and on Sunday from 11am to 6pm.

NORDSTROM, in the Westside Pavilion, 10830 W. Pico Blvd, West Los Angeles. Tel. 213/470-6155.

⭐ Considered to have one of the best children's-shoe departments in town, Nordstrom offers trendy styles along with basic and conservative choices, as well as good stocking and tight selections. Open Monday through Friday from 10am to 9:30pm, on Saturday from 10am to 7pm, and on Sunday from 11am to 6pm.

Also in Glendale in the Glendale Galleria at 200 West Broadway (tel. 818/502-9922).

WESTSIDE KIDS, 11677 San Vicente Blvd., Brentwood. Tel. 213/207-6977.

This clothing store has a good selection of the latest shoe styles for kids up to age 10. Sizes start at 0 and go to 6 for boys, to 9 for girls. Open Monday through Saturday from 11am to 7pm, and on Sunday from noon to 5pm.

SHOPPING MALLS

THE BEVERLY CENTER, 8500 Beverly Blvd., West Hollywood. Tel. 213/854-0070.

This is L.A.'s largest fully enclosed shopping complex. Its two flagship stores are The Broadway and Bullock's. Between them are approximately 200 shops and restaurants. On the eighth floor is the 13-screen Cineplex movie theater, fast-food stands, and sit-down restaurants. Starkey's Deli serves pizza by the slice and has a fairly large video arcade in the rear. On the street level are the popular Hard Rock Café, California Pizza Kitchen, and Irvine Ranch Market, the market to the stars and anyone else who can afford its prices.

Strollers and wheelchairs are available at the information booth, located on the sixth floor under the escalators near the middle of the center. Parking entrances are on La Cienega Boulevard, San Vicente Boulevard, and Beverly Boulevard. Parking costs $1 for the first 3 hours. Valet parking is available at the Beverly Boulevard and La Cienega Boulevard entrances.

Shops are open Monday through Friday from 10am to 9pm, on Saturday from 10am to 8pm, and on Sunday from 11am to 6pm. The theaters and restaurants are open after shopping hours.

CENTURY CITY SHOPPING CENTER & MARKETPLACE, 10250 Santa Monica Blvd., Century City. Tel. 213/277-3898.

L.A.'s last outdoor shopping center is always bursting with families on weekends. In addition to the boutiques, toy and book stores, and pet shops are first-run movie theaters and a huge international open-air food hall. Bullock's and The Broadway are the main department stores. Parking is plentiful, and there's even that priceless southern California phenomenon, valet parking, near the Little Santa Monica Boulevard entrance. Other parking entrances are on Constellation Boulevard and on Century Park West. Free 3-hour parking is available with validation (no purchase necessary). No strollers are available.

Open Monday through Friday from 10am to 9pm, on Saturday from 10am to 6pm, and on Sunday from 11am to 6pm. Restaurants and theaters are open later.

SANTA MONICA PLACE, 395 Santa Monica Place, Santa Monica. Tel. 213/394-5451.

This three-story mall is bright and open and filled with more than 160 shops and restaurants. Robinson's and The Broadway are the department-store anchors. The highlight of the mall is the ground-floor level, where you might find an elaborate sand sculpture, a Christmas extravaganza, or a wishing pond. Andrew loves to visit the Gamekeeper and See's Candy, and Elizabeth's choice is The Very Very Beast. Plenty of parking. Open Monday through Friday from 10am to 9pm, on Saturday from 10am to 6pm, and on Sunday from 11am to 6pm.

WESTSIDE PAVILION, 10800 W. Pico Blvd., West Los Angeles. Tel. 213/474-6255.

This center has one of the best food courts in the city, offering almost anything you could want to eat. With Nordstrom and May Company as the anchor stores (located on either end of the shopping mall), the shops in the Westside Pavilion run the gamut in price. One of our favorites is WaldenKids, which has an area where the kids can play on the floor to try out some of the goodies before mom or dad purchases them. There are plenty of children's clothing and toy stores. You'll also find the Samuel Goldwyn Pavilion Cinemas with four theaters, one of which often shows children's films. Free parking or valet parking; rooftop parking is good for stroller access, but no strollers are available.

Open Monday through Friday from 10am to 9:30pm, on Saturday from 10am to 7pm, and on Sunday from 11am to 6pm.

SPORTING GOODS

ADVENTURE-16 WILDERNESS CAMPING OUTFITTERS, 11161 W. Pico Blvd., West Los Angeles. Tel. 213/473-4574.

This is an excellent place to visit if you're in the market for backpacking, camping, or mountaineering gear. Open Monday through Friday from 10am to 9pm, on Saturday from 10am to 6pm, and on Sunday from noon to 5pm.

GOLDEN BEAR SKATE SHOP, 10712 Washington Blvd., Culver City. Tel. 213/838-6611.

In the market for roller blades or ice skates? Golden Bear Skate Shop has an excellent reputation, and plenty of street hockey and other hockey gear. Open Monday through Friday from 10am to 6pm and on Saturday from 10am to 5pm.

HORIZONS WEST SURF AND WEAR, 2011 Main St., Santa Monica. Tel. 213/392-1122.

Visit Horizons for surf and boogie boards, skateboards, and some children's clothes. Open daily until 7pm—opening time depends on surfing conditions, so call ahead!

NATURAL PROGRESSION, 1734 Colorado Ave., Santa Monica. Tel. 213/829-5952.

You'll probably agree that this is surf heaven, as you make your way through the many surfboards and wetsuits. Spring suits and wetsuits are available for juniors, but there are no children's sizes. Hours vary depending on the surf—call ahead.

OSHMAN'S SPORTING GOODS, 11110 W. Pico Blvd., West Los Angeles. Tel. 213/478-0446.

This is a good store for basic sporting goods, tennis shoes, sports clothes, and some children's ski wear. Open Monday through Friday from 9am to 9pm and on Saturday and Sunday from 9am to 6pm. Also in the Westside Pavilion, 10800 West Pico Blvd., West L.A. (tel. 213/474-2321).

RIP CITY SKATES, 2709 Santa Monica Blvd., Santa Monica. Tel. 213/828-0388.

Stop by for skateboards, roller blades, and everything that goes with them. Open Monday through Saturday from 10:30am to 6pm and on Sunday from noon to 4pm.

SPORTS CHALET, in the Beverly Connection, 100 N. La Cienega Blvd., West Hollywood. Tel. 213/657-3210.

This is our choice for a family sporting-goods store. You'll find everything from colorful Obermayer ski clothes for kids, to outdoor sports equipment of all types—skis and snowboards; rollerblades; scuba gear; backpacking, mountaineering, and camping supplies; and bikes. There are some Flapdoodles clothes for kids, as well as outerwear and even Scout uniforms. The staff is well versed and most helpful. Open Monday through Saturday from 10am to 9pm and on Sunday from 10am to 6pm.

TOYS

AGES & STAGES, 8950 W. Olympic Blvd., Beverly Hills. Tel. 213/274-4301.

The specialties here are personal service and unique toys. There is also clothing for children sizes 0 to 6x. Throughout the week, classes in art and music and a fairytale theater are conducted in the store; call for schedules. Open Monday through Saturday from 10am to 6pm and on Sunday from 10am to 4pm.

ALLIED MODEL TRAINS, 4411 S. Sepulveda Blvd., Culver City. Tel. 213/313-9353.

The true model-train enthusiast will appreciate this store, built to look like Los Angeles's Union Station and totally devoted to model trains and all the paraphernalia that goes with them. This is not a toy store, per se, but there is a large selection of European trains and accessories. Open Monday through Thursday and on Saturday from 10am to 6pm, on Friday from 10am to 9pm.

DISNEY STORE, in the Century City Shopping Center, 10250 Santa Monica Blvd., Century City. Tel. 213/556-8035.

Couldn't stop to buy that favorite Disney toy or sweatshirt when you were in Fantasyland? Don't worry. Everything you ever wanted with a mouse or duck on it can be found here: Viewmasters, stuffed animals, sweatshirts, T-shirts, pajamas, watches, videos, books, and lots of toys. Open Monday through Friday from 10am to 9pm, on Saturday from 10am to 6pm, and on Sunday from 11am to 6pm.

F.A.O. SCHWARZ, in the Beverly Center, 8500 Beverly Blvd., West Hollywood. Tel. 213/659-4547.

It's fun to walk in here and watch what's going on. One or more toys are always being displayed by the staff. This store has items other toy stores don't carry. Collector dolls, the newest Nintendo and other system games, huge stuffed animals, Brio wooden toys, and a good selection of music items are available. Open Monday through Friday from 10am to 9pm and on Saturday and Sunday from 10am to 6pm.

THE GAME KEEPER, in the Westside Pavilion, 10800 West Pico Blvd., West Los Angeles. Tel. 213/475-1753.

Most of the games here are geared toward adults, although family games, such as "USA Trivia" can be found. They have a nice selection of unusual chess sets for the serious game player, as well as a variety of hand-held puzzles and mindteasers. Customer service is emphasized, and gift certificates, game lessons, and free UPS shipping are available. Open Monday through Friday from 10am to 9:30pm, on Saturday from 10am to 7pm, and on Sunday from 11am to 6pm.

IMAGINARIUM, in the Century City Shopping Center, 10250 Santa Monica Blvd., Century City. Tel. 213/785-0227.

Hold onto your hats if you visit this store on the weekend! Because the kids are allowed to play with the toys, and even work with arts and crafts, the place is always full—and fun. You really get to see what your children and other youngsters like as you watch them pick and choose what to play with. No violent toys here: there are many science-related items and travel toys, and a nice book selection. Open Monday through Friday from 10am to 9pm, on Saturday from 10am to 6pm, and on Sunday from 11am to 6pm.

Other locations are in Santa Monica in Santa Monica Place at 395 Santa Monica Place (tel. 213/393-6500), and in Sherman Oaks in the Fashion Square at 14000 Riverside Drive (tel. 818/995-7445).

LAKESHORE CURRICULUM MATERIALS STORE, 888 Venice Blvd., Culver City. Tel. 213/559-9630.

This is a fabulous stop for a variety of educational books, toys, workbooks, records, and arts and crafts supplies. There are many materials you can't find in most children's book or toy stores. Open Monday through Friday from 9am to 5:30pm and on Saturday from 9am to 5pm.

TOYS 'Я' US, 1833 S. La Cienega Blvd., Los Angeles. Tel. 213/558-1831.

Almost every imaginable toy brand can be found in this huge warehouse-like store. Prices are usually less than in the other retail toy stores. They also carry well-priced diapers, formula, outdoor equipment, sporting goods (for kids), bicycles, electronics, bedding, and clothing. Open Monday through Saturday from 9:30am to 9:30pm and on Sunday from 10am to 7pm.

There's another branch in Culver City at 11136 Jefferson Boulevard (tel. 213/398-5775).

THE WOUND AND WOUND TOY COMPANY, 7374 Melrose Ave., West Hollywood. Tel. 213/653-6703.

If you can't find the windup toy of your dreams here, then it just doesn't exist. Adults love this place, which is filled with the usual and the unusual. Their slogan is "We do not stop playing because we grow old—we grow old because we stop playing." Even if you don't come to buy, it's a fun place to browse. Open Monday through Thursday from 11am to 10pm, on Friday and Saturday from 11am to midnight, and on Sunday from noon to 8pm.

CHAPTER 6

THEIR KIND OF ENTERTAINMENT

1. THEATER & DANCE
2. COFFEEHOUSES
3. CLUBS
4. CONCERT VENUES
5. SPECTATOR SPORTS
6. STORY HOURS

Home to the first motion picture and still the major film production center in the world, Los Angeles also prides itself on the talents of its culturally diverse population in other areas of the arts. In addition to film, TV, and music production, Los Angeles boasts live theater, dance, and music performances of all types year round. There is always something going on, much of it alluring to the entire family.

Each Sunday the "Calendar" section of the *Los Angeles Times* lists "Family Attractions and Events for Children."

Tickets to most events are available either at the box office or through **TicketMaster** (tel. 213/480-3232) or **Ticketron** (tel. 213/410-1062). Have your credit card number ready when you call. You can also contact the following companies: **Teletron** (tel. 213/410-1062), **First Class Tickets** (tel. 213/477-8977), **Ticket Time** (tel. 213/473-1000), and **Front Row Center** (tel. 213/478-0848). Most hotel concierges can secure tickets to any event.

1. THEATER & DANCE

FOR KIDS

BOB BAKER MARIONETTE THEATER, 1345 W. 1st St., downtown. Tel. 213/250-9995.
This 250-seat arena theater is the longest-running permanent theater of its kind in the United States. Make reservations for the daily shows.
Prices: Tickets, $8 (including refreshments and an after-show discussion about the marionettes).

LOS ANGELES CHILDREN'S THEATRE, various locations throughout Los Angeles. Tel. 213/469-6663.
The Children's Theatre presents several performances for children of various ages

throughout the year. Call or check the *Los Angeles Times* Sunday "Calendar" section for schedules.

LOS ANGELES JUNIOR PROGRAMS, various locations throughout Los Angeles. Tel. 213/271-6402.

Every performance of music, drama, comedy, or puppetry is geared to teach children an appreciation of the theater. Performances are open to children in grades one to six, although most performances are geared to the lower grades. Children under 5 are not allowed. The Wadsworth Theater at UCLA is a good location to visit.
Prices: Tickets, $3. Subscription series discount.

ODYSSEY THEATER ENSEMBLE, 2055 S. Sepulveda Blvd., West Los Angeles. Tel. 213/477-2055.

The Glorious Players, a very professional group of actors (many of whom are also teachers), perform thought-provoking plays for children. Call for program information.

OPEN HOUSE AT THE HOLLYWOOD BOWL, 2301 N. Highland Ave., Hollywood. Tel. 213/850-2000.

Children as young as 3 (we recommend not younger than 5) can visit this beautiful outdoor venue weekdays in the summer. There are performances by folk dancers, puppeteers, musicians, and other performers from around the world. A hands-on workshop themed to the presentation of the day follows each performance. Single show tickets are available, but try to get them in advance. While you're there, visit the Bowl itself, where you might be lucky enough to sit in on a rehearsal of the Los Angeles Philharmonic.
Prices: Tickets, $3.

SANTA MONICA PLAYHOUSE, 1211 4th St., Santa Monica. Tel. 213/394-9779.

The Family Theater Series offers matinees for children as young as 2.
Prices: Tickets, $6.

SERENDIPITY THEATRE CO., at the Coronet Theatre, 366 N. La Cienega Blvd., West Hollywood. Tel. 213/652-9199.

This new children's theater company offers a seven-play season of new and familiar plays for various age groups. Everything from Judy Blume's *Tales of a Fourth Grade Nothing* to the timeless *Androcles and the Lion*. Single tickets are available at the box office. Performances are on weekends.
Prices: Tickets, $10 adults, $6 children 13 and under.

THEATER WEST, 3333 Cahuenga Blvd., North Hollywood. Tel. 818/761-2203.

During the school year, children's musicals are performed every Saturday at 1pm. Most of the 1-hour plays have audience participation and are appropriate for children ages 2 to 9.

FOR THE WHOLE FAMILY

LONG BEACH CONVENTION & ENTERTAINMENT CENTER, 300 E. Ocean Blvd., Long Beach. Tel. 213/436-3636.

The center produces a wide variety of performances from ballet to theater to pop concerts to symphony and opera. Call for show information.

THE MUSIC CENTER, 135 N. Grand Ave., at 1st St., downtown. Tel. 213/972-7211.

The Music Center is Los Angeles's grand complex of three theaters—the Dorothy Chandler Pavilion, the Ahmanson Theatre, and the Mark Taper Forum. The theaters present a mix of the Los Angeles Philharmonic, Broadway theater, experimental theater, ballet, and other live performances. There are often presentations suitable for the entire family. To get tickets by mail for any of the theaters, write 2 weeks in advance to the Box Office, 135 North Grand Avenue, Los Angeles, CA 90012. Or you can get tickets through Ticketron (tel. 213/642-4242) or Teletron (tel. 213/410-1062).

PANTAGES THEATRE, 6233 Hollywood Blvd., Hollywood. Tel. 213/410-1062, or 213/642-4242 for tickets.

The Pantages features at least one or two performances for families during the year. Check the "Calendar" section of the Los Angeles Times. It's worth popping in just to see the interior of this magnificent building, built in 1929 as a movie house.

PASADENA CIVIC AUDITORIUM, 300 E. Green St., Pasadena. Tel. 818/793-2122.

Although many of the performances here are adult-oriented, there are often major plays children will love, such as My Fair Lady. Check the Los Angeles Times.

UCLA CENTER FOR THE PERFORMING ARTS, University of California. Tel. 213/825-9261.

Single tickets are available to various performances. The Family Series performances appeal to a variety of age groups. Theater, dance, professional storytelling, and singing make up some of the offerings. Ticket prices vary depending on the show.

2. COFFEEHOUSES

Remember beatniks and bohemians? The coffeehouses in those days offered poetry and readings of all types, and today they are making a come-back in Los Angeles. The '90s versions often combine poetry readings with music—live performances and sometimes tapes. Some are hip, others serious. There are a couple usually suitable for ages teen and up.

JAVA, 7286 W. Beverly Blvd., Wilshire District. Tel. 213/931-4943.

Great coffees and desserts are served in a low-key atmosphere. Poetry readings appropriate for teens and adults are hosted twice a week. Call for details. Open Sunday through Thursday from 9am to 2am and on Friday and Saturday from 10am to 4am.

THE LIVINGROOM, 110 S. La Brea Blvd., Wilshire District. Tel. 213/933-2933.

An extremely hip atmosphere that caters to club-goers and celebrity gazers alike, from teens to adults, the Livingroom gets very lively, especially on Friday and Saturday nights. They often host live bands (call for schedules). Open Sunday through Thursday from 8:30am to 2:30am and on Friday and Saturday from 8:30am to 4am.

3. CLUBS

COMEDY & JAZZ CLUBS

THE BAKED POTATO, 3787 Cahuenga Blvd. W., North Hollywood. Tel. 818/980-1615.

This small jazz club serves 18 varieties of baked potatoes along with its very popular live music. There is no age limit. Open nightly from 7pm to 1am.
Admission: Cover varies.

THE GROUNDLING THEATRE, 7307 Melrose Ave., West Hollywood. Tel. 213/934-9700.

Adults and teenagers will appreciate the talent at the Groundling, one of the city's best improvisational theaters. Numerous TV and film stars have started out here. Call for show times.
Admission: $10–$17.50.

LA CONNECTION, 13422 Ventura Blvd., Sherman Oaks. Tel. 818/784-1868.

This 100-seat intimate theater is famous for its "Saturday Night Live"–style performances. The *Los Angeles Times* calls it the "teen hot spot," while the *Daily News* touts it as being one of the best places to take the kids. Children as young as 8 have attended the performances. No food or alcohol is served, but you can bring your own food. Shows are Saturday and Sunday; call for reservations.
Admission: $6–$10, depending on the show.

McCABE'S, 3101 Pico Blvd., Santa Monica. Tel. 213/828-4497.

An L.A. institution, McCabe's includes a guitar shop, a music school, and a concert hall. Weekend concerts begin at 8pm and might be jazz, folk, R&B, or bluegrass. There's no age limit and no alcohol is served. Open Monday through Thursday from 10am to 10pm, on Friday and Saturday from 10am to 6pm, and on Sunday from 1am to 5pm.
Shows: Fri and Sun at 8pm and 10:30pm, cover charge $12.50–$15. All major credit cards.

SECOND CITY, 214 Santa Monica Blvd., Santa Monica. Tel. 213/395-8416.

This improvisational comedy club is especially popular with teenagers. Many of the performers come straight from Chicago's legendary Second City. There's no age limit, and on Friday they have a two-for-one college discount. Call for seasonal hours and prices.
Admission: Varies.

DANCE CLUBS & NIGHTCLUBS

MARILYN'S, 220 S. Lake Ave., Pasadena. Tel. 818/796-8662.
 With KROQ 'n' Roll Friday and KPWR Saturday, this club keeps teens dancing with popular tunes and current hits. It's strictly for 16- to 21-year-olds; ID required. No alcohol is served.
 Admission: $6 ($8 after 9:30pm Sat).

THE NATURAL FUDGE COMPANY, 5224 Fountain Ave., Hollywood. Tel. 213/669-8003.
 Natural foods compliment an eclectic variety of entertainment that includes comedy and live music. There's no age limit. Open Monday through Saturday from 5pm to 2am.
 Admission: Cover varies.

PALOMINO, 6907 Lankershim Blvd., North Hollywood. Tel. 818/764-4010.
 This restaurant/club hosts a variety of bands, and is best known as a leader in country music. Its barbecue restaurant opens at 7:30pm. There is no age limit here and alcohol is served with ID. Call for details on shows.
 Admission: Cover varies.

THE ROXY, 9009 Sunset Blvd., West Hollywood. Tel. 213/276-2222 or 213/278-9457.
 Teenagers have been flocking to the Roxy for years. There's no minimum age, so you'll have to decide whether the performers are appropriate for your kids. Well-established and new performers are featured. Liquor is served. Tickets are only available at the door before the shows, but call ahead because selected show tickets are available through Ticketron (tel. 213/642-4242).

DOUG WESTON'S TROUBADOR, 9081 Santa Monica Blvd., West Hollywood. Tel. 213/276-6168.
 Shows here lean toward hard rock and heavy metal. Food is available. All ages can dance to records on Monday night from 9pm to 2am. Live groups are scheduled the rest of the week. Call 213/276-1158 Tuesday through Friday between 2 and 6pm for specific show information.
 Admission: $9, including drink minimums.

4. CONCERT VENUES

GREEK THEATER, 2700 N. Vermont Ave., Griffith Park. Tel. 213/410-1062.
 The famed Greek is an outdoor amphitheater nestled in the woods of Griffith Park and offering a wide range of musical fare from jazz to popular to rock. The season runs from late May to early October. Tickets are available through Ticketron (tel. 213/642-4242), or at the box office Monday through Friday from 10am to 6pm.

UNIVERSAL AMPHITHEATER, Universal City. Tel. 818/980-9421.
This indoor theater is set on the Universal Studios lot, located off the Hollywood Freeway (U.S. 101) in Universal City. Everything you can think of is performed here. The Amphitheater box office is located in the parking lot of the site, above the Hilton Hotel and Towers, and is open daily from 1 to 9pm. Tickets are also available through TicketMaster (tel. 213/480-3232), local May Company stores, and Music Plus stores.

WILTERN THEATER, 3790 Wilshire Blvd., Mid-Wilshire. Tel. 213/380-5005.
You might discover classical, folk, pop, or jazz concerts at the Wiltern during your visit. The restored art deco building houses a relatively intimate theater. Shows run throughout the year. Tickets are available through TicketMaster (tel. 213/480-3232), or you can contact the box office (tel. 213/380-5005).

5. SPECTATOR SPORTS

BASEBALL The **L.A. Dodgers** play National League baseball at Dodger Stadium, 1000 Elysian Park Avenue, downtown (tel. 213/224-1400). The season lasts from April through October. Tickets—priced at $5 to $7—are available by mail from the Dodger Stadium Ticket Office, P.O. Box 51100, Los Angeles, CA 90057 (add $2 to each order for postage and handling); or you can order through TicketMaster (tel. 213/480-3232) or Ticketron (tel. 213/642-4242). You can also purchase tickets in person at the Dodger Ticket Office, 1750 Stadium Way, Monday through Saturday from 8:30am to 5:30pm.

The **California Angels** play baseball at Anaheim Stadium, 2000 South State College Blvd., Anaheim (tel. 714/634-2000) from April through October. Purchase tickets at the box office Monday through Saturday from 9am to 5:30pm; through TicketMaster (tel. 213/480-3232), or by phone by calling 714/740-2000.

BASKETBALL The Los Angeles **Lakers** play their home games at the Great Western Forum, 3900 West Manchester Boulevard, Inglewood (tel. 213/419-3160). Unfortunately, tickets are usually sold out well in advance. You can try for tickets by mail, at least 1 month in advance, from the Forum Box Office, P.O. Box 10, Inglewood, CA 90306 (tel. 213/419-3182). The Forum Box Office is open daily from 10am to 6pm.

The **Clippers** play NBA basketball in the Los Angeles Sports Arena, 3939 South Figueroa Street, downtown (tel. 213/748-8000). The season is October through April. Tickets can be purchased at the gate or through TicketMaster (tel. 213/480-3232).

FOOTBALL The **Los Angeles Raiders** make their home in the Los Angeles Memorial Coliseum, 3939 South Figueroa Street, downtown (tel. 213/322-5901 for Raiders information, or 213/747-7111 or 213/748-6136 for the Coliseum Sports Arena). The Raiders season is September through December. For tickets—priced at $25, $18, and $10—send a stamped, self-addressed envelope with a money order as early as possible to: Raiders Tickets, 332 Center Street, El Segundo, CA 90245. You can purchase them in person at the El Segundo office—but for cash only. You can also get tickets through Ticketron (tel. 213/642-4242) and TicketMaster (tel. 213/480-3232).

HOCKEY, SOCCER, TENNIS   The **Los Angeles Kings** (ice hockey), the **L.A. Lasers** (soccer), and the **L.A. Strings** (tennis) all play at the Great Western Forum, 3900 West Manchester Boulevard, Inglewood (tel. 213/419-3160). Tickets for the Kings ($7 to $18.50), Lasers ($7 to $18.50), and Strings ($7 to $18.50) are available by mail, 1 month in advance, from the Forum Box Office, P.O. Box 10, Inglewood, CA 90306 (tel. 213/419-3182). The Forum Box Office is open daily from 10am to 6pm.

6. STORY HOURS

CHILDREN'S BOOK AND MUSIC CENTER, 2500 Santa Monica Blvd., Santa Monica. Tel. 213/829-0215.
There's a story hour here each Saturday beginning at 10am for children ages 2 to 7.

CHILDREN'S BOOK WORLD, 10580½ Pico Blvd., Los Angeles. Tel. 213/559-2665.
Kids ages 3 to 8 will enjoy these story hours the second Saturday of each month, beginning at 10:30am.

CULVER CITY LIBRARY, 4975 Overland Ave., Culver City. Tel. 213/559-1676.
Each Tuesday there's a 7pm story hour for toddlers. Preschoolers can listen to stories appropriate to them on Tuesday nights at 7:30pm and Thursday mornings at 10am.

HAPPILY EVER AFTER CHILDREN'S BOOKSTORE, 2640 Griffith Park Blvd., Los Feliz. Tel. 213/668-1996.
These free story hours are held the first and third Wednesday of each month from 10:30am to 11am.

WEST LOS ANGELES REGIONAL LIBRARY, 11360 Santa Monica Blvd., West Los Angeles. Tel. 213/312-8323.
Kids ages 3 to 6 will enjoy the bedtime stories here every Wednesday evening at 7pm.

WILL AND ARIEL DURANT LIBRARY, 1403 N. Gardner St., Los Angeles. Tel. 213/876-2741.
Story hour, for all ages, is held on the first Tuesday of each month at 7pm.

CHAPTER 7

WHERE KIDS LIKE TO EAT

1. ON THE RUN

2. COOKIES, CANDIES & ICE CREAM

3. KID-RATED RESTAURANTS

Where do kids *really* like to eat? Well, the Golden Arches (McDonald's) probably wins hands down in many families. In Los Angeles it's not hard to find one—or any of its competitors. We've listed a couple of locations below so that you'll be prepared should your little ones have a Big Mac Attack.

But some kids' tastebuds have grown more sophisticated than that—or at least more adventurous. They may still want a cheeseburger and fries, or a regular old pizza (heaven forbid California designer pizza!), but they may be more willing to try new places.

We've listed restaurants and fast-food establishments in many areas of town, in different price ranges, and usually with a variety of services appropriate to families. Some typify the fun and casualness of Los Angeles; others are traditional favorites. A spot without a children's menu might be listed because the price is right, the food is particularly good, it's a fine choice with older children, or it's close to a sightseeing venue and has been recommended as family-friendly.

Remember, prices go up—even occasionally, down—management changes, and servers come and go. When in doubt, don't hesitate to call the restaurant and ask if they recommend a certain time to come with youngsters, whether you can request quick service, and any other questions that relate to your family's needs.

1. ON THE RUN

Much of the eating we do while sightseeing is on the run, so we've come up with some fast—and cute—L.A. places for you and the kids. Since these are typical fast-food eateries, we don't list amenities such as highchairs, and we don't worry about reservations.

In addition to the eateries listed below, remember that many of the shopping centers have food halls with lots of eating choices. One of the best is the **Century City Shopping Center & Marketplace,** 10250 Santa Monica Boulevard, Century City (tel. 213/553-5300), on the Little Santa Monica Boulevard side of the Mall, between Century Park West and Avenue of the Stars. The food hall here—open Monday through Saturday from 10am to 9pm (some restaurants stay open till midnight), and on Sunday from 11am to 10pm—is filled with almost every imaginable type of food: deli selections, pizza and other Italian choices, salads, baked potatoes, stir-fry, Japanese food, burgers, Mexican dishes, Indian delicacies, special coffees, and fudge. Seating is indoors and outdoors. It's a good place to take the kids because there's something for everyone—and the people-watching is great.

As for the Golden Arches, there's a centrally located **McDonald's** at 6345 Wilshire Boulevard in the Mid-Wilshire District (tel. 213/655-6116), and another across from the Westside Pavilion at 5930 West Pico Boulevard in West Los Angeles (tel. 213/933-1089). For other locations, consult the White Pages of the telephone directory.

THE BURGER THAT ATE LA, 7624 Melrose Ave., West Hollywood. Tel. 213/653-2647.

Cuisine: AMERICAN.
$ Prices: Average $4. No credit cards.
Open: Daily 11:30am–10pm.

Who can resist a place with a name like this? Wait until you see the architecture! Yes, it really looks like the burger did consume L.A. It's mostly outdoor eating, and folks line up for the next available umbrella table. Inside there's a long counter, but no tables. The burgers are good. Smother them with hickory sauce, or get chicken, tuna, or ham sandwiches. It's at the corner of Stanley Avenue and Melrose Avenue. There's limited street parking.

CARNEYS EXPRESS LIMITED, 8351 Sunset Blvd., Hollywood. Tel. 213/654-8300.

Cuisine: AMERICAN.
$ Prices: $1.50–$4. No credit cards.
Open: Daily 11am–midnight.

Carneys serves food children love in a place where they feel comfortable—an authentic Union Pacific railway car set on a train track. There are outside tables, but most youngsters prefer to eat in the main car. The fare is simple: good old cheeseburgers and double burgers served with chili, hot dogs, tuna melts, chicken sandwiches, and a vegetarian combo—all self-service. Yummy ice-cream or orange-juice bars and frozen chocolate-dipped bananas are for dessert. Owner Bill Wolf and his staff will do just about anything to accommodate families, including warming bottles and baby food. A parking lot is behind the restaurant.

There's also a Carneys at 12601 Ventura Boulevard, Studio City (tel. 818/761-8300).

FATBURGER, 450 S. La Cienega Blvd., West Hollywood. Tel. 213/652-8489.

Cuisine: AMERICAN.
$ Prices: 40¢–$3.45. No credit cards.
Open: Daily 24 hours.

Burgers, from the ordinary to the out of the ordinary, can be found here on La Cienega at San Vicente Boulevard, near the Beverly Center. The Double King Burger with the works must be sampled, although kids may prefer a good old-fashioned cheeseburger. Fatburger also serves hot dogs and sandwiches.

There's another branch in the Mid-Wilshire District at 5001 Wilshire Boulevard (tel. 213/939-9593).

JEREMIAH P. THROCKMORTON GRILLE, 255 S. Beverly Dr., Beverly Hills. Tel. 213/550-7111.
   Cuisine: AMERICAN.
$ Prices: $1.95–$3.85. No credit cards.
   Open: Mon–Sat 11am–9pm, Sun noon–6pm.
It's quick, it's nice, it's comfortable, and it's convenient. Pick a Hebrew National hot dog, a burger, or hot and cold sandwiches. Sit at the counter and watch them make the food. You'll find it between Wilshire Boulevard and Olympic Boulevard in Beverly Hills. Street parking available.

JOHNNY ROCKET'S, 7507 Melrose Ave. Tel. 213/651-3361.
   Cuisine: AMERICAN.
$ Prices: 95¢–$6.50. No credit cards.
   Open: Mon–Fri 11am–midnight, Sat–Sun 11am–2am.
Here you will find '50s nostalgia L.A. style, complete with juicy burgers and creamy malts. Probably the hippest diner of its kind in town, Rocket's is a great place to sit at the counter and watch the chefs cook up chili fries for you and spread peanut butter and jelly for the kids. This location has outdoor tables. Be prepared for a wait during peak hours. It's at the corner of Gardner Avenue and Melrose Avenue. Street parking available.

   Other locations are in Westwood at 10959 Weyburn Boulevard (tel. 213/824-5656), in West Los Angeles in the Century City Shopping Center at 10250 Santa Monica Boulevard (tel. 213/788-9020), and in Beverly Hills at 474 North Beverly Drive (tel. 213/271-2222).

LA SALSA, 11075 W. Pico Blvd., West Los Angeles. Tel. 213/479-0919.
   Cuisine: MEXICAN.
$ Prices: 75¢–$5.75. No credit cards.
   Open: Sun–Thurs 7am–10pm, Fri–Sat 7am–midnight.
For your 1st, or 51st, Mexican craving, try one of the La Salsa locations. You'll find a broad range of Mexican favorites made from the freshest ingredients, including some with a twist, like the vegetarian taco. All items are prepared "health consciously," and they gladly accommodate dietary requests. You'll find this Salsa on the corner of Pico and Sepulveda Boulevard near the Overland exit from the Santa Monica Freeway (I-10) west.

   Other locations are in Beverly Hills at 9631 Little Santa Monica Boulevard (tel. 213/276-2373), in Marina del Rey in the Marina Market Place at 13455 Maxell Avenue (tel. 213/306-2414), and in Malibu at 22800 Pacific Coast Highway (tel. 213/456-6299).

PINK'S CHILI DOGS, 709 N. La Brea Ave., Hollywood. Tel. 213/931-4223.
   Cuisine: AMERICAN/HOT DOGS.
$ Prices: $1–$5. No credit cards.
   Open: Daily 7am–3am.
   The most famous hot dog stand in L.A., Pink's is a Hollywood icon. Since 1939, movie stars, schoolchildren, businesspeople, and out-of-towners have been stopping at this family-owned landmark to feast on the renowned Chili Dog, or the more exotic 12-inch Jalapeño Dog. There is also an array of hamburgers, side orders, and floats, as well as New York and Chicago Dogs for the homesick. Orders are usually prepared and served with a smile in less than 30 seconds. Pink's has

La Jolla Ave.
Sweetzer Ave.
Melrose Ave.
Rosewood Ave.
Beverly Blvd.
3rd St.
La Cienega Blvd.
San Vicente Blvd.
Santa Monica Blvd.
Olympic Blvd.
Stanley Dr.
Burton Way
Carson Rd.
Sunset Blvd.
Robertson Blvd.
Clark Dr.
Melrose Ave.
Dorrington Ave.
Rosewood Ave.
Beverly Blvd.
La Peer Dr.
Almont Dr.
Dayton Way
Clifton Way
Wilshire Blvd.
Charleville Blvd.
Gregory Way
Doheny Dr.
Alden Dr.
3rd St.
Oakhurst Dr.
Palm Dr.
Sierra Dr.
Maple Dr.
Elm Dr.
Alta Dr.
Arden Dr.
Hillcrest Rd.
Palm Dr.
Public Library
Crescent Dr.
Canon Dr.
Maple Dr.
Elm Dr.
Camellia Ave.
Foot Hill Rd.
City Hall
Post Office
Visitors Bureau
Rodeo Dr.
Beverly Dr.
Alpine Dr.
Rexford Dr.
Crescent Dr.
Bedford Dr.
Blvd.
Canon Dr.
Wilshire Blvd.
Linden Dr.
Beverly Dr.
Rodeo Dr.
Camden Dr.
Lasky Dr.
Coldwater Canyon
Bedford Dr.
Roxbury Dr.
Linden Dr.
Santa Monica Blvd.
Walden Dr.
Will Rogers Memorial Park
Lomitas Ave.
Lexington Rd.
Benedict Canyon Drive

Baskin-Robbins 2
Beverly Center 12
Beverly Connection 13
The Cheesecake Factory 1
Daily Grill 13
Ed Debevic's Short Orders/Deluxe 8
Fatburger 15
Hard Rock Café 11
Island's 17
Jeremiah P. Throckmorton Grille 6
Johnny Rocket's 10
Larry Parker's Beverly Hills Diner 7
Lawry's The Prime Rib 9
Louise's Trattoria 4
Nate 'N Al Delicatessen 5
RJ's, The Rib Joint 3
Souplantation 2
Tail of the Pup 16

its own free parking with—oh so L.A.—an attendant! It's between Santa Monica Boulevard and Melrose Avenue.

TAIL O' THE PUP, 329 N. San Vicente Blvd., West Hollywood. Tel. 213/652-4517.
   Cuisine: AMERICAN.
$ **Prices:** 20¢–$3.50. No credit cards.
   Open: Mon–Sat 6am–6pm, Sun 6am–5pm.

This fast-food eaterie with its kitschy hot-dog architecture has survived all the development around it. Rather than closing when the big Beverly Center went up on its former location, it picked up and moved nearby, just north of the intersection of San Vicente and Beverly Boulevard. Be sure to drive by when it's closed to see the hot-dog architecture at its best. Their selection of hot dogs, burgers, and sandwiches are served out of the famed stand. There are only a few tables. Parking lot available.

TITO'S, 11222 Washington Place, West Los Angeles. Tel. 213/391-5780.
   Cuisine: MEXICAN.
$ **Prices:** 45¢–$2.30. No credit cards.
   Open: Daily 9am–11:30pm.

Possibly the best burritos in town can be found here on the corner of Washington Place and Sepulveda Boulevard. Locals line up around the block at lunchtime for everything from guacamole and chips to a simple taco. Despite the crowds, there's plenty of seating here for families.

2. COOKIES, CANDIES & ICE CREAM

BASKIN-ROBBINS, 271 N. Canon Dr., Beverly Hills. Tel. 213/273-3422.

This ice-cream establishment is known for its 31 flavors. Now many of its locations carry fat-free versions and frozen yogurt. Stop at this location and you might even see one of your favorite stars. Open daily from 11am to 10pm.

For other locations, consult the telephone directory.

BEN & JERRY'S, 2441 Main St., Santa Monica. Tel. 213/450-0691.

Made from Vermont cream, the ice cream here comes in flavors that have a sense of humor and a feel for popular cravings, with blends like Chocolate Chip Cookie Dough. There are 34 tempting flavors, but go ahead and take your time to choose—the service is extremely friendly here. Open Sunday through Thursday from noon to 11pm and on Friday and Saturday from 11am to midnight.

There's another Ben & Jerry's in Brentwood at 11740 San Vicente Boulevard (tel. 213/447-0695).

BLUE CHIP COOKIES, in the Century City Shopping Center, 10250 Santa Monica Blvd., Century City. Tel. 213/286-2583.

As the name implies, chocolate-chip cookies are the specialty here. They have 15 varieties, with temptations like the chocolate-chip macadamia-nut cookie. Open

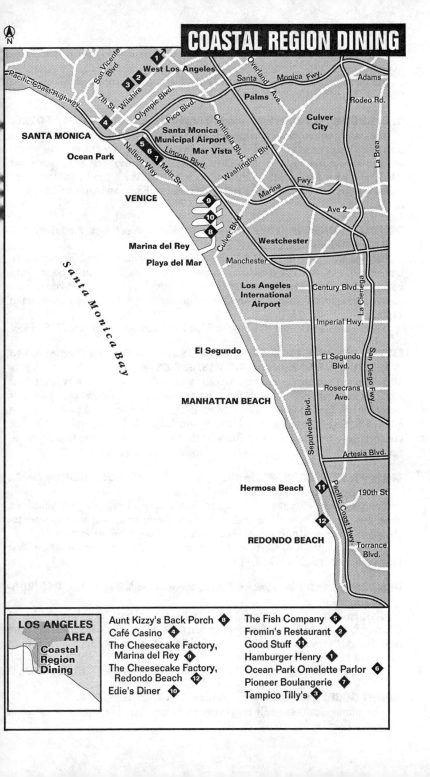

Monday through Friday from 10am to 9pm and on Saturday and Sunday from 10am to 6pm.

Another branch is in the Marina Market Place, at the corner of Maxella and Glencoe, Marina del Rey (tel. 213/822-4844).

C. C. BROWN'S, 7007 Hollywood Blvd., Hollywood. Tel. 213/464-9726.

The founder of hot fudge in Los Angeles in 1906, C. C. Brown's is a legend in its own right. It still retains the distinctive air of an old-fashioned ice-cream parlor where you can choose from a bevy of delicious sundaes. They also serve sandwiches and salads, and have a collection of their own chocolates, which can be mailed. Open Monday through Thursday from 1 to 10:30pm and on Friday and Saturday from 1pm to midnight.

DOUBLE RAINBOW, 1898 Westwood Blvd., West Los Angeles. Tel. 213/470-6232.

Dubbed the "Best in the U.S.," the premium ice cream served here has won numerous prizes. According to local "experts," the Chocolate Peanut Butter Swirl comes in first. Open Monday through Thursday from 8am to 11pm, on Friday from 8am to midnight, on Saturday from 11am to midnight, and on Sunday from noon to 11pm.

There's another Double Rainbow at 7336 Melrose Avenue (tel. 213/655-1986).

LITTLE JOHN'S ENGLISH TOFFEE HOUSE, in the Farmers Market, 6333 W. 3rd St., Mid-Wilshire. Tel. 213/936-5379.

Browsing through the Farmers Market, you can't be sure which will get your attention first, the smell of freshly dipped caramel apples or the sight of large vats of chocolate. At Little John's, established in 1921, candy lovers, especially kids, can enjoy watching an assortment of sweets—including fudge and other chocolate concoctions—being made. Open Monday through Friday from 9am to 6:30pm, on Saturday from 10am to 6:30pm, and on Sunday from 9am to 5pm.

MRS. FIELD'S COOKIES, in the Beverly Center, 8500 Beverly Blvd., West Hollywood. Tel. 213/659-4221.

Fresh out of the oven and delicious, Mrs. Field's Cookies will satisfy everyone from chocolate-chip lovers to those with a taste for the more exotic, such as a white-chocolate-chip macadamia-nut cookie. Open daily from 10am to 9pm.

Another location is in West Los Angeles in the Westside Pavilion at 10800 West Pico Boulevard (tel. 213/470-7100).

PENGUINS, 1133 Westwood Blvd., Westwood Village. Tel. 213/208-3338.

The best-known frozen yogurt in Los Angeles is served here. They have a variety of different flavors each day and fun toppings that include crushed Butterfingers and fresh fruit. For kids, they have small servings called Baby Penguins for $1. Open daily from 11am to 10:30pm.

There's another Penguins at 7115 West Sunset Boulevard (tel. 213/851-1343).

ROBIN ROSE, 215 Rose Ave., Venice. Tel. 213/399-1774.

The unusual (and unusually tasty) array of flavors offered here put this ice-cream

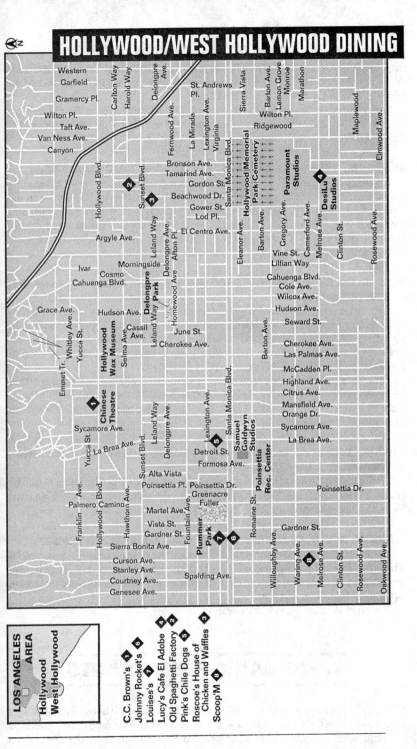

HOLLYWOOD/WEST HOLLYWOOD DINING

LOS ANGELES AREA

Hollywood
West Hollywood

C.C. Brown's **1**
Johnny Rocket's **6**
Louises's **7**
Lucy's Cafe El Adobe **4**
Old Spaghetti Factory **2**
Pink's Chile Dogs **5**
Roscoe's House of
Chicken and Waffles **3**
Scoop'M **8**

establishment on the map. The ice creams with liquor, like Bailey's Irish Cream, are especially popular, although kids will swear by the Devil's Food Cookies and Cream or the White Chocolate. Open Sunday through Thursday from 11am to 11pm and on Friday and Saturday from 11am to midnight.

Other locations are in Santa Monica at 221 Arizona Avenue (at the 3rd St. Promenade) (tel. 213/576-1888), and in Brentwood at 11819 Wilshire Boulevard (tel. 213/445-2771).

SCOOP 'M, 7555½ Melrose Ave., Los Angeles. Tel. 213/651-4886.

Ice-cream aficionados can exercise their imaginations here. With a blending machine, an assortment of ice cream and frozen yogurt flavors, and delectable fruits, candies, and cookies, you can create your own flavor. Kids will love this one, and rumor has it that New York Cheesecake with Strawberries is the flavor of choice. Open Sunday through Thursday from 11am to 11pm and on Friday and Saturday from 11am to midnight.

SEES, in the Beverly Center, 8500 Beverly Blvd., West Hollywood. Tel. 213/657-1010.

One of Los Angeles's best-known candy stores, Sees is famous for its suckers—chocolate, peanut butter, and butterscotch—which are especially popular with kids. They also specialize in assorted chocolates and have gift assortments available for mailing. Open Monday through Friday from 10am to 9pm, on Saturday from 10am to 8pm, and on Sunday from 11am to 6pm.

Other locations are in Century City in the Century City Shopping Center at 10250 Santa Monica Boulevard (tel. 213/277-9228), in Santa Monica at 261 Santa Monica Place (tel. 213/395-4728), West Los Angeles in the Westside Pavilion, 10800 Pico Boulevard (tel. 213/470-2973).

STAN'S DONUTS, in Westwood Village, 10948 Weyburn Ave., Westwood. Tel. 213/208-8660.

Fresh-baked doughnuts from the basic to the not-so-basic can be found here. The Peanut Butter Chocolate Donuts are especially decadent, as are their Cinnamon Sticks. Muffins are also available. Open daily from 6am to midnight.

THRIFTY, 300 N. Canon Dr., Beverly Hills. Tel. 213/273-7293.

Located in Thrifty's Drugstore, this is perhaps the only place left in Los Angeles where you can still get a good old-fashioned ice-cream cone for 35¢. They have at least 20 back-to-basics flavors, and the kids usually agree that Rocky Road is the best. Open daily from 9am to 10pm.

For other locations, check the telephone directory.

3. KID-RATED RESTAURANTS

With 5,000 or more restaurants of every ethnic persuasion to choose from, finding a place to eat is never a problem in the Los Angeles area. The hard part is making a decision. Since space prohibits listing every family restaurant, consider this an hors d'oeuvrerie. Unless otherwise noted, the welcome mat is out for kids of all ages at any of the following establishments.

BEVERLY HILLS

EXPENSIVE

LAWRY'S THE PRIME RIB, 55 N. La Cienega Blvd. Tel. 213/652-2827.

Cuisine: AMERICAN. **Reservations:** Recommended.

$ Prices: Main courses $17–$23. AE, CB, DC, MC, V.

Open: Dinner only, Mon–Thurs 5–11pm, Fri–Sat 5pm–midnight, Sun 3–10pm.

Children's Services: Children's portions, booster seats.

Walking into Lawry's is like entering a Georgian manor house decorated on a grand scale with plush carpets, traditional English paintings, and candelabra-style chandeliers. The restaurant is divided into two dining areas. Huge silver serving carts are brought to your table so that chefs can carve your selection to your specifications.

We usually request one of the booths, which are ornately upholstered and well padded, offering privacy from neighboring diners and allowing us greater peace of mind when the kids get a tad noisier than we wish. Tables are comfortable too, complete with padded high-back chairs.

Lawry's secret to success is that it serves only one entrée—prime rib. For 52 years Lawry's has served standing rib roasts that have been dry-aged for 2 to 3 weeks. Cuts include English, Lawry, California (for light eaters), and Diamond Jim Brady (extra thick with a bone). Each dinner comes with the house salad (prepared at the table), mashed potatoes, traditional Yorkshire pudding, and creamed horseradish.

The children's portion, at $12.95, is almost the same size as the California-cut adult portion, and comes with a beverage and dessert. The full bar offers nonalcoholic drinks as well as standard cocktails.

We have only one suggestion about bringing youngsters here: You must be prepared for a leisurely meal. A 2-year-old may do fine for an hour, but even the best-natured toddler may get restless or even troublesome when it extends beyond that.

Lawry's is on Restaurant Row, half a block north of Wilshire Boulevard. Valet parking is available.

RJ'S, THE RIB JOINT, 252 N. Beverly Dr. Tel. 213/274-RIBS.

Cuisine: AMERICAN. **Reservations:** Recommended.

$ Prices: Dinner main courses $9–$19. AE, V.

Open: Lunch/dinner Mon–Sat 11:30am–11pm; Sun 4–11pm; brunch Sun 10:30am–3pm.

Children's Services: Sassy seats, booster seats, children's portions.

Everything at RJ's is done on a grand scale—including the portions. The exposed-brick saloon-style main dining room opens to an enormous bar with a floor-to-ceiling display of bottles (over 500 brands), where customers wait for tables while they munch on peanuts in the shell. Wooden tables and booths line the room, and the walls are decorated with black-and-white celebrity photos and large back-lit stained-glass hangings.

RJ's famous Green Grocery salad bar is a truly extraordinary assortment of salad fixings, presented among a symphony of fresh fruits and vegetables. The last time they counted, there were over 80 items, including such yummy treats for kids as fruit

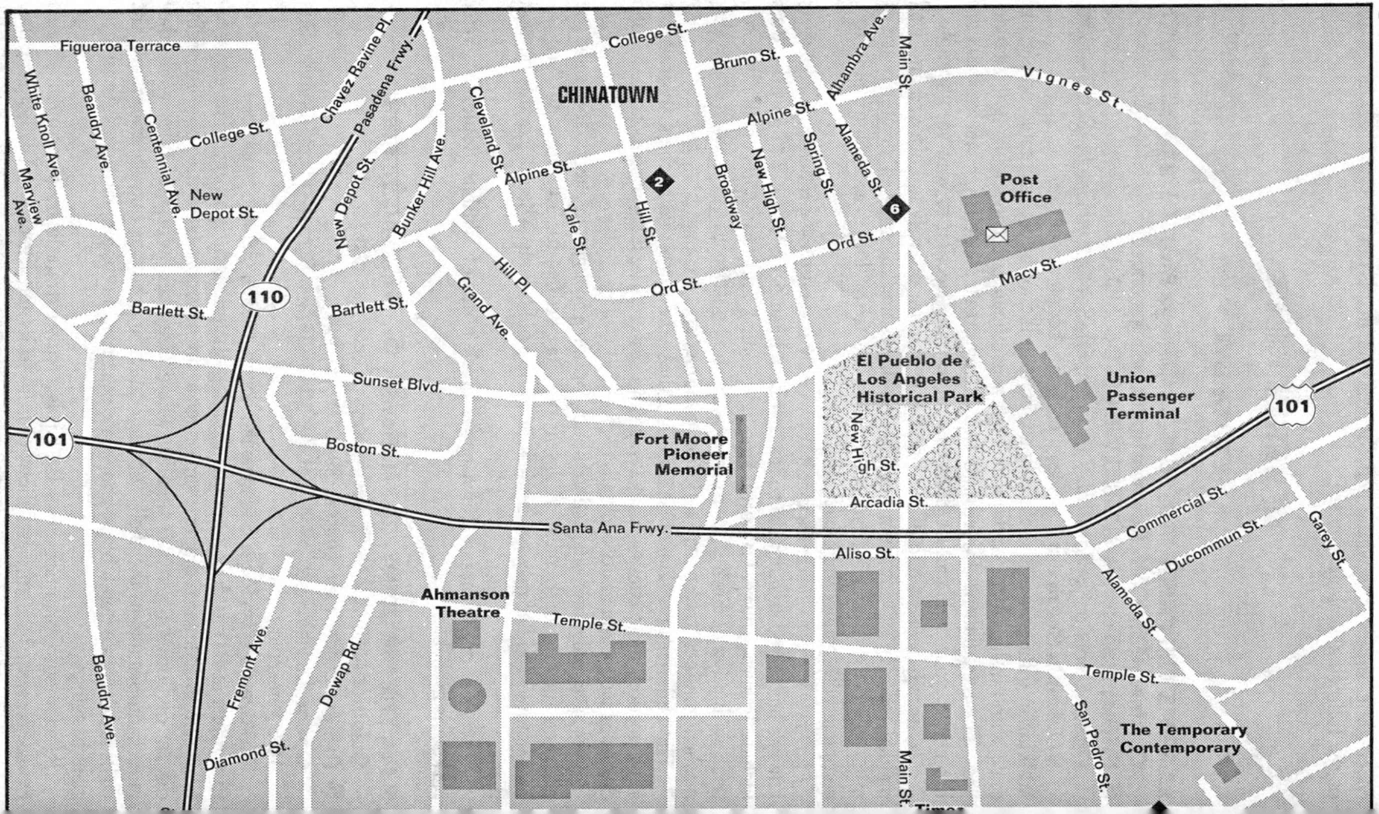

CHINATOWN
Figueroa Terrace
College St.
Bruno St.
Alhambra Ave.
Main St.
Vignes St.
Chavez Ravine Pl.
Pasadena Frwy.
White Knoll Ave.
Beaudry Ave.
Centennial Ave.
Marview Ave.
New Depot St.
Cleveland St.
Alpine St.
Spring St.
Alameda St.
New High St.
Broadway
Hill St.
Yale St.
Bunker Hill Ave.
Post Office
Ord St.
Macy St.
110
Bartlett St.
Grand Ave.
Hill Pl.
Sunset Blvd.
El Pueblo de Los Angeles Historical Park
Union Passenger Terminal
101
Boston St.
Fort Moore Pioneer Memorial
Arcadia St.
Santa Ana Frwy.
Commercial St.
Ducommun St.
Garey St.
Aliso St.
Ahmanson Theatre
Temple St.
Fremont Ave.
Dewap Rd.
Diamond St.
San Pedro St.
The Temporary Contemporary

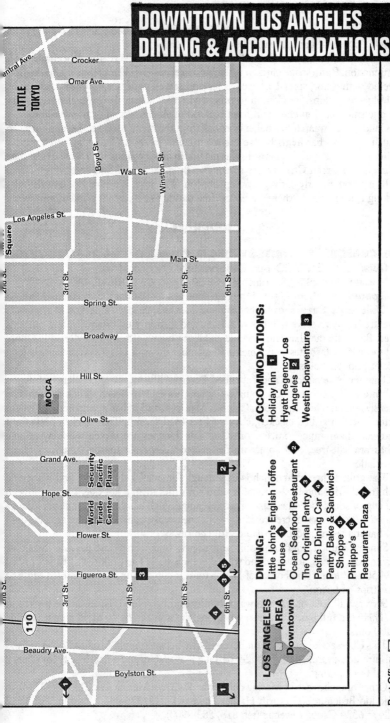

DOWNTOWN LOS ANGELES
DINING & ACCOMMODATIONS

LITTLE TOKYO

Crocker
Omar Ave.
Boyd St.
Wall St.
Winston St.
Los Angeles St.
Square
Main St.
2nd St.
3rd St.
4th St.
5th St.
6th St.
Central Ave.
Spring St.
Broadway
Hill St.
MOCA
Olive St.
Grand Ave.
Security Pacific Plaza
Hope St.
World Trade Center
Flower St.
Figueroa St.
110
Beaudry Ave.
Boylston St.

ACCOMMODATIONS:

Holiday Inn **1**
Hyatt Regency Los Angeles **2**
Westin Bonaventure **3**

DINING:

Little John's English Toffee House ◆4
Ocean Seafood Restaurant ◆2
The Original Pantry ◆3
Pacific Dining Car ◆4
Pantry Bake & Sandwich Shoppe ◆5
Philippe's ◆6
Restaurant Plaza ◆7

LOS ANGELES AREA
Downtown

Post Office ⊠

compote, dates, grated coconut, and fresh fruit. There are two soups to choose from as well. The salad bar can easily be a meal in itself.

Known for hickory-smoked ribs, RJ's offers pork back ribs and beef ribs or a combination. Rattlesnake chicken is the No. 1 seller—chicken breasts cut into strips, covered with a hot, spicy barbecue sauce and served with rice and beans, coleslaw, and blue-corn chips. In addition to other styles of chicken, there are also steaks (try the one smothered in chili) and fresh seafood (including scampi and swordfish).

Children are treated to smaller portions from the menu for $4 to $8, and they can munch on salad-bar items before the main course arrives. On Friday and Saturday nights a strolling magician performs his magic. To avoid waiting for a table or standing in line at the Green Grocery, try to come early—between 5 and 7pm.

RJ's is on Beverly Drive between Dayton Way and Wilshire Boulevard. Valet parking is available, or there's 2 hours' free parking in a city lot a few doors south.

MODERATE

THE CHEESECAKE FACTORY, 364 N. Beverly Dr. Tel. 213/278-7270.
  Cuisine: INTERNATIONAL. **Reservations:** Not accepted.
$ Prices: Lunch $5–$8; brunch $7–$8.50; dinner $5–$16. AE, MC, V.
  Open: Mon–Thurs 11am–11pm, Fri–Sat 11am–12:30am, Sun 10am–11pm.
  Children's Services: Highchairs and boosters; children's portion at brunch.
"We are happy to serve families with kids, and kids love us!" they say, and our kids agree. But sadly they have no separate children's menu, although they've added more and more kids' favorites to the menu. Remember the wait can be excruciatingly long here at popular hours.

The newly remodeled and expanded Beverly Hills location has plenty of action and interesting conversation going on among its mostly Beverly Hills crowd. The extensive menu offers American, Chinese, Mexican, and Italian specialties. You might go for Yucatán grilled chicken, coconut beer-fried shrimp, Thai chicken pasta, or a sandwich, hamburger, omelet, or salad. Lite lunches are served weekdays. Some dishes are salt-free, and some are designated acceptable to the American Heart Association.

The grilled-cheese sandwich is big enough for small kids to split, and it's served with french fries and fresh vegetable salad. Or order them a hot dog, a half sandwich and cup of soup, individual-size pizzas (evenings only), hamburgers, or a simple pasta marinara. For dessert there are 35 different cheesecake concoctions, fudge cake, mud pie, banana splits, and other wonderful choices.

Sunday brunch offers not only egg dishes, but a breakfast pasta, a breakfast burrito, lox, onions, and eggs, and stuffed French toast. The Children's Brunch, priced at $4.50, includes a small order of French toast, a cup of fruit, one scrambled egg, and two strips of bacon.

Servers will split orders and warm bottles and baby food. Food can be packed to go. There is a full bar. Without reservations, the wait can be 20 to 45 minutes during peak hours.

This Cheesecake Factory is on Beverly Drive between Santa Monica Boulevard and Wilshire Boulevard. Metered street parking is available, and a nearby city lot offers 2 hours' free parking.

Other branches are in Marina del Rey at 4142 Via Marina (tel. 213/306-3344), in Redondo Beach at 605 North Harbor Drive (tel. 213/376-0466), and in Woodland Hills at 6324 Canoga Avenue (tel. 818/883-9900).

LARRY PARKER'S BEVERLY HILLS DINER, 206 S. Beverly Dr. Tel. 213/274-5655.

  Cuisine: AMERICAN. **Reservations:** Not accepted.

$ Prices: $6–$24.95. AE, DC, MC, V.

  Open: Daily 24 hours.

  Children's Services: Children's menu; highchairs and boosters.

The food is only part of the experience here. Not your flash-in-the-pan trendy diner, this small all-night restaurant was built in 1947 and claims to have served over four million people. Helium balloons bob on the ceiling, a jukebox plays constantly (and each table has its own selection box as well), neon signs and old pictures line the walls, and old-fashioned pink bubble gum comes with the check. Incongruous to the casual atmosphere is one Hollywood-style amenity—free limousine service (for five people or more) provided to and from the restaurant Monday through Friday from 10am to 3pm. Another only-in–Los Angeles trademark—there are telephones at each table.

You shouldn't have any trouble making everyone in the family happy here. The 20-page menu (yes, 20 pages!) epitomizes the fun and diversity of Los Angeles. Mom may order lox, eggs, onions, and a bagel; dad may select a meatloaf sandwich or a stuffed croissant; Gramps might choose one of the 15 burgers; Gram may eat soft tacos or Szechuan shrimp; and Uncle David may go for one of the vegetarian dishes. And the list of salads (more than 30 of them) is truly amazing. The children's menu includes macaroni and cheese and "pisquetti" (spaghetti) at $3 to $3.50.

Servers will warm bottles and baby food, and chat with you to keep you occupied while the kids are climbing all over. They may charge you $2 extra for split orders.

The diner is on South Beverly Drive between Wilshire Boulevard and Olympic Boulevard. Metered street parking is available, or you can park for free for 2 hours in a city lot a few doors away.

LOUISE'S TRATTORIA, 342 N. Beverly Dr. Tel. 213/274-4271.

  Cuisine: ITALIAN. **Reservations:** Not accepted.

$ Prices: Main courses $6–$13; pizza $8.75–$16. MC, V.

  Open: Mon–Thurs 11am–10pm, Fri–Sat 11am–11pm, Sun 4:30–10pm.

  Children's Services: Booster seats, Sassy seats, highchairs.

All the Louise's locations are unpretentious open rooms. The food is satisfying, and the prices are reasonable. One nice thing about these neighborhood trattorias is that your kids can have an individual slice of pizza ($1.50) or a whole one, and you can have your chicken fiorentina, marsala, chianti, cacciatore, or one of four other ways. There's also a large list of homemade pasta dishes. You might try capellini with scallops in shiitake-mushroom sauce, tagliatelle primavera with goat cheese, or a simple rigatoni with grilled vegetables. Al forno dishes feature lasagne, manicotti, and eggplant parmigiana. Ravioli can be prepared several ways, and there's calzone—pizza dough filled with ricotta and mozzarella cheese, folded, and baked.

But back to the pizzas. They're so good that every time we go back and say we're going to order something else, we end up with the pizza. In addition to the traditional choices and one vegetarian selection, there are California-style pizzas: One has barbecued chicken and another has veal sausage, shiitake mushrooms, and basil.

This trattoria is on North Beverly Drive between Santa Monica Boulevard and Wilshire Boulevard. There's metered street parking, or you get 2 hours' free parking in a nearby city lot.

Other locations are in Hancock Park at 232 North Larchmont Boulevard (tel.

213/962-9510), in West Hollywood at 7505 Melrose Avenue (tel. 213/651-3880), in Santa Monica at 1008 Montana Avenue (tel. 213/394-8888), in Brentwood at 264 26th Street (tel. 213/451-5001), and in West Los Angeles at 10645 Pico Boulevard (tel. 213/475-6084).

NATE 'N AL DELICATESSEN, 414 N. Beverly Dr. Tel. 213/274-0101.

Cuisine: DELI. **Reservations:** Not accepted.
$ Prices: $3.50–$12.50. CB, DC, MC, V.
Open: Sun–Fri 7:30am–8:45pm, Sat 7:30am–9:30pm.
Children's Services: Highchairs, booster seats.

This Beverly Hills institution is an atypical East Coast deli restaurant. No one yells and screams at the counter, and the corned beef is a little dry. But mom and dad will love it because the rest of the food is good and the people-watching is even better. Although most families come here on the weekends, on some weekday mornings you'll find a local grandpa or mom or dad here with junior before school. You'll also see some of the "old guard" Hollywood types.

On weekends the wait to get a table can be 20 to 30 minutes. Get your name on the waiting list, smile nicely at the hostess (who might get a bagel to assuage your toddler's hunger), and then take a walk. Once you sit down, you'll be able to get crackers or a bagel right away for the kids. Service is quick and friendly.

There's no children's menu, but they're willing to split most items. Many youngsters go straight for the chicken soup. Cottage-cheese and potato pancakes are popular items too. Familiar peanut butter or grilled-cheese sandwiches, hot dogs, and hamburgers are available as well.

Adults can choose typical deli items, including cream cheese and lox, blintzes, and pastrami and roast beef sandwiches. Breakfast is served all day. There are specials for dinner, but take the kids here for breakfast or lunch. Pound-cake lovers should save room for the marble pound cake.

The kitchen will split orders and warm baby food and bottles. There's also counter service for take-out items—order there or call ahead.

You'll find Nate 'n Al's on North Beverly Drive between Santa Monica Boulevard and Wilshire Boulevard. There's metered street parking, or park free for 2 hours in a city lot a few doors away.

INEXPENSIVE

ED DEBEVIC'S SHORT ORDERS/DELUXE, 134 N. La Cienega Blvd. Tel. 213/659-1952.

Cuisine: DINER FOOD. **Reservations:** Accepted only for weekday lunch.
$ Prices: $4.45–$6.45. MC, V.
Open: Mon–Fri 11:30am–11pm, Sat–Sun 11:30am–1am.
Children's Services: Booster seats, highchairs.

You don't really come here for the food, you come for the theatrics and for a trip back to the 1950s. It's a great place to go with the children—the diner decorations keep them busy and the noise level is perfect for them. Sundays are packed with youngsters.

People come for the hamburgers, of which there are eight different kinds. There are also sandwiches, chili, eggs, hot dogs, and side orders of cheese fries, and fries with gravy or chili. Of course, a diner wouldn't be complete without such deluxe plates as chicken fried steak, chicken pot pie, and roast turkey dinner. The salad bar is excellent. Janey orders the world's smallest hot-fudge sundae for an exorbitant 49¢! There are many other decadent desserts to try.

This Ed Debevic's is on La Cienega's Restaurant Row between Wilshire Boulevard and San Vicente Boulevard. There's valet parking and limited metered street parking.

There's another branch in Torrance at 23705 South Hawthorne Boulevard (tel. 213/378-5454).

WESTSIDE

This area includes Century City, Westwood, Brentwood, and West Los Angeles.

EXPENSIVE

ANNA'S ITALIAN RESTAURANT, 10929 Pico Blvd., West Los Angeles. Tel. 213/474-0102.
   Cuisine: ITALIAN. **Reservations:** Recommended.
$ **Prices:** Lunch $5–$10; dinner $7–$20. AE, CB, MC, V.
   Open: Mon–Thurs 11:30am–11pm, Fri 11:30am–midnight, Sat 4pm–midnight, Sun 4–11pm.
   Children's Services: Highchairs, booster seats.

A favorite with neighborhood families as well as those who come from miles away, Anna's is always filled with activity. Despite the red-checkered tablecloths, red-leather booths, and old chandeliers, this is not your romantic candlelit Italian restaurant, so bring the kids and relax. We've taken a sleeping infant here and kept him in the stroller while we enjoyed dinner. The waiters weren't crazy about having to serve around the stroller, but they were accommodating, and our 5-year-old Elizabeth put them through their paces.

If you like marinara salad, this is the place to order it. Anna's version has large chunks of seafood tucked into the well-dressed greens. But, then, everything here is good.

The lunch menu offers pizza, pasta, salads, sandwiches, omelets, veal, and fish, as well as weekday specials that include soup or salad. Anna's dinner choices include steaks, poultry, seafood, and 11 styles of veal, all of which come with soup or salad, spaghetti, and vegetable. There are also pizzas, pasta dishes, and large salads, and weekday dinner specials.

We usually share our food with the little ones, or order pizza to split for older kids. The folks at Anna's will warm bottles and baby food, bring warm sourdough bread to the table, and make special children's drinks.

Anna's is on Pico Boulevard, two blocks west of Westwood Boulevard. There's street parking during the day, valet parking at night.

MODERATE

JUNIOR'S DELI, 2379 Westwood Blvd., West Los Angeles. Tel. 213/475-5771.
   Cuisine: DELI. **Reservations:** Accepted only for parties of six or more.

$ Prices: Breakfast $2.25–$10.25; lunch and brunch $4–$15; dinner $5–$13. MC, V.

Open: Sun–Thurs 6am–11pm, Fri–Sat 6am–12:30am.

Children's Services: Children's menu, highchairs, booster seats, Sassy seats.

How about a place that serves two million eggs a year? Or almost 2 tons of coffee a month? Not only is the food fresh and delicious here, but the servers are fantastic with kids. This is a real family place. In fact, owner Marvin Saul says he developed the children's menu in response to his regular customers who said that they couldn't bring their children because it became too costly to feed three kids from the regular menu. He asked other customers what they'd like to see on the menu, and then he created it. It offers peanut butter and jelly, grilled cheese, hot dogs, pancakes, and other traditional kid favorites for around $3 or $4. Or they'll gladly let you split and share adult portions. Maybe the greatest draw for the kids (and for the sugar-loving adults in our family) is the cinnamon-bread French toast. It's baked with thick rings of cinnamon and sugar so that when it's dipped in the egg and grilled, it melts into a sinful goody. There are regular and petite orders.

All the fish is flown in from New York, and there are many imported delicacies in addition to the popular deli items. There are more than 300 choices on the menu for breakfast, lunch, and dinner, from old-fashioned chicken-in-the-pot to low-cholesterol roast turkey drumsticks. Corned beef, pastrami, and matzo brei are not forgotten.

The wait is at least 15 minutes during popular times; on weekends, try to get there before 9:30am.

Junior's is just north of the intersection of Pico Boulevard and Westwood Boulevard. There's limited metered street parking, and a small parking lot adjacent.

MARIO'S ITALIAN RESTAURANT, 1001 Broxton Ave., Westwood Village. Tel. 213/208-7077.

Cuisine: ITALIAN. **Reservations:** Suggested.

$ Prices: Lunch $6.75–$12.50; dinner $10–$22.50 (for lobster tail). AE, CB, MC, V.

Open: Mon–Thurs 11:30am–11:30pm, Fri 11:30am–12:30am, Sat noon–12:30am, Sun noon–11:30pm.

Children's Services: Highchairs, booster seats.

An institution in Westwood Village, Mario's has seen nearly three decades of students, professors, tourists, and families come through "the Village." Traditional red-and-white-checkered tablecloths and a festive atmosphere greet you.

While they don't have a children's menu, they will gladly prepare half orders of pasta. Children love the mini-size pizzas and the hamburger main course.

Mom and dad might want to try the house specialty: linguine Sorrento (with langostino, shrimp, and clams cooked in a bag), or farfalle (bowtie pasta with pesto and sun-dried tomatoes). Dinners include minestrone soup or salad, pasta, and vegetable; pasta courses include soup or salad and bread. Pizza prices begin at $6.75.

Mario's is at the corner of Broxton Avenue and Weyburn Avenue, in the center of Westwood Village. There are pay parking lots nearby.

ROSIE'S BARBECUE GRILLERY, 11845 W. Olympic Blvd., West Los Angeles. Tel. 213/473-8533.

Cuisine: AMERICAN. **Reservations:** Accepted only for parties of six or more.

$ Prices: Lunch $4.75–$9; dinner $10–$15. AE, MC, V.
Open: Daily 11am–10pm.
Children's Services: Children's menu, booster seats, highchairs.

All our children enjoy eating at Rosie's because it's unpretentious, open, and full of other families. While they wait for their order, the kids busy themselves with the coloring/activity book that comes with the children's menu.

The all-you-can-eat salad bar is enormous (50 items) and sure to please everyone. The main-course treat is the delicious barbecue—anyway you like it—ribs, chicken, or sandwiches. There are also hamburgers and a delicious tri-tip dinner. Early bird specials are served from 4 to 6pm.

Kids 11 and under get to choose from a nice variety: baby back, beef, or spare ribs; a hot dog; barbecue beef sandwich; hamburger; chicken; grilled cheese; the salad bar; or the salad bar with soup. All their meals include a drink and ice cream, and are served with fries and beans or coleslaw, for $2.95 to $5.95.

Rosie's is in the Westside Towers office building on Olympic Boulevard near the corner of Bundy Drive. The building has validated underground parking, or there's limited metered street parking.

INEXPENSIVE

EARTH, WIND & FLOUR, 1776 Westwood Blvd., Westwood. Tel. 213/ 470-2499.

Cuisine: ITALIAN. **Reservations:** Not accepted.
$ Prices: $3.50–$15.45 (for a large pizza with five toppings). AE, DC, MC, V.
Open: Mon–Thurs. 11:30am–11pm, Fri–Sat 11:30am–midnight, Sun 4–11pm.
Children's Services: Highchairs, booster seats.

Some of our family's favorite pizza comes from this neighborhood restaurant. Very casual, this is a place with sawdust on the floors and a rustic cabinlike interior of rough-wood walls and hanging plants. Great for a Sunday quick bite.

The menu is simple, the service is fast, and the food is good. In addition to wonderful Boston-style pizza, they'll tempt you with pasta (eight different sauces and six different pasta types), chicken, salads, and a sampling of sandwiches and burgers. A family of four can easily have dinner for under $20.

The restaurant is on Westwood at Santa Monica Boulevard. There's a parking lot available. A second branch is located in Santa Monica at 2222 Wilshire Blvd. (tel. 213/829-7829).

FLAKEY JAKE'S, 2347 S. Sepulveda Blvd., West Los Angeles. Tel. 213/477-0405.

Cuisine: AMERICAN. **Reservations:** Not accepted.
$ Prices: Around $5. MC, V.
Open: Mon–Thurs 11am–11pm, Fri–Sat 11am–midnight, Sun 11am–10pm.
Children's Services: Children's menu, highchairs, booster seats.

S The food is good here, and there's plenty of it. You'll find a small video-game room for the kids and a high noise level. Not surprisingly, this hamburger place tops the list of our children's favorites.

In fast-food style, you place your order, get your beverages, and grab a table. In addition to burgers, there are hot dogs, chicken (fried, teriyaki, and grilled lemon), fish, entrée-size baked potatoes, even a few salads. Flakey Jake's has its own bakery and its own butcher shop, where it makes all the bread and grinds all the meat used for the sandwiches.

The Jake Junior (hamburger or hot dog, fries, and a beverage with free refills) runs $2.50. On weekends that price drops and includes a small scoop of ice cream as well. The lunch special, Lite Bite (served daily), includes a main course, salad, drink, and fries from $4.60. All beverage refills are free.

Flakey Jake's is on the corner of Sepulveda and Pico Boulevard. There's a free parking lot.

ISLANDS, 10948 W. Pico Blvd., West Los Angeles. Tel. 213/474-1144.
Cuisine: AMERICAN. **Reservations:** Not accepted.
$ Prices: $4–$6.50. AE, MC, V.
Open: Mon–Thurs 11:30am–11pm, Fri–Sat 11:30am–11:30pm, Sun 11:30am–10pm.
Children's Services: Children's menu, highchairs, booster seats.

Islands comes complete with tropical atmosphere—ceramic parrots hang overhead, servers wear island clothes, and photographs of surfers riding the great waves line the walls.

This fun, lively eatery boasts gourmet hamburgers, soft tacos, chicken sandwiches, and great salads. Burgers come in many configurations, and there are five varieties of chicken sandwiches. Everybody must have at least one side order of Islands fries. The portions are large and can easily be split between two children. But the little surfers aged 12 and under may choose from the "Gremmie menu," which features a small burger or hot dog for $2. There's a full bar, which will also prepare special children's drinks.

The lunch wait can be about 15 minutes; to avoid a dinner wait, try to get there before 7pm (6:30pm on Sunday). Once seated, you'll be served quickly.

Islands is on Pico near Veteran Avenue. There's limited street parking before 6pm and valet parking after 6pm.

Other locations are in Marina del Rey at 404 Washington Street (tel. 213/822-3939); in Beverly Hills at 350 South Beverly Boulevard (tel. 213/556-1624); and in Manhattan Beach at 3200 Sepulveda Boulevard (tel. 213/546-4456).

THE COASTAL REGION

This area stretches from Malibu in the north to Redondo Beach in the south, including Santa Monica and Marina del Rey.

EXPENSIVE

CHEZ MELANGE, 1716 Pacific Coast Hwy. (Calif. 1), Redondo Beach. Tel. 213/540-1222.
Cuisine: CONTINENTAL. **Reservations:** Recommended.
$ Prices: Appetizers $1.50–$8.95; main courses $7.95–$19.95; Sun brunch $5–$15. AE, MC, V.
Open: Breakfast Mon–Fri 7–11am; lunch Mon–Fri 11:30am–3pm; dinner Mon–

Thurs 5–11pm, Fri–Sat 5–11:30pm, Sun 5–10:30pm; brunch Sat 7:30am–3pm, Sun 8am–2:30pm.

Children's Services: Sassy seats, highchairs, boosters, crayons and coloring items.

Located in the Palos Verdes Inn, this is an upscale restaurant, with Victorian tearoom appeal and an excellent local reputation, that's perfect for Sunday brunch. Children are welcome here, and although there are no kids' items on the menu, they will accommodate any requests they can.

The menus change daily, so you may want to call in advance to get a brief listing. All items are served with a touch of class and imagination. Lunches are particularly popular and, like the dinners, include a variety of appetizers, salads, pizza, pasta, and fresh fish. Specialties like lamb ravioli are particularly inviting. The breakfast list is quite extensive, and you can choose from fresh baked goods, fruit, cereals, and breakfast classics like "pancakes of the day" for $5.50. Children can get small stacks of pancakes. No-yolk omelets and scrambled egg whites are two thoughtful health-conscious choices. At brunch you can sample a Greek omelet, oysters, eggs Benedict, and other specials, which change weekly.

THE FISH COMPANY, 174 Kinney St., Santa Monica. Tel. 213/392-8366.

Cuisine: SEAFOOD. **Reservations:** Accepted.
$ Prices: Lunch $8.50; dinner $14.50. AE, MC, V.
Open: Lunch Mon–Fri 11:30am–4pm, Sat–Sun 11:30am–3pm; dinner Mon–Thurs 4–10pm, Fri 4–11pm, Sat 3–11pm, Sun 3–10pm.
Children's Services: Children's menu, booster seats, highchairs.

This is a great place to go for seafood. The staff at this casual, airy restaurant with a high wooden ceiling, wooden floors, and tasteful nautical decorations, is perfectly comfortable with children. There are two glassed-in kitchen areas where you can take the kids to watch the cooks. There's also a small plant-filled patio on the side of the restaurant.

The children's menu has coloring activities, and consists of charcoal-broiled shrimp or whitefish, chicken strips, or a quarter-pound cheeseburger, each for $4.95.

The lunch menu offers items from the oyster bar, seafood salads, and a few sandwiches. Mesquite-broiled fresh fish and chicken teriyaki, calamari, and a good ole hamburger are other tempting choices. At dinner you can get much of the same, plus lobster, scampi, cioppino, seafood fettuccine, a Pritikin plate, and a light-eater's plate, consisting of choice pieces of fish. There are plenty of desserts here—or take a stroll down Main Street after dinner and have your treat at one of the ice-cream shops.

The Fish Company is on Kinney Street, a block west of Main Street, south of Ocean Park Boulevard and north of Rose Avenue. There's street parking, or validated parking for 2 hours in the lot two blocks south.

GLADSTONE'S 4-FISH, 17300 Pacific Coast Hwy., Malibu. Tel. 213/GL4-FISH.

Cuisine: SEAFOOD. **Reservations:** Recommended.
Directions: Take the Santa Monica Freeway (I-10) and turn north on the Pacific Coast Highway (Calif. 1) until you reach Sunset Boulevard.
$ Prices: Appetizers $8–$10; main courses $8.95 to market price for lobster. AE, DC, MC, V.

Open: Sun–Thurs 7am–11pm; Fri–Sat 7am–midnight.
Children's Services: Booster seats.

This is the ultimate in California casual, with sawdust on the floors, large wooden booths with benches, and leaded-glass panels throughout. Request a window table in advance for a superb view of the beach and water beyond. On Saturday and Sunday mornings the place is simply brimming with families who get an early breakfast and spend the rest of their day at the beach. With all this popularity, the place can become very noisy, and you'll probably have to wait for your table even if you make a reservation. This isn't as much of a problem during the day because next to the restaurant is a ramp to a little beach where you can stroll while you wait. In the evenings, however, come early. We've waited as long as an hour—even with a reservation.

The kitchen says they'll make anything on the menu from 7am on—including seafood—but we prefer traditional breakfasts, ranging in price from $5.95 to $11.95 and including eggs, omelets, and French toast.

The six different seafood salads are heavenly, and the huge assortment of fish and shellfish will delight seafood lovers. Main courses can be simple (mesquite-broiled sea bass) or more elaborate (fresh salmon steamed in parchment with tomatoes, onions, mushrooms, and scallions). The steamed clams are brought to the table in a cute little metal bucket. Of course, the menu also features shrimp, clams, oysters, mussels, crab, and lobster. Steaks and burgers are also available. Dinners include choice of salad, bread, and potato or vegetable.

Follow Sunset Boulevard to the ocean. Valet parking is offered.

MODERATE

AUNT KIZZY'S BACK PORCH, in the Villa Marina Shopping Center, 4325 Glencoe Ave., Marina del Rey. Tel. 213/578-1005.

Cuisine: SOUTHERN. **Reservations:** Not accepted.
$ Prices: Lunch $7; brunch $12; dinner $12. No credit cards.
Open: Lunch Mon–Sat 11am–4pm; dinner Sun–Thurs 4–10pm, Fri–Sat 4pm–midnight; brunch Sun 11am–3pm.
Children's Services: Children's portions, highchairs, booster seats.

This is where to come for some real down-home cookin'. It's not very big, and certainly not fancy. The emphasis here is on food—good southern food, based on recipes handed down from friends and relatives. Daily lunch specials (which come with two fresh vegetables, and rice and gravy or cornbread dressing and gravy), might be smothered pork chops on Monday, smothered steak on Tuesday, meatloaf on Wednesday, chicken and dumplings on Thursday. Fried chicken is a daily special. At dinner try catfish and hushpuppies, or red beans and rice and hot links. As you'd expect, the desserts are homemade and rich—sweet-potato pie, pineapple-coconut cake, and sweet peach cobbler.

Kids can have the macaroni and cheese or a child's portion of anything on the regular menu for $6.95. There's a $3 charge for splitting an order.

The buffet-style Sunday brunch features salads, breakfast items (like grits, scrambled eggs, and grilled country potatoes with onions), baked or fried chicken, barbecued beef ribs, smothered pork chops, and plenty of good vegetables. Most children will love the buttery, sugary candied yams they serve at an additional price. Brunch includes dessert and a beverage. Children are charged half price.

There's plenty of parking in the shopping center lot.

CARLOS AND PEPE'S, 22706 W. Pacific Coast Hwy., Malibu. Tel. 213/456-3105.

Cuisine: MEXICAN. **Reservations:** Not accepted.

$ Prices: A la carte $3.75–$6.75; main courses and dinners $4.25–$14.75. AE, DC, MC, V.

Open: Mon–Sat 11:30am–11pm; Sun 11am–11pm.

Children's Services: Booster seats.

This Mexican restaurant graciously welcomes children. The terra-cotta floors, artificial palm trees, and parrots decorate the interior. But the real kid pleaser is the aquarium filled with tropical fish. Every seat has an ocean view, and the restaurant is adjacent to a path to the beach. In fact, some parents take a window table overlooking the sand and let the older kids play outside while they have their meal.

The food is familiar, so there's no problem finding goodies for the kids. We usually choose à la carte orders of tacos, enchiladas, and quesadillas. Hamburgers and omelets are also served here. Come before 6pm with the kids for the shortest wait.

Take the Santa Monica Freeway (I-10) and turn north on the Pacific Coast Highway (Calif. 1); the restaurant is between Cross Creek Road and Carbon Canyon, 1 mile south of the pier. Valet parking is offered.

THE CHEESECAKE FACTORY, 4142 Via Marina, Marina del Rey. Tel. 213/306-3344.

Cuisine: INTERNATIONAL. **Reservations:** Not accepted.

$ Prices: Lunch $5–$8; brunch $7–$8.50; dinner $5–$16. AE, MC, V.

Open: Mon–Thurs 11:30am–11:30pm, Fri–Sat 11:30am–12:30am, Sun 10am–11pm.

Children's Services: Children's brunch; highchairs, boosters.

The Marina del Rey location, just north of Washington Boulevard and west of Lincoln Boulevard, is large and features a patio overlooking the marina, perfect for dining with children. Unlike its Beverly Hills counterpart, it serves "mini–roadside sliders" (tiny hamburgers), taquitos, and mini-quesadillas, any of which might be perfect for your child.

The wait here can be lengthy during peak periods. Valet parking is available.

For further information about the restaurant, see the Cheesecake Factory listing in the "Beverly Hills" section, above.

THE CHEESECAKE FACTORY, 605 N. Harbor Dr., Redondo Beach. Tel. 213/376-0466.

Cuisine: INTERNATIONAL. **Reservations:** Accepted Mon–Thurs for parties of 10 or more.

$ Prices: Appetizers $4.95–$7.95; main courses $5.95–$16. AE, MC, V.

Open: Mon–Thurs 11:30am–11pm, Fri–Sat 11:30am–12:30am, Sun 10:30am–11pm; brunch Sun 10am–2:30pm.

Children's Services: Children's brunch, Sassy seats, booster seats, highchairs.

The menu selections here are the same as the Beverly Hills and Marina del Rey locations (see "Beverly Hills," above), but the atmosphere is different. The wonderful cheesecake variations, plus lunch, dinner, and Sunday brunch, are served in this spacious eatery, located along the Redondo Beach Harbor. When putting your name in for a table you may want to request a window seat for a lovely view of the boats on the water.

They don't have a children's menu here, but portions tend to be large, so you may want to share. Also, Lite Lunches, which are smaller portions of certain menu items, are available Monday through Friday until 5pm. A children's brunch is offered.

This is not the place to come if you're in a hurry, whether it be for lunch or for brunch. The wait can be long (up to an hour and a half), but worth it for the marvelous view and relaxing atmosphere. Valet parking is offered, or you can park in the restaurant lot.

MALIBU INN AND RESTAURANT, 22969 Pacific Coast Hwy., Malibu. Tel. 213/456-6106.
   Cuisine: INTERNATIONAL/SEAFOOD. **Reservations:** Not accepted.
$ **Prices:** Lunch $3–$6; dinner $7–$13. AE, MC, V.
   Open: Mon–Thurs 6am–3pm; Fri–Sat 6am–10pm; Sun 6am–9pm.
   Children's Services: Children's menu, booster seats, Sassy seats.

This nice, moderately priced restaurant is on Calif. 1 just south of Cross Creek Road. As you open the saloon-style doors, it's like stepping into a Victorian-style greenhouse. Wood floors, carved posts, and celebrity photographs make up the eclectic interiors.

Lunch and dinner items include omelets and creative sandwiches and salads. At dinner, there's seafood, chowder, fish and chips, fajitas (chicken or shrimp), and teriyaki chicken. On weekends the wait is about 20 minutes to an hour. To avoid the weekend wait, come before 9am or after 2pm. A parking lot is available.

TAMPICO TILLY'S, 1025 Wilshire Blvd., Santa Monica. Tel. 213/451-1769.
   Cuisine: MEXICAN. **Reservations:** Accepted.
$ **Prices:** $4.50–$14.25. AE, MC, V.
   Open: Daily 11:30am–10pm.
   Children's Services: Children's menu, highchairs, booster seats.

Most people agree that southern California is one of the best places to eat Mexican food. Fortunately, Mexican restaurants generally welcome children. You'll feel as if you've entered a home south of the border with its high ceilings, tile floors, and lace curtains when you arrive at Tampico Tilly's. Both tables and booths are available, and there are several dining areas from which to choose. (The "library" in the back is quaint and quiet—we request the main room because there's lots of activity here.)

Our kids virtually dive into the bowl of tortilla chips that's served as soon as you are seated. The menu is diverse, offering an enormous assortment of great, tame Mexican food. We love the Monterey salad (with crabmeat, shrimp, and avocado) and the crab enchilada tomatillo (crab rolled in a corn tortilla with tomatillo sauce). Other dishes include tostadas, burritos, tacos, fajitas, and enchiladas. They even offer eight Mexican omelets ranging in price from $4.50 to $9.75.

For dinner, you can order many of the same dishes offered at lunch, but with larger portions and including soup or salad, rice, and beans. You may also choose from several traditional Mexican steak dishes and other main courses. For children under 12 there's a kid's menu with four items (taco, cheese enchilada, hamburger, or grilled-cheese sandwich) for $3.50 to $4.

Servers will warm baby bottles and baby food in the kitchen, and there's a full bar (music and dancing in the evening). Valet parking is offered, and limited street parking is available.

This Tampico Tilly's is at the corner of Wilshire Boulevard and 11th Street. There's another Tampico Tilly's on the third level of the Santa Monica Place Shopping Center, 395 Santa Monica Place (tel. 213/393-1404).

INEXPENSIVE

CAFE CASINO, 1299 Ocean Ave., Santa Monica. Tel. 213/394-3717.

Cuisine: FRENCH/CONTINENTAL. **Reservations:** Accepted only for large groups.

$ Prices: Breakfast $3–$4; lunch around $6; dinner $9–$10. MC, V.

Open: Sun–Thurs 7am–10pm, Fri–Sat 7am–11pm.

Children's Services: Highchairs, booster seats.

Café Casino is an American extension of Casino de France, one of the largest food distributors in Western Europe. This location, across from Palisades Park, is a perfect place to stop on a Sunday morning before an outing to the Santa Monica Pier or a trek to Malibu. We've spent many a marvelous morning sipping our first cups of coffee while the kids watched the joggers and seagulls. The large whitewashed patio area outdoors is a perfect spot. It's shielded from the wind by glass, and has heat lamps should the need arise. It's also a lovely setting for an early dinner at sunset.

Serving French and continental cuisine, this gourmet cafeteria offers delicious food, while allowing you to get in and out quickly. The only hangups are the long line (at times) waiting to file past the gratin provençal, quiche, and croissants, and having to maneuver a baby stroller through the line if you are the lone adult.

While there isn't a children's menu, the side orders are so varied that you shouldn't have trouble pleasing the kids. For breakfast, there's cereal and such traditional items as sausage, French toast, and delectable fresh fruit, as well as the more sophisticated eggs Benedict. For lunch, there is cheese, bread, and more fresh fruit sitting alongside the salade niçoise, croissant sandwiches, and salmon basquais. For dinner, the kids can have soup or share your roast beef, snapper, or beef bourguignon.

There's validated parking in the building lot.

There are other Café Casino branches, including one in Westwood Village at 1145 Gayley Avenue (tel. 213/208-1010).

EDIE'S DINER, 4211 Admiralty Way, Marina del Rey. Tel. 213/823-5339.

Cuisine: AMERICAN. **Reservations:** Not accepted.

$ Prices: $4–$6. AE, CB, DC, MC, V.

Open: Daily 24 hours. **Closed:** Mon midnight to 6am Tues.

Children's Services: Children's portions, highchairs.

The typical diner decor is enhanced by an outdoor patio overlooking the boats. Table-attached jukeboxes challenge you to remember the words to "Itsy-Bitsy, Teeny-Weeny, Yellow Polka Dot Bikini." The four-page menu includes the blue-plate special of southern fried chicken with vegetable, mashed potatoes and gravy, soup, roll, and butter. There are also waffles, hot dogs, chili burgers (and most any other configuration of burger), and sandwiches, plus wonderful soda-fountain treats. For small appetites, there's a mini-burger or two pieces of chicken for $2, and a child's portion of ice cream or fries. The management will warm bottles and baby food. The average wait is 20 minutes.

The diner is on Admiralty Way between Bali Way and Palawan Way. Both valet and self-parking are available.

FROMIN'S RESTAURANT, 1832 Wilshire Blvd., Santa Monica. Tel. 213/829-5443.

Cuisine: DELI. **Reservations:** Accepted only for parties of five or more.

$ Prices: $5–$11. MC, V.

Open: Daily 6:30am–10pm.

Children's Services: Children's menu, highchairs, booster seats.

This is one of those kosher-style delis that's perfect on a Sunday morning when you're craving bagels and cream cheese. For some reason, there's less of a crowd at breakfast than at lunch or dinner, so that's when we come here most often.

The children's menu is extensive, with breakfast, lunch, and dinner items ranging from $2.15 to $4.15. The adult portions are good-size, and the servers will be happy to split orders. They'll bring the kids a bagel on request (or pickles in the afternoon and evening). For omelet lovers, there are 20-plus varieties to choose from (ham and cheese, bologna, pastrami, and Reuben, for instance), and if that doesn't suffice, you can create your own extravaganza from 17 different ingredients.

There are also traditional breakfast offerings; deli platters with lox, whitefish, and bagels; soups; 13 different salads; burgers; and a huge assortment of sandwiches. Choose from typical deli fare (salami, sardine, cold roast beef) to triple-decker and hot creations.

At night you can order à la carte or a complete dinner (with soup or salad; potato, coleslaw, or vegetable; and bread and butter; plus dessert and beverage). There are such dishes as sweet-and-sour rolled cabbage, corned beef and cabbage, chicken in a pot, fish, and boiled beef. Early-bird and senior-citizen dinners are available.

This Fromin's is on Wilshire Boulevard at 19th Street, and a parking lot is available. There's another branch in Encino at 17615 Ventura Boulevard (tel. 818/990-6346).

GOOD STUFF, 13th and the Strand, Hermosa Beach. Tel. 213/374-2334.

Cuisine: CONTINENTAL. **Reservations:** Not accepted.

$ Prices: Appetizers $1.65–$3.25; breakfast $2.30–$5.50; lunch $2.50–$7.75; dinner $3.95–$8.95. AE, MC, V.

Open: Daily 7am–9pm.

Children's Services: Children's menu, booster seats, Sassy seats, highchairs.

Located right on the beach with a casual atmosphere that typifies California, this eatery is especially popular with families. Surrounded by windows, you may be able to catch a game of beach volleyball while making your way through an avocado-bacon cheeseburger. It does get crowded here, especially on weekends, but waiting for a table is the perfect excuse to take a stroll along the water.

This is also a great place for breakfast if you plan to spend the day on the beach.

They have everything from thick sliced cinnamon-swirl French toast with two eggs and bacon or sausage at $4.25, to a good dose of the Californian favorite, granola with fruit. Dinner features nightly specials and treats such as calamari steak with pasta parmesan, served with soup or salad.

The "Kid Stuff" selections (for youngsters under 12) are limited to breakfasts of an egg, one pancake, and milk ($1.95), French toast ($1.65), or an egg, toast, and bacon ($1.95). Lunch is a grilled-cheese sandwich or peanut butter and honey ($1.95). At dinner there are plenty of burgers for them to try, but no children's menu.

HAMBURGER HENRY, 3001 Wilshire Blvd., Santa Monica. Tel. 213/ 828-3000.

Cuisine: AMERICAN. **Reservations:** Accepted.

$ Prices: $4–$9. AE, MC, V.

Open: Daily 7am–1am; brunch Sat 10am–3pm, Sun 9am–3pm.

Children's Services: Children's menu, highchairs, booster seats.

We were first drawn to Hamburger Henry for the unusual—and delicious—hamburger creations. Ever try an applenut burger? You can even get turkey burgers for non-beef eaters. There are also good old-fashioned burgers, plus sandwiches, salads, soups, and main dishes. The array of Belgian waffles and omelets is equally inviting.

There's a special children's price for the salad bar. Kids pay $3.75, which includes frozen yogurt and toppings. With over 40 salad items (including potato salad, carrot salad, macaroni salad, and tuna salad), plus fruit, soup, and a tostada bar, you can see why families gather here. Children can also choose a burger, peanut-butter sandwich, grilled-cheese sandwich, or scrambled eggs (all with fries, milk, and fresh fruit) for $2.75. There are Shirley Temple cocktails.

Your server will gladly warm baby bottles or baby food, and will split adult portions between kids.

Hamburger Henry is on Wilshire Boulevard a half mile west of Bundy Avenue. There is free parking.

OCEAN PARK OMELETTE PARLOR, 2732 Main St., Santa Monica. Tel. 213/399-7892.

Cuisine: AMERICAN. **Reservations:** Not accepted.

$ Prices: Average $4.50. AE, MC, V.

Open: Daily 6am–3pm.

Children's Services: Booster seats.

This small, quaint spot with an outdoor patio is a satisfying choice for breakfast or lunch. It serves good old-fashioned breakfasts (Annie May's homemade biscuits and gravy, for example), salads, and sandwiches, as well as an array of omelets. It's hard to find better prices. The three-egg omelets include potatoes and an English muffin. There is some street parking or a metered parking lot in back.

PIONEER BOULANGERIE, 2012 S. Main St., Santa Monica. Tel. 213/ 399-7771.

Cuisine: BISTRO. **Reservations:** Accepted only for the dining room.

$ Prices: Dining room, $5–$13; cafeteria, $4.25–$7. AE, DC, MC, V.

Open: Dining room, daily 11am–3pm; cafeteria, daily 7am–8:30pm.

Children's Services: Highchairs, booster seats.

Known for its great baked goods, Pioneer is a Basque-style eatery with a wonderful assortment of eating possibilities under one roof. There is a cafeteria with two patios (one is enclosed), a wine shop, a gourmet food and candy shop, a bistro, and a bakery, where you can watch the bakers kneading dough and working their magic.

The menu in the cafeteria and bistro features continental, seafood, Italian, and French themes, depending on the day. The cafeteria offers sandwiches, salads, omelets, and daily specials. The bistro offers seafood, stews, pasta, and soup.

There's no children's menu, but that presents no real problem because of the diverse list of side orders and baked goods.

Parking is in an adjacent lot; enter on Bicknell Street.

HOLLYWOOD, MID-WILSHIRE, WEST HOLLYWOOD

EXPENSIVE

THE DAILY GRILL, in the Beverly Connection, 100 N. La Cienega Blvd., West Hollywood. Tel. 213/659-3100.
   Cuisine: AMERICAN. **Reservations:** Not accepted.
$ **Prices:** Main courses $7–$19. AE, MC, V.
   Open: Mon–Thurs 11am–11pm, Fri 11am–midnight, Sat 10am–midnight, Sun 10am–10pm.
   Children's Services: Highchairs, booster seats.

It didn't take long for this big, bright New York–style grill to catch on with the 30- and 40-something crowd of parents. Many of them were already familiar with the fashionable Grill in the Alley in Beverly Hills, from which these more casual—and less expensive—restaurants were spun off. Come any time between 6 and 8pm and you're sure to see families with children in all age ranges, even though there is no children's menu and the portions are large and pricey.

Families like the fact that the waiters and waitresses are excellent, the wait is usually no more than 15 or 20 minutes, and the food is consistently good. White and black tile floors, wooden booths, Venetian blinds, and art deco–like hanging lamps contribute to the traditional look of the place. Butcher's paper on the tables allows busy hands to draw (although that was not its original intention). The food consists of hearty, standard grill fare such as steaks and chops, plus a great garlic chicken (and seven other varieties), seafood, and fish. Hamburgers are thick and satisfying; salads come in small and main-course sizes. Share a plate of fried potatoes and onions (for two or four people) while you wait for your order. The daily specials include chicken; meatloaf and mashed potatoes; calves' liver, bacon, and onions; short ribs; and Joe's Special—a traditional San Francisco dish consisting of ground beef, spinach, and eggs. Leave room for dessert, if you can. Our favorite is the double-chocolate layer cake. Some people swear by the rice pudding.

This Daily Grill is across from the Beverly Center, just north of La Cienega Boulevard and 3rd Street. There's validated parking in the lot.

Another location in Brentwood is at 11677 San Vicente Boulevard, (tel. 213/442-0044).

GENGHIS COHEN, 740 N. Fairfax Ave., West Hollywood. Tel. 213/653-0640.
   Cuisine: CHINESE. **Reservations:** Accepted.
$ **Prices:** Main courses $7.50–$15. AE, MC, V.
   Open: Lunch Mon–Fri noon–3pm; dinner Mon–Sat 5–11:30pm, Sun 5–10pm.

Children's Services: Highchairs, booster seats.

The food here is worth the price. Genghis Cohen gets its share of music studio people, Melrose wanderers, and the Westside chic. The dining room is large, the tables are spread out, and there are big, comfy booths—plus the service is prompt and helpful.

There's no children's menu, but most dishes are suitable for sharing. If you like duck, try it crispy. Or sample the candied garlic shrimp, crackerjack shrimp, spicy garlic lamb, or orange-peel chicken. Or you can order Szechuan ribs, Beijing barbecued chicken, or the three-flavor moo shu (which they call their famous Oriental fajitas!). They'll make your Szechuan choices as hot as you want, and they don't use MSG in anything. There's a bar for ordering Shirley Temples.

Genghis Cohen is on Fairfax half a block north of Melrose Avenue. Parking is available in a small adjacent lot.

MODERATE

EL CHOLO, 1121 S. Western Ave., Mid-Wilshire. Tel. 213/734-2773.

Cuisine: MEXICAN. **Reservations:** Highly recommended.

$ Prices: Dinner main courses $7–$12.25. AE, MC, V.

Open: Mon–Thurs 11am–10pm, Fri–Sat 11am–11pm, Sun 11am–9pm.

Children's Services: Specially priced items, highchairs, booster seats.

The story of El Cholo goes back to 1927 when it opened across the street from its present location with six booths and a counter. What you see now was the actual house, currently decorated in the style of a Spanish hacienda. The various dining rooms are named after employees who stayed with El Cholo more than 30 years.

The bar has inviting stuffed chairs and couches, perfect while waiting for your table (which you'll have to do for 40 minutes to an hour without a reservation). There are also tabletop video games and a big-screen TV. On our last visit a caricaturist created complementary drawings for the kids. The lively dining rooms are comfortable for children, and on Monday you can listen to the mariachis serenade your whole family.

This award-winning restaurant is famous for its margaritas and green-corn tamales (served June through September only). In addition to the traditional Mexican appetizer selections, there are crab or beef taquitos at $5 per order. Main courses include fajitas, combination plates (with enchiladas, tamales, tacos, and chile relleños), the special Sonora-style enchilada, tostadas, a taco tray for two, and chimichangas.

There is no children's menu, but if your child is under 12, tell your server you want the children's-priced items. They'll make a taco, cheese enchilada, chile relleño, or tamale with rice, beans, or french fries for $5.25. Special children's drinks are available. Servers will split adult portions for children at no charge, and will warm baby food and bottles.

El Cholo is on South Western Avenue between Pico Boulevard and Olympic Boulevard. There's free parking in a lot across the street.

HARD ROCK CAFE, 8600 Beverly Blvd., West Hollywood. Tel. 213/276-7605.

Cuisine: AMERICAN. **Reservations:** Not accepted.

$ Prices: Main courses $5.50–$12.50. AE, MC, V.

Open: Mon–Thurs 11:30am–11:30pm, Fri–Sat 11:30am–midnight, Sun noon–11:30pm.

Children's Services: Children's menu, highchairs.

If you are traveling with teenagers, you must make a pilgrimage to the Hard Rock. Known throughout the world, it's one of L.A.'s most popular casual restaurants—and teens love it. The green Cadillac plunging through the roof and the lines of people outside make the restaurant easy to spot.

Once inside you'll be bombarded by loud rock music and surrounded by rock 'n' roll decor. (This isn't a place to take very young children who are noise-sensitive.) The big barnlike room seems to hold hundreds of people. Once you get a table (the wait can be long on weekends and at prime times), you'll probably be doing so much looking around at the eclectic crowd that it'll be hard to concentrate on the menu, which will satisfy everyone's tastes.

There are plenty of meal-size salads and five different hamburgers on fresh whole-wheat buns. The lime-grilled chicken is good, but the watermelon-basted baby back ribs are better. There is also fresh fish and sandwiches, served with salad and fries. The children's menu (for kids 12 and under) is limited, but a great buy—a burger or grilled-cheese sandwich (both are regular size) with fries and watermelon goes for $2.95. Be sure to make room for the desserts—homemade apple pie with ice cream or melted cheese, chocolate devil's food cake, strawberry shortcake, a banana split, or a homemade brownie.

This version of the Hard Rock Café is on the street level of the Beverly Center, at the corner of Beverly Boulevard and San Vicente Boulevard. There's plenty of parking in the Beverly Center lot ($1).

HUNAN TASTE, 6031 W. San Vicente Blvd., Mid-Wilshire. Tel. 213/936-5621.

Cuisine: CHINESE. **Reservations:** Accepted but not necessary.

$ Prices: Lunch specials $4–$5; dinner main courses average $8. AE, MC, V.

Open: Sun–Thurs 11:30am–10pm, Fri–Sat 11:30am–10:30pm.

Children's Services: Highchairs, booster seats.

Chinese restaurants make great family dining experiences, and the Hunan Taste is no exception. This friendly neighborhood restaurant, where you see lots of the same faces over and over again, is perfect for a Sunday-night—or any-night—dinner. The restaurant is bright and cheerful, with linen-covered tables set far apart, and a comfortable, casual atmosphere.

Owner and chef Tommy Yan (a veteran of three well-known L.A. Chinese restaurants) is known for his velvet shrimp Peking style and his hot-and-sour soup, but kids seem to like almost everything served here. Some are more partial to the three-ingredients dish, others to almond chicken. As the restaurant's name suggests, the dishes here are prepared Hunan style, so be sure to specify if you want milder versions of spicy dishes. Your waiter will be happy to suggest combinations of orders for the best sharing opportunities. A few good choices are General Tso's chicken, Mongolian-style lamb, and velvet shrimp. Ask about the weekly specials.

We've made Hunan a lunch stop before the Los Angeles County Museum of Art and Page Museum. Such lunch specials as beef with broccoli, cashew chicken, hot braised shrimp, and other Hunan-style dishes come with soup, appetizer, and fried rice. Or you can order off the regular menu.

The staff will gladly warm baby bottles and baby food, and Shirley Temples are cheerfully provided. If you are staying in a hotel in the area, you might consider ordering take-out.

The Hunan Taste is at the intersection of Fairfax Avenue, Olympic Boulevard, and San Vicente Boulevard. There's parking in a free lot.

INEXPENSIVE

CANTER'S, 419 N. Fairfax Ave., Mid-Wilshire. Tel. 213/651-2030.
Cuisine: DELI. **Reservations:** Accepted.
$ Prices: Average $6. No credit cards.
Open: Daily 24 hours.
Children's Services: Highchairs, booster seats.

Canter's, which is one of Los Angeles's oldest delis, is usually filled with an eclectic crowd—families, local would-be celebrities, neighborhood residents, and tourists.

In addition to oatmeal, egg dishes, Belgian waffles, and matzo brei, there's Canter's fresh baked goods (a slice of pumpernickel-raisin bread can't be beat!). Traditional hot and cold deli sandwiches, soups, fish dishes, hot dogs, hamburgers, and steak sandwiches are on the menu. A plate of lox and cream cheese is the most expensive item on the menu at $9.50. Take-out is available at the counter.

They will split orders in the kitchen for two children, will warm bottles and baby food, and will make special children's drinks at the bar.

Canter's is on North Fairfax Avenue two blocks north of Beverly Boulevard. There's validated parking in Canter's lot two doors south.

CHAO KRUNG RESTAURANT, 111 N. Fairfax Ave., Mid-Wilshire. Tel. 213/939-8361.
Cuisine: THAI. **Reservations:** Not necessary.
$ Prices: Appetizers $4.25–$6.25; main courses $4.25–$10.95. AE, MC, V.
Open: Lunch Mon–Fri 11:30am–3pm; dinner daily 5–10pm.
Children's Services: Highchairs, booster seats.

As a special treat, we bring Janey and her friends to this friendly neighborhood restaurant for chicken satay (marinated chicken on a stick). They sometimes go through two orders each ($4.95 per order)! We like the barbecue dishes, and especially the noodles. Pad Thai, pad see ew, and noodle bowl are favorites. There are also 20 seafood selections, vegetarian dishes, and spicy curry choices.

The restaurant is lovely, and the kids like to talk about the colorful art on the walls depicting Thai life. Take-out is available. Beer and wine are served.

Chao Krung is across from CBS Studios, between Beverly Boulevard and 3rd Street. Street parking.

DUPAR'S RESTAURANT, in the Farmers Market, 3rd St. and Fairfax Ave., Mid-Wilshire. Tel. 213/933-8446.
Cuisine: AMERICAN. **Reservations:** Not accepted.
$ Prices: Breakfast $3.25–$7. AE, MC, V.
Open: Daily 6am–10:30pm.
Children's Services: Highchairs, booster seats.

DuPar's has been an L.A. institution for more than 50 years. This location, seemingly the most popular, is filled with booths and a counter. Breakfast is the best time to visit—the pancakes are outstanding and the coffee is good and strong. The short order of pancakes is plenty for one child, or split it between two light eaters. You can also choose omelets, French toast (comes in short-order size, too), cereals, or eggs. If you really want to be naughty, pick from the unreal bakery goods, such as a made-on-the-premises butterhorn (crescent) or bear claw, or perhaps a doughnut or two. The Sunday-morning wait averages about 20 minutes. There's a free parking lot.

LUCY'S CAFE EL ADOBE, 5536 Melrose Ave., Hollywood. Tel. 213/462-9421.

Cuisine: MEXICAN. **Reservations:** Accepted only for six or more.

$ Prices: Full dinners $8–$9. AE, MC (they ask that you leave the gratuity in cash).

Open: Mon–Sat 11:30am–11pm.

Children's Services: Children's menu, booster seats.

This homey neighborhood restaurant, made famous by the Jerry Brown–Linda Ronstadt duo, is made up of wooden booths and dark-paneled walls. Family owned and run, Lucy's is now serving the second and third generation of customers—locals and celebrities.

The food is simple, the margaritas great. Specialties such as chile Colorado (fresh chopped beef with red chile sauce), ropa vieja (shredded beef in sauce), and gallina en mole (breast of chicken in mole sauce) come with soup, salad, rice, beans, tortillas, and butter. There are seven variations of enchilada dinners, as well as à la carte selections. Children under 12 can order a taco, enchilada, or meat patty with rice, beans, soup, or salad, each $6. Bottles and baby food can be warmed, and special children's drinks made. The wait is 10 to 30 minutes.

Lucy's is across from Paramount Studios. A parking lot is available.

OLD SPAGHETTI FACTORY, 5939 Sunset Blvd., Hollywood. Tel. 213/469-7149.

Cuisine: ITALIAN. **Reservations:** Not accepted.

$ Prices: Lunch $2.50–$5.25; dinner $4.50–$7. No credit cards.

Open: Lunch Mon–Fri 11:30am–2pm; dinner Mon–Thurs 5–10pm, Fri–Sat 5–11pm, Sun 4–10pm.

Children's Services: Children's menu, highchairs, booster seats.

This is like walking into a turn-of-the-century museum. Children will have a ball looking at all the ornate decorations: All love the 1918 trolley car, where you can request a table.

Lunch and dinner offer many of the same items; only the price is different. In addition to the nine different spaghetti dishes at lunch, you have your choice of fettuccine Alfredo, spinach tortellini with Alfredo sauce, pasta salad, sausage or meatball sandwich, and soup. Complete dinners include salad, bread, beverage, and spumoni. An à la carte dish of spaghetti with meat sauce and bread is available for $4.10. An under-12 dinner for kids consists of spaghetti with meat or tomato sauce. Baby food and bottles will be warmed upon request. During peak periods the wait is 15 to 30 minutes; on weekends, 30 to 45 minutes.

The Old Spaghetti Factory is on Sunset Boulevard between Vine Street and Western Avenue. A parking lot is available.

ROSCOE'S HOUSE OF CHICKEN AND WAFFLES, 1514 N. Gower St., Hollywood. Tel. 213/466-7453 or 213/466-9329.

Cuisine: SOUTHERN. **Reservations:** Not accepted.

$ Prices: $3.50–$7.75. AE, CB, MC, V.

Open: Sun–Thurs 9am–11pm, Fri–Sat 9am–3am.

Children's Services: Highchairs, booster seats.

The name reflects their specialties, and both are served in many different ways. From delicious chicken smothered with gravy and onions, accompanied by grits and biscuits, to fresh chicken livers, a waffle, potato salad or fries, you'll find large portions at reasonable prices. There's also a chicken burger and chicken sandwiches served all day. Baby bottles and baby food can be warmed; orders can be split for two kids. The busiest time is 11:30am to noon.

It's between Hollywood Boulevard and Sunset Boulevard on North Gower Street. Street parking available.

SOUPLANTATION, in the Beverly Connection, 8491 W. 3rd St., Hollywood. Tel. 213/655-0381.
   Cuisine: AMERICAN. **Reservations:** Not necessary.
   $ Prices: Lunch $5.95; dinner $6.95. MC, V.
   Open: Sun–Thurs 11am–9pm, Fri–Sat 11am–10pm.
   Children's Services: Special prices, highchairs, booster seats.

Souplantation was made for families. This serve-yourself restaurant offers a wholesome variety of food at fabulous prices. The salad bar is big and the items fresh; there are also pasta and specialty salads. The soup bar features several selections of hearty soups; the bakery has fresh breads and rolls. The kids love the dessert bar, where they can make their own frozen-yogurt sundaes or can choose fresh fruit. The best part is that children under 5 eat free, and kids under 12 eat for only $2.99.

Souplantation is in the Beverly Connection at the corner of 3rd Street and La Cienega Boulevard. Parking is free in the Beverly Connection lot.

Other locations are in Pasadena at 201 South Lake Avenue (tel. 818/577-4798), in Marina del Rey at 13455 Maxella (tel. 213/305-7669), and in Brentwood at 11911 San Vicente Boulevard (tel. 213/476-7080).

DOWNTOWN

PACIFIC DINING CAR, 1310 W. 6th St. Tel. 213/483-6000.
   Cuisine: AMERICAN. **Reservations:** Accepted.
   $ Prices: Breakfast $4.50–$12.25; main courses $10.95–$29 at lunch, $25–$35 at dinner. AE, MC, V.
   Open: Breakfast Mon–Fri 11pm–11am, Sat–Sun 11pm–4pm; lunch Mon–Thurs 11am–4pm; afternoon tea daily 3–5:30pm; dinner daily 24 hours.
   Children's Services: Highchairs, booster seats.

Weekend breakfast time is when you'll find the most families with children dining here. Although it's open 24 hours a day, don't expect a coffeeshop—the ambience is more luxurious, and the prices are quite high. Weekdays, L.A.'s major powerbrokers spend their breakfast time here making major deals.

Set in an enlarged replica of a real railway dining car, this restaurant has been serving food in this location since 1923. Through the years it became famous for its aged meats. Although the coffee is no longer 10¢, and you can't get a sirloin steak for 65¢ anymore, it still draws a loyal crowd of diners for breakfast, lunch, dinner, and after-theater supper. The rooms are handsome and the atmosphere subdued. We like to sit in the area near the entrance, the original railwaylike car, with windows on one side.

Breakfast features mostly egg dishes such as fresh avocado scramble, Swiss eggs, and omelets. Our kids love the pancakes and the homemade blueberry and bran muffins. You can also get a bowl of yogurt, granola, or Familia muesli. Preserves, marmalade, and apple butter are made on the premises.

Lunch and dinner feature seafood, steaks, and veal. Dinner selections include spareribs, shrimp diavolo, chicken dishes, and hamburgers. Main courses come with a potato, but vegetables are à la carte.

Management is willing to warm baby bottles and baby food in the kitchen, and will prepare special children's drinks at the bar.

This 24-hour place is on West 6th Street between Alvarado Street and Figueroa Street. Valet parking is available. A new Pacific Dining Car is in Santa Monica at 2700 Wilshire Boulevard (tel. 213/453-4000).

THE ORIGINAL PANTRY, 877 S. Figueroa St. Tel. 213/972-9279.

Cuisine: AMERICAN. **Reservations:** Not accepted.

$ Prices: Breakfast $3.75; lunch $6; dinner $8. No credit cards.

Open: Daily 24 hours.

Children's Services: Highchairs, booster seats.

Not many Los Angeles restaurants can claim more than 66 years of business without having closed their doors once. Walking into this place is like entering a time warp and reemerging in the 1930s. It's not diner style, mind you, but there's real linoleum on the floors and Formica on the tables. Waiters in white shirts, aprons, and black bow ties know their business, which is to serve generous portions of real American food. Locals know that the Pantry's hallmark is the line out the door. The menu changes daily, but basically you'll get hearty breakfasts, plus hamburgers, steaks, cutlets, ham, rib roast, pork, lamb, soup, and salads at reasonable prices. They'll gladly split orders in the kitchen or warm baby bottles and baby food.

The Original Pantry is at the corner of 9th Street and Figueroa Street. It has a parking lot.

PANTRY BAKE & SANDWICH SHOPPE, 875 S. Figueroa St. Tel. 213/ 627-6879.

Cuisine: AMERICAN. **Reservations:** Not accepted.

$ Prices: $2.25–$5.25. No credit cards.

Open: Daily 6am–9pm.

Children's Services: Highchairs, booster seats.

This sister restaurant to the Original Pantry has the same 1930s feel. It has a large quick-service counter area for snacks and fast meals. The main difference of the Bake Shoppe is that it serves a lighter lunch than its next-door neighbor, with such fare as sandwiches; breakfast and dinner items are the same at both places.

PHILIPPE'S, 1001 N. Alameda St. Tel. 213/628-3781.

Cuisine: AMERICAN. **Reservations:** Not accepted.

$ Prices: Breakfast 35¢–$4.25; lunch averages $3.25. No credit cards.

Open: Daily 6am–10pm.

Children's Services: Highchairs.

S This is a good place to try after a visit to the Children's Museum. Like the Pantry, Philippe's is an L.A. tradition, this one dating back to 1908. The setting is informal, the tables are long and to be shared, and the floors are covered with sawdust. The restaurant draws a clientele that ranges from Los Angeles celebrities to downtown workers.

"Self-serve" is the word here. Pay and order at the counter and choose eggs, French toast, or fresh baked goods for breakfast. At lunch or dinner, sample the famous Philippe's French-dip sandwiches. They come in pork, beef, ham, lamb, turkey, or tuna. Coffee is still Depression-priced at 10¢. Don't miss the candy counter!

Phillipe's is near Olvera Street and Chinatown. Park in the back or on the street.

CHINATOWN

OCEAN SEAFOOD RESTAURANT, 750 N. Hill St. Tel. 213/687-3088.
Cuisine: CHINESE. **Reservations:** Accepted at dinner only.
$ Prices: Lunch $2.50–$10; dinner $5–$20. MC, V.
Open: Daily 8:30am–10pm.
Children's Services: Highchairs, booster seats.

It is said by local reviewers that this is *the* place for dim sum in Los Angeles. New on the L.A. scene, Ocean Seafood is a good place to introduce your children to the wonders of that Chinese breakfast food. Dim sum selections are $1.50 each.

Lunch might be anything from sticky rice in lotus leaf to braised e-fu noodles with crabmeat. If all else fails to enthrall your kids, the Chinese chicken noodles in soup will probably be a hit.

Because Ocean Seafood prepares more than 300 dishes in the gourmet Cantonese style of Hong Kong, you can imagine that dinner is a cornucopia of exotic selections. Here are just a few: In addition to crispy Peking duck, priced very reasonably at $20 for a whole bird, there is lemon chicken (in half and full orders) sweet-and-sour pork, braised sea cucumber with preserved shrimp eggs, pan-fried lobster with ginger and green onions, Geoduck clam Japanese style, and squab steamed with wine sauce. There are several desserts you may never have heard of: almond Jello, coconut and bird's-nest soup, or sweetened red-bean soup with lotus.

Nothing here is spicy and everything is very fresh. The family will get to watch dishes prepared at the table. Bottles and baby food will be warmed upon request.

Ocean Seafood is on North Hill Street between Alpine Street and Ord Street. There's both valet and street parking.

LITTLE TOKYO

RESTAURANT PLAZA, 356 E. 1st St. Tel. 213/628-0697.
Cuisine: JAPANESE. **Reservations:** Accepted.
$ Prices: Lunch $4.75–$19.50; dinner averages $13. AE, MC, V.
Open: Daily 11:30am–9:30pm.
Children's Services: Highchairs, booster seats.

This is a real find when you want to take the kids for authentic Japanese food. This restaurant is actually a combination of several restaurants, each specializing in a different cuisine: sushi, noodles, tempura, teriyaki, bento (traditional Japanese lunch-in-a-box), and nabe (dishes cooked in a pot).

Whenever we eat here, we feel as if we've spent an hour in Tokyo. The dining room, while larger than a traditional Japanese restaurant, exudes an air of the Orient. Maybe it's because Japanese is spoken all around you; maybe it's the paper lanterns hanging from the ceiling or the small indoor gardens.

All food is attractively presented, the way it would be in Japan. Sushi is neatly—and colorfully—arranged on raised rectangular plates. Makunouchi bento comes in a lacquered luncheon box with rice and pickles. Teriyaki and tempura are artistically presented amid slivered cabbage and colorful orange slices.

You'll find Restaurant Plaza on the second floor of Japanese Village Plaza. There's plenty of parking nearby.

PASADENA

ROBIN'S, 395 N. Rosemead Blvd. Tel. 818/351/8885.
Cuisine: AMERICAN. **Reservations:** Not accepted.
$ Prices: $4.25–$10.95. MC, V.
Open: Sun–Thurs 7am–11pm, Fri–Sat 7 am–1am.
Children's Services: Children's menu, booster seats, highchairs.

Robin's is a true neighborhood family restaurant. There seems to be something for everyone, including discounts for senior citizens, a special prize for the kids, and a complimentary jar of baby food for the infants.

In addition to the burgers and salads, there are stir-fry selections, fajitas, and barbecued ribs and chicken. Dinner specials list fish, steak, chicken, liver and onions, spaghetti, and beer-battered shrimp. Most popular are the Family Nites, when you get all-you-can-eat selections until 10pm. Sunday is fried-chicken night, Wednesday and Friday it's beer-batter fish, Monday you get steak, and Tuesday is barbecued beef ribs. Thursday is shrimp night.

And that's not all. Children 12 and under get their own menu for breakfast, lunch, and dinner, with prices ranging from $1.99 for a junior cheeseburger to $2.99 for fried chicken and fries. There's even a vegetable stir-fry listed among the choices.

Robin's is on Rosemead at Michalinda Boulevard. Parking is free.

ROSE CITY DINER, 45 S. Fair Oaks Ave. Tel. 818/793-8282.
Cuisine: AMERICAN/DINER. **Reservations:** Not accepted.
$ Prices: Breakfast $1.55–$5.95; lunch/dinner $3–$9.55. No credit cards.
Open: Daily 6:30am–2am.
Children's Services: Booster seats.

This cute, lively, noisy diner is a perfect family restaurant when you're strolling through Old Pasadena. There's the typical diner counter and booths and tables of all sizes. Old Quaker Oats boxes are used as decorations; Bazooka bubble gum comes with the check. Look up at the ceiling, then do your own. (You'll know what we mean when you see it.)

Breakfast is served all day. Eggs and omelets come with hash browns, toast, or biscuits. Little readers are sure to spot the chocolate-chip pancakes. Chicken fried steak, chicken pot pie, meatloaf and gravy, and chili and macaroni are a few choices under deluxe plates. There are also hot and cold sandwiches, burgers, a hot dog, and salads. If you still have room, we dare you to try something from the dessert menu!

The Rose City Diner is in Old Pasadena on South Fair Oaks Avenue between Green Street and Colorado Boulevard. Valet parking is available; stree parking is limited.

SOUPLANTATION, 201 S. Lake Ave. Tel. 818/577-4798.
See the Souplantation listing under "Hollywood, Mid-Wilshire, West Hollywood," above.

UNIVERSAL CITY/BURBANK

VICTORIA STATION, 3850 Lankershim Blvd., Universal City. Tel. 818/ 760-0714.

Cuisine: AMERICAN. **Reservations:** Suggested.

$ Prices: Lunch/brunch $6.50–$16.50; dinner $13–$22. AE, MC, V.

Open: Mon–Thurs 11:30am–10pm, Fri–Sat 11:30am–11pm, Sun 11:30am–3pm for brunch and 4–10pm for dinner.

Children's Services: Children's menu, highchairs, booster seats.

Young children delight in the fact that they're eating inside a replica of a famous train depot. Victoria Station, as the name suggests, re-creates the ambience of the famous London railroad station. In fact, you can eat inside one of the original Flying Scotsman fleet of British railway cars.

Specializing in carved-to-order prime rib (you can have it with the bone in) and continental cuisine, Victoria Station caters to families. Junior Conductor dinners for children 12 and under offer a cheeseburger, barbecued ribs, chicken sticks, or prime rib for $4.95 to $8.95. All meals come with fries and a beverage. Add $2 for the unlimited salad bar.

In addition to the prime rib, there's barbecued beef or pork ribs, fresh seafood, and chicken selections. Adult dinners include salad bar or soup du jour, baked potato or chestnut wild rice, and fresh vegetables. Lunch offerings include top sirloin, honey grilled chicken, chicken stir-fry, or shrimp Victoria (large shrimp sautéed with garlic, white wine, and lemon). Quiche and burgers are also served.

For brunch, omelets, quiche, stuffed French toast, and gourmet egg dishes are offered. You can also order prime rib or the fresh catch of the day.

Children's nonalcoholic drinks are served from the bar; servers will warm baby bottles or baby food, and will gladly bring crackers to the table if your kids are hungry.

Victoria Station is atop the hill at Universal Studios, next to the Universal Studios tours. Valet parking is offered, or there's parking in the Universal Studios lot ($5).

FUNG LUM RESTAURANT, 222 Universal Terrace Pkwy., Universal City. Tel. 818/763-7888.

Cuisine: CHINESE. **Reservations:** Highly recommended.

$ Prices: Main courses $4.50–$8.50 at lunch, $7–$23 at dinner; Sun brunch $11.95. AE, MC, V.

Open: Lunch Mon–Sat 11:30am–2:30pm; dinner Mon–Thurs 5–10pm, Fri–Sat 5–11pm, Sun 3–10pm; brunch Sun 11am–3pm.

Children's Services: Highchairs, booster seats.

Looking like an Oriental palace, this is a "must" on your list of interesting restaurants to visit. Enter through ornate hand-carved doors; Moongates (arched entryways) lead to exquisite gardens, and inside are embroidered silk decorations and panels inlaid with coral and ivory. As formal as it looks, it's still a fine place to take the family. The main dining room seats 500 comfortably.

Cantonese is the primary Chinese cuisine served here, although Hunan and Szechuan selections are also prepared. Familiar dishes such as chicken chow mein, fried rice, and moo shu chicken should please the kids. At dinner there are many duck dishes, 11 kinds of soup, a huge list of seafood, and vegetable, chicken, beef, and pork dishes. You could visit over and over again and still not taste everything on the menu.

For $35 you can have the celebrated shark's-fin soup with shredded chicken, or whole winter-melon soup, which has to be ordered in advance and serves 10 people.

Sunday brunch features a buffet and nonstop champagne. Children are charged half price. Baby bottles and baby food can be warmed; special children's drinks are prepared at the bar. Even with a reservation, be prepared for a wait.

Fung Lum is on the side of the hill leading up to Universal Studios. Valet parking is offered.

TONY ROMA'S A PLACE FOR RIBS, 100 Universal City Plaza, Universal City. Tel. 818/777-3939.
   Cuisine: BARBECUE. **Reservations:** Not accepted.
$ **Prices:** Lunch $5–$12; dinner $9–$15. AE, DC, MC, V.
   Open: Lunch daily 11am–4pm; dinner daily 4–11pm.
   Children's Services: Children's menu, highchairs, booster seats.

The ever-reliable Tony Roma's offers consistent quality, fast service, and a welcoming attitude toward kids. This attractive location has lots of large picture windows and a lovely view on clear days.

The menu has a mouthwatering assortment of barbecued ribs and chicken, and a few other grilled dishes. Dinners include coleslaw and tangy ranch-style beans, baked potato, or fries. Lunches include most of the same choices. The terrific little children's menu also doubles as a page to color, and offers chicken-in-a-basket, burgers, chicken fingers, and ribs, all with fries for $3 to $5. Servers will be glad to let you split adult portions, and they'll warm baby bottles and baby food in the kitchen.

This Tony Roma's is next to the Universal Studios entrance. Park in the Universal Studios lot ($5).

Other Tony Roma's are in Santa Monica at 319 Santa Monica Boulevard (tel. 213/393-0139) and in Redondo Beach at 20720 South Avalon Street (tel. 213/329-5723).

CHAPTER 8

WHERE KIDS PREFER TO STAY

1. FAMILY-FRIENDLY HOTELS
2. CAMPING

Los Angeles is so large that one of your main considerations when choosing lodgings will probably be location. We have listed hotel choices in the most accessible areas of town—Beverly Hills, the Westside, the Coastal Region (Santa Monica and Marina del Rey), West Hollywood, Universal City, downtown, Hollywood, and at the airport.

Note: If you only have a couple of days in the Los Angeles area and you're planning on spending most of your time at Disneyland, you should consider staying near the park. For information on hotels in Anaheim, near Disneyland, see Section 6, "Orange County," in Chapter 9.

HOTELS   In general, you'll find that hotel prices here are comparable to those in most large cities; thus you won't find as many budget-priced accommodations as you might in a smaller, less popular town. But expense is relative—what may be expensive to one family isn't to another. In this chapter we've listed our hotel recommendations first by location and then by price. Some price ranges will overlap. An "expensive" hotel might end up being "very expensive" if some of the lowest priced rooms are not available. Even a "moderate" hotel may become expensive if children are charged, if the cost of parking is high, or if you must pay for a rollaway or crib. On the other hand, a "very expensive" or "expensive" hotel might become more affordable if you can take advantage of weekend or holiday specials, or family plans. Read each listing carefully to determine which ones meet your needs.

Price categories are as follows: "Very Expensive," $200 to $400 per night for a double room; "Expensive," $150 to $200; "Moderate," $75 to $150; "Budget," less than $75.

Note: All rates are subject to change, and *the rates given do not include the Los Angeles hotel tax of 12.5%.* When you make your reservation, be sure to inquire about family plans, weekend or holiday specials, corporate rates, AAA discounts, senior rates, and any other discounts you might be eligible for.

B&Bs   Bed-and-breakfast accommodations are practically nonexistent in L.A., and those that do exist are geared more for couples who want to spend a romantic weekend away. Thus we have not included them in this guide.

CAMPING   Family camps will take you well out of town. We have included a few camping listings at the end of this chapter. For even more information on camping and other lodging facilities in California, see *Frommer's California with Kids.*

1. FAMILY-FRIENDLY HOTELS

BEVERLY HILLS

VERY EXPENSIVE

BEVERLY HILLS HOTEL AND BUNGALOWS, 9641 Sunset Blvd., Beverly Hills, CA 90210. Tel. 213/276-2251, or toll free 800/283-8885. Fax 213/281-2919. 268 rms and bungalows. A/C TV TEL

$ Rates: $230–$320 single or double (depending on size, view, and furnishings); from $395 suite; three- and four-bedroom bungalows go to $3,100 per night. Additional person $20; crib $20 per stay. AE, DC, MC, V. **Parking:** Valet parking.

Who hasn't heard of the Beverly Hills Hotel, that pink stucco California mission-style legend that embodies early Hollywood? The legend began in 1912, when developer Burton Green (who named Beverly Hills after his home in Beverly Farms, Massachusetts) opened the doors of the city's first major structure, before it became the exclusive area it is today. It wasn't until 1920, when Mary Pickford and Douglas Fairbanks created their famous country home, Pickfair, that other movie stars started to make their way to Beverly Hills. The hotel played host to many of the great and famous. In fact, the acclaimed Polo Lounge got its name because Will Rogers, Darryl Zanuck, and Tommy Hitchcock frequented the restaurant after their polo matches. It's still a watering hole for the powerful and popular.

The swimming pool and cabaña club are reminiscent of bygone days as well. Enormous in size, the pool area is surrounded by 22 private cabañas, surely the repository of Hollywood stories and secrets we wish we were privy to. You can rent a cabaña for $100 per day.

No two rooms in the hotel are identical, but they are all tastefully decorated and most are large. The first-floor rooms have enormous private patios with umbrella tables, chaise longues, and chairs. Rooms have at least two TVs (one in the bathroom), two or three telephones, and game tables and chairs. Some have love seats; others have sofa beds.

The legendary bungalows are like private little homes, separated from the main building and tucked into the lush foliage of the gardens. Each bungalow has a main suite with its own entrance. To this can be added one, two, even three connected guest bedrooms with baths, each with its own entrance. Each bungalow has a kitchen or kitchenette; most have wet bars and full dining areas.

Dining/Entertainment: Only one of the several hotel restaurants is suited for kids, the Fountain Coffee Shop. The small, casual old-fashioned–looking soda fountain serves breakfast, lunch, and snacks. We don't recommend the Polo Lounge for young children, although your teenagers might enjoy star gazing; it offers indoor and outdoor seating for breakfast and lunch, and late supper is also served here. The Dining Room is an elegant gourmet dinner house. Get a baby-sitter for this one too. Poolside food service is available.

Services: Men's and women's hair salons, car rental, limousine service, 24-hour room service, concierge, laundry and valet, on-call physician, baby-sitting services.

Facilities: Swimming pool, cabaña club, business services, gift shop.

BEVERLY HILTON, 9876 Wilshire Blvd., Beverly Hills, CA 90210. Tel. 213/274-7777, or toll free 800/HILTONS. Fax 213/285-1313. 592 rms and suites. A/C MINIBAR TV TEL

$ Rates: Poolside cabaña rooms, $195 single; $215 double. Poolside lanai rooms, $170 single; $190 double. Junior suites, $195 single; $215 double. One- and two-bedroom suites $300–$600. Children—regardless of age—sleep free in their parents' room. Additional adults $20 per night; cribs and rollaways free. Ask about special packages; on the Family Plan, two rooms for the family are charged at the single rate for each room. AE, CB, MC, V. **Parking:** $12 per day.

Conrad Hilton opened this famed hotel in 1955 to a throng of guests that included stars and business tycoons. But regular folks have always been catered to as well. Today the hotel, at the intersection of Wilshire Boulevard and Santa Monica Boulevard, is even more inviting since its $35-million renovation.

One of the two outdoor heated swimming pools is Olympic size, with a shallow end and a large surrounding garden area. The other, a circular pool with a fountain in the center, is 5 feet deep in all spots. The enclosed patio area surrounding it is perfect for children who want to play. Kids under 16 are admitted to the fitness center with a parent.

Guest rooms are located in one of three buildings: the main building, the garden lanai area (rooms around the main pool), and the Palm Court building (with rooms near the fountain pool). Rooms in the main building have balconies large enough to accommodate lounge chairs, and most have an inviting view. These rooms are generally priced higher than the other two locations.

Each room has a desk, mini-refrigerator/honor bar, two telephones, and remote-control television with free HBO, ESPN, and CNN. Bathrooms have marble floors and counters, tub/showers, and bathroom amenities. Bathrobes are provided in most rooms. Rooms with two double beds may have a balcony and a view of Century City; these have two overstuffed chairs and an end table. The rooms with king-size beds feature love seats. Garden lanai rooms, with two double beds, are very large, accommodating a desk and a table and chairs. Junior suites have two baths, a king-size bed, and a sofa bed. One- and two-bedroom suites have two entrances (one directly into the bedroom) and two baths.

Dining/Entertainment: The hotel has three restaurants, a coffee shop, and two lounges. The romantic L'Escoffier Room serves classic French food, and has a lovely view of the city (leave the kids with a sitter, though). Trader Vic's offers Polynesian cuisine, and while a bit on the pricey side, it's a treat for the kids with its festive decor. The poolside Mr. H Restaurant has a tempting array of buffets as well as an à la carte menu for breakfast, lunch, and dinner. Café Beverly serves breakfast, lunch, and dinner and has a children's menu. Both restaurants and the café have highchairs and boosters.

Services: Concierge, multilingual staff, baby-sitting, room service (until 2am), complimentary Lincoln Town Car or Rolls-Royce service within a 2-mile radius, men's and women's salons, car-rental and airline offices, currency exchange, airport shuttle.

Facilities: Fitness center, two outdoor heated swimming pools, gift shop, boutiques.

FOUR SEASONS HOTEL AT BEVERLY HILLS, 300 S. Doheny Dr., Los

Sacramento
★

CALIFORNIA

Los Angeles ◉

Bay View Plaza Holiday Inn **15**

Beverly Hills Hotel and
Bungalows **1**

Beverly Hilton **2**

Beverly Laurel Motor Hotel **23**

Beverly Plaza **21**

Brentwood Suites Hotel **5**

Century Plaza Hotel & Tower **4**

Century Wilshire Hotel **6**

Comfort Inn, Coastal Region **18**

Days Inn Hotel, Los Angeles
Airport **27**

Del Capri Hotel **7**

Four Seasons Hotel at
Beverly Hills **24**

Holiday Inn, Downtown **28**

Holiday Inn Hollywood **25**

Holiday Inn Westwood Plaza
Hotel **8**

Hollywood Roosevelt Hotel **33**

Hyatt Regency Los Angeles **29**

Jamaica Bay Inn **16**

Le Dufy **19**

Le Parc Hotel **20**

Loews Santa Monica
Beach Hotel **11**

Los Angeles Airport Hilton and
Towers **30**

Marina del Rey Hotel **12**

Marina International Hotels
and Bungalow **13**

Miramar Sheraton Hotel **14**

Pacific Shore Hotel **17**

Quality Inn, Airport **31**

Ramada Hotel Beverly Hills **3**

Royal Palace Westwood **9**

Sheraton Universal **26**

Travelodge Los Angeles West **10**

Westin Bonaventure **32**

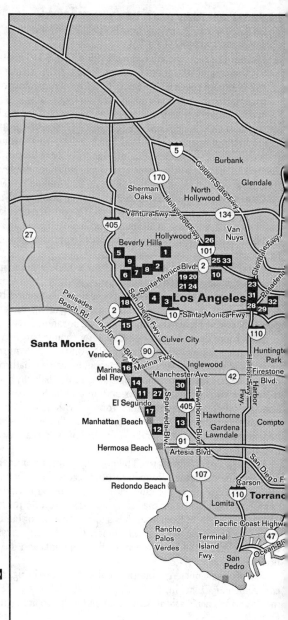

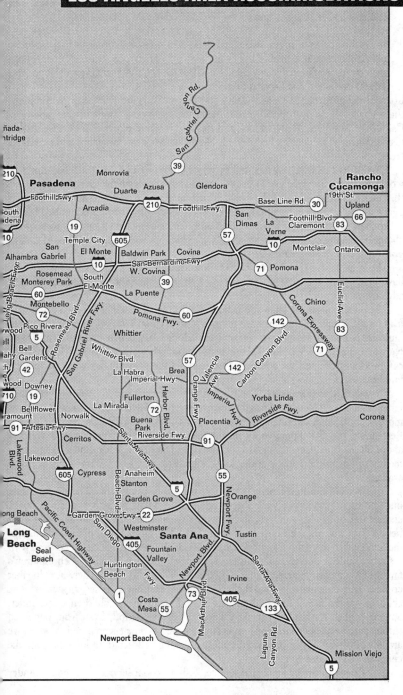

LOS ANGELES AREA ACCOMMODATIONS

Angeles, CA 90048. Tel. 213/273-2222, or toll free 800/332-3442. Fax 213/859-3824. 285 rms and suites. A/C MINIBAR TV TEL

$ Rates: $225–$330 single; $250–$355 double; $500–$2,000 suite. Children stay free in their parents' room. Additional adults $25; cribs and rollaways free. Specials and weekend rates available; the Family Plan offers two rooms (usually connecting) each at the single-occupancy rate. AE, CB, DC, MC, V. **Parking:** Valet parking $13.50 per night; self-parking free.

Located at the corner of Doheny Drive and Burton Way, the Four Seasons combines the richness of a European manor with the easygoing ambience of southern California. Antiques, marble floors, and fresh flowers and plants indoors give way to lush, manicured gardens and courtyards filled with Mexican fan palms and jacaranda trees.

Elegant as the hotel is, the staff is very family oriented, so you need not feel worried about your children. The staff is trained to anticipate the guests' needs—and that includes those of the kids. There is such attention to detail that the staff often personally interviews baby-sitters before recommending them to hotel guests. There is a brochure of children's services and family amenities offered by the hotel at no charge, including car seats and strollers. Older kids are welcome to use board games, pool toys, and playing cards.

The large rooftop pool has a nice shallow area for kids. This is a favorite place to have lunch with the little ones. You can even do your morning exercises directly adjacent to the pool.

The plush rooms are large and beautifully decorated. Each has French doors that lead to a balcony. The rooms have remote-control color TVs, refrigerator/minibars, multiline phones (at least two in a room), terrycloth robes, hairdryers, and a full line of bathroom amenities. We like the Four Seasons rooms best; they have a parlor area that can be closed off, and the additional television in the parlor makes them perfect for families.

Dining/Entertainment: The Café is very informal and is open for breakfast, lunch, dinner, and late into the night; prices range from $8 to $18. Windows Lounge is more sophisticated, offering appetizers, afternoon tea, and cocktails. At the Gardens Restaurant, the fine dining room on the premises, the international menu averages about $8 for breakfast, about $15 for lunch, and $18 to $27 for dinner. Alternative menus for people on low-calorie, low-cholesterol, and low-sodium diets are also available.

An extensive children's menu is available at all hotel restaurants. There's a separate one for room service as well. Prices range from $5.50 to $10. Ice-cream floats, cheesecake, hot-fudge sundaes, and brownies are among the goodies available. And believe it or not, the kids have their own china! The ultimate kid-pleaser, though, is the Sunday brunch, with a genuine 2½-foot-high children's buffet table covered with a special tablecloth and centerpieces. The buffet selection includes such children's favorites as chicken fingers, peanut-butter sandwiches, and pizza. There are alphabet cookies and chocolate beyond belief—M&Ms, Hershey's Kisses, brownies. The children's buffet is $17 for children 5 to 11, and no charge for children 4 and under. Sunday brunch for adults costs $34. Large tables of seafood, fresh fruit, peppered sirloin, pastry-wrapped veal and loin of lamb, as well as omelets prepared to order, are artfully displayed. We've watched the adults debating between the adult tables and the children's selections!

Services: Courtesy limousine service, 24-hour room service, concierge, laundry and valet services, baby-sitting, complimentary shoeshine, twice-daily maid service; hairdryers, refrigerators, and terrycloth robes in the rooms.

Facilities: Rooftop pool, exercise facilities, business services, car- and limousine-rental offices, gift shop.

MODERATE

RAMADA HOTEL BEVERLY HILLS, 1150 S. Beverly Dr., Los Angeles, CA 90035. Tel. 213/553-6561, or toll free 800/2-RAMADA. Fax 213/277-4469. 260 rms. A/C TV TEL

$ Rates: $100–$110 single; $110–$120 double; $175 suite. Children under 12 stay free in their parents' room. Additional adults $10 per night; cribs free; rollaways $10. The Family Plan offers one room, for up to four, at reduced rates; ask about special weekend rates. AE, CB, DC, MC, V. **Parking:** Free.

At Pico Boulevard and Beverly Drive, 1 mile west of Robertson Boulevard, the Ramada is close to central Beverly Hills, and is as good a location as you can get in the city. Kids will like the outdoor heated swimming pool, which gets sun all afternoon. Guests can request privileges at a nearby fitness club, which also features a children's class.

The attractively decorated rooms have either oak or cherrywood furniture, a game table and desk, and a color TV in the armoire, with free cable and pay movies. All rooms above the fourth floor have views. All have tub/shower combinations and bathroom amenities.

Dining/Entertainment: Summerfield's serves breakfast, lunch, and dinner with prices ranging from $2.75 (breakfast) to $15 (dinner). The little children's menu offers such favorites as spaghetti, hamburgers, hot dogs, chicken, and sandwiches for $1.75 to $2.25. Breakfast is also available.

Services: Room service (6am to 10pm), baby-sitting referrals, 1-day valet service, bathroom amenities, privileges at nearby fitness club.

Facilities: Outdoor heated swimming pool, gift shop.

THE WESTSIDE REGION

VERY EXPENSIVE

CENTURY PLAZA HOTEL & TOWER, 2025 Ave. of the Stars, Los Angeles, CA 90067. Tel. 213/277-2000, or toll free 800/228-3000. Fax 213/551-3355. 750 rms and suites (hotel), 322 rms (tower). A/C MINIBAR TV TEL

$ Rates: Century Plaza, $175–$202 single; $205–$235 double; $300–$1,025 suite. Tower, $225–$265 single; $255–$295 double; $1,100–$1,300 suite; Plaza Suite $5,000. Children 18 and under stay free in their parents' room. Additional adults $25; cribs free; rollaways free for children, $25 for adults. Ask about special weekend rates. AE, CB, DC, MC, V. **Parking:** Valet parking $15 per day; self-parking $8 per day.

Located two blocks south of Santa Monica Boulevard in the heart of Century City, this curving 20-story structure sits on 14 acres of tropical gardens, interlaced with reflecting pools and fountains. Designed by the celebrated Japanese architect Minoru Yamasaki, the Century Plaza opened in 1966, and in 1984 the $85-million Tower at the Century Plaza was added. Since its opening the hotel has played host to the wealthy and powerful, and to every U.S. president. You're as likely to see a television or movie "shoot" in one of the patio areas as you once were able to spot stars on Hollywood Boulevard.

Plush furnishings, inlaid marble floors, and an exceptional collection of fine art and rare antique pieces grace the colonnaded lobbies and richly decorated public areas. A pianist plays in the grand lobby during the afternoon. Lest you think this is all too grand for your little ones, the hotel staff is accommodating and friendly to children. Alert the reservationist you are bringing your children and they'll get their own amenity pack filled with such goodies as jacks and a ball, an inflatable beach ball, and crayons and coloring books. Each building has its own spacious pool area.

Rooms in the Century Plaza are inviting, with their plush carpets, custom-designed fabrics, oversize lounge chairs, and stunning armoires. Every room has a spacious balcony, three telephones, wall safes, desk, and 25-inch remote-control TV with cable channels. Tower rooms are larger and are similarly furnished.

Dining/Entertainment: Café Plaza, the informal restaurant reminiscent of a sidewalk café in Paris, is perfect for families. Prices range from $10 to $15 for breakfast, lunch, and dinner, and box lunches are available to take to the beach or on a hike. The Garden Pavilion, also open for three meals, overlooks the reflecting pools and hotel gardens. Breakfast prices are $10 to $12, lunch is $8.25 to $13, and dinner goes for $20 to $25; Sunday brunch is $23.75 for adults, $19 for kids. The Terrace Restaurant, in the Tower, is open daily for lunch ($7 to $14), and Monday through Saturday for dinner ($20 to $25). All these restaurants have highchairs and boosters and will provide children's portions.

For truly fine dining, hire a baby-sitter and reserve a table at La Chaumière at the Tower. With the ambience of a European club, amid alderwood paneling, upholstered burled-elm chairs, and five enormous 18th-century French paintings, guests dine on classic French and nouvelle California cuisine. It's open for both lunch and dinner; main dishes range from $11 to $16 at lunch, $16 to $35 at dinner.

Services: Concierge staff, baby-sitting, multilingual staff, twice-daily maid service, same-day laundry and valet, complimentary shoeshine (the Tower), 24-hour room service, amenity pack for children.

Facilities: Business center, pools, shopping arcade.

MODERATE

BRENTWOOD SUITES HOTEL, 199 N. Church Lane, Los Angeles, CA 90049. Tel. 213/476-6255, or toll free 800/235-8990. Fax 213/471-4285. 60 suites. A/C TV TEL

$ Rates (including continental breakfast): $78–$85 single; $86–$95 double. Children under 12 stay free in their parents' room. Additional guests $8; cribs free; rollaways $8 per night. AE, CB, DC, MC, V. **Parking:** Free.

Although its location is wonderfully convenient, just north of Sunset Boulevard at the San Diego Freeway (I-405), this all-suite hotel is literally right next to the freeway. However, there is a Plexiglas sound wall around most rooms to block out most of the noise, so that once you're in the rooms the sound is muffled. As it has a 95% occupancy rate, many people obviously do not find this a drawback at all. Ironically, because of its position near the freeway, it was built into the hills so the back of the rooms look out onto a wooded area with a tree-lined trail for walking.

The motor inn has very large rooms, with two highback chairs, an eating table, and a small but complete kitchen with a dishwasher. The "king suites" (or "town-house suites") are split-level units that are much like apartments. In addition to the kitchen, there is a king-size bed upstairs (with a TV and phone), and a full-size sofa bed downstairs in the living-room area. The living room also has a TV, a telephone, and four comfortable chairs. The bathrooms are a good size.

Services: Car-rental service.

Facilities: Heated pool, spa, sauna, coin-operated laundry.

CENTURY WILSHIRE HOTEL, 10776 Wilshire Blvd., Los Angeles, CA 90024. Tel. 213/474-4506, or toll free 800/421-7223. Fax 213/474-2535. 99 rms. A/C TEL TV

$ Rates (including continental breakfast): $65–$75 single; $75–$85 double; $80–$95 junior suite ($475–$550 weekly); $125–$150 suite ($750–$875 weekly). Additional guests above double occupancy $5 each; cribs and rollaways $10 per night. AE, DC, MC, V. **Parking:** Free.

This charming European-style hotel exudes a homey ambience that's inviting to families. The staff takes the time to get to know the guests (some of whom stay for weeks and even months), and take pleasure in assisting them. The hotel draws an eclectic mix: the staff of consulates (who stay while looking for permanent residences), traveling businesspeople, and families. The location is great—right on Wilshire Boulevard (between Selby Avenue and Westwood Boulevard) outside Westwood Village, easily accessible to the beach, the freeway, and Beverly Hills.

The heated pool, good for lap swimming, with a nice shallow area for the kids, sits in a large garden with palm and banana trees. There are plenty of chaise longues and umbrella tables. The full continental breakfast can be enjoyed in the garden courtyard or in the breakfast room that opens onto the garden.

Rooms are clean and airy, with lace curtains and comfortably worn furniture. Some have balconies with poolside views. All have stall showers; some have separate bathtubs. Rooms with two double beds are spacious. Junior suites and one-bedroom suites have fully equipped kitchens that will meet your basic needs (no dishwasher). The suites have full dining areas and plenty of storage space.

Services: Multilingual staff, valet service, baby-sitting.

Facilities: Heated pool.

DEL CAPRI HOTEL, 10587 Wilshire Blvd., Los Angeles, CA 90024. Tel. 213/474-3511, or toll free 800/44-HOTEL. Fax 213/470-9999. 81 units. A/C TV TEL

$ Rates: $74–$79 single; $84–$89 double; kitchenette suites, $94–$104 single, $104–$114 double. Children under 12 stay free in their parents' room. Additional adults $10 per night; cribs free; rollaways $10. AE, CB, DC, MC, V. **Parking:** Free.

This is an excellent accommodation for the price, and is a charming place to spend several days. With its great location (at Westholme Avenue and Wilshire Boulevard in Westwood), garden patio, heated pool, newly refurbished rooms, and excellent prices, it's a great deal.

Rooms are sleek and unusual, with lacquered furniture, cylindrical side tables and coffee tables, decorated in tan, light rose, and mint green. Each room has a combination whirlpool tub/shower, cable color TV with a free movie channel, and game tables with chairs. Over half the rooms have small but complete kitchens. These kitchenette suites are like compact one-bedroom apartments with a sofa bed in the parlor. There's plenty of room to spread out, and both the parlor and bedroom have a TV. You can request kitchenette suites with different bed configurations, so let the reservationist know how many children you'll have with you and their ages when you make your plans. There are even some suites that connect with another bedroom.

Facilities: Heated pool.

HOLIDAY INN WESTWOOD PLAZA HOTEL, 10740 Wilshire Blvd., Los Angeles, CA 90024. Tel. 213/475-8711, or toll free 800/472-8556. Fax 213/475-5220. 300 rms. A/C MINIBAR TV TEL

$ **Rates:** $110–$118 single; $128–$138 double; $150–$350 suite. Children under 18 stay free in their parents' room. Cribs free; rollaways $10. AE, CB, DC, MC, V.
Parking: Valet parking $3; self-parking free.

This fabulous location, three blocks east of Westwood Boulevard at Selby Avenue and Wilshire Boulevard in Westwood, is within walking distance of Westwood Village and, like the Century Wilshire, is close to the freeway and the beach. Complimentary transportation is available to Century City, UCLA, Brentwood, and Beverly Hills.

Our favorite part of the hotel is the charming ground-level promenade arcade, housing the gift shop, video games, and exercise room (which can be used by kids under 14 when accompanied by an adult). It leads outside to the lovely pool and spa; the pool is heated year round and has a great shallow area for young kids.

Standard rooms have two double beds with Queen Anne–style furniture, side chairs, and a game table and desk. You can also choose a room with one queen-size bed and a small couch. Suites come with one or two baths, and depending on the suite, may have a large living room with a couch, desk, and comfortable chairs. Free cable TV is in each room, as is pay-per-view SpectraVision. There are tub/shower combinations and the usual bathroom amenities.

Dining/Entertainment: Café Le Dome serves breakfast, lunch, and dinner from 6:30am to 10:30pm. It has an extensive children's menu with prices ranging from $1.25 to $3.50.

Services: Concierge, room service (6:30am to 2:30pm and 5 to 10pm), complimentary morning newspaper, complimentary transportation within a 3-mile radius.

Facilities: Heated pool, spa, exercise room, gift shop, video games.

BUDGET

ROYAL PALACE WESTWOOD, 1052 Tiverton Ave., Los Angeles, CA 90024. Tel. 213/208-6677, or toll free 800/631-0100. Fax 213/824-3732. 35 rms. A/C TV TEL

$ **Rates:** $67–$70 single; $73–$76 double; minisuites, $75 single, $81 double; one-bedroom suites, $90 single, $96 double. Children under 12 stay free in their parents' room. Additional adults $6 per night; cribs and rollaways $6. AE, CB, DC, MC, V. **Parking:** Limited free parking.

Located one block north of Wilshire Boulevard in the heart of Westwood Village, the Royal Palace is a small, simple motor inn. You are paying for an ideal location within walking distance of more than 80 restaurants, 20 first-run movie theaters, and many shops and department stores. You're also on one of the few convenient major bus routes that will take you to the beach, Century City, and Beverly Hills.

Each room has a small but complete kitchenette with an eating area. The standard rooms with one queen-size bed are on the small side if you have to bring in a crib. If you can afford it, go for a room with two queen-size beds, as these are much larger rooms that will accommodate a crib and don't cost that much more. The suites feature a queen-size sofa bed with a very small bedroom in which a king-size bed and dresser just fit. The closet space is very large. Suites also have complete kitchens and nice bathrooms. Cable TV channels are available in all rooms.

TRAVELODGE LOS ANGELES WEST, 10740 Santa Monica Blvd., Los Angeles, CA 90025. Tel. 213/474-4576, or toll free 800/255-3050. Fax 213/470-3117. 55 rms. A/C TV TEL

$ Rates: $57–$63 single, $64–$68 double with a queen- or king-size bed, $68 with two twin beds, $68–$72 with a queen-size bed plus two twin beds, $75–$79 with two queen-size beds. One or two children under 17 stay free in parents' room if no additional beds are requested. Cribs free; rollaways $7. AE, CB, DC, MC, V. **Parking:** Free.

This is a clean little two-story motel conveniently situated at Overland Boulevard and Santa Monica Boulevard in West L.A., and within walking distance of fast-food establishments. There is a small heated pool (gated and locked), and refrigerators are in all rooms. Rooms are comfortable, newly remodeled, and what you'd expect from a budget motel in pricey West Los Angeles. Units have game tables, color TVs, instant coffee makers, radios, and showers; some have tub/shower combinations. Connecting rooms are available.

THE COASTAL REGION

VERY EXPENSIVE

LOEWS SANTA MONICA BEACH HOTEL, 1700 Ocean Ave., Santa Monica, CA 90401. Tel. 213/458-6700, or toll free 800/223-0888. Fax 213/458-6761. 349 rms and suites. A/C MINIBAR TV TEL

$ Rates: $155–$285 single; $175–$305 double; from $300 suite. Children under 18 stay free in their parents' room. Additional adults $20 per day; cribs free. AE, CB, DC, MC, V. **Parking:** Valet $10 per day; self-parking $8 per day.

Loews is the only beachfront hotel in Los Angeles. On Ocean Avenue between Pico Boulevard and Colorado Avenue, overlooking the Pacific, this airy, lavish hotel is just two blocks from the Santa Monica Pier.

The hotel offers a complete children's program during the summer called the "Splash Club," designed for children between 5 and 12 years old. The club operates from 10am to 4pm, 7 days a week (based on demand) and costs $25 per day per child, including lunch and snack. The club staff takes kids to the historic Santa Monica Pier where they ride the carousel and play arcade games. They tour the kitchen and take cooking classes in pizza making and cookie baking. And they play in the hotel's private playground and swimming pools with pool and beach toys the hotel provides. The hotel offers arts and crafts, puppet shows, treasure hunts, and kite flying. The kids can be enrolled in the Friday- and Saturday-night programs, from 7 to 10pm, for an additional fee. Reserve the Splash Club in advance.

Each of the hotel's rooms and suites has three TVs, three phones (two phone lines—a reminder of home for those of you with preteens and teens), bathrobes, and all the amenities you'd expect of a first-class hotel. Request rooms with either a king-size bed or two doubles.

Dining/Entertainment: There are two restaurants in the hotel, and poolside snack service.

Services: Children's program during the summer, concierge, twice-daily maid service, 24-hour room service, dry cleaning, shoeshine, beauty salon services, baby-sitting, bike and roller-skate rental.

Facilities: Indoor/outdoor swimming pool, Jacuzzi, fitness center.

EXPENSIVE

MARINA DEL REY HOTEL, 13534 Bali Way, Marina del Rey, CA 90292. Tel. 213/301-1000, or toll free 800/882-4000 or 800/8-MARINA. Fax 213/301-8167. 159 rms and suites. A/C TV TEL

$ Rates: $120–$185 single; $140–$205 double; $350–$400 suite. Children under 12 stay free in their parents' room if additional beds are not needed. Cribs free; rollaways $15. AE, DC, MC, V. **Parking:** Free.

Ah, to be so close to the city and yet feel so far away . . . that's the Marina Del Rey Hotel, the only hotel in the marina that's right on the water. As you drive to the end of Bali Way, you're encircled by masts of sailboats and yachts. At the end, between Lincoln Boulevard and Admiralty Way, sits the three-story white stucco building with royal-blue awnings and a rather grand entryway, all set on the main canal of the Marina del Rey harbor. Inside, a small three-story atrium lobby gives the upper floors a sense of openness. There's a seating area on each floor that serves as a mini-lobby with couches, tables, and a patio. Outside the grounds are beautiful, and almost every room has a view. The swimming pool has a large shallow area and lots of room for kids to play; the adults can relax, surrounded by water and boats.

All the rooms have remote-control color TV with free cable channels and Select TV. There are pay movies with locks so that children can't turn on the movies without your consent. Most of the rooms have balconies with chairs and a table so you can enjoy the view and sea breeze. The rooms themselves have nice bathrooms done in marble, tub/shower combinations, separate vanity areas, and closets with floor-to-ceiling mirrors. Accommodations are good-sized and comfortable, recently remodeled (1990). Those with two double beds have enough space for the kids and their toys; the room with a king-size bed has adequate space for a crib or rollaway. Suites are available and can connect to rooms with two double beds.

Dining/Entertainment: The Dockside Café is a glassed-in room facing the water that serves a variety of breakfast and lunch items, with prices ranging from $4.50 to $9.95. The Crystal Seahorse is the small waterfront terrace restaurant that serves dinner nightly; prices range from $14.50 to $19.50. Both restaurants have highchairs and boosters.

Services: Room service, laundry and valet service, car-rental desk, Marina cruise-line service, shuttle service to the airport.

Facilities: Swimming pool, putting green, gift shop, ice machines; refrigerators, irons, and hairdryers free upon request.

MARINA INTERNATIONAL HOTELS AND BUNGALOWS, 4200 Admiral-

ty Way, Marina del Rey, CA 90292. Tel. 213/301-2000, or toll free
800/882-4000. Fax 213/301-6657. 135 rms. A/C TV TEL
$ **Rates:** $100–$145 single; $120–$180 double; $170 junior suite (double occupancy); $198–$288 bungalow or suite. Children under 16 stay free in their parents'
room. Additional adults $15; cribs and rollaways free. AE, DC, MC, V. **Parking:**
Free.

This small hotel, in a pleasant garden setting at the corner of Palawan Way and
Admiralty Way, across the street from a calm sandy beach, is just perfect for families.
Although a bit pricey, it's probably the best value in this price range if you want
something near the water. You have your choice of rooms in the main building or a
garden bungalow.

The two-story lobby resembles a large cheery sitting room or enclosed patio.
There's a huge skylight and plants that continue the outdoor effect. You can enjoy
happy-hour appetizers served in the adjacent lounge. The pool area is very pretty and
is tucked away and safe, and there's a large shallow area for the kids.

The very large rooms are done in a sunny southwestern motif in light sand and
turquoise colors that add to the life of the place. Plantation shutters filter the light and
give privacy. All rooms have balconies and come with free remote-control cable TV,
Select TV, and pay movies. There are game tables and chairs, desks, and AM/FM
clock radios. Bathrooms have marble floors; most come with tub/shower combinations (but specify your needs, because some bungalows have showers only). There are
complete bathroom amenity baskets.

Bungalows are located in a charming, flower-filled courtyard where there is ample
space for kids to wander. The ones on the ground floor have balconies that are
cordoned off by planters so that toddlers won't wander off. Bungalows are split-level
rooms with a loft, cathedral ceilings, and large windows. There are huge walk-in
closets, two TVs, two telephones, a double bed, and a sofa bed.

Dining/Entertainment: The Crystal Fountain Restaurant is open for breakfast,
a deli lunch buffet, and a prime rib dinner buffet. They have highchairs and boosters,
but no children's menu. Prices range from $3.25 to $7.25 for breakfast, around $7 for
lunch, and $7.50 to $16 for dinner. The typical buffet brunch runs $12.95.

Services: Airport shuttle service, 24-hour room service, baby-sitting.

Facilities: Swimming pool, vending and ice machines, nearby self-service laundry
and shopping center.

**MIRAMAR SHERATON HOTEL, 101 Wilshire Blvd., Santa Monica, CA
90401. Tel. 213/394-3731,** or toll free 800/325-3535. Fax 213/458-7912.
305 rms, 60 suites. A/C MINIBAR TV TEL
$ **Rates:** Poolside bungalows, $125 single, $145 double; Palisades rooms, $155
single, $175 double; Ocean Tower rooms, $165 single, $170 double; Palisades
one-bedroom suites, $160 single, $185 double. Ocean Tower suites start at $275.
Children under 18 stay free in their parents' room. Additional adults $20; cribs free.
AE, CB, DC, MC, V. **Parking:** Free.

The Miramar sits on the bluff across the street from Palisades Park at the end of
Wilshire Boulevard at Ocean Avenue, and close to the Santa Monica Pier and all the
Santa Monica beaches. Its rich history began over 100 years ago when U.S. Sen. John
P. Jones bought the land for $1 and built a private mansion (completed in 1889) on the
spot and called it Miramar ("view of the sea"). Jones, a prosperous politician, struck it
rich in the silver mines. Looking for a place to build a railroad and harbor so he could

carry his silver to be minted in San Francisco, he chose Santa Monica Bay as the port for his endeavor. With his partner, Col. Robert Baker, he founded the city of Santa Monica. At the Miramar, political figures and other luminaries have come and gone, including Susan B. Anthony, Mark Twain, and Greta Garbo, who were all drawn to the ocean view and the hotel's lovely tropical gardens. The story goes that Betty Grable was discovered at the hotel.

You can choose accommodations from the two towers or the small garden bungalows. The Ocean Tower and Palisades rooms are newly renovated and come two ways—traditional, with dark woods and elaborate moldings; or in light pastels with rattan and bleached-wood furniture, and polished brass fixtures. You can select from rooms with a king-size bed or with two double beds. Each room has an honor bar/refrigerator, game table, color TV, in-room safe, and bathroom amenities. Most have tub/shower combinations, but request one specifically if it's important to you.

Dining/Entertainment: The Café is open from 6:30am to midnight. The children's menu offers breakfast for $1.25 to $2, and lunch and dinner dishes run $1.25 to $2.50. The little menu includes games and mazes to keep the kids occupied.

The Garden Room is a delightful poolside eatery open for lunch on weekdays from 11:30am to 2pm. The International Room offers elegant dining from 6 to 10pm, and the Stateroom Lounge is open for cocktails nightly, serving complimentary hors d'oeuvres during the week from 5 to 8pm. Children must be accompanied by an adult.

Services: Concierge, 24-hour room service, complimentary newspaper, laundry and valet service, nightly turn-down, limousine and car rentals, men's and women's hair salons.

Facilities: Swimming pool, gift shops, boutiques.

MODERATE

BAY VIEW PLAZA HOLIDAY INN, 530 Pico Blvd., Santa Monica, CA 90405. Tel. 213/399-9344, or toll free 800/HOLIDAY. Fax 213/399-2504. 309 rms and suites. A/C MINIBAR TV TEL

$ Rates: $75–$115 single; $75–$125 double; $250 suite. Children 18 and under stay free in their parents' room. Cribs free; rollaways $10. AE, CB, DC, MC, V.
Parking: Free.

This full-service hotel, with its four-story atrium-style lobby, is done in contemporary Santa Fe style. It's not too big, but you'll have plenty of space to stroll with the kids.

Of the 309 rooms and suites, four have private outdoor Jacuzzis. The rooms are standard size, and most have balconies. Each has cable color TV with remote control and pay-per-view movies, bathroom amenities, and nice views. Some of the accommodations have sofa beds; some have two bathroom sinks and vanities. Most rooms have a tub/shower combination, and most are equipped with a minibar/refrigerator.

Dining/Entertainment: The BayView Café serves breakfast, lunch, and dinner, featuring such American standards as hotcakes, burgers, and seafood. Breakfast costs $4.25 to $8, lunch is $6 to $10, and dinner runs $7.75 to $18.25. The Café has highchairs, boosters, and a children's menu. The piano bar is open nightly, with complimentary hors d'oeuvres served from 5pm.

Services: Room service (6am to 11pm), baby-sitting, complimentary afternoon hors d'oeuvres, bathroom amenities.

Facilities: Two swimming pools, two Jacuzzis, fitness room, gift shop, beauty salon.

JAMAICA BAY INN, 4175 Admiralty Way, Marina del Rey, CA 90292.
Tel. 213/823-5333. Fax 213/823-1325. 42 rms. A/C TV TEL

$ Rates: $90–$115 double with two queen-size beds, $90–$125 double with a king-size bed, $100–$145 deluxe double with a king-size bed and a queen-size sofa bed. Children under 12 stay free in their parents' room. Cribs free; rollaways $10. AE, CB, DC, MC, V. **Parking:** Free self-parking.

For a nice basic room without a lot of extras, the Jamaica Bay Inn is an appropriate choice. Directly on the beach at Palawan Way and Admiralty Way, the motel has a coffee shop (with highchairs and boosters), a bar, and a nice swimming pool and patio. Watch the little ones, though—the recreation area is not enclosed.

The second-story bayside rooms have extraordinary views of either the beach or the city. Ceilings are high, and the rooms are away from the hubbub of the downstairs walk-through lobby. The spacious, bright units have color TV, king- or queen-size beds, and a balcony or patio. Deluxe rooms have a game table and chairs, wet bar, refrigerator, and microwave oven. Rooms with two queen-size beds have lots of extra space for the kids to play in.

Dining/Entertainment: The coffee shop is open from 6am to 11pm. The menu runs from $3 to $8 for breakfast and lunch, and $6 to $11 for dinner.

Services: Room service (6am to 11pm).

Facilities: Swimming pool.

PACIFIC SHORE HOTEL, 1819 Ocean Ave., Santa Monica, CA 90401.
Tel. 213/451-8711, or toll free 800/241-3848. Fax 213/394-6657. 168 rms. A/C MINIBAR TV TEL

$ Rates (including continental breakfast): $110–$120 single; $120–$130 double. Children 12 and under stay free in their parents' room. Additional adult $10; cribs free; rollaways $10 per night. AE, DC, V. **Parking:** Free.

The big attraction at the Pacific Shore, on Ocean Avenue at Pico Boulevard, is its proximity to the beach, which is across the street. It has an unimpeded view of the ocean, so that even second-floor ocean-view rooms have a great vista. This is very much a family-oriented establishment: The staff will refer you to a baby-sitting agency. You can request refrigerators when you make your reservation, at $10 per night. The swimming pool area is pleasant and spacious, and the shallow end of the pool can be cordoned off to keep little swimmers out of the deep end.

The rooms are decorated in California pastels and accented with rattan furniture. They all have cable color TV, pay-per-view in-room movies, AM/FM radios, small desks, tub/shower combinations, and bathroom toiletries. The best family rooms are those with two double beds, but there are also rooms with king-size beds. Connecting rooms can have a king-size bed and two double beds. In fact, you can connect three rooms: those with two double beds on either side and one with a king-size bed in the middle.

Dining/Entertainment: A Baker's Square restaurant is adjacent to the hotel. These are nice coffee shops with reasonable prices. A complete children's menu has main dishes for about $1.75. And room service provides a children's menu.

Services: Guest laundry, same-day valet service, baby-sitting, room service (7am to 10pm).

Facilities: Swimming pool and spa area, gift shop.

BUDGET

COMFORT INN, 2815 Santa Monica Blvd., Santa Monica, CA 90404. Tel. **213/828-5517,** or toll free 800/228-5150. Fax 213/829-6084. 101 rms. A/C TV TEL.

$ Rates: $55–$75 single; $65–$85 double. Children under 17 stay free in their parents' room. Cribs and rollaways $10. AE, CB, DC, MC, V. **Parking:** Free.

Ⓢ This well-kept and clean motel on Santa Monica Boulevard at Yale Street, is an excellent choice for the money. Although it isn't within walking distance of the beach (which is 10 minutes away), it's just minutes by car from Westwood, Brentwood, and Santa Monica. It has a large swimming pool with a good-size shallow area. There's plenty of room for kids to wander or play on the patios, and tables are provided. The staff is friendly and is used to families.

The rooms are tidy and surprisingly good-sized. All have tub/shower combinations, coffee makers, oversize closets, and game tables. Request a room on the third floor, which is generally brighter. Rooms with two double beds are especially large and have plenty of room for a crib. The units with king-size beds have small love seats. Adjoining rooms are available.

WEST HOLLYWOOD

VERY EXPENSIVE

LE DUFY, 1000 Westmount Dr., West Hollywood, CA 90069. Tel. **213/657-7400,** or toll free 800/424-4443. Fax 213/854-6744. 103 rms. A/C MINIBAR TV TEL

$ Rates: $185–$225 single or double. Children under 12 stay free in their parents' room. Additional guests $25; cribs and rollaways free. AE, CB, DC, MC, V. **Parking:** $6 daily with in-and-out privileges.

The advantages of Le Dufy are that it is centrally located in a quiet residential area (on Westmount Drive a block west of La Cienega Boulevard and a block north of Santa Monica Boulevard), is fairly small, and offers apartmentlike accommodations that are very comfortable and affordable, especially for longer stays. The pool, spa, and garden on the rooftop provide good views.

The contemporary apricot-and-lavender suites, all converted apartments, are furnished with king-size beds, pullout sofas in the living room, gas fireplaces, remote-control cable TVs, and private balconies. There's a small eating area and a long, narrow living room. In the executive suites the bedroom is semiprivate, divided by a curtain; in the one-bedroom suites it's completely private. Kitchens are standard, but request dishes and pots and pans ahead of time. Hairdryers and full-length mirrors are provided, along with every woman's dream for a hotel amenity—a makeup mirror with makeup lights.

Dining/Entertainment: The Café du Soleil is the hotel's small restaurant, offering moderately priced California-style cuisine. It's open from 7am to 11pm and also provides room service. A children's menu is available.

Services: Coin-operated laundry, daily valet service, hairdryers, baby-sitting, room service.

Facilities: Pool, spa.

LE PARC HOTEL, 733 N. West Knoll Dr., West Hollywood, CA 90069.

Tel. 213/855-8888, or toll free 800/424-4443. Fax 213/659-7812. 154 rms. A/C MINIBAR TV TEL

$ Rates: $165–$175 single or double; $205–$235 one-bedroom suite. Children under 12 stay free in their parents' room. Additional guests $25; cribs and rollaways free. AE, CB, DC, MC, V. **Parking:** $6 daily with in-and-out privileges.

You may wonder why we are recommending yet another all-suite hotel, one in the same general neighborhood and owned by the same people. Like its sibling hotel, Le Parc is set in a quiet residential neighborhood, north of Melrose Avenue and a block west of La Cienega Boulevard, convenient to Beverly Hills, downtown, and many local attractions. This all-suite hotel (actually a converted apartment building) hides a small outdoor pool, sundeck, spa, and tennis court on the roof.

The warm, comfortable rooms come with gas fireplaces, two phone lines, and nice-size closets. In the standard executive suites, and the slightly larger deluxe suites, the bedrooms are a step up from the living area, separated by a curtain, and there is a hide-a-bed in the living room. While there is enough room for a crib, adding a rollaway would be difficult. The deluxe suites have two remote-control TVs; the standard suites, one. All have cable stations and VCRs, and movies are available at the front desk. One-bedroom suites have completely private bedrooms.

All sorts of snacks are available in the cocktail cabinet in your generous-size kitchenette (which you must request). Management will supply appliances, cookware, and dishes at your request, and room service will do the dishes. Some suites have a full-size refrigerator as well.

Dining/Entertainment: Café Le Parc is open only to guests. Although there are no children's menus, breakfast choices will appeal to most youngsters. Lunch, with a French menu, also offers the ever-faithful cheeseburger. Dinner is for the sophisticated—and rich—only. There are boosters and highchairs. In the evening, complimentary cocktails and hors d'oeuvres are served in the restaurant.

Services: Baby-sitting, valet.

Facilities: Outdoor pool, sundeck, spa, tennis court, videocassette library.

MODERATE

BEVERLY PLAZA, 8384 W. 3rd St., Los Angeles, CA 90048. Tel. 213/658-6600, or toll free 800/62-HOTEL, 800/33-HOTEL in California. Fax 213/653-3464. 98 rms and suites. A/C MINIBAR TV TEL

$ Rates: Standard rooms, $110 single, $120 double; superior rooms, $125 single, $135 double; deluxe rooms, $155 single, $165 double. Children under 12 stay free in their parents' room. Additional guests $10; cribs free; rollaways $10. Ask about special weekend rates. AE, CB, DC, MC, V. **Parking:** $5 daily with in-and-out privileges.

This hotel is well located at 3rd Street and Orlando Avenue, one block east of La Cienega Boulevard, just adjacent to Beverly Hills. Complimentary van service (by appointment) will shuttle you to and from anywhere within a 5-mile radius. There is a tiny, shallow pool perfect for young children. Poolside food service is provided.

Almost half the rooms are designated no-smoking. Good-size double rooms with two queen-size beds can be rented with connecting units. You'll find space for a crib in a standard room, but a rollaway would be tight. The decor is French provincial, and rooms are furnished with a writing desk plus a small table and two chairs.

Remote-control TVs with cable channels and minibars are hidden behind cabinets and armoires. All rooms have VCRs, or one can be requested at the front desk; there are adult and children's movies for rent in the lobby. Minisuites are roomy and are equipped with a king-size bed and double-size hide-a-bed in addition to the standard furnishings. All rooms have hairdryers and phones in the bathrooms. Tub/shower combinations are featured in the small bathrooms, and closet doors double as full-length mirrors.

Dining/Entertainment: Rembrandt's serves three meals a day. We're told that lots of families dine here, but other than chicken in a basket (at $7) and a hamburger ($5.50), there isn't much on the menu for youngsters. There are excellent casual neighborhood restaurants within walking distance.

Services: 24-hour room service, VCRs, hairdryers, terrycloth robes, complimentary shuttle.

Facilities: Small pool, health club, sauna, beauty salon.

BUDGET

BEVERLY LAUREL MOTOR HOTEL, 8018 Beverly Blvd., Los Angeles, CA 90048. Tel. 213/651-2441, or toll free 800/962-3524. 52 rms. A/C TV TEL
$ Rates: $51 single; $57 double. Kitchenette rooms $10 extra. Extra children and adults $5; cribs and rollaways $3. AE, CB, DC, MC, V. **Parking:** Free.

This is an older family-run motel with rooms that overlook a small pool/courtyard area. On Beverly Boulevard, three blocks west of Fairfax Avenue, it's within walking distance of many small restaurants, and there is one on the premises (with limited hours) not owned by the hotel. You can get room service, but you may not charge it to your room. A coin-operated laundry is one block away.

Corner rooms with kitchenettes are great for families. Dishes and small pots are provided, but bring your own coffeepot. There are two double beds (with room for a crib or rollaway) and tub/shower combinations. Watch out for the floor heater if you have crawlers or toddlers with you. Many of the double rooms have been redecorated and have tiny microwaves and refrigerators. These rooms, with two double beds, would be crowded with a crib or rollaway. Most have large shower stalls. If you need a tub, be sure to request one in advance.

UNIVERSAL CITY

SHERATON UNIVERSAL, 333 Universal Terrace Pkwy., Universal City, CA 91608. Tel. 818/980-1212, or toll free 800/325-3535. Fax 818/985-4980. 446 rms and suites. A/C MINIBAR TV TEL
$ Rates: $150–$190 single; $170–$210 double; from $210 executive suite; $400 large suite. Connecting rooms available. Children 17 and under stay free in their parents' room. Cribs free; rollaways $15. AE, CB, DC, MC, V. **Parking:** $7.50 per day.

The Sheraton is located just off the Hollywood Freeway (U.S. 101) at Lankershim Boulevard and Ventura Boulevard, on the lot of Universal Studios, perched high above the San Fernando Valley floor. Many of the rooms literally overlook the famous studio and others have views of the Hollywood Hills. Rooms are located in either the 20-story tower or in the two-story poolside lanai buildings. The enchanting outdoor pool area is surrounded by clusters of tall palm trees and umbrellas, offering shade to outdoor diners and a wonderful area for sun worshippers. The pool has a large shallow area and lots of space.

Rooms are spanking new, light and bright, set off with pastels and light-wood furniture. You can choose a room with a king-size bed (with a comfortable overstuffed chaise longue), two double beds, and parlor suites that have king-size beds with full-size sectional couches. Deluxe suites have a sleeping room that closes off, and a parlor. All rooms have a fancy phone system with "call waiting," a direct-dial to hotel services, and phone jacks that allow you to move the phone around the room. Remote-control TV comes with free HBO and video checkout, and pay SpectraVision. All bathrooms have tub/shower combinations as well as the usual toiletries.

Dining/Entertainment: The hotel's restaurant, Californias, serves breakfast ($2.50 to $10.50), lunch ($7 to $11), and dinner (averaging $16). Kids can get a hot dog or hamburger for around $3. In addition, numerous good restaurants are within walking distance.

Services: Concierge, 24-hour room service, laundry and valet, complimentary shuttle service to Universal Studios Tours, toiletry amenities.

Facilities: Gift shop, outdoor pool.

DOWNTOWN

HYATT REGENCY LOS ANGELES, 711 S. Hope St., Los Angeles, CA 90017. Tel. 213/683-1234, or toll free 800/233-1234. Fax 213/629-3230. 485 rms and suites. A/C TV TEL

$ Rates: $175 single; $200 double; $225–$550 suite. Children under 18 stay free in their parents' room. Additional adults $25; cribs and rollaways free. Inquire about weekend and holiday rates. AE, CB, DC, MC, V. **Parking:** $12 daily, with in-and-out privileges.

The rooms here are quite lovely, having gone through a $30-million renovation. The hotel is centrally located at Hope Street and 7th Street, downtown. It's connected to the Broadway Plaza Shopping Center (open daily), a welcome treat for parents always in search of interesting adventures for their tots. Hold on tight to your teenagers when you exit the lobby, because Judy's boutique across from the entrance is quite "the thing."

The hotel's Camp Hyatt program offers a frequent-stay plan for kids, which includes a welcome package, a weekend supervised-activity program, and the opportunity for families to purchase a connecting room at half the price of the parents' room (if available).

The hotel's health club is geared toward adults, and the sundeck adjacent to it is very limited in size. The spa is extremely small and is better suited to aching muscles than to rambunctious children.

Rooms are spacious and newly furnished with mahogany armoires and brass accents. The large bathrooms have been redone in marble. Remote-control TV and complimentary cable stations are standard. VCRs can be rented. In addition to the dataport for a PC hookup, there is call-waiting telephone service. A big surprise for a downtown hotel is that the windows open! But they open at the bottom only, and although they don't open all the way, you should be careful with very small, curious, crawling infants.

Rooms with king-size beds have space for a crib, but with a rollaway would be crowded. Most families, we're told, rent either the corner rooms with king-size beds—which are a half again as big as a regular king-bedded room, and come with a refrigerator—or rooms with two queen-size beds. There are connecting rooms available for even larger families. Suites are lovely and feature a bedroom and sitting alcove, plus a living room and dining room, wet bar, refrigerator, stereo, and a bath and a half. Some suites seat six in the dining rooms. Bathrooms in the suites are carpeted and have wonderful lighting.

Dining/Entertainment: The Brasserie restaurant, on the lobby level, is definitely appropriate for families. Featuring American bistro-style cooking, it's open for breakfast, lunch, and dinner. Boosters and highchairs are provided, and the children's menu is extensive and reasonable.

Services: Twice-daily maid service, evening turn-down service, triple-sheeted beds, 1-day valet service, baby-sitting, Camp Hyatt for kids, 24-hour room service.

Facilities: Health club, sundeck, spa, dataport for PC hookup.

WESTIN BONAVENTURE, 404 S. Figueroa St., Los Angeles, CA 90071. Tel. 213/624-1000, or toll free 800/228-3000. Fax 213/612-4800. 1,500 rms and suites. A/C MINIBAR TV TEL

$ Rates: $150–$185 single; $175–$210 double. Children 18 and under stay free in their parents' room. Additional adults $25; cribs and rollaways free. Ask about special packages and weekend rates. AE, CB, DC, MC, V. **Parking:** $18.15 daily with in-and-out privileges.

The Bonaventure's round mirrored towers, on Figueroa Street between 4th Street and 5th Street, are visible almost anywhere in the downtown area. With nearly 1,500 guest rooms, 20 restaurants, five lounges, and more than 30 retail shops, it's like a small city—there's always something to look at and someplace to wander. The shopping gallery hosts everything from jewelry stores and art galleries to bookstores and T-shirt shops. The lobby is a six-level atrium with six reflection pools. There's a large fenced-in outdoor pool and patio on the fourth level with room to romp. For guests who miss their exercise, there is a state-of-the-art fitness center accessible via a skybridge.

All the rooms have been refurbished and fitted with custom-made armoires housing the minibar and remote-control TV. The headboard provides one convenient spot for phone, lights, and music. A mirrored wall adds space, while mirrored closets make finding those lost toys much easier. Bathrooms are generously sized and have tub/shower combinations. Connecting rooms and no-smoking rooms can be requested. Choose between rooms with twin, queen-size, or king-size beds. The hotel prides itself on the fact that no room is more than seven doors from an elevator—an important fact when you're dragging teddy bears, infant seats, 16 Barbie dolls, and the kids.

Dining/Entertainment: The Sidewalk Café in the Lobby Court is perfect for families. Children are given crayons and a coloring mat, and are offered a complimentary Shirley Temple. The Little Leaguer menu includes Tony the Tiger and toast for breakfast, a Bruin basket for lunch (hamburger, fries, and a salad), and a Tommy Lasorda special for dinner (ravioli, roll, and salad). Meals range from $3 to $4.50, including beverage. The breakfast buffet is $9.75 for adults and $4.85 for children. If the kids tire of this restaurant, there are dozens more on Levels 4 and 6, including delis, falafel, Chinese, and health-food emporiums. There is always live entertainment featured during lunch and in the evening on stage in the lobby next to the café.

Weekend brunch is a show in itself. There's an enormous selection of hot and cold buffet items; kids can choose from fried chicken, corn dogs, and ribs. The giant Jell-O mold produces giggles, while Chocolate Fantasy Island and its 24 decadent chocolate desserts produce sighs. A Dixieland band, a mime, and "U.B.E.," the giant elephant, hand out balloons and play tricks. Brunch prices are $17.95 for adults and $1 per year of age for those children 10 and under.

Room service is available 24 hours a day, with a separate children's menu available for lunch and dinner. The hotel will also pack a picnic lunch for the beach or park, or you can get take-out sandwiches from the numerous restaurants in the gallery.

Services: 24-hour room service, valet, concierge.

Facilities: Shopping arcade, fitness and tennis center, outdoor pool, car-rental desk.

HOLIDAY INN, 750 Garland Ave., Los Angeles, CA 90017. Tel. 213/ 628-5242, or toll free 800/HOLIDAY. Fax 213/628-1201. 204 rms and suites. A/C TV TEL Location: 8th and Garland, downtown.

$ Rates: $76–$90 single; $82–$96 double. Children under 18 stay free in their parents' room. Additional adults $8; cribs free; rollaways $5. Ask about "Great" rates, which offer discounts. AE, CB, DC, MC, V. **Parking:** Free.

For a modestly priced hotel in downtown Los Angeles, at 8th Street and Garland Avenue, this unpretentious, well-kept hotel with a pool is a good choice. Standard rooms and rooms with king-size beds can accommodate a crib, but a rollaway might be a squeeze. Consider renting a connecting room if your family is large. The clean and comfortable rooms are furnished with reading chairs and a small table and chairs, and have individual heaters and air conditioners, free cable channels, and pay-movie channels. The front desk can refer you to outside baby-sitters; there are coin-operated laundry facilities.

Dining/Entertainment: The Garland Restaurant overlooks the pool and is open for all three meals. It has a varied menu, offering everything from steak and shrimp to sandwiches and salads. Kids under 11 can eat for $1—for breakfast they can have an egg and bacon or pancakes; at lunch and dinner there's grilled cheese and fries, a piece of chicken, or a hamburger. Boosters and highchairs are provided. Room service is available.

HOLLYWOOD

HOLLYWOOD ROOSEVELT HOTEL, 7000 Hollywood Blvd., Hollywood, CA 90028. Tel. 213/466-7000, or toll free 800/950-7667. Fax 213/462-8056. 350 rms and suites. A/C TV TEL.

$ Rates: Tower rooms, $105–$150 single, $125–$165 double; cabaña rooms, $125–$150 single, $150–$175 double; concierge floor, $150–$200 single or double; suites, $160–$275 single, $180–$350 double; $1,500 Celebrity Suite. Children of all ages stay free in their parents' room. Cribs free; rollaways $15. AE, CB, DC, MC, V. **Parking:** Valet parking $8 per night.

This hotel epitomizes Tinsel Town when it was in its heyday. Site of the first Academy Awards presentation, it was renovated in 1985 and carefully restored to its original glory. Although the area isn't great for walking around at night (Hollywood Boulevard between La Brea Avenue and Highland Avenue), the hotel is located diagonally across from the Chinese Theatre and within easy access of the Hollywood Freeway (U.S. 101), downtown, and Beverly Hills.

The two-story lobby, with its hand-painted ceilings and Spanish wrought-iron grillwork, remains. It's a large lobby with ample seating for good people-watching. Be sure to take a walk by the Olympic-size pool to see the David Hockney painting on the bottom. There's plenty of room for lounging around the pool, but only a tiny grassy area for wandering toddlers. Poolside food service is available, and the exercise room is adjacent. Ask the concierge to arrange baby-sitting.

Rooms are decorated in soft, relaxing colors; some have art deco touches. Standard accommodations have room for a rollaway or crib. Request either two double beds or a king-size bed. Some Tower rooms have connecting doors. Cabaña rooms open to the outside gardens (keep this in mind if you're traveling with young wanderers). Remote-control TVs and SpectraVision are standard. Rooms differ in terms of size and location. The three-room Star Suites have great art deco furniture. The two-room Hollywood Suites are furnished in country French, and there is a two-story Celebrity Suite.

Dining/Entertainment: Although neither the Stargazer Café nor Theodore's has a children's menu, the Stargazer has enough choices to keep most kids satisfied for breakfast and lunch; prices are quite reasonable. Room service, however, offers only limited choices for youngsters.

Services: Poolside food service, baby-sitting, room service, concierge, valet.

Facilities: Olympic-size pool, exercise room.

HOLIDAY INN HOLLYWOOD, 1755 N. Highland Ave., Hollywood, CA 90028. Tel. 213/462-7181, or toll free 800/465-4329. Fax 213/466-9072. 470 rms and suites. A/C TV TEL

$ Rates: $85 single; $97 double; $126 minisuite. Children under 18 stay free in their parents' room. Additional adults $12; cribs free; rollaways $10. Ask about special summer rates. AE, CB, DC, MC, V. **Parking:** Free parking, and room for motor homes in the lot.

This Holiday Inn is appropriate for families who want to stay in a moderately priced hotel centrally located to many southland attractions, but again it's not in an area we recommend for wandering about at night. The hotel offers a small fenced-in outdoor pool area. Baby-sitting can be arranged with an outside agency through the housekeeping department.

The modern rooms are simple and compact. All come with two double beds or one king-size bed, and there is room for a crib or rollaway. Rooms with king-size beds are furnished with either sofa beds or small couches. Remote-control TV and in-room movies are standard features. Request an in-room safe for $4 per day. There are adjoining rooms suitable for large families. Or rent one bedroom and a minisuite, which has a bedroom and a seating area.

Dining/Entertainment: The Show Biz Restaurant is the place to take the family for breakfast, lunch buffets (both under $9), and evening dinner (with reasonably priced hamburgers and sandwiches). Children's menus are provided, and there's a variety of selections at lunch and dinner that will appeal to those who don't opt for the buffet. Windows on Hollywood is a more formal restaurant on the revolving top floor—only sophisticated tastebuds need attend. Room service has selections for the kids.

Services: Baby-sitting, room service.
Facilities: Outdoor pool, laundry rooms, soda and ice machines, hairdryers and extra phones available upon request.

THE AIRPORT AREA

For all the following, take the Century Boulevard exit from the San Diego Freeway (I-405).

LOS ANGELES AIRPORT HILTON AND TOWERS, 5711 Century Blvd., Los Angeles, CA 90045. Tel. 213/410-4000, or toll free 800/HILTONS. Fax 213/410-6250. 1,200 rms and suites. A/C MINIBAR TV TEL

$ Rates: $125–$155 single; $135 double; Tower rooms, $150 single, $160 double; $280–$515 suite. Children, regardless of age, stay free in their parents' room. Additional adults $15 per night; cribs and rollaways free. Ask about special weekend packages and summer rates. AE, CB, DC, MC, V. **Parking:** Valet parking $7 per day; self-parking $5 per day with in-and-out privileges.

We're told that this is the largest airport hotel in the world, and despite its formal-looking lobby with a contemporary fountain and baby grand piano, children are welcome here. In addition to the large outdoor pool with its self-service eating area, there are three garden terraces where children can entertain themselves (and you can order room service). The Family Fitness Center, with racquetball courts, massage facilities, and workout equipment, provides child care. The hotel concierge will also arrange baby-sitting through an outside agency. A small video arcade on the same level as the health club is sometimes a welcome diversion. The Galleria, part of the Centroplex complex of shops and restaurants adjacent to the hotel, makes for good strolling.

Clean, nicely lighted rooms come with remote-control TV and free cable stations. Refrigerators are available for $10 per night. Rooms with king-size beds can accommodate a rollaway and a crib, while rooms with two double beds could fit one or the other. Features include mirrored closet doors, sleek and clean bathrooms with tub/shower combinations, a big lighted mirror, and rattan furniture. A parlor is a good choice for large families; it's quite roomy and has a sofa bed, refrigerator and wet bar, table, chairs, and a desk. It can connect to one or two sleeping rooms.

Dining/Entertainment: Café L.A. is on the lobby level and open 24 hours. It's a perfect choice for families. While there's no children's menu, they offer smaller portions at half the price for kids under 12. Main courses run $10 to $20. The Galleria, next door, offers food service Monday through Saturday.

Services: Room service (6am to 2am), baby-sitting, concierge, valet service, complimentary 24-hour airport shuttle.

Facilities: Family Fitness Center, video arcade, outdoor pool, four spas.

DAYS INN HOTEL/LOS ANGELES AIRPORT, 5101 Century Blvd., Los Angeles, CA 90304. Tel. 213/419-1234, or toll free 800/325-2525. Fax 213/677-7871. 252 rms. A/C TV TEL.

$ Rates: $79 single; $85 double. Children 17 and under stay free in their parents' room. Additional adults $10; cribs and rollaways $6. Ask about special weekend rates. AE, CB, DC, MC, V. **Parking:** Free.

You'll be happy to know that kids under 12 sleep *and* eat free here. Not surprisingly, the Days Inn is attractive to lots of families. At the fenced-in outdoor pool, you can arrange to have food delivered from the restaurant, which stays open for breakfast, lunch, and dinner.

There are no suites or adjoining rooms. Units with two double beds, fine for a family of three or four, have tiny outside decks, separate vanities, and chairs and a table. Cable TV channels are in all the rooms. A crib or rollaway would fit in a single, but would be crowded in a room with two double beds.

QUALITY INN, at the Los Angeles International Airport, 5249 W. Century Blvd., Los Angeles, CA 90045. Tel. 213/645-2200, or toll free 800/228-5151. Fax 213/641-8214. 300 rms. A/C TV TEL.

$ **Rates:** $58 single (one bed); $65 double (two beds); $75 suite. Children under 16 stay free in their parents' room. Additional adults $10; cribs free; rollaways $10. Ask about special weekend rates. AE, CB, DC, MC, V. **Parking:** $3 per day with in-and-out privileges.

Prices here are excellent for what you get. Rooms aren't huge, but a family of three or four could stay comfortably. The hotel is near major freeways and close to Marina del Rey. A large pool, not fenced in, provides relief on a hot day. Baby-sitting can be arranged through an agency.

Single rooms, with one queen-size bed, have room for a crib. The rooms with two double beds are what we recommend for a small family; there are adjoining rooms for larger families. Or for longer stays, suites have one king-size bed and a pullout sofa. Cable TV with movies and direct-dial telephones are standard.

Dining/Entertainment: Of the two restaurants in the hotel, Brandi's serves dinner only, and has reasonably priced sandwiches on the menu. Tivoli Garden is open for breakfast and lunch. The Palm Court Lounge serves snacks, soups, and sandwiches from 11am to 1am. Room service is available.

2. CAMPING

To make reservations for any of the state campgrounds, call MISTIX (tel. toll free 800/444-PARK). If you need further information about campsites, call the State Park Headquarters (tel. 818/706-1310).

LEO CARRILLO STATE BEACH, on the Pacific Coast Hwy., 28 miles west of Santa Monica. Tel. 213/457-1324 or 818/706-1310.

This is the best camping in the area, nestled into the canyon near the beach. Camp on the beach or in the canyon at one of the 100 developed campsites, all rented on a first-come/first-served basis. There is a 31-foot limit for RVs or trailers. There are no hookups, but the campground does have a dump station, and rest rooms and hot showers are available. The camp convenience store is open daily from 7am to 7pm in summer. There are ranger-led nature walks on Sunday, and campfire programs on Saturday night in the summer.

CIRCLE X RANCH, 2896 Yerba Buena Rd., Malibu. Tel. 818/597-9191.

The 23 rural campsites here in the Santa Monica Mountains offer beautiful scenery and great hiking. You have to walk in 1½ miles. They are rented on a first-come/first-served basis.

MALIBU CREEK STATE PARK CAMPGROUND, Calabasas, south of Mulholland Hwy. Tel. 818/706-1310 or 818/706-8809.

Also in the Santa Monica Mountains are these 55 developed family campsites. First come, first served.

EASY EXCURSIONS

How can you visit Los Angeles and not see Disneyland? Well, you probably can't—which is why we listed the park first among "Kids' Top 10 Attractions" (see Section 1 in Chapter 4). But what about Palm Springs, Newport Beach, and Catalina? Of course, you can't see everything, so you must pick and choose those excursion destinations of most interest to your family. Each of the following is an easy drive—or in the case of Catalina, an easy boat trip—away. In this chapter we've covered the highlights of these spots and other surprises for you.

Should you choose to spend some more time in the more distant of these areas, we've also offered some suggestions for lodging.

1. PASADENA

Pasadena is Los Angeles's bulwark of tradition. Originally founded in 1886 as a resort community, called the Indiana Colony, Pasadena was a sunny sanctuary for industrialists and other members of the moneyed classes who came from points east to spend their winters. In fact, the area on South Orange Grove Boulevard near the Rose Bowl used to be called Millionaire's Row because of the many gorgeous mansions there. In decades past, Los Angeles society was centered exclusively in Pasadena. There's still a lot of wealth here, although there are now other such pockets of society in this big metropolis.

GETTING THERE Pasadena is approximately 10 driving miles from downtown Los Angeles via the Pasadena Freeway (I-110).

INFORMATION Contact the **Pasadena Convention and Visitors Bureau,** 171 South Los Robles Avenue, Pasadena, CA 91101 (tel. 818/795-9311), or the **Pasadena Chamber of Commerce,** 117 East Colorado Boulevard, Suite 100, Pasadena, CA 91105 (tel. 818/795-3355), for information on accommodations and attractions in the area.

WHAT TO SEE & DO

Plan to spend a full day in Pasadena, perhaps starting with Sunday brunch, or ending at one of the restaurants we've listed in Chapter 7.

In appreciation of the beauty of its once-splendid downtown buildings, Pasadena has restored a 10-block section to recapture its original glory. Called **Old Pasadena,** the area is bordered by Pasadena Avenue, Arroyo Parkway, Holly Street and Union Street, and Del Mar Boulevard. The historic buildings are not only interesting for their architecture and interiors, but they now house an eclectic group of restaurants, boutiques, and art galleries. It's a nice place to take a walk after Sunday brunch. This is where you'll find the **Rose City Diner** (for details, see Section 3, "Kid-Rated Restaurants," in Chapter 7). Or you can sample a chocolate-chip bagel at **Goldstein's Bagel Bakery,** 86 West Colorado Boulevard. You'll have to search for the **Heminger's Fudge & Chocolate Co.** counter as it's tucked away at 42 East Colorado Boulevard. An ice-cream cone or frozen yogurt is a must—try the **Pasadena Creamery** at 50 West Colorado Boulevard.

Pasadena is also well known for its museums, gardens, theater, and music. Two of its most famous museums are the Huntington Library and the Norton Simon Museum, both of which are known worldwide. And two other Pasadena attractions were detailed in Chapter 4, "What Kids Like to See and Do": **Kidspace,** a small hands-on, participatory museum for children 2 to 12 (see Section 2, "More Attractions"), and the **Descanso Gardens,** a great place for a stroll or tram tour (see Section 4, "Letting Off Steam"). But what most people think of when they hear of Pasadena is the Rose Bowl and Rose Parade, officially known as the Tournament of Roses.

THE TOURNAMENT OF ROSES. Tel. 818/449-ROSE (year-round 24-hour hotline for parade and game information).

⭐ The Tournament of Roses has been held each New Year's Day since 1890, at which time Pasadena streets are filled with the colors of millions of flowers covering lavishly decorated floats. **The Rose Parade:** Each year the parade attracts about 60 floats, 22 bands, and 230 equestrians, and is watched by more than a million curbside spectators and more than 125 million television viewers. In addition to the colorful floats, you see the Rose Queen and her Court (seven beautiful young women chosen from a field of about 1,000 full-time students of the Pasadena Area Community College District), as well as various celebrities riding on the floats. The parade's grand marshals of the past have tended to be celebrities, too.

If you're planning to be in Los Angeles at this time, you may want to think about camping out for curbside viewing of the parade. Kids love to do this. Thousands of people flock to the parade route the night before, secure a good viewing spot, talk it up with other hardy campers, catch a few winks of sleep in a sleeping bag, and then wake up to the New Year's Day excitement. (If New Year's Day falls on a Sunday, the parade and game are held on the following Monday, January 2.) If a hotel room sounds more comfortable, be sure to make your hotel and grandstand seat reservations far in advance. Expect a 3- to 5-night minimum stay, payable in advance, for hotel rooms in Pasadena. (Contact the Pasadena Convention and Visitors Bureau or the Pasadena Chamber of Commerce—see "Information," above—for information on hotels and motels in the area.)

The parade starts at 8:20am, lasts until 10:30am, and runs along Colorado Boulevard. **Grandstand-seat tickets** can be purchased for $24 to $35 from Sharp Seating Co., P.O. Box 68, Pasadena, CA 91102-0068 (tel. 818/795-4171), or at a substantially higher price from Ticketron. Tickets go on sale February 1 for the next year, and the good seats tend to sell out by early summer. To avoid the driving mayhem, you can take a chartered bus in from Santa Monica Lines (tel. 213/458-

1975), Gardena Bus Lines (tel. 213/321-0165), or Long Beach Public Transportation (tel. 213/591-8753); call at least 2 months in advance for reservations. If you do drive, be sure to park by 6:30am to get to your seats.

The parade has substantial RV accommodations, available through Sharp Seating (see above). The **Good Sam RV Club** (tel. 818/991-4980) sells packages to RV users.

The Rose Bowl: The Rose Bowl college football game, played after the parade, pits the winner of the Pacific 10 (on the West Coast) against the winner of the Big 10 (in the Midwest) conference, a tradition that was begun in 1902.

Tickets to the game are distributed primarily to loyal fans of the universities involved, but you can participate in a drawing of the sale of 3,500 end-zone seats by mailing a postcard with your name and address to: **Rose Bowl Ticket Drawing,** P.O. Box 91386, Pasadena, CA 91109. Postcards must be postmarked between September 1 and October 1 for the November drawing.

Viewing the Floats: If you don't like the crowds but want a closer view of the festivities, you can take the kids for a look at the floats before or after the parade. The **Tournament of Roses Association,** 391 South Orange Grove Boulevard, Pasadena, CA 91184 (tel. 818/449-4100 or 213/681-3724), publishes a brochure, available in November each year, of locations, hours, and admission charges to five float-construction sites (the best time to go is 2 days before the parade up to the time the floats are moved to the formation area).

After the parade, the floats are on display on Sierra Madre Boulevard, between Washington Boulevard and Villa Avenue. You can see them on parade day from 1:30 to 4pm, and the next day, from 9am to 4pm. If you're not going to the game or parade, you're best off waiting until the next day for viewing. Park on nearby residential streets.

HUNTINGTON LIBRARY, ART COLLECTIONS, AND BOTANICAL GARDENS, 1151 Oxford Rd., San Marino. Tel. 818/405-2100.

There are essentially three major parts to the Huntington Library, each of which is worth a separate visit: the library, the art galleries, and the botanical gardens.

Older kids who know just a bit about art and literature will appreciate the Huntington much more than the little ones, who will easily get bored here. It's a good idea to pick up the short self-guiding-tour booklets before embarking on this cultural wonderland.

The **Huntington Library** is an institution devoted entirely to the study of British and American history and literature. It contains 600,000 reference and rare books; many thousands of photographs, prints, and microforms; and nearly 2.5 million valuable individual manuscripts. Many of the subjects your children are already studying in school come alive for them in this wonderful library. Even the 14-year-old who was with us was fascinated by the most reliable manuscript in existence of Chaucer's *Canterbury Tales* (circa 1410); the Gutenberg Bible (circa 1455); one of only three animal-skin copies still in existence in America; and *Shakespeare's Comedies, Histories, and Tragedies* (the First Folio), printed in 1623. In addition, there are documents by Benjamin Franklin, George Washington, Euclid, Milton, Galileo, Thomas Paine, Abraham Lincoln, Robert Frost, James Joyce, W. B. Yeats—even a draft of the U.S. Constitution (1787).

The art collections are prized as well. The **Huntington Art Gallery** is devoted primarily to British art of the 18th and early 19th centuries, and houses a multitude of masterpieces. Kids seem to love Gainsborough's *Blue Boy* and Lawrence's *Pinkie,* which face each other. This gallery also features furniture, decorative objects, and sculpture from the same period.

The Scott Gallery for American Art is much newer, having opened in 1984. Here American paintings from the 1730s to the 1930s are featured, including the work of such artists as Stuart, Copley, Bingham, and Cassatt. Renaissance paintings and 18th-century French sculpture, tapestries, porcelain, and furniture are found in the Arabella Huntington Memorial Collection, housed in the west wing of the main library building.

The **Huntington Botanical Gardens** are equally impressive. They occupy about 130 acres and consist of one wondrous garden after another. There's the Rose Garden, with its 1,100 varieties arranged historically from around A.D. 1000. And there are various international gardens—the Australian Garden, the Subtropical Garden, the Desert Garden, and the Palm Garden (a must-see because this is, after all, Los Angeles).

There is restaurant service available from 1 to 4pm. Picnics are not allowed, and pets are not permitted. The Huntington is stroller-accessible.

Admission: Free; a donation of $5 per adult is suggested.

Open: Tues–Sun 1–4:30pm (Sun visitors must make reservations in advance). **Closed:** Major hols. **Directions:** Take the Pasadena Freeway (I-110) to the end; the Huntington is on Allen Avenue, off California Boulevard.

NORTON SIMON MUSEUM, 411 W. Colorado Blvd. Tel. 818/449-6840.

The Norton Simon holds an abundance of excellent artwork, some contemporary but mostly classical: Matisse, Picasso, Raphael, Rubens, Rembrandt, and others. This may be your child's first opportunity to view such a large collection of rare masterpieces. Children over 7 will enjoy this museum. The sixth-grader in our group liked the statues the best, especially the three rooms of Degas' miniature *modeles.*

There are 30 galleries and a sculpture garden—about 1,000 works of art all together. Plan to spend as much time here as your child's concentration will allow. We break up the viewing by spending time in the outdoor sculpture garden, which is a tranquil spot for the kids to roam if they get restless. You may be surprised at how much culture they can soak up just by walking among the sculptures.

There are no eating facilities, but you may leave and return on one admission. It's stroller-accessible, and ample parking is available.

Admission: $4 adults, $2 students with ID and senior citizens, free for children under 12.

Open: Thurs–Sun noon–6pm. **Directions:** Take the Foothill Freeway (I-210) or the Ventura Freeway (Calif. 134) to their intersection; the museum is nearby, on Colorado Boulevard at Orange Grove Boulevard.

PACIFIC ASIA MUSEUM 46 N. Robles Ave. Tel. 818/449-2742.

This is a little gem of a museum devoted to past and present Asian and Pacific art. Built in 1929 in the Chinese Imperial Palace courtyard style, the museum is listed in the National Register of Historic Places. Let the kids know that the garden they see at the museum is an authentic Asian courtyard garden, one of only two such gardens in the United States.

In addition to the special exhibitions and changing displays from its permanent collection, the museum has a special Student's Gallery designed especially for children, with displays interesting to many age groups. Some of the objects can be handled, and there are hands-on experiences and workshops available at various times.

On the third Saturday of every month the museum sponsors Free-Day, Fun-Days, with free family programs. There may be dance performances, an origami workshop, a demonstration of the art of fan making, or other programs featuring the cultural arts of many different Asian and Pacific countries.

Admission: $3 adults, $1.50 students with ID and seniors, free for children under 12.

Open: Wed–Sun noon–5pm; tours given Sun. **Directions:** Take the Foothill Freeway (I-210) to the Orange Grove Boulevard exit; the museum is 2½ blocks south.

WHERE TO EAT

Because it's an easy drive to Pasadena for dinner or Sunday brunch, we've included Pasadena restaurants among the Los Angeles restaurants (see Section 3, "Kid-Rated Restaurants" in Chapter 7).

2. LONG BEACH

Home of the *Queen Mary* and the *Spruce Goose,* Long Beach is also home to what was once the richest oil strike in North America. When you arrive in town, notice the high-rise "condos" offshore. At night they look like pretty islands, lit with colorful lights and surrounded by palm trees and fountains. They are really decorated oil-drilling platforms.

Long Beach makes a pleasant 1-day excursion. Its downtown is experiencing a renaissance that denizens hope will be appealing to tourists. Downtown Long Beach's Pine Avenue is becoming the trendy place to be for merchants and restaurateurs, and the first phase of the Greater Los Angeles World Trade Center was recently completed downtown. Long Beach Harbor has become one of the most important shipping ports for the Pacific Rim trade.

GETTING THERE   Long Beach is just 30 miles south of Los Angeles on the San Diego Freeway (I-405), the Harbor Freeway (I-110), the Long Beach Freeway (I-710), or the Pacific Coast Highway (Calif. 1).

INFORMATION   The staff at the Convention Council will be happy to add to our listings of what's appropriate and appealing for kids. Call or visit the **Long Beach Area Convention and Visitors Council,** One World Trade Center, No. 30, Long Beach, CA 90802 (tel. 213/436-3645); the office is open Monday through Friday from 8:30am to 5pm. A new **Visitor Center** has opened at 3387 Long Beach Boulevard, just off the San Diego Freeway (I-405) (tel. 213/426-6773), open daily from 9am to 5pm.

If you plan to be in the area for a while, be sure to contact the **Long Beach**

Convention and Entertainment Center, 300 East Ocean Boulevard (tel. 213/432-2233 or 213/436-3660), to find out what's on the schedule. Everything from the *Nutcracker* performed by children and "Sesame Street Live" goes on here. Or call the 24-hour **Telephone Arts Line** (tel. 213/499-7722) for information on events all over town.

WHAT TO SEE & DO

QUEEN MARY and SPRUCE GOOSE, Long Beach Harbor, at the end of the Long Beach Freeway (I-710). Tel. 213/435-3511.

Without question, the *Queen Mary* and *Spruce Goose* are the two most popular sightseeing attractions in Long Beach. Today they are part of the same complex at Long Beach Harbor.

The **Queen Mary** was the biggest, best, and fastest of its time, and was truly the most elegant sailing vessel on the sea. It also played a significant role in World War II, and it could outrun German torpedoes. Take the kids on the Shipwalk, a self-guided tour of the upper and lower decks, the sun deck, and the sports deck. You'll also see the wheelhouse, World War II displays, an audiovisual presentation of the story of the vessel, and other exhibits. The Captain's Tour is a personalized small-group tour for $5 extra; it lasts 90 minutes and takes you behind the scenes to areas usually off-limits. New to the ship is a multimedia presentation and new exhibits about the darker side of the ship's history, "Ghosts, Myths & Legends of the *Queen Mary*." These tales of the supernatural are included in the general admission fee. Besides housing a 390-room hotel created from converted staterooms, the vessel has four restaurants and two bars.

The **Spruce Goose** was Howard Hughes's 400,000-pound contribution to the war effort, built to transport American troops out of the range of German U-boats. Constructed of wood, it flew only once, in 1947, and was then placed in a specially built hangar. Standing on platforms, you can see into the flight deck and cargo bay. Many displays and audiovisual presentations surround the plane, which is now housed in the world's largest geodesic aluminum dome.

Also part of the *Spruce Goose/Queen Mary* complex is **Londontown Village,** a themed center of boutiques and snack bars.

Admission: $17.50 adults and children over 11, $14 seniors, $9.50 children 5–11, free for children under 5.

Open: July 4–Labor Day, daily 9am–9pm (box office closes at 8pm); the rest of the year, daily 10am–6pm (box office closes at 4pm).

LONG BEACH CHILDREN'S MUSEUM, 445 Long Beach Blvd., in the Long Beach Plaza. Tel. 213/495-1163.

If your children are infants to age 11, you'll want to take them to this hands-on learning center. It has an infant-toddler area for youngsters up to age 3, a dress-up attic to stimulate the imagination, 32,000 Legos (give or take a few), a special art café, a music room, and much, much more for the curious.

Admission: $2.95 per person over 1 year of age, free for toddlers under 1.

Open: Thurs–Sat 11am–4pm, Sun noon–4pm.

RANCHO LOS ALAMITOS, 6400 Bixby Hill Rd., Tel. 213/431-3541.

History buffs might be interested in seeing Rancho Los Alamitos, the oldest adobe structure of its kind in California. Tours are available. In June, the city sponsors California Ranch Day at the structure; there are live animals, and kids get to participate in "hands-on" ranching and farming demonstrations. Call for this year's June date.

Admission: Call for current charges.

Open: Wed–Sun 1–5pm.

MORE ATTRACTIONS

SHOPPING   At the end of the Long Beach Freeway (I-710), **Shoreline Village,** 407 Shoreline Village Drive, at Pine Avenue (tel. 213/590-8427), makes an interesting stop when you're in the area. Set on 7 acres, this turn-of-the-century themed shopping center features restaurants, seaside cafés, shops, and an early-1900s carousel.

WATER SPORTS   Long Beach has a very active water-sports life. In addition to 5 miles of pure southern California beaches to enjoy, **Alamitos Bay** offers 7 more miles of beaches. **Marine Stadium,** at Marina Park, 5255 Appian Way (tel. 213/594-0951), is the place for waterskiing. Right next door is a "tame" beach, frequented by parents and little kids, called **Mother's Beach.** And **Marina Park** is also the place to rent pedalboats and kayaks. Take windsurfing lessons at the **Long Beach Windsurf Center,** 3850 East Ocean Boulevard (tel. 213/433-1014).

WHALE-WATCHING CRUISES   You can go whale-watching from December to April. **Queen's Wharf,** 555 Pico Avenue (tel. 213/432-8993), operates 65- and 85-foot vessels for up to 128 passengers. Reservations are recommended for both whale-watching and sport fishing.

Or you can search for whales from aboard a sailboat or powerboat with **Spirit Cruises,** Berth 75, Ports O' Call, in nearby San Pedro (tel. 213/831-1073). Weekday and weekend cruises are guaranteed—if you don't see a whale, you can take another cruise for free.

3. SAN PEDRO

Pack up the kids for a journey to the seaside area of San Pedro. This can easily be combined with your day in Long Beach. San Pedro Bay is home to one of the world's largest artificial harbors—**Los Angeles Harbor.** But San Pedro offers more than cargo and freighters: From downtown San Pedro (known as Old San Pedro), you can choose among numerous ocean views. **Angels Gate Park,** near the Point Fermin Lighthouse, hosts the Korean Bell of Friendship (considered the largest Asian bell in existence), given to the city by the Republic of (South) Korea.

GETTING THERE   Right next to Long Beach, San Pedro is 30 miles south of Los Angeles on the San Diego Freeway (I-405), the Harbor Freeway (I-110), or the Pacific Coast Highway (Calif. 1).

INFORMATION The Los Angeles Convention & Visitors Bureau, ManuLife Plaza, 515 South Figueroa St., 11th Floor, Los Angeles, CA 90071 (tel. 213/624-7300), is your best bet for advance information. They have brochures printed in English, French, German, Japanese, and Spanish and will answer written inquiries.

While in San Pedro, you might try the Chamber of Commerce, 390 West 7th St. (tel. 213/832-7272), if you have a last-minute question or two.

WHAT TO SEE & DO

CABRILLO MARINE MUSEUM AND AQUARIUM, 3720 Stephen White Dr. Tel. 213/548-7562.

Located within a stone's throw of the ocean, the Cabrillo Museum provides children of all ages a glimpse of the marine life of southern California. There are 34 seawater aquariums that are home to hundreds of marine species and plantlife. The elaborate displays—kelp forests, rocky shores, and sandy habitats—are arranged especially for children and can be viewed from all sides. Skilled guides explain the exhibits at the children's level. The high point of our trip is the touching pool, where the children get to hold anemones, sea stars, and sea cucumbers.

You might want to avoid the tours since they rush you through the exhibits. There are a variety of children's programs, ranging from 1-day workshops to week-long sessions. Call for information. There's also a gift shop.

Don't leave yet. Across the parking lot from the museum is a grassy area and a wonderful beach. **Cabrillo Beach** (tel. 213/832-1179) has very gentle waves because it's inside the breakwater that protects the harbor. It offers perfect swimming for young children, yet has enough action to let them dodge the low-breaking waves. You'll also want to check the tide tables and try to be there during low tide so you can wander through the tidepools on the rocks. *Careful, though—it's slippery.*

Admission: Museum and beach, free; parking costs $5.50.

Open: Museum, Tues–Fri noon–5pm, Sat–Sun 10am–5pm; the last touch-tank hour is 3:30pm, which is when the gift shop closes, too. **Closed:** Thanksgiving and Christmas Days.

LOS ANGELES MARITIME MUSEUM, Berth 84, at the foot of 6th St. Tel. 213/548-7618.

Located near Ports O' Call (see "More Attractions," below), this museum offers your school-age seafaring tykes (and older) a glimpse at ship models (approximately 700), seaman's knots, and other exhibits relating to ships of all kinds.

Admission: By donation; parking is free.

Open: Tues–Sun 10am–5pm.

MORE ATTRACTIONS

FOR STROLLS, SHOPPING, AND DINING Located at Berth 77 and the main channel of Los Angeles Harbor, **Ports O'Call Village** (tel. 213/831-0287), and the **Whaler's Wharf** offer a pleasant few hours. Cobblestone streets and waterfront dining make you feel as if you've suddenly landed in an old New England seaport town. There are three villages, each with its own flavor. One has huge fresh fish markets and open-air barbecues where you can have the fish cooked to order. Many people buy drinks and enjoy the delectable fish on the open-air decks.

Altogether the villages have 15 restaurants (which include a wide variety of fast-food and light-snack places), 75 shops, and boathouses for harbor cruises and whale-watching trips. Our favorite stop is **Candy Town** (tel. 213/514-2669). This emporium offers everything from imported chocolates to sweet dinosaur eggs. Strolling throughout the villages are dancers, musicians, and clowns. The Village is open daily 11am to 9pm in summer, until 7pm the rest of the year. There's plenty of free parking.

HARBOR CRUISES   To get a sense of the harbor, take the **L.A. Harbor Cruise** (tel. 213/831-0996). This 1-hour sojourn goes all around the harbor passing the Vincent Thomas Bridge, Todd Shipyards, and Angel's Gate Lighthouse. Our 7-year-old especially liked the supertankers and freighters we passed. School-age children do well for about half the trip; after that it's a bit of a struggle to keep them entertained. We brought snacks and little trinkets for them to play with.

Tours depart at noon and 1, 2, 3, and 4pm. But call ahead for schedule information. Fares are $7 for adults, $3 for children 2 to 12; under-2s, free.

4. CATALINA

"Twenty-six miles across the sea. . . ." Actually, it's 22 miles across the sea to Santa Catalina Island, the island of romance.

First discovered by Juan Cabrillo in 1542, it wasn't until 1892 that the island was purchased and turned into the Santa Catalina Island Company for the purpose of becoming a pleasure resort.

The island was once home to the Catalina Indians and to sea otters, both of which were wiped out by the Russians and their accompanying tribes of fierce Aleut and Kodiak Indians. It was also home to pirates, cattle- and sheepherders, fur traders, and miners.

The year 1919 marked the beginning of its prime development phase, when William Wrigley, Jr., bought controlling interest in the company. He was instrumental in preserving the island's wilderness. The Santa Catalina Island Conservancy was organized in the early 1970s to preserve and protect the wilderness areas—over 42,000 acres. It was the Wrigleys who really made the island a popular vacation spot.

Catalina is easy to do in a day, although we've given you lodging alternatives should you decide to stay overnight.

GETTING THERE

   By Boat   To go by boat from Los Angeles, you have your choice of Catalina Cruises or Catalina Express. Liquid Dramamine is in order for these trips, as well as extra plastic bags and a change of clothes for the kids.

   Catalina Express, which leaves from Berth 95, Los Angeles Harbor in San Pedro, or from next to the *Queen Mary* in Long Beach (tel. 213/519-1212, 213/510-1212 on the island, or toll free 800/540-4753 in California), offers a 90-minute trip on a small boat. This is the one we recommend because it has stabilizers for a more comfortable trip. Airline-style seats, cabin attendants, and refreshments are provided. In winter there are 4 to 6 departures daily; in summer, as many as 10. Call for specific schedules. Reservations are required. Round-trip fares from San Pedro are $30.30 for adults, $22.80 for children 2 to 11; under 2, $2.60. From Long Beach, adults pay $35.30; children, $26.30; kids under 2, $2.80.

Catalina Cruises (tel. 213/253-9800 in Los Angeles or 213/410-4441 in the Long Beach/South Bay area) leaves from Long Beach year round, and in the summer also from Berth 95 in San Pedro. You can also reserve tickets through Ticketron (tel. 213/410-1062 in Los Angeles or 714/634-1300 in Orange County). Departures are daily and the trip takes 2 hours one way. There's a snack bar and cocktails. Reservations are a must, especially during summer. Round-trip fares are $27.50 for adults, $17 for children 2 through 11, $1.50 for under-2s.

From Orange County you can leave from the Balboa Pavilion in Newport Beach: Call **Catalina Passenger Service** (tel. 714/673-5245).

By Plane   To go by air is certainly faster, though more expensive.

Helitrans (tel. 213/548-1314, or toll free 800/262-1472) takes you over in a jet helicopter from Berth 95 in San Pedro every hour on the hour. The **Island Express** (tel. 213/491-5550) jet-helicopter service leaves from San Pedro and from Long Beach (from a helipad near the *Queen Mary*). Call for reservations. The trip takes 15 minutes. Round-trip fares for both companies are $96 for adults and children; under 2, free.

San Diego Seaplanes (tel. 619/453-8833) will transport you to Avalon from San Diego, Orange County, Long Beach, Torrance, and Los Angeles. Call for reservations and rates.

INFORMATION   Before you leave, you can get maps, brochures, and information on island activities from the **Catalina Chamber of Commerce & Visitors Bureau,** P.O. Box 217, Avalon, CA 90704 (tel. 213/510-1520). A very useful 60-page booklet about the area is offered at no charge.

After you arrive, you'll find the **Visitors' Information Center** right in the center of town (see "What to See & Do," below, for details).

ISLAND LAYOUT   You are now on an island 21 miles long and 8 miles wide. The island's main port and only town is **Avalon,** which boasts an average of 267 days of sunshine yearly, and an average high temperature of 76° and an average low of 58° June through October. Mid-October and mid-April are its wet months. Summers rarely get above 80°; winters, rarely below 50°. In summer Avalon's population of a little over 2,000 swells to 6,000 weekdays, and sometimes up to 10,000 on weekends.

Avalon is about a square mile in size. The interior of the island is wild, beautiful, and pristine—and off-limits to private vehicles and to hikers and campers without permits. Protected by the Catalina Conservancy, whose job it is to preserve it for posterity, it is accessible by tour bus or permit.

Two Harbors, on the other side of the island at the Isthmus, is a remote, peaceful location for camping, hiking, and water activities.

You'll find that addresses aren't used much here. Instead, directions are given according to certain landmarks and piers. The natives are friendly and are glad to point you in the right direction.

GETTING AROUND   Autos are not allowed on the island except by special permit held by residents. But Avalon is an easy place to get around **on foot.** Reasonably priced **taxis** are always available.

Many families with one or two kids are seen in gasoline-powered golf-cart-type vehicles rented from **Cartopia Cart Rentals,** 615 Crescent Avenue (tel. 213/510-2493). Drivers 25 years old and up can rent these four-passenger vehicles for $25 per hour all year round. It's open daily during the summer season from 9am to 5pm; off-season, from 9am to 4pm. Cash or traveler's checks only.

Brown's Bikes, right under the Holly Hill House (tel. 213/510-0986), rents bikes by the hour or the day, and there are lockers. A limited number of child carriers and helmets are available. You'll pay $4 to $10 per hour for adult bikes, and $4 for children's bikes. Strollers and wheelchairs can also be rented. Open daily in summer from 9am to 5pm and in winter from 10am to 4pm.

WHAT TO SEE & DO

There's much more to see and do in Catalina with kids than you might expect.

GUIDED TOURS

After you leave the pier, your first stop should be the **Visitors' Information Center,** located on Crescent Avenue across from the Green Pleasure Pier (tel. 213/510-2000, or toll free 800/4-AVALON). You'll find information on land and water tours here, and you can purchase tickets for different tours at one time. The Visitors' Center is open daily from 8am to 5pm, year round.

Tours leave a minimum of twice a day—some, 10 or 12 times a day on weekends. You can make reservations. You may want to purchase your tickets by phone with a credit card, or by mail. Write to: Catalina Sightseeing Tours, P.O. Box 737 Reservations, Avalon, CA 90704.

The Visitors' Information Center suggests a half-day outing combining the Glass Bottom Boat Tour, the Avalon Scenic Tour, and the Coastal Cruise to Seal Rocks. You need to decide whether your children can handle all that in a half day. We spread it out over 2 days with our toddler. Children over 5 could certainly handle all the water tours in a day, but it would be too much to do in just half a day. Inquire about special prices for combination tours.

LAND TOURS The Visitors' Center staff will direct you to the bus terminal (for the land tours), which is a short walk past the center. You can leave your strollers at the terminal. Soft drinks and sandwiches are available at the terminal, but you can't take them on the buses. There are also rest-room facilities here.

The **Avalon Scenic Tour** shows you some of the highlights of Avalon. The 50-minute tour is taken in an open-air, tram-style bus, and is fine for a sleeping infant or a child who can sit still for an hour—but there are no stops during the tour. Fare is $5 for adults, $4.50 for seniors, $3.25 for children 5 to 11, and free for kids under 5.

Children over 7 enjoy the **Skyline Drive Tour** because they can catch a glimpse of the buffalo and other animals that roam the 42,000 acres of the Conservancy. The guide narrates the tour, explaining what rare plants and trees you are seeing, as well as outlining the history of the island. The road to the top is pretty scary (the kids love it!).

About 40 minutes into the tour, there's a stop at the Airport-in-the-Sky, Catalina's commercial and private airport. This 1¾-hour tour will take you 10 miles into the Conservancy, which is only accessible by tour or hiking. Adults pay $10.50; seniors, $9.50; for children 5 to 11, $7; under 5, free.

If you have the time, and if the kids can sit on a bus for a while, consider taking the **Inland Motor Tour.** This half-day tour is a good way to see the remote wilderness and herds of buffalo. In addition to a stop at the Airport-in-the-Sky, you'll visit El Rancho Escondido, where you'll be treated to a performance by the Arabian horses that are raised here. There are several bathroom stops. The cost is $19.50 for adults, $18 for seniors, $12.50 for children 5 to 11, and free for kids under 5.

WATER TOURS   Water tours leave from the Green Pleasure Pier directly across from the Visitors' Center. There are rest-room facilities and food stands here. Strollers can't be taken on the boats.

The **Coastal Cruise to Seal Rocks** is a 1-hour boat trip that cruises close to shore. From May through September the sea lions return to the area, and the vessel is able to reach their sunning area. The cruise also passes the Amphibian and Helicopter Terminal, where the children are likely to watch a seaplane take off or land. This tour is fine for toddlers and children, but teens might find it a bit boring. There are no rest-room facilities on board. Adults pay $5; seniors, $4.50; children 5 to 11, $3.25; under 5, free.

The **Glass-Bottom Boat Trip** is a 40-minute ride, and just perfect for short attention spans! The waters off Catalina are so clear that you'll have no trouble spotting the various sea creatures. The guide explains what you're seeing and points out special animal and plant life. Adults are charged $5 ($6 for evening trips); seniors, $4.50 ($5 in the evening); children 5 to 11, $3.25 ($4 for evening trips); under 5, free.

The **Flying Fish Boat Tour** draws quite a few families. Running from mid-May through September, this 55-minute evening tour can be fascinating. The boat shines a 40-million-candlepower searchlight on the water, attracting the flying fish to sail through the air. Be sure to dress warm—by September it gets chilly in the evenings, and the water spray makes it even colder on this open boat. There are no bathroom facilities on board. The fare is $6 for adults, $5 for seniors, $4 for children 5 to 11; under 5, free.

OTHER ACTIVITIES

BEACHES AND WATER SPORTS   Beach lovers have only two choices on the Avalon side of the island. Although hordes of tourists enjoy the beach on either side of the Green Pleasure Pier on summer weekends, we prefer the **Descanso Beach Club,** on the other side of the Casino (tel. 213/510-2780). You can bicycle there pretty easily. Here you'll spend your day at a private beach where you can rent towels and a beach chair. Showers and changing rooms are available. Rafts, snorkels, and boogie boards can be rented, and you can play volleyball. There are also family cookouts nightly during the summer. Descanso provides the condiments, baked potato, salad bar, and rolls. You bring the main dish and grill it on their barbecue pit (make reservations). There is also a sidewalk café and open-air bar. Admission to the beach is $1.50 for adults, 50¢ for children under 12. Cookout prices are $6.50 for adults, $3.50 for children.

Brave souls who want to stay at the beach by the Pleasure Pier have various beach-supply rentals available to the right of the pier. Sand chairs, umbrellas, mats, tubes, floats, and even beach towels can be rented, in summer only, from 9am.

Visit **Joe's Rent-A-Boat** on the Green Pleasure Pier (tel. 213/510-0455) for rowboats, pedalboats, 16-foot runabouts, and 15-h.p. sportsters. Paddleboards, which are also available, are a favorite with the teens. Joe's doesn't take reservations, but the wait is usually no more than a half hour on a busy sumner weekend. It's open from the weekend before Easter Sunday to the month of October, daily from 6am to 7pm; closed the rest of the year. Hourly rates are $5 for paddleboards, $10 for rowboats, $20 for runabouts, $25 for a sportster, and $10 for pedalboats.

Water bikes and two-person jet boats are available at **Jet Sprint Catalina, Inc.,** at Hamilton Cove (tel. 213/510-0791); take the shore boat from the end of the Green Pleasure Pier to The Float. Kids have to be a minimum of 14 years old for the Yamaha water bikes, and must have a parent's signed authorization. Water bikes rent for $40 per half hour, $60 per hour. Open April through October, daily from 8am to 6pm.

If you're interested in diving in Catalina's beautiful waters, there are two places to call. One is **Argo Diving Service** (tel. 213/510-2208). The other is **Island Charters** (tel. 213/510-0600, or toll free 800/262-DIVE). **Catalina Diver's Supply** (tel. 213/510-0330) rents equipment.

Are you ready for parasailing? It's not as scary as it looks. They say it's safe enough for even 4-year-olds—it's your decision. Contact **Island Cruzers,** 107 Pebbly Beach Road (tel. 213/510-1777). The boats take six people per hour, every hour. The parasailing itself lasts 8 to 10 minutes, and the charge is $35 per ride for adults and children alike. Children must weigh at least 60 pounds to go up.

LAND ACTIVITIES   You might want to take the time to play miniature golf at **Golf Gardens,** one block from the beach in the Island Plaza (tel. 213/510-1200). This is an 18-hole golf course, perfect for the whole family. Open daily from Easter to mid-June and from mid-September to October, daily and evenings from mid-June to mid-September. Open winter weekends and holidays when weather permits. Times vary, so call first or drop by and check the sign out front.

Hiking in Catalina is best for families in good condition, or as part of your camping experience. In the interior of the island, routes follow existing roads and Jeep trails. From Avalon into the interior, the trail gains 1,450 feet of elevation in less than 3 miles. From Two Harbors it climbs only 800 feet in 2 miles, but the route is longer.

It's best to contact the **Los Angeles County Department of Parks and Recreation** in Avalon (tel. 213/510-0688) or the **Catalina Camp and Cove Agency** in Two Harbors (tel. 213/510-0303) before you plan to hike on the island. The Los Angeles agency is located in the Island Plaza in Avalon, and is open Monday through Friday from 9am to 1pm and 2 to 4pm. The Two Harbors office is open daily from 8:30am to 4:30pm. Permits are required for hiking. Ask the park staff about the accessibility of certain trails for children.

If you decide to hike, be aware that temperatures change drastically during certain times of the year—it may be extremely hot in the interior, but only 60°F at the beach. Bring layers of clothing and sunscreen—and don't forget to bring water.

Another way to see the island is on horseback. **Catalina Stables** on Avalon Canyon Road, six blocks from the ocean (tel. 213/510-0478), offers 1½-hour guided rides into the mountains behind the golf course. Although children don't need prior riding experience, they must be strong enough to handle these horses. (They are well-trained, gentle horses, but the 5-mile ride covers some difficult terrain.) The minimum age is 8; the maximum weight limit is approximately 200 pounds; you must have closed-toe shoes—no sandals. Groups are limited to eight people. Reservations must be made in person and can be made only on the day you plan to ride. The stables are open in summer, daily from 9am to 3pm; in winter, daily from 10am to 2:30pm, weather permitting. Rates are $25 per person (adult or child).

TWO HARBORS

Located on the other side of the island, Two Harbors is a secluded, noncommercial area. Catalina Express from San Pedro (tel. 213/519-1212, or toll free 800/540-4753), and Catalina Cruises from Long Beach (tel. 213/514-3838), can take you directly to Two Harbors. Catalina Safari Bus will take you there from Avalon (tel. 213/510-2800). Or it will transport you to one of two campsites (see "Camping" under "Where to Stay," below). Round-trip fares to and from Avalon are $28.30 for adults, $20.40 for children 2 to 11. The same phone number will give you information on Catalina Safari Tours. You can choose between snorkeling trips by boat from Two Harbors or naturalist-led hikes and short walks. This is a great way to introduce the kids to the natural side of the island.

Once you have arrived in Two Harbors, you'll find nearly empty beaches. You can snorkel, dive, hike, and even camp. There's a general store open daily from 8am to 5pm, and a snack bar open from 8am to 3pm.

WHERE TO STAY

PAVILION LODGE, 513 Crescent (P.O. Box 737), Avalon, CA 90704. Tel. 213/510-1788, or toll free 800/4-AVALON. Fax 213/510-7254. 75 rms. A/C TV TEL

$ Rates: Mid-June through mid-Sept, $99 single or double; end of Mar to mid-June and mid-Sept to the end of Oct, $75 single or double; Nov to the end of Mar, $59 single or double. Children stay free in their parents' room. Cribs free; rollaways $10. DISC, MC, V.

The hotel's large garden court with lawn chairs makes an inviting spot to relax while watching the kids play. The newly remodeled rooms have air conditioning and some are connecting; all have refrigerators and free Showtime and Disney Channel cable TV. There is no restaurant on the premises, but the hotel—located just across from the beach—is within easy walking distance of many eateries. Baby-sitting can be arranged through the front desk.

CAMPING

There are five campgrounds on the island. The first is in Avalon, two are in the interior, and the other two are in Two Harbors. For reservations in Avalon, contact the **Los Angeles County Department of Parks and Recreation** (tel. 213/510-0688).

Hermit Gulch is the closest campground to town. It accommodates 230 people and has water, toilets, hot showers, vending machines, and picnic tables. Sites are $7 per person per night. **Black Jack** campground is approximately 2½ miles from the airport and is at a 1,500-foot elevation. Some 75 campers can stay here, and there are toilets, water, and picnic tables. Reservations are $7 per person per night. **Little Harbor** is on the opposite side of the island. You can get to the beach easily from here. There are 150 sites, with toilets, picnic tables, and cold showers. Reservations are $6 per night per person, 50¢ for children under 14.

Contact the **Catalina Camp & Cove Agency** (tel. 213/510-0303) for reservations in the two Two Harbors campsites. **Two Harbors Camping** is a quarter mile from the Two Harbors pier and accommodates 250 campers. Sites have barbecue pits, picnic tables, water, and rinse-off showers. **Parson's Landing,** 7 miles west of Two Harbors, is more primitive and accessible only by foot or boat. It has room for 150 campers. There are pit toilets and a water tank. Stoves and lanterns can be rented in Two Harbors.

WHERE TO EAT

Although there aren't many restaurants in town with children's menus, your crew won't go hungry.

THE CHANNEL HOUSE, 205 Crescent Ave., Avalon. Tel. 213/510-1617.
   Cuisine: CONTINENTAL. **Reservations:** Accepted only in winter.
$ Prices: Lunch $5–$10; dinner $13–$21. AE, MC, V.
   Open: Easter week through Sept, lunch daily 11:30am–2:30pm; dinner daily from 5pm. Oct–Easter week, dinner only, Wed–Sun from 5pm.
   Children's Services: Children's menu (dinner only), highchairs, booster seats.
This big, friendly place is perfectly located right on the main street. You can sit in either the garden-like open-air room in front, or in the newly refurbished inside dining room.

At lunch there are hamburgers, salads, and sandwiches. The children's menu (dinner only) offers a choice of spaghetti, a burger and french fries, or fried chicken for $6 or $7. Adults can sample pasta, seafood, ribs, steak, or the house speciality—duck à l'orange. Soup and salad included.

Adult portions can be split, baby bottles and baby food can be warmed in the kitchen, and special children's drinks can be made. In summer, arrive between 5 and 6pm if you have hungry children in tow.

THE BUSY BEE, 306 Crescent Ave., Avalon. Tel. 213/510-1983.
   Cuisine: AMERICAN. **Reservations:** Not accepted.
$ Prices: Breakfast $4.50–$8; lunch $7; dinner $7.50–$13. AE, CB, DC, DISC, MC, V.
   Open: Summer, Mon–Fri 8am–11pm, Sat–Sun 8am–10pm; winter, daily 8am–8pm, depending on the weather.
   Children's Services: Highchairs, booster seats.
Eating outside is always fun in Catalina. At the Busy Bee, eating outside means that the kids can occupy themselves watching the harbor and feeding the pushy seagulls that congregate beneath the dock. The atmosphere is nautical and casual. Breakfast selections include eggs, omelets, buttermilk pancakes, and Belgian waffles. For lunch there are Mexican dishes, a large selection of salads and hamburgers, hot sandwiches, and health foods. The dinner menu is quite limited—steak, barbecued chicken,

corned beef and cabbage, and pasta. There are numerous homemade dessert selections.

5. SANTA BARBARA & THE SURROUNDING AREA

SANTA BARBARA

North of Los Angeles lie some easily accessible areas that make marvelous weekend trips. Santa Barbara is a treasure of a town in a gorgeous setting with the ocean on one side and the Santa Ynez Mountains on the other. The temperatures are almost perfect, and there are activities for every season. Its Andalusian-like look of red-tile roofs and white Spanish buildings complements the easy-going attitude of its inhabitants. To this add fantastic wide beaches and a wonderful, long bike path and you have a near-perfect city.

GETTING THERE Santa Barbara is just 90 miles north of Los Angeles by car on Calif. 1 or U.S. 101.

The **Santa Barbara Airport** is served by a number of local and national carriers. If you choose to visit Santa Barbara before Los Angeles, the **Santa Barbara Airbus** can whisk you to and from Los Angeles International Airport (tel. 805/964-7759 or 805/964-7374, or toll free 800/423-1618). Major rental-car companies are located at the airport and in town.

Amtrak (tel. toll free 800/USA-RAIL) serves Santa Barbara direct from Los Angeles, San Diego, and San Francisco. Be sure to make your reservations a month in advance—this is the same train that travels up the coast, and it books up quickly.

There is also **Greyhound Bus** (tel. toll free 800/237-8211) service linking major cities with Santa Barbara.

INFORMATION Before you arrive you may want to contact the **Santa Barbara Conference and Visitors Bureau,** 510 State Street, Suite A, Santa Barbara, CA 93101 (tel. 805/966-9222). When in town, stop by the **Santa Barbara Visitor Information Center,** 1 Santa Barbara Street (tel. 805/965-3021), to find out all the facts you need. The center is open daily from 9am to 5pm.

CITY LAYOUT **State Street** is one of the main shopping streets in town, its hub between Victoria Street and the ocean. State Street is lined with boutiques, cafés, snack shops, bookstores, a balloon store, a toy store, T-shirt shops, and Mexican import shops. On **Brinkerhoff Avenue** you'll find a large number of antique stores.

State Street and **Cabrillo Boulevard** is the point at which Stearns Wharf begins and the Santa Barbara Trolley stops (more information in "What to See & Do," below). This is where you'll find the statue of the dolphin, a good point to use as a meeting place when the family separates to do different things.

The main streets downtown are one way, running east and west. All of Santa Barbara is a dream to get around in. Signs aim you toward important points of interest. Cabrillo Boulevard leads you to most of the important streets; you can find them off **U.S. 101** too, but that can get extremely crowded, especially during the summer.

GETTING AROUND　　It seems that everyone in Santa Barbara has a bicycle, and the bicycles here get plenty of use. Just about everywhere you look there are families pedaling those Italian Pedalinas, cute red four-wheel cycles with canvas tops. Junior (up to 50 pounds) sits in the front and mom and dad do all the work pedaling. But the Pedalinas aren't just limited to family fun. Teenagers like to rent them too, and go tooling down the beach.

Bicycles are easy to rent in Santa Barbara. Stop at **Cycles-4-Rent,** 101 State Street (tel. 805/966-3804). Cycles-4-Rent also operates out of Fess Parker's Red Lion Inn at a stand located poolside. Or visit **Beach Rentals,** directly across the street from Stearns Wharf at 8 West Cabrillo Boulevard (tel. 805/963-2524).

A trolley trip is another fun way to see the city or get from one point to another. The **Santa Barbara Trolley** is no exception. Catch it at the dolphin statue, State Street and Cabrillo Boulevard (tel. 805/565-1122). The 90-minute narrated tours take you (not in this order) through Montecito, past the Court House, up State Street, by La Cumbre Shopping Plaza, make a stop at the Mission, and end back at Stearns Wharf. If your flock gets antsy, you can get on or off the trolley at any time along the route. Tours leave every 90 minutes beginning at 10am.

SPECIAL EVENTS　　For 5 days in early August each year, it's fiesta time in Santa Barbara. **Old Spanish Days in Santa Barbara** is an exciting street celebration, created to preserve and perpetuate the city's heritage, which began with its Spanish roots. One of Santa Barbara's important fiestas was the 1920 celebration of the dedication of the Santa Barbara Mission—that's how far back these fiestas go. During the 5-day celebration there are two parades (including the Children's Parade, with more than 2,000 children participating), a children's variety show, free performances, and a rodeo. A special marketplace is set up, and dancing takes place in the streets into the night. Everywhere you look there are tortilla stands, piñatas, and women dressed in traditional lace mantillas. Contact the office of Old Spanish Days in Santa Barbara, 1122 North Milpas Street, Santa Barbara, CA 93101 (tel. 805/962-8101), for the dates of this year's fiesta. And if you plan to stay over during the fiesta, make reservations as far in advance as possible, because the town gets booked up 100%.

WHAT TO SEE & DO

In addition to the following four "sights," there's a lot of beach and water activity in Santa Barbara. Read on.

SANTA BARBARA ZOOLOGICAL GARDENS, 500 Niños Dr., off Cabrillo Blvd. Tel. 805/962-5339, or 805/962-6310 for recorded information.

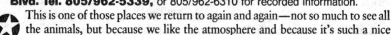
This is one of those places we return to again and again—not so much to see all the animals, but because we like the atmosphere and because it's such a nice place to let the kids wander and play.

The miniature train ride ($1 for adults, 50¢ for children) and farmyard are always a huge success. The children's zoo is a particularly nice one, and it's especially popular with the youngsters who love to chase the goats.

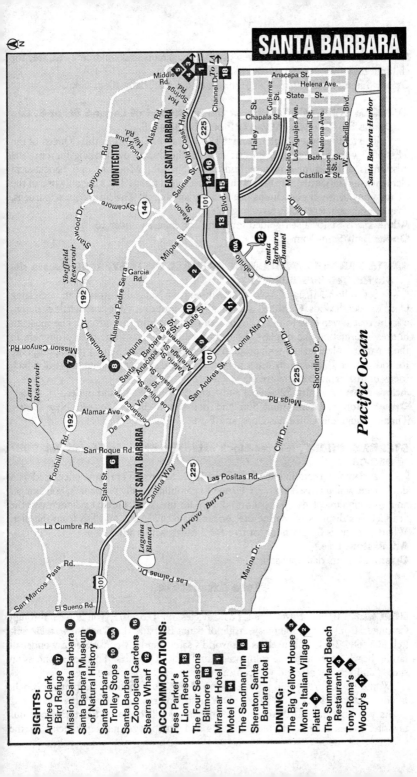

SANTA BARBARA

SIGHTS:
Andree Clark
Bird Refuge ⑰
Mission Santa Barbara ⑧
Santa Barbara Museum
of Natural History ⑦
Santa Barbara
Trolley Stops ⑩ ⑩A
Santa Barbara
Zoological Gardens ⑯
Stearns Wharf ⑫

ACCOMMODATIONS:
Fess Parker's
Lion Resort ⑬
The Four Seasons
Biltmore ⑱
Miramar Hotel ①
Motel 6 ⑭
The Sandman Inn ⑥
Sheraton Santa
Barbara Hotel ⑮

DINING:
The Big Yellow House ③
Mom's Italian Village ②
Piatti ⑤
The Summerland Beach
Restaurant ④
Tony Roma's ⑨
Woody's ⑪

Pacific Ocean

Admission: $4 adults and children over 12, $2 seniors and children 2–12, free for children under 2.
Open: Summer, daily 9am–6pm; the rest of the year, daily 10am–5pm.

MISSION SANTA BARBARA, at the upper end of Laguna St. at E. Los Olivos St. Tel. 805/682-4713 or 805/682-4715.

The tenth of the 21 Franciscan missions built in California, this "Queen of the Missions" was founded in 1786. Set in a striking locale overlooking the city, the mission is a beautiful structure built with Spanish, Moorish, and neoclassical elements, and its gardens are exceptionally lovely and tranquil. It's the only one of the 21 missions to be in continuous use as a parish church. The little rooms, gardens, chapel, and cemetery don't take long to see.
Admission: $1 for a self-guided tour, free for children under 16.
Open: Daily 9am–5pm.

SANTA BARBARA MUSEUM OF NATURAL HISTORY, 2559 Puesta del Sol Rd. Tel. 805/682-4711.

Set in lush Mission Canyon, the Museum of Natural History is an interesting place to take the kids. Outside is a fascinating 72-foot touchable blue-whale skeleton, a sight that never fails to elicit "oohs" and "aahs" from our group. The museum houses information and displays about the Chumash Indians (the tribe prominent in these parts), a planetarium with programs every Saturday and Sunday (not appropriate for kids under 7), and many other permanent and changing exhibits, most of which focus on the Santa Barbara area.
Admission: $3 adults, $2 seniors and teens, $1 children 12 and under.
Open: Mon–Sat 9am–5pm, Sun and hols 10am–5pm. **Closed:** New Year's, Thanksgiving, and Christmas Days, and Fiesta.

STEARNS WHARF, a three-block extension of State Street. Tel. 805/963-0611.

A Santa Barbara landmark built in 1872, Stearns Wharf was once used as a dock from which passengers were ferried to gambling boats. Nowadays, you can get an ice-cream cone; have your palm read; stop for breakfast, lunch, or dinner; visit the Sea Center's displays of marine life; or rent bait and tackle and fish from the pier. Wharf parking is $2 per hour, or free for 2 hours with a validation.
Admission: Free.
Open: 24 hours daily (wharf).

More Attractions

BEACHES If you travel from Los Angeles on U.S. 101, you'll pass through Carpinteria. Just a few minutes outside of Santa Barbara, the **Carpinteria Beach** (tel. 805/684-2811) bills itself as the world's safest, and it's considered a wonderful family beach because of the calm waters and lack of riptides. There are concession stands and rest rooms, and you can camp here.

Would-be surfers should go to **Rincon Point,** just south of Carpinteria Beach, famous for having perfect waves, and the best winter waves for surfers.

As you continue north through Montecito, you'll come to **East Beach,** our favorite. It has dozens of volleyball nets and fun playground equipment. At the

Cabrillo Bath House at East Beach (you can't miss it), you can rent just about anything you need for a day in the sun, including beach chairs and umbrellas. A parking lot is adjacent, and there's food service and rest rooms.

You can't miss Chase Palm Park, before you get to the pier, with its grassy areas perfect for playing Frisbee and having picnics. Just past the pier is **West Beach,** considered the best spot for windsurfing (parking and rest rooms available); then comes **Leadbetter Beach,** with a parking lot, picnic areas, and rest rooms. The Sea Cove Café, on the beach, is good for an outdoor snack.

If you continue farther north, you'll come to **Arroyo Beach,** one of the nicest beaches in the area, with parking, picnic areas, and rest rooms. You can surf here, too.

A BICYCLE TOUR A 3⅓-mile, two-lane bikeway beginning on Cabrillo Boulevard is easy to navigate and leads you through the beaches, crossing the boulevard at Milpas Street. Heading east, you'll come to the **Andrée Clark Bird Refuge,** 1400 East Cabrillo Boulevard, a 42-acre preserve of ducks and other waterfowl, and little islands dotting the lagoon. We like to spend an hour or so walking through the preserve on the separate footpath.

On our way back, we sometimes ride to the Santa Barbara Zoo, but only when we've rented standard bikes rather than the Pedalinas. You can also ride up Stearns Wharf, but we don't do that with the Pedalinas either.

For details on bike rentals, see "Getting Around," above.

HARBOR CRUISES AND WHALE WATCHING Harbor cruises are less available in Santa Barbara than elsewhere on the coast but they are possible. Call **Captain Don's Harbour Cruises** (tel. 805/969-5217) for a fully narrated tour on the *Harbour Queen.*

One of the most special once-a-year events is California whale watching. Join the **Santa Barbara Museum of Natural History** (tel. 805/682-4711) on its selected excursions in February and March. You can't make phone reservations, but you can call to find out this year's dates and to request a reservation form. But do this well in advance—these are special trips, led by naturalists and museum docents, and they fill up early. You'll board the *Condor,* at Sea Landing, at 9am for a 2½-hour trip. Adults pay $16; children 12 and under, $12.

The **Condor,** Sea Landing, Breakwater (tel. 805/963-3564), also goes out on whale-watching trips not sponsored by the museum. These trips are available from February to the first of May, daily during the height of the season.

WATER SPORTS **Sailing** is a wonderful activity to pursue in Santa Barbara, and you can partake of it even if you've never sailed before. There are a number of companies offering everything from customized family trips to individual lessons. **Windsurfing** is also popular, and there are plenty of services offering lessons and rentals. **Sportfishing** and **scuba diving** round out the water activities.

To arrange fishing or diving trips, call Sea Landing (tel. 805/963-3564; 24hr recording plus operator assistance). For further information about water sports, telephone the Conference and Visitors Bureau at 805/966-9222.

WHERE TO STAY

Very Expensive

FOUR SEASONS BILTMORE, 1260 Channel Dr., Santa Barbara, CA

93108. Tel. 805/969-2261, or toll free 800/332-3442. Fax 805/969-5715. 186 rms, 75 suites. MINIBAR TV TEL

$ Rates: $250–$375 standard room; $325 cottage room; $425 junior suite; $650–$1,700 other suites. Children under 18 and extra adults stay free. Cribs and rollaways free. AE, CB, DC, DISC, MC, V. **Parking:** Valet.

This is certainly one of the best and most beautiful places in the deluxe category to stay with a family. Built as a private residence in the early 1900s, the Biltmore sits off the Olive Mill Road exit from the Ventura Freeway (U.S. 101), on 19 lush acres with views of both the ocean and the Santa Ynez Mountains. The hacienda-style main building, the clusters of smaller individual cottages, the extraordinary gardens and walkways, the grand lobby, and the Patio dining room are painstakingly maintained. Just walking through the gardens of fuchsias, roses, impatiens, tropical trees, and other plants—which, you can tell, have been here for years—creates serenity and is actually a perfect activity with a young child.

Inquire about the "Kids Four All Seasons" summer children's program (ages 5 to 12). There is also a Star Fish program with a focus on swimming. The concierge can provide numerous family amenities from sundries to games and toys.

Dining/Entertainment: The Patio restaurant is set in a glass-enclosed courtyard, with a retractable ceiling; al fresco dining is available when weather permits. Adults can order salads, full main courses, and a few sandwiches. There is a great children's menu with reasonable prices. Room service has children's selections, but you must ask for them. There is poolside food service and take-out from the Raft. If adults want a special night out alone, the elegant La Marina restaurant features nouvelle cuisine and an ocean view.

Services: 24-hour room service, concierge, baby-sitting, laundry service.

Facilities: Tennis courts, shuffleboard, croquet, putting green, bikes (free), two swimming pools, sundeck, spas; terrycloth robes, hairdryers, makeup mirrors, and two telephones in each room.

Expensive

FESS PARKER'S RED LION RESORT, 633 E. Cabrillo Blvd., Santa Barbara, CA 93103. Tel. 805/564-4333 or 805/547-8010, or toll free 800/879-2929. Fax 805/564-4964. 360 rms and suites. A/C MINIBAR TV TEL

$ Rates: $180–$250 standard room single or double; $225 and $280 deluxe room single or double; $340–$700 suite. Children under 18 stay free in their parents' room. Additional guests $15; cribs free; rollaways $15. Package plans available. CB, DC, DISC, MC, V. **Parking:** Valet or self-parking.

The Red Lion is just cross from the beach and minutes from the zoo and town. You can't miss it as you drive up Cabrillo Boulevard—it's the one painted that gorgeous pink with the huge rotunda in front. There's a big heated fenced-in pool and spa, poolside barbecues on weekends, Pedalinas and standard bikes available for rent poolside, three night-lit tennis courts, a health club and sauna, a putting green, and shuffleboard court. The concierge can arrange activities and baby-sitting.

Even standard rooms here are oversized. Along with the standard cable channels is the Disney Channel, HBO, and pay-per-view movies. Every room has a double vanity. Deluxe rooms have small sitting areas and the bathrooms are huge. All rooms are soundproof.

Dining/Entertainment: The coffee shop–style Café Los Arcos is open long hours and has a children's menu.

Services: Room service (6am to 11pm), baby-sitting.

Facilities: Heated pool, spa, health club, sauna, bicycle rentals, tennis courts, putting green, shuffleboard.

Moderate

MIRAMAR HOTEL, U.S. 101 at San Ysidro Rd., Santa Barbara, CA 93102. Tel. 805/969-2203, or toll free 800/322-6983. Fax 805/969-3163. 212 rms, suites, and cottages. TV TEL **Directions:** Take the Pacific Coast Highway (Calif. 1) to the San Ysidro turnoff.

$ Rates: $70–$125 standard room single or double; $100–$285 cottage single or double. Children 12 and under stay free in their parents' room. Additional guests over 12 $8 per night; cribs $10; rollaways free. May–Oct, 2-night minimum stay on weekends, 3 nights on hols. AE, MC, V. **Parking:** Free.

Families have been heading for the blue-tile roofs of the Miramar Hotel for years. The two pools, rooms right on the beach, grassy play areas, and roomy cottages have created its popularity. In summer the hotel anchors a raft off the beach for guests' use. There's always a lifeguard and beach equipment. You can also rent bikes and play tennis, paddle tennis, table tennis, or shuffleboard.

Newly refurbished poolside rooms have one double bed and one twin downstairs, or two double beds upstairs. Oceanfront rooms are big, with two double beds and room for a crib. These rooms can connect with a parlor that sleeps two and has a full kitchen. This could then connect to yet another bedroom, making it a full suite that can sleep 10. Cottages come in various configurations from a one-bedroom cottage with a kitchenette and a fireplace to a three-bedroom cottage. Most cottages have small wood decks. Light sleepers should note: A train comes through the grounds in the middle of the night.

Dining/Entertainment: An authentic railcar houses a diner that serves up light meals. There's also a full-service dining room open for breakfast, lunch, and dinner.

Services: Room service.

Facilities: Two pools, bicycle rentals, tennis courts, table tennis, paddle tennis, shuffleboard.

SHERATON SANTA BARBARA HOTEL, 1111 E. Cabrillo Blvd., Santa Barbara, CA 93103. Tel. 805/963-0744, 213/278-8014 in Los Angeles, or toll free 800/325-3535. Fax 805/962-0985. 173 rms, 5 suites. A/C MINIBAR TV TEL

$ Rates: July to early Sept, $119–$184 single or double; mid-Sept to June, $89–$169 single or double; $250–$475 suite. Children under 17 stay free in their parents' room. Extra adults $10 per night; cribs and rollaways free. AE, CB, MC, V. **Parking:** Free self-parking.

Soft desert hues and casual wood furniture decorate this comfortable hotel, which is conveniently located off the Ventura Freeway (U.S. 101) just across the street from East Beach, and within walking distance of the Santa Barbara Zoo. Rooms vary in size, so let the reservationist know your needs. There are plenty of connecting rooms.

Room service and poolside food service are available. Zack's at the Beach serves breakfast, lunch, and dinner. A children's menu is offered at lunch. There's complimentary coffee service in the lobby from 6 to 9am.

A small fenced-in heated pool looks out to the ocean; the health club includes a weight room, Jacuzzi, sauna, massage room, showers, and lockers. There are bike rentals on the property.

Budget

MOTEL 6, 443 Corona del Mar, Santa Barbara, CA 93103. Tel. 805/564-1392 or 505/891-6161. 52 rms. TEL TV

$ Rates: $37.95 single; $43.95 double. Children under 18 stay free in their parents' room. Additional adults $6; cribs free; no rollaways. AE, CB, DC, DISC, MC, V. **Parking:** Free.

⑤ This Motel 6 has as its claim to fame the distinction of being the first Motel 6 ever built. It's always booked (because of its wonderful location behind the Sheraton Santa Barbara Hotel within walking distance of the beach), so it's necessary to make reservations far in advance. There's a small, fenced-in heated pool near the parking lot, and lots of vending machines.

Four corner rooms are larger than the standard units and have partial ocean views. Singles have room for a crib; it would be a tight squeeze in a double—you'd be better off to get connecting rooms. Rooms are clean and tidy, and come with color TVs with a movie channel, and small dressing areas.

SANDMAN INN, 3714 State St., Santa Barbara, CA 93105. Tel. 805/687-2468, or toll free 800/457-2880 in California. Fax 805/687-6581. 110 rms, 8 suites, A/C TV TEL.

$ Rates: (including continental breakfast, wine, and cheese): $66–$74 single; $84–$110 double; $105–$130 minisuite or suite. Children under 16 stay free in their parents' room. Additional adults $5 per night; cribs free; rollaways $5. Weekly and monthly rates available. AE, DC, MC, V. **Parking:** Free.

About 15 minutes from the ocean, and within blocks of a big shopping center, the Sandman is a good budget choice. It has two fenced-in swimming pools and a spa. There is room service beginning at noon, and a restaurant is on the premises. A poolside room with a king-size bed is nice for a small family; the minisuite or two-room units are best for larger families. Color TV with basic cable channels is standard in all rooms.

WHERE TO EAT

PIATTI, 516 San Ysidro Rd., in Montecito. Tel. 805/969-7520.
   Cuisine: ITALIAN. **Reservations:** Accepted. **Directions:** Take the San Ysidro Road exit off U.S. 101.
$ Prices: Dinner main courses $7.50–$16.95. MC, V.
   Open: Lunch Mon–Fri 11:30am–2:30pm; Sat–Sun noon–2:30pm; dinner Sun–Thurs 5–10pm, Fri–Sat 5–11pm.
   Children's Services: Booster seats.

Piatti is trendy, suburban, rustic, and contemporary all rolled into one. We'd suggest it for school-age kids and up. There's indoor and al fresco dining, a small open-air kitchen, and a young, extremely professional staff to serve you. The food is delicious and fresh. There are familiar choices, such as angel-hair pasta with fresh tomatoes, basil, garlic, and olive oil; a grilled veal chop; and ravioli filled with spinach and ricotta; as well as many specialties—*beef* scaloppine; whole peppers stuffed with spaghetti, black olives, cheeses, and tomato sauce; and lasagne al pesto (this is made with grilled zucchini, tomato pasta, sun-dried tomatoes, pine nuts, and assorted cheeses). Salads are enticing, there's a nice selection of antipasti, and several pizza and calzone selections are baked in their special oven. Children often split the pizza, salad, or spaghetti, we're told. The restaurant serves lots of kids at Saturday and Sunday lunch; for dinner, the best time to come with children is usually between 5 and 7pm. There is a parking lot.

TONY ROMA'S, 26 W. Anapamu St. Tel. 805/963-3278.

Cuisine: BARBECUE. **Reservations:** Accepted. **Directions:** Take the Chapala Street exit off U.S. 101 and drive north to Anapamu Street.

$ Prices: Main courses $5–$13.95; Sun brunch $11.95. MC, V.

Open: Sun–Thurs 11am–10pm; Fri–Sat 11am–midnight. Brunch Sun 10am–2pm.

Children's Services: Children's menu, table toys, crayons, highchairs, boosters.

A statement on the menu reads: "Children are our special guests at Tony Roma's, too. That's why we have a special menu just for kids." Can't get more welcoming than that, can you? If you've been to a Tony Roma's in another city, you'll recognize the menu selections. This downtown Santa Barbara location adds a few things. On the special summer lunch menu, you'll discover chicken salad Oriental, a barbecued-turkey sandwich, and a barbecued-sausage sandwich, in addition to the regular offerings on the year-round menu, such as lunch and dinner portions of the famous ribs, barbecued chicken, salads, and fish. Dinner is much of the same.

The kid's choices are simple: chicken fingers, a hamburger, child's portion of ribs, or crisp ravioli pockets filled with ground beef—all with fries—priced between $2.95 and $4.95. Kid-style drinks can be ordered too, made with a mix of juice and soda or cream. Little ones get entertained with crayons and little table toys. Baby bottles and baby food will be warmed upon request.

Sunday brunch comes with complimentary champagne and a huge selection of ribs, made-to-order omelets, barbecued or marinated chicken, salads, fish, French toast, breakfast meats and potatoes, a variety of appetizers, and just-baked breads and desserts. Adults are charged $11.95; kids under 10 pay only $3.95.

Seating is indoors or out. There is a full bar and an extensive wine list. When you call for reservations, ask about weekly specials—when we were there, kids ate free at Saturday lunch, and the restaurant offered an all-you-can-eat rib night for $9.95. There's street parking, or you can use City Lot No. 5, behind the restaurant.

MOM'S ITALIAN VILLAGE, 421 E. Cota St. Tel. 805/965-5588.

Cuisine: ITALIAN. **Reservations:** Accepted only for three or more, and strongly recommended during the summer. **Directions:** Take the Milpas Street exit off U.S. 101; it's at Milpas Street and Cota Street.

$ Prices: Dinner main courses $6.50–$13.95. MC, V.

Open: Lunch Tues–Fri 11:30am–2:30pm; dinner Tues–Sun 5–10pm.

Children's Services: Children's menu, highchairs, booster seats.

This old-fashioned neighborhood restaurant is a wonderful place to take the family for dinner. Although there is seating for 250 people, the attitude is small-town friendly. You can tell Mom's constantly gets repeat customers because regulars know the buspersons by name, and servers who aren't busy can be spotted calming fussy children.

The children's menu, for kids 10 and under, consists of spaghetti, ravioli, roast tri-tip (a beef roast, a local favorite), halibut, breaded veal cutlets, ground sirloin with mushroom gravy, and a couple of other pasta choices. Prices range from $4.75 to $8.95.

Adults have a large selection to choose from. There are full dinners of chicken à la cacciatore, beef spezzatini, veal scaloppine, and other fish, chicken, and steak dinners, which come with vegetables and potatoes, bread, and butter. Pasta dinners include a salad and bread and butter. Many of these dishes are vegetarian. There's also a yummy lasagne and Mom's eggplant parmigiana, a favorite. You can get a number of deluxe dinner courses à la carte.

Baby bottles and food can be warmed, and special children's drinks can be made at the bar. Servers bring bread right away so kids can munch, and the children get suckers on their way out. Street parking is available.

WOODY'S, 229 W. Montecito St. Tel. 805/963-9326.
Cuisine: BARBECUE. **Reservations:** Mon–Fri nights only. **Directions:** Take U.S. 101 to the Chapala Street exit and turn left to Montecito Street.
$ Prices: Lunch $3.75–$4.75; dinner $3.75–$12.95. MC, V.
Open: Mon–Sat 11am–11pm; Sun 11am–10pm.
Children's Services: Children's menu, highchairs (plastic-wrapped), booster seats.

It may be a little hard to find, but it's worth it. The place is lively and the price is right. Sawdust covers the floor, red-and-white-checkered plastic tablecloths cover the tables, and there's a big-screen TV for entertainment. Walls are lined with old skis and license plates, pails, signs, etc. There's plenty for little eyes to look at while you stand in line to place your order.

The "Kids Stuff" menu, for "Woody's little buddies under 12," includes a hot dog, a kidburger, or one-quarter chicken ($2.50 to $3.45).

Other options, for everyone, include ribs, chicken, smoked duckling, barbecued beef, turkey and tri-tip, eight styles of hamburgers, and chili served several ways. Main courses include barbecue beans, fries, and bread, and you can order an extra portion of ribs for only $4.25 with any dinner. Lunches include coleslaw, beans, or fries. If these aren't enough, there's also a salad bar, sausage sandwiches, chicken wings, fish, and shrimp. Beer and wine are served.

They will warm bottles and baby food. There's street parking, or you can park in the lot across the street after 5pm.

In Nearby Summerland

The following two choices are in suburban Summerland, about 12 miles south of downtown Santa Barbara on U.S. 101; take the Summerland exit.

THE BIG YELLOW HOUSE, 108 Pierpont Ave., Summerland. Tel. 805/ 969-4140.
Cuisine: AMERICAN. **Reservations:** Accepted.
$ Prices: Breakfast, $4.50–$9.25; lunch $3.95–$9.25; dinner $7–$16.95. AE, MC, V.
Open: Sun–Thurs 7:30am–9pm, Fri–Sat 7:30am–10pm.

Children's Services: Children's menu, highchairs, booster seats.

Located just outside Santa Barbara and minutes from Montecito, this is an excellent choice for breakfast, lunch, or dinner. The service is efficient and friendly, and the charming restaurant is occupied by its own ghost, named Hector. The house itself, which is more than 100 years old, has an interesting history (read all about it on the back of the menu).

Besides the standard French toast and buttermilk pancakes for breakfast, there's also grandma's fruit stacks—a stack of hot apples, blueberries, strawberries, and bananas with whipped cream—or blueberry hotcakes with honey–wheat-germ topping. Homemade corned-beef hash, huevos rancheros, and standard egg dishes round out the offerings.

If you come for lunch, there's a kids' burger with chips for $3.25. Or order off the main menu: a basket of chicken (fried chicken is the specialty here), salads, tempura beer-batter fish, standard-sized hamburgers, homemade chili, and hot and cold sandwiches.

Dinner is a great time to come with the family. Adults get broiled tri-tip (a local beef favorite), famous fried chicken, pork chops, chicken breast, prime rib, fish, seafood, pot roast, or a vegetarian platter, all with soup or salad, a vegetable, mashed potatoes and gravy, and a fresh-baked corn muffin. You can order any size portion of a main course for your children and the server will determine the price by weight. Or order the kid's hamburger, which is $2.95 at dinner. Adults can add two pieces of fried chicken to any dinner selection for an additional $3.25, so if you have a very light eater, order the extra chicken with your main course. Kids get a free dessert sherbet cone.

Baby bottles and baby food can be warmed, and special drinks can be made. A parking lot is available.

SUMMERLAND BEACH RESTAURANT, 2294 Lillie Ave., Summerland. Tel. 805/969-1019.

Cuisine: AMERICAN. **Reservations:** Accepted only for parties of six or more.
$ Prices: $3–$4.75. MC, V.
Open: Mon–Fri 7am–3pm, Sat–Sun 7am–4pm (opens at 6am in summer).
Children's Services: Children's menu, Sassy seats, booster seats.

Only breakfast and lunch are served in this turn-of-the-century–style restaurant decorated with wooden benches and booths, stained-glass windows, stenciled wall decorations, and hanging plants and ceiling fans. Portions are large and can be split, but there's a children's menu for the 12-and-under set. Junior French toast, eggs, or a cheese omelet will wake them up. Each $2.25 breakfast comes with either fresh fruit, sausage or bacon, or potatoes (depending on the main dish), plus a muffin. Grilled cheese or a turkey "samwich" are the luncheon items ($2.25 and $2.95).

The regular menu lists 10 versions of omelets, which include potatoes, an English muffin, and fresh fruit and are priced quite reasonably at $4.85. Or there's oatmeal, Belgian waffles (served with or without a fruit topping), and French toast (either topped with powdered sugar and cinnamon, or made out of cinnamon-swirl bread). Lunch consists of a variety of healthy sandwiches (like apples, raisins, and tuna mixed with honey-mustard dressing and served on raisin bread), salads, and hamburgers (besides the traditional burgers, there's one served with peanut butter, bacon, and Jack cheese!).

Servers will bring extra plates for splitting meals at no charge, and will gladly warm baby food and bottles in the kitchen.

There's a parking lot, and some street parking is available.

VENTURA/OXNARD

The Ventura/Oxnard area is within easy driving distance of Los Angeles and Santa Barbara. From Los Angeles, take the Ventura Freeway (U.S. 101) north—or from Santa Barbara, take U.S. 101 south—to the Rose Avenue exit going west. Go right on Gonzales Road and take that all the way to Harbor Boulevard. At Harbor Boulevard, turn right for Ventura, left for Oxnard.

Some people make Oxnard or Ventura their base, others visit for the day. Ventura and Oxnard are only about 10 or 15 minutes apart on Harbor Boulevard.

VENTURA

What to See & Do

THE CHANNEL ISLANDS Located just off the coast of Ventura is one of the area's main attractions. The Channel Islands are a group of eight islands off the California coast, five of which comprise **Channel Islands National Park.**

You'll want to start out at the **Visitor Center,** at 1901 Spinnaker Drive (tel. 805/644-8262). Not only will you get information on the islands, plus maps and brochures, but the children will also enjoy the little museum of marine life that includes an indoor tidepool and displays of Chumash Indian artifacts. Special weekend programs provide interesting facts about the animals and birds that inhabit the area. These programs are conducted by park rangers and are most appropriate for youngsters over 6. A free 25-minute film about the islands is shown, and some children will enjoy this. The Visitor Center is open daily from 8am to 5:30pm.

Next door to the Visitor Center is **Island Packers,** 1867 Spinnaker Drive, Ventura, Ca 93001 (tel. 805/642-1393 for reservations, 805/642-7688 for information), the official park concessionaire. This is where you'll get information and make reservations to tour the islands. Island Packers runs boats to Santa Cruz, Anacapa, and Santa Barbara islands regularly during spring and summer and at scheduled times the rest of the year. They take small groups to the islands on basic, open boats to capture the feel of the environment. You will not be embarking on plush cruise boats. There are rest rooms on board, but no food service. There's a deli/snack shop near the embarkation point.

The islands are virtually unsullied by development—their natural state has been maintained. These rugged islands are wonderful fun for boys and girls who love to explore, but come prepared: Wear layered clothing for warmth, and shoes with good gripping soles for walking. If you intend to hike, be prepared to carry young children. Tell the kids they'll be seeing some very precious sea and land mammals, plants, endangered brown pelicans, and exquisite wildflowers. Because the islands are undisturbed, the sea life is abundant. Kids are fascinated by the teeming life in the tidepools. Rock formations, giant sea caves, and steep cliffs vary among the different islands, and some can be seen as the boat gets closer to the islands. Happily, there are no souvenir shops on the islands and no stores. On some of the islands there's not even fresh water, so you'll have to fill your own canteens ahead of time.

STROLLING, SHOPPING, SNACKS Once you're back on the mainland, you may want to visit **Ventura Harbor Village,** 1559 Spinnaker Drive, off Harbor

Boulevard in Ventura Harbor (tel. 805/644-0169), a quaint village of shops selling souvenirs and gifts. Of particular interest to the kids are the shells, kites, and nautical items. Adjacent to the Ventura Yacht Club and overlooking the harbor, it's a charming spot for an afternoon stroll. There are lots of restaurants, including many places to eat outdoors. Keep your eyes open for the **Carousel Market,** which has an indoor carousel surrounded by shops selling cotton candy, popcorn, hot dogs, and souvenirs. Look for boat rentals along Spinnaker Drive.

The Village gets crowded on weekends, and parking, even in the lot, can try your patience. Stores are open daily from 10am to 6pm; restaurant hours vary.

HARBOR CRUISES Every hour on the hour, 40-minute cruises of Ventura Harbor are available on the *Harbor Queen* or the *Bay Queen* (tel. 805/642-7753), which are docked at 1567 Spinnaker Drive in Ventura Harbor Village adjacent to the Coastal Cone Co. Tours depart in the winter on Saturday and Sunday from noon to 5pm; in summer, Tuesday through Sunday from noon to 5pm. Fares are $4 for adults, $3 for children under 12; under 2, free.

Where to Eat

Although there are numerous fast-food restaurants in the vicinity, two sit-down restaurants deserve a mention.

LA MARINA CANTINA, in Ventura Harbor Village, 1567 Spinnaker Dr. Tel. 805/658-7067.

Cuisine: MEXICAN. **Reservations:** Not accepted.
$ **Prices:** Lunch $3.25–$6.75; dinner $7.50–$10.50. MC, V.
Open: Mon–Fri 11am–10pm, Sat 9am–11pm, Sun 9am–10pm.
Children's Services: Children's menu, booster seats, highchairs.

La Marina has an outdoor patio and a view of the harbor from its spot at the top of the lighthouse. The Mexican food is simple and delicious, and the prices are reasonable. There's a children's menu priced at $2.50 with several popular selections. Management will gladly split orders, warm baby food and bottles, and make special children's drinks. There's parking in the Ventura Harbor Village lot.

CHRISTY'S, in Ventura Harbor Village, 1559 Spinnaker Dr. Tel. 805/642-3116.

Cuisine: AMERICAN.
$ **Prices:** Average $4.50. MC, V.
Open: Daily 7am–3pm.
Children's Services: Boosters, highchairs.

This is another good choice. Open for breakfast and lunch, Christy's serves eggs, omelets, sandwiches, salads, and burgers. There's no harbor view or children's menu, but the food is good. They keep a stock of children's books to entertain the kids. Parking is in the Village lot.

OXNARD

The primary connection between Ventura and Oxnard is Harbor Boulevard, a 4-mile stretch with a well-marked bike trail on each side of the road.

Oxnard's **Channel Islands Harbor** is the city's main waterfront recreation area. There are 7 miles of uncrowded beaches just north of the harbor, and slips for more than 2,500 pleasure boats. Sportfishing boats and boat rentals are plentiful at South Victoria Avenue, Channel Islands Landing.

INFORMATION A small **Visitor Center,** located at 3600 South Harbor Boulevard, in the Marine Emporium, Suite 215, Channel Islands Harbor, Oxnard, CA 93035 (tel. 805/985-4852), can give you maps and special-event information. Or contact the **Oxnard Convention and Visitors Bureau,** 400 Esplanade Drive, Oxnard, CA 93030 (tel. 805/485-8833).

SPECIAL EVENTS If you plan to be in the area in the spring, be sure to allow time for the annual **Strawberry Festival,** a 2-day event that attracts more than 50,000 people. Everything revolves around that tasty fruit, including strawberry shortcake–eating contests and the judging of the outstanding strawberry blonde (there's one of these contests for 5- to 12-year-olds, too). There are bands, dances, arts and crafts displays, and tons of strawberry products for sale. The Oxnard Convention and Visitors Bureau (see "Information," above) can give you this year's exact dates.

What to See & Do

If you want to go biking on the Harbor Boulevard bicycle paths, you can rent a bicycle at **Cycles 4 Rent,** 2800 South Harbor Boulevard, at the front of the shopping center (tel. 805/652-0462). There are some children's beach cruisers, plus adult mountain bikes, pedalinas (quadricycles), and tandems. Helmets are free. It's open in summer, Monday through Friday from 10am to 6pm and on Saturday and Sunday from 9am to sunset; in winter, on Saturday and Sunday only.

McGRATH STATE PARK AND BEACH, off Harbor Boulevard.

The beach is a 10-minute walk from the parking lot. Pretty and peaceful, and equipped with barbecue pits and picnic tables, McGrath is a day-use park, but also has a campground (174 developed sites). The public beach makes a great morning or afternoon stop. There's also a nature trail and other hiking areas in the park.

Admission: $4 per car for day use, $12 overnight, $2 for walk-in camping. Make campsite reservations through MISTIX (tel. toll free 800/446-PARK).

GULL WINGS CHILDREN'S MUSEUM, 418 W. 4th St. Tel. 805/483-3005.

Children can let their imaginations run wild in this small, but full, hands-on museum in a small building in the older section of Oxnard. Geared for kids ages 3 and older, the museum has a designated section, with its own puppet theater, just for toddlers. The older children make special crafts, play familiar and foreign instruments, and learn various ways to create sound, use the stage to become junior thespians, dig in the sand for fossils, and learn what it would be like to have a physical disability. A science section allows kids to experiment, and various communications exhibits teach them the new and old ways of getting a point across. Special activities are housed in numerous cupboards just begging to be opened. Strollers must be left at the door; street parking is available.

Admission: $3 adults, $1.50 children 3 and up, free for under-3s.

Open: Wed–Sun 1–4pm. **Closed:** Major hols, as well as Presidents' Day weekend, Ventura County Fair Day, and Sept 1–16.

Where to Stay

MANDALAY BEACH RESORT AND CONFERENCE HOTEL, 2101 Mandalay Beach Rd., Oxnard, CA 93035. Tel. 805/984-2500, or toll free 800/582-3000. Fax 805/984-8339. 250 suites. A/C TV TEL **Directions:** Take the Victoria Avenue exit off U.S. 101N; turn left on Victoria Avenue, right on Gonzales Road to Harbor Boulevard, left on Harbor to Costa de Oro Road, right into the hotel.

$ Rates: (including complimentary breakfast and afternoon beverages): $135–$240 single; $145–$250 double; $450–$500 two-bedroom suite. Children under 12 stay free in their parents' room. Additional guests 12 and over $10 nightly; cribs $10 the first night, $5 each night thereafter; no rollaways. Inquire about packages. AE, DC, DISC, MC, V. **Parking:** Free.

This is the deluxe hotel of choice for many Angelenos. This all-suite hotel is located on a good swimming beach, but it also has a large free-form pool and two huge spas set in secluded, plant-filled areas. Lush foliage, waterfalls, and streams give the Spanish-style buildings a tropical feel. And the lobby, with its three-story-high ceiling, makes a pleasant place to wander with restless toddlers.

There are numerous hotel sports activities, bike rentals, a video arcade, and billiard and Ping-Pong tables. On Saturday and busy holiday weekends a clown or magician entertains the children—and adults—during the complimentary cocktail hour. Weekends, everybody gets involved in kite-flying or hula-hoop contests on the beach, and small prizes are awarded. Contact the concierge about other special children's activities that might be scheduled during your stay. The concierge can also refer baby-sitters.

Standard suites come with two full bathrooms, a living room with a queen-size hide-a-bed, two color TVs, multiline phones, a small dining area, and a kitchenette with a compact microwave and a small refrigerator. The use of the VCR is free, and tapes are available for rent in the lobby. You'll find coffee in the room, and you can request microwavable dishes.

Dining/Entertainment: The hotel restaurant is lovely for lunch and dinner. The children's menu is limited, but quite adequate, and there are booster seats and highchairs. The lounge will serve snacks and main courses all day, and there is evening entertainment.

Services: Room service, concierge, baby-sitting.

Facilities: Pool, two spas, bike rentals, video arcade, table games.

Where to Eat

While there are many fast-food establishments scattered throughout the area, you might want to stop for more substantial fare. Or you may want to visit the area just for brunch and a view of the harbor. Here are a couple selections:

TUGS, in the Marine Emporium at Channel Islands Harbor, 3600 S. Harbor Blvd. Tel. 805/985-TUGS.

Cuisine: AMERICAN. **Reservations:** Only for parties of six or more.

$ Prices: Breakfast $2.75–$7.95; lunch $3–$10; dinner $11–$16; Sun brunch $4–$7.50. MC, V.

Open: Daily 8am–10pm.

Children's Services: Highchairs, booster seats.

This is your best bet for a moderately priced restaurant that's comfortably casual, with some outdoor seating and a view of the harbor. It doesn't have a children's menu, but most kids will be satisfied with the selections. Breakfast choices include the standard pancakes and waffles, plus corned-beef hash and eggs, omelets, and steak and eggs. At lunch there is chowder, salads, fried seafood dishes, sandwiches, and burgers.

Dinner adds a couple of steak and chicken choices, but consists of mostly seafood and fish. There's an interesting afternoon menu of appetizers served form 3 to 5pm that's perfect for early eaters ($3.95 to $6.50). Sunday brunch selections add tostadas, eggs Benedict, and seafood crêpes to the regular choices.

Servers will split dishes for two children and will warm baby bottles and baby food. There is free parking nearby.

THE WHALE'S TALE, 3950 Bluefish Circle. Tel. 805/985-2511.

Cuisine: CONTINENTAL. **Reservations:** Accepted.

$ Prices: Lunch $4–$9; dinner $9–$26. AE, CB, DC, MC, V.

Open: Lunch Mon–Sat 11:15am–3pm; dinner Mon–Thurs 5–10:30pm, Fri–Sat 5pm–midnight, Sun 4–10:30pm; brunch Sun 10:30am–2:30pm.

Children's Services: Children's menu, booster seats, highchairs.

The Whale's Tale is an excellent restaurant with a superb view of the marina. The choices here are mainly seafood and beef, and there's a great salad bar set up in a replica of a fishing boat. The portions are large and the food is good. Young travelers will be kept busy while you wait for your food with the crayons and mini-coloring books provided by the restaurant. (If the kids return the crayons, they get a balloon and candy.) There's a children's menu priced at $5 to $10 (or ask about selections not on the menu). There's even a Sunday-brunch menu just for youngsters pegged at $4 to $6.

Upstairs in the Whale's Tale is a shellfish bar for light eating. You could easily make a lunch or dinner out of selections such as iced and hot shellfish, sandwiches, salads, burgers, and daily specials. Prices up here range from $4.75 to $13. The Shellfish Bar serves food Monday through Thursday from 11am to 11pm, on Friday and Saturday from 11am to midnight, and on Sunday from 10:30am to 11pm. A parking lot is available.

THE OJAI VALLEY

Ojai (pronounced O-high) was named by the Chumash Indians many, many years ago. The translation—the nest—is really quite appropriate, because the town's quiet, pastoral character, and its valley setting, really do make it seem as comfortable as a nest.

Ojai is the place to spend the day bicycle riding, hiking, or taking leisurely drives on picture-perfect backcountry roads. It's a town of art galleries, artists' studios, antiques stores, and alternative-living centers.

GETTING THERE Ojai is a day trip from Los Angeles, or part of a day from Santa Barbara or Oxnard. The 85-mile drive from Los Angeles is an easy one. The exit off U.S. 101 is about 10 minutes outside Oxnard. The two-lane highway to Ojai passes through picturesque little towns. Or incorporate a visit to Ojai with one to Ventura and Oxnard, 14 miles away. Santa Barbara is 20 miles north.

INFORMATION You can't miss the Spanish mission-style architecture of the Arcade, the main shopping area in town. There, stop by the **Ojai Chamber of Commerce,** 338 East Ojai Avenue (Calif. 150), Ojai, CA 93023 (tel. 805/646-8126), for a free copy of *The Visitor's Guide to the Ojai Valley.* The chamber has detailed lists of bike and hiking trails and campgrounds. The office is open Monday through Friday from 9:30am to 4:30pm, on Saturday from 10am to 5pm, and on Sunday from 10am to 4pm.

WHAT TO SEE & DO

There's nice shopping in and around the **Arcade.** Across from the center of the Arcade on Ojai Avenue is **Libbey Park,** where you'll want to picnic if you've come just for the afternoon. It's a charming park with lots of oak trees, a nice picnic area, and a children's playground. It's also the site of many of Ojai's cultural events, which you might want to enjoy during your visit.

BICYCLING Bicycling is one of the most popular activities in town. There are a number of roads for pedaling, including the paved bike trail that begins at **Fox Street** and continues for about 5 miles. The tree-filled neighborhoods and groves of eucalyptus trees make a perfect setting for a family ride. If you don't have bikes, join the rest of the people who use this as a walking trail.

You can also take an easy ride through orange and avocado groves by taking **Ojai Avenue** east and making an easy loop around the east side of town. This is a very popular route for biking because of the flat, paved road and the surrounding perfume of oranges.

Camp Comfort Park, 2 miles south of town, is a good place to stop for a picnic during a ride. Take Creek Road from the foot of South Montgomery Street.

You can rent a bike from **The Bicycle Doctor,** 212 Fox Street, two blocks from the Arcade (tel. 805/646-7554). He has two small boy's bikes, but no child carriers and no helmets. Open Monday, Tuesday, and Thursday through Saturday from 9am to 5pm and on Sunday from 9am to 3pm. Adult and children's bikes rent for $5 per hour, or $15 per day.

A TROLLEY RIDE If you don't feel like walking, jogging, or bicycling, or if you want to see the whole town, grab a ride on the **Ojai Trolley** (tel. 805/646-8126). It runs a limited number of days a week, so call first. Or pick up a schedule at city hall, the post office, the library, or the visitors center. Fare is 75¢ for adults, 60¢ for children, 30¢ for seniors—and anyone over 75 rides free.

HIKING, FISHING, BOATING Besides the **Los Padres National Forest,** there are other places for day hikes in the area. One is **Matilija Lake,** about 6 miles from Ojai. Take Calif. 33 north toward Taft to Country Campground No. 1. Take the quarter-mile hike to the lake from the old road at the end of the campground. There are plenty of rest stops along the way, which also make great places to picnic.

Plan to spend the entire day at the **Lake Casitas Recreation Area,** 11311 Santa Ana Road, Ventura (tel. 805/649-2233), just 5 miles from Ojai. Take Calif. 33

south to Calif. 150; turn right and go 4 miles to the entrance. Set on 6,200 acres in the Ojai Valley, Lake Casitas is used as a reservoir. No swimming or waterskiing is allowed, but you can camp, fish, hike, and picnic.

Fishing licenses, bait, and equipment rental are available at the **Boat, Bait & Tackle Shop** (tel. 805/649-2043), where you can also rent boats. There are rowboats, a 10-passenger patio-deck boat, and motorboats of varying sizes and horsepower suitable for fishing or just a leisurely ride around the lake. Rentals are by the hour, 5 hours, or the day. You can reserve a boat ahead of time for a full-day rental by mailing in a full-day deposit. Contact **Casitas Boat Rentals,** 11311 Santa Ana Road, Ventura, CA 93001 (tel. 805/649-2043), for current rates and deposit information.

The recreation area is open year round. Day use is $3 per vehicle.

Lake Casitas also has 400 campsites for public use (see "Where to Stay," below, for details).

WHERE TO STAY

OJAI VALLEY INN & COUNTRY CLUB, Country Club Road, Ojai, CA 93023. Tel. 805/646-5511, or toll free 800/422-OJAI. Fax 805/646-7969. 218 rms and suites. A/C MINIBAR TV TEL **Directions:** Take U.S. 101 to Calif. 150, take that to Calif. 33, and then follow the signs to Ojai.

$ Rates: $180–$220 standard room single or double; $240 deluxe room single or double; $310 junior suite and one-bedroom parlor; $350–$760 cottage or suite. Children of any age stay free in their parents' room. Extra adults $20 per night; cribs and rollaways free. Summer family packages and holiday packages available. AE, CB, DC, MC, V. **Parking:** Free.

The setting of this inn is one of the most beautiful in California. In fact, the surrounding valley and Topa Topa mountain range are what attracted director Frank Capra for his 1937 film *Lost Horizon*. To him, these 200 gorgeous acres really were Shangri-La.

The inn's brochure claims that "Children of all ages are always welcome at the Inn. . . ." It's true. Youngsters get the use of a big playground with a jungle gym, swings, and a sandbox, as well as a children's program tailor-made for ages 5 to 12. The complimentary sessions are offered during the summer, the Christmas holidays, Spring Break, and on Thanksgiving weekend—every day except Monday. Most of the usual children's activities are offered except for water activities, and the program is run no matter how many children sign up.

The rambling resort has all sorts of rooms. Some have mountain views; some face the fairway or are set on the fairway. Some have fireplaces, terraces, or patios. There are two-bedroom cottages, one-bedroom suites, connecting rooms, and units with sofa beds. Your best bet is to explain your family's needs when you make your reservation and let them put you in the most appropriate of the 218 rooms and suites. Accommodations are roomy and are equipped with a king- or two queen-size beds. A coffee maker, a stocked minibar, a hairdryer, and robes are welcome features.

Dining/Entertainment: The inn's policy is that children 4 to 12 order off the regular menus for half the price, and those under 3 eat free. There is also a children's menu. There are two dining rooms to choose from, and Janey was comfortable and treated well in both. Outdoor dining during nice weather is a real treat. Room service also has a children's menu. Poolside food service is also convenient.

Services: 24-hour room service, evening turn-down, laundry service.

Facilities: Par-70 golf course, eight tennis courts (four night-lit), sauna, spa, fitness center, two swimming pools, jogging/bicycle trail, bicycle rentals, children's program.

Camping

At **Lake Casitas Recreation Area,** 11311 Santa Ana Road, Ventura (tel. 805/649-2233), just 5 miles from Ojai, there are more than 400 campsites available on a first-come/first-served basis. The fee is $10 per vehicle per night. Coin-operated showers and rest rooms are plentiful, and you'll find a park store, a snack bar, a first aid station, pay phones, and fish-cleaning sinks on the grounds. If you aren't camping out, come just for a picnic or a hike. The recreation area is open year round. Day use is $3 per vehicle.

WHERE TO EAT

There are several places to eat in town, and they range from the super-casual to the "dressed up casual." On the more "dressed up" side is the **Ojai Valley Inn & Country Club** restaurant (see "Where to Stay," above).

ROGER KELLER'S, 331 E. Ojai Ave. Tel. 805/646-7266.

Cuisine: CALIFORNIAN. **Reservations:** Accepted but not necessary.

$ Prices: Lunch $4.75–$6.95; dinner $4.75–$14.95. AE, MC, V.

Open: Mon–Thurs 11:30am–9pm, Fri 11:30am–10pm, Sat 10am–10pm, Sun 10am–9pm.

Children's Services: Children's menu, booster seats, highchairs.

Roger Keller's qualifies in the mid-casual range. Palm trees, pastel paintings, and ceiling fans decorate this one-room restaurant, which also has its own French bakery on the premises. The California cuisine is light, and there are a variety of choices. The selection includes a Cobb salad, grilled-chicken sandwich, or a combination of a half-chicken/walnut salad on a croissant with either soup or salad. Hot specialties include chicken fettuccine parmesan, Sicilian-style spaghetti, or a spa-cuisine special (healthy vegetables sautéed with lemon and garlic in a cholesterol-free oil and sprinkled with fresh parmesan cheese). A starter of pepper pâté might entice you in the evening, followed by coconut-mango chicken, beef filet wrapped in pastry, or spicy orange shrimp. The spa-cuisine special is served in the evening, and there are hamburgers, salads, and fresh fish. The restaurant serves wine and beer only.

Although the children's menu seems limited, don't let that stop you from trying the restaurant. Children are very welcome at Roger Keller's. Their own menu comes with crayons, kids are gladly fed first (if that's your request), and servers make sure the chef knows that youngsters are at the table so food preparation time can be gauged. The menu offers grilled-cheese sandwiches on whole-wheat bread or a hot dog, each $2.50. Sunday selections include French toast, pancakes, or scrambled eggs, each $2. Kids can order a hamburger at any time for $4.75. Roger and his staff will make almost anything you want for the youngsters. Servers will happily warm baby bottles and baby food.

Street parking is available.

SODA BAR & GRILL, 219 E. Matilija St. Tel. 805/646-7632.

Cuisine: AMERICAN.

$ Prices: $2–$5.20. No credit cards.

Open: Mon–Sat 6am–8pm, Sun 7am–5pm.

Children's Services: Highchairs, booster seats.

Around the corner from the Arcade (park in the Arcade lot) is a cute, casual place for a quick bite and a soda or sundae. There's a jukebox in the center of the room and a few video games to keep everyone occupied. Sit at the counter or in one of the '50s-style booths. "Mitey Bites" are perfect for little appetites—they're little hamburgers with "everything" for 75¢ (you can also buy them by the bag). There are quarter-pound burgers, sandwiches, hot dogs, croissant sandwiches, chicken and chips, and salads. Save room for banana splits, sundaes (Janey loved the mini-size sundaes), shakes, floats, pies, or fudge brownies. Bottles and baby food can be warmed.

JOVONE'S DELI, in the Arcade. Tel. 805/646-0207.

Cuisine: DELI.

$ Prices: $1.50–$5. No credit cards.

Open: Mon–Fri 6am–8pm, Sat 7am–8pm, Sun 7am–5pm.

Children's Services: Booster seats.

Another quick-stop restaurant—which is also a great place for take-out picnic food—Jovone's is a favorite with the locals. No children's menu here, but there are enough choices for everyone. At breakfast there's a huge selection of omelets as well as full breakfasts. For the toddlers, you can get a side order of pancakes for 80¢. There's also an eclectic mix of bagels to eat here or to go—ever tried a chocolate chip bagel?—and with scallion- or honey-walnut-raisin–flavored cream cheese! At lunch there are hot and cold sandwiches (in large or small sizes), hamburgers, and Mexican food. You can also order small or large salads, pizza bagels, hot dogs, or grilled-cheese sandwiches.

6. ORANGE COUNTY

The name Orange County conjures up images of family outings and vacation fun. For most of us, Orange County made it on the map in 1955 when Disneyland opened its gates. At that time orange groves graced the roadsides and the area's famous beach cities were almost unknown.

Today, with a population of over 2 million, Orange County boasts more than 35 million visitors a year, making it one of the country's premier vacation destinations—and people aren't coming just to see Disneyland. They're also interested in Knott's Berry Farm and the Movieland Wax Museum, among other attractions. They travel to see the Los Angeles Rams and the California Angels. They come to play on the beaches and stroll through the tidepools of the fabulous 42-mile coastline that's now being called the Côte d'Orange.

INFORMATION   For up-to-the-minute information about the area, you'll want to contact the **Anaheim Area Visitor and Convention Bureau,** 800 West Katella Avenue (P.O. Box 4270), Anaheim, CA 92803 (tel. 714/999-8999). These folks know a great deal about Orange County, and if there's anything they don't know, they'll point you in the right direction.

ANAHEIM

GETTING THERE The easiest way to get to Anaheim by car is via the Santa Ana Freeway (I-5). If you're coming from either Los Angeles or San Diego, exit at Harbor Boulevard; to get to Buena Park, exit at Beach Boulevard south.

INFORMATION For everything you'd want to know about the Anaheim area, ask the good people at the **Anaheim Area Visitor and Convention Bureau** (see "Information," above).

WHAT TO SEE & DO

Anaheim attractions are so popular and well known, and Anaheim is so close to Los Angeles, that most people just lump the activities from the two cities together. To make it simple, we've listed the major Anaheim activities like Disneyland and the Movieland Wax Museum in with the Los Angeles activities in Chapter 4.

WHERE TO STAY

Expensive

ANAHEIM HILTON HOTEL & TOWERS, 777 Convention Way, Anaheim, CA 92802. Tel. 714/750-4321. Fax 714/740-4460. 1,600 rms and suites. A/C TV TEL **Directions:** Take the Harbor Street exit off the Santa Ana Freeway (I-5); follow the signs to the Convention Center.

$ Rates: $120–$140 single; $140–$160 double; $300–$1,075 suite. Children of any age stay free in their parents' room. Additional adults $20 per night; cribs and rollaways free. Ask about special packages. AE, CB, DC, DISC, MC, V. **Parking:** Valet ($7 per night).

The Hilton is in a perfect location—across the street from the Convention Center, 2 minutes from Disneyland (complimentary shuttle service), and 15 minutes from Knott's Berry Farm. The three-story atrium lobby seems tailor-made for children who may need to burn off some energy. There's a lovely recreation area on the fifth floor with a huge fenced-in pool and four Jacuzzis, open year round. Food service and showers are nearby. Rooftop gardens and sun decks give you many options for a before-dinner walk. A game center houses video games and pool tables.

Most interesting for families is the Hilton's Kids Klub, a program in effect from June through Labor Day. Registered children are entitled to free Disney movies every day in the Kids Klub Disney Theatre, complete with popcorn and punch. They can also check in at the Kids Klub room to enjoy arts and crafts or sports programs, and to meet other kids. There are tours of the hotel and other special things just for kids. Children must be between 5 and 13.

Accommodations are comfortable and roomy. Rooms with two double beds have space for a crib or rollaway. Bathrooms are small, with tub/shower combinations. Rooms have remote-control TV and complimentary cable stations. On the lanai level,

LOS ANGELES AREA

Orange County

ACCOMMODATIONS:

Anaheim Hilton Hotel & Towers **1**
Anaheim Plaza Resort Hotel **2**
Best Western Bay Shores Inn **3**
Best Western Stovall's Inn **4**
Dana Point Resort **5**
Disneyland Hotel **6**
The Inn at the Park **7**
Newport Beach Marriott Hotel and Tennis Club **8**
Newporter Hyatt **9**
Quality Hotel and Conference Center **10**
Raffles Inn & Suites **11**
Sheraton–Anaheim Hotel **12**

DINING:

B.J.'s Chicago Pizzeria **1**
Crab Cooker **2**
The Cottage **3**
Flakey Jake's **4**
Peppers Restaurant **5**
Reuben E. Lee Showboat **6**
Ruby's **7**
Spaghetti Station **8**
Tony Roma's **9**
Tony Roma's, Newport Beach **10**
Villa Nova **11**

ATTRACTIONS:

Balboa **1**
  Balboa Island
  Balboa Pavilion
  Balboa Pier
  Boardwalk
  Fun Zone
Corona del Mar Marine Life Refuge **2**
Newport Dunes Aquatic Park **3**
South Coast Plaza **4**
Upper Newport Bay Ecological Reserve **5**

N

East Whittier Los Angeles
710   19   Santa Fe Springs   La Habra
South Gate Downey 42
Lynwood
Compton   42   La Mirada Fullerton
Bell 5
Paramount flower Norwalk Buena Park
Artesia Freeway 91 Fullerton Municipal A
Artesia 5
North Long Beach Lakewood Cerritos Santa Ana
19 Hawaiian Gardens 39 4 9 8
Long Beach Airport 605 Cypress Anaheim 1 2
Stanton
Los Alamitos 10 6 7
22 Garden Grove Freeway 11 12
Long Beach 405 Westmins
Bolsa Chica State Beach Pacific Coast Highway 39 San Diego Freeway Foun Valle
Sunset Beach
Huntington Beach Costa
Huntington State Park

PACIFIC OCEAN

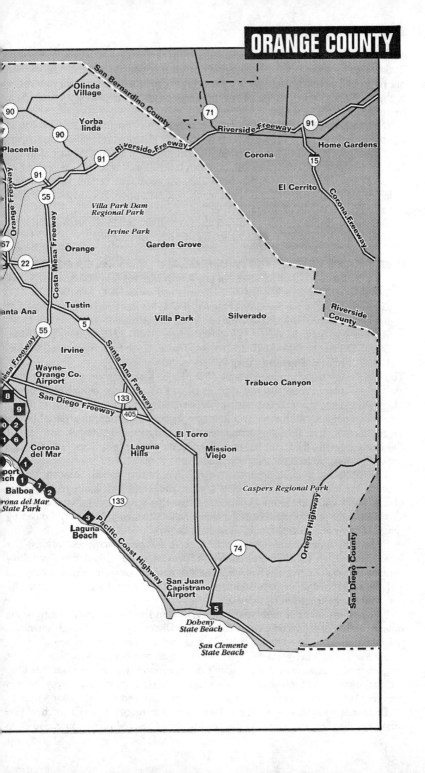

ORANGE COUNTY

rooms open out to the garden, but watch this with the toddlers—there are no screens. Rooms aren't soundproof, so be sure to request that you're not assigned a room over one of the ballrooms. Because the hotel is so big, it can be a long way from your room to the elevators; if your children are at the carrying age, you might want to request a room closer to the elevators.

Dining/Entertainment: The hotel features three restaurants, a sushi bar, a nightclub, and two bars. The Café Oasis is especially pleasant for families and is open until 2am. Hasting's Grill serves continental cuisine for lunch (prices start at $7.25) and dinner (from $15.50). Pavia has northern Italian food, with dinners starting at $10.50. Room service is available until 2am. At breakfast, certain items can be ordered as a child's portion and you'll be charged half price. For lunch and dinner there's a special children's menu.

Services: Room service, laundry and dry cleaning, children's program.

Facilities: Swimming pool, four spas, sun decks, game center.

DISNEYLAND HOTEL, 1150 W. Cerritos Ave., Anaheim, CA 92802. Tel. 714/778-6600, 213/636-3251 in Los Angeles, or toll free 800/854-6165. Fax 714/956-6582 or 714/956-6597. 1,132 rms and suites. A/C MINIBAR TV TEL **Directions:** Take the Santa Ana Freeway (I-5) to the Ball Road exit; the hotel is at the intersection of Cerritos Avenue and West Street.

$ Rates: Mid-June to Aug, $120–$195 single; $120–$215 double. Sept–Jan, $99–$175 single; $99–$195 double; $400 suite. Cribs free; rollaways $15. AE, CB, DC, MC, V. **Parking:** Valet ($7 per night).

The hotel's very name produces a smile, but it's one hotel that you should save your nickels and dimes for so you can experience it. Known as the official hotel of the Magic Kingdom, the magical aura of Disneyland permeates this 60-acre family recreation complex. With three swimming pools, a small marina, an artificial beach, 11 restaurants, free family entertainment, 30 shops and boutiques, and a full children's program, the resort has enough going on that we sometimes find ourselves neglecting other activities in Anaheim and Buena Park.

The complex is built around a lovely mini-marina called Seaports of the Pacific—and it's a child's delight. Here's where you'll find a miniature replica of the *Queen Mary* with tiny remote-control tugboats that scurry around her. There are also two-seater pedalboats. Nearby a state-of-the-art video-game center houses 64 games. There are also free family shows (see below).

During the summer and holiday season, there are special activities for kids. The Mouseketeer Club for children between the ages of 4 and 12 is designed to allow parents to have their evenings free while the kids have fun on their own. The program includes supervised dinner, activities, and crafts from 5pm to midnight. Rates are $7 per child per hour (including dinner).

Some rooms have balconies (most have a view of Disneyland, the gardens, or the hotel marina). All rooms have color TV with the Disney channel, plus bath amenities, hairdryers, and a stocked honor bar (which cannot be used as a refrigerator).

Standard rooms are good-sized. Most come with two double beds, though some king-size and queen-size beds are available. Some rooms in the Oriental Gardens sleep six. Parlor rooms and junior suites vary in size. The suites have refrigerators and wet bars. For other rooms, refrigerators are complimentary and supplied upon request.

Dining/Entertainment: The Disney Character meals (in Chef's Kitchen) give little ones the chance to meet the likes of Mickey Mouse, Minnie Mouse, and Pooh

Bear. During the summer and holidays there's a breakfast buffet, and dinner is served nightly. At other times character breakfasts are held on Saturday and Sunday; dinners, on Friday and Saturday. For breakfast, adults pay $10.95 and children are charged $6.95. Dinner prices are $14.95 for adults and $7.25 for children. Reservations are not required.

With 11 restaurants and lounges on the premises, you're sure to find plenty to satisfy your appetite. All restaurants have Mickey highchairs and booster seats. All the lounges except two are geared to children, and feature Shirley Temple and Roy Rogers drinks. Sgt. Preston's Yukon Saloon and Dancehall is a stage show suitable for the kids. There are two shows nightly. Finger food is served, and there is no cover charge.

In addition, there are also free family shows in Seaports of the Pacific. Probably the most unusual is the Dancing Waters Show, in which water, lights, and music create a dazzling effect. These shows are nightly at 9 and 10pm during the summer, at 8 and 9pm the rest of the year.

Services: 24-hour room service, laundry and dry cleaning, photo processing, baby-sitting referrals, children's program.

Facilities: Three swimming pools, video-game center, 10 tennis courts, white sand beach, volleyball, Ping-Pong, shops and boutiques, car-rental desk, small marina.

Moderate

ANAHEIM PLAZA RESORT HOTEL, 1700 S. Harbor Blvd., Anaheim, CA 92802. Tel. 714/772-5900, or toll free 800/228-1357. Fax 714/772-8386. 300 rms and suites. A/C TV TEL

$ Rates: $77–$92 single; $92–$107 double; $92–$117 triple or quad; $200–$325 suite. Children under 18 stay free in their parents' room. Cribs free; rollaways $10. AE, CB, DC, DISC, MC, V. **Parking:** Free.

This is a favorite hotel with visitors. Directly across from the Disneyland entrance, the gardens and grounds are spacious, the Olympic-size swimming pool and the surrounding area are quite lovely, and the rooms are extremely pleasant and large. And it's moderately priced for this location. There is a video-game room, a Disney specialty gift shop, and shuttle service to and from Disneyland. Complimentary cable television, including the Disney channel, and in-room coffee/tea makers are standard. Baby-sitting service can be arranged through the front-desk staff; there is a coin-operated laundry for guest use. The hotel's Palm Court café serves breakfast, lunch, and dinner.

THE INN AT THE PARK, 1855 Harbor Blvd., Anaheim, CA 92802. Tel. 714/750-1811. Fax 714/971-3626. 500 rms and suites. A/C TV TEL **Directions:** Take the Santa Ana Freeway (I-5) to the Harbor Boulevard exit.

$ Rates: $88–$118 single; $98–$128 double; $125–$135 minisuite; $225–$425 suite. Children under 18 stay free in their parents' room. Cribs free; rollaways $15 per night. AE, CB, DC, DISC, MC, V. **Parking:** $4 per day.

Located on 4 acres of grounds, the Inn at the Park is an attractive hostelry, with a friendly attitude toward kids. The nicely landscaped pool area has a large patio with lots of chaise longues and a pretty little gazebo for shade. The kids also enjoy the video-game room. Other amenities include free shuttle to and from Disneyland, a gift shop with Disney memorabilia, and help arranging for baby-sitting.

Each room has remote-control TV and pay-per-view movies, plus a game table with chairs. Every room has a balcony—with a view of either the gardens or

Disneyland. During the summer, we request a room facing Disneyland and enjoy the summer fireworks from the park. There are a variety of suites to choose from (all with refrigerators and sofa beds), or you can connect three regular guest rooms (and have three baths).

Dining/Entertainment: For dinner, the Overland Stage Restaurant looks as if it was lifted out of Disney's Frontierland, complete with antique prints of the Old West, hanging lanterns, rich velveteen tapestries, and a lovely grandfather clock. The dinner menu consists of steaks, chops, lobster, and prime rib. The inn's moderately priced coffee shop serves breakfast, lunch, and dinner.

Services: Room service (7am to 11pm), baby-sitting, Disneyland shuttle.

Facilities: Pool, gift shop, video-game room.

SHERATON-ANAHEIM HOTEL, 1015 W. Ball Rd., Anaheim, CA 92802. Tel. 714/778-1700, or toll free 800/325-3535. Fax 714/535-3889. 500 rms and suites. A/C MINIBAR TV TEL **Directions:** Take the Santa Ana Freeway (I-5) to the Harbor Boulevard exit.

$ Rates: $90–$110 single; $105–$125 double; $285 suite. Children under 18 stay free in their parents' rooms. Cribs free; rollaways $10. AE, CB, DC, DISC, MC, V. **Parking:** Free.

You'll know this hotel as soon as you see it from the freeway—it's designed to resemble a medieval castle. Although the lobby is small, the outdoor areas are large, complete with grassy, flower-lined courtyards, a rose garden, a little pond with a bridge, and inviting sitting areas. While parents are more impressed with the complete concierge service and room service, the kids fancy the video-game room. And of course there's a large heated swimming pool. Shuttle service to and from Disneyland and help with arranging a baby-sitter are other bonuses.

Some rooms open out onto the swimming pool; others open onto the grassy areas or indoor hallways. Guest rooms are generously sized and tastefully decorated. In-room amenities include cable color TV, in-room pay movies, and a complimentary toiletry basket. Refrigerators are available upon request. You can reserve connecting rooms and suites.

Dining/Entertainment: The hotel has a moderately priced coffee shop, which has a children's menu with prices from $3.25 to $5. Gerber baby foods are available for $1. Full meals are also served and start at $6.25. There is also a quick-serve deli. Classy Adrienne's restaurant serves continental cuisine; main dishes start at $11 (there are no children's portions here). Highchairs and boosters are available everywhere.

Services: Room service, concierge, baby-sitting, Disneyland shuttle.

Facilities: Heated pool, video-game room.

Budget

BEST WESTERN STOVALL'S INN, 1110 W. Katella Ave., Anaheim, CA 92802. Tel. 714/778-1880. Fax 714/778-3805. 290 rms and suites. A/C TV **Directions:** Take the Santa Ana Freeway (I-5) to the Ball Road exit; the hotel is at the corner of West Street and Katella Avenue.

$ Rates: $68–$75 single or double in high season (June–Aug), $55–$65 single or double in low season; $110–$150 suite. Children under 18 stay free in their parents' room. Cribs free. AE, CB, DC, DISC, MC, V. **Parking:** Free.

A good budget alternative is this Best Western, located close to Disneyland. Stovall's is a large, basic motor inn with clean rooms, two swimming pools, two whirlpools, and a small wading pool. Other nice touches include a bathroom at the swimming pool and topiary gardens surrounding much of the property. (Yes, they even have sculpted Disney characters.) Catering to the traveling family, there is same-day photo processing at the gift store, sightseeing tour and car-rental assistance, and coin-operated laundry machines for guest use. (Valet service is also available.) Another nice feature is the VCR-rental facility. There's free shuttle service to and from Disneyland. And the front desk will help you arrange for baby-sitting.

There's no restaurant on the premises, but Coco's Coffeeshop is next door. This is an inexpensive way to feed the family.

Services: Baby-sitting, Disneyland shuttle, sightseeing and car-rental assistance, valet laundry.

Facilities: Two swimming pools, two whirlpools, wading pool, VCR-rental desk, coin-operated laundry.

QUALITY HOTEL AND CONFERENCE CENTER, 616 Convention Way, Anaheim, CA 92802. Tel. 714/750-3131, or toll free 800/777-1455. Fax 714/750-9027. 284 rms and suites. A/C TV TEL Directions: Take the Santa Ana Freeway (I-5) to the Harbor Boulevard exit; hotel is adjacent to Convention Center, two blocks from Disneyland.

$ Rates: $62–$85 single or double; from $150 suite. Children 18 and under stay free in their parents' room. Additional adults $10 per night; cribs free; rollaways $10. AE, CB, DC, DISC, MC, V. **Parking:** Free.

This is an excellent choice in the budget-priced range. Clean, tastefully decorated, and completely renovated within the last few years, the inn is located only a few blocks from Disneyland. The heated pool is quite large, and has lots of chaises and chairs for sitting and lounging. Amenities include room service, shuttle service to Disneyland, and a video-game/vending machine area for the kids. Baby-sitting can be arranged through the front desk.

All rooms have balconies, and some face Disneyland. Those balconies are large enough to accommodate a few chairs, so you can enjoy Disneyland's summer fireworks from your hotel room if you can't enjoy them from the park. The rooms also have color TVs and tub/shower combinations, and at the time you book, you can request a refrigerator (no extra charge). Two-bedded rooms have just enough space to add a crib. There are family suites available with a king-size bed and a sofa bed. Connecting rooms are also available. Each floor has ice and soft-drink machines.

Dining/Entertainment: There are two restaurants—the Tivoli Gardens Café, which serves breakfast and lunch, and Captain Greenhorn's Gourmet restaurant. Both have highchairs and booster seats. Tivoli has a children's menu.

Services: Room service (6am to 10pm), baby-sitting, video-game/vending-machine area, Disneyland shuttle.

Facilities: Pool.

RAFFLES INN & SUITES, 2040 S. Harbor Blvd., Anaheim, CA 92802. Tel. 714/750-6100. Fax 714/740-0639. 122 rms and suites. A/C TV TEL Directions: Take the Santa Ana Freeway (I-5) to the Katella Avenue exit; the inn is two blocks south of Disneyland.

$ Rates: (including continental breakfast): $64–$89 single or double; $85–$109 minisuite; $130–$165 family suite. Children under 18 stay free in their parents' room. Additional beds $5; cribs free. AE, CB, DC, DISC, MC, V. **Parking:** Free.

⑤ This is the best bet for your money in the budget category. The complimentary continental breakfast is served in a charming little parlor room off the swimming pool area. This room is open during the summer and on winter evenings serve as a game room, with a sitting room upstairs. There is free shuttle service to Disneyland, and the front desk will help you arrange everything from tours to baby-sitting.

The rooms are very clean and definitely different, and all units have double sinks and tub/shower combinations. There are a variety of rooms to choose from. Family suites can sleep six people; these have large living rooms with sofa sleepers and lots of room, enough even for two rollaways. These suites have master bedrooms with king-size beds, plus sinks and vanity areas; the kitchenettes are outfitted with the basics. Minisuites have small parlor rooms with sofa sleepers and refrigerators. The bedrooms have either king- or queen-size beds.

Services: Baby-sitting, Disneyland shuttle, tour services.
Facilities: Pool.

WHERE TO EAT

While your kids may want to spend all their waking hours at the theme parks and fast-food parlors, the adults in our group sometimes yearn for another choice.

PEPPERS RESTAURANT, in the Plaza Alicante, 12361 Chapman Ave. (at Harbor Blvd.), in Garden Grove. Tel. 714/740-1333.
   Cuisine: MEXICAN. **Reservations:** Accepted.
$ Prices: Main courses $3.75–$9 at lunch, $5.50–$12.95 at dinner; Sun brunch $12.95. AE, MC, V.
   Open: Lunch Mon–Sat 11am–4pm; dinner Mon–Thurs 4–10pm, Fri–Sat 4–11pm; brunch Sun 10am–2pm.
   Children's Services: Children's menu, booster seats, highchairs.

Peppers is a perfect example of an adult restaurant where you can comfortably include the kids. It's lively and fun, charming and sophisticated. Balloons, potted plants, and ceiling fans complement the soft-pink and burgundy decor. A large noisy bar is on the other side of the reception area, out of the way of the diners.

Tortilla chips are brought immediately, and the service is prompt and efficient, even at the busiest hours. The children's menu items include hamburgers, hot dogs, grilled-cheese sandwiches, cheese enchiladas, burritos, or tacos for $3 (includes a beverage and ice cream). Mom and dad get to choose from an array of Mexican dishes, including such specials as filet mignon, camarones Merida, or fajitas. Lunch has many of the same selections, plus tostadas, huevos (eggs), and salads. Be sure to leave room for something indecently rich on the dessert menu—deep-fried ice cream, Kahlúa mousse, or white-coffee toffee are just a few suggestions. The "all you can eat" Sunday brunch costs $12.95 for adults, $6 for kids 10 and under.

The kids love the complimentary shuttle that picks them up from their hotel and takes them back after dinner. Baby bottles and food will be warmed in the kitchen upon request. A parking lot is available.

TONY ROMA'S, 1640 S. Harbor Blvd. Tel. 714/520-0200.

Cuisine: BARBECUE. **Reservations:** Not accepted.
$ Prices: Breakfast $2.65–$4.95; lunch $3.95–$9.95; dinner $4.95–$13.95. AE, DC, MC, V.
Open: Mon–Fri 11am–midnight, Sat–Sun 7am–midnight. Breakfast Mon–Fri is seasonal, so call ahead.
Children's Services: Children's menu, highchairs, booster seats.

This large restaurant just across from the Disneyland entrance boasts the same good food that the other locations have. All dinner main courses come with coleslaw and a choice of beans, french fries, rice, or baked potato. Choose from ribs and chicken, grilled shrimp, marinated breasts of chicken, New York steak, steamed vegetables, or an old-fashioned burger. For lunch you can choose from similar items at lower prices.

The adorable children's menu offers the kids chicken fingers, burgers, ribs, or chicken with fries and slaw for $2.95 to $4.95.

Reservations are not accepted, so it's best to come before 6pm to avoid the 15- to 45-minute wait. Parking is free in the lot.

SPAGHETTI STATION, 999 W. Ball Rd. Tel. 714/956-3250.

Cuisine: ITALIAN. **Reservations:** Accepted only for parties of 8 or more.
Directions: Take the Santa Ana Freeway (I-5) to the Ball Road exit.
$ Prices: Lunch $4.65–$12.25; dinner $5.95–$13.55. AE, MC, V.
Open: Lunch Mon–Fri 11am–2pm; dinner daily 4:30–10pm. **Closed:** Thanksgiving and Christmas days.
Children's Services: Children's menu, highchairs, booster seats.

Like a scene from the Old West, the Spaghetti Station greets you outside the door with a sign reading WELCOME PARDNER and a topiary of a stagecoach. Enter the eatery and you step into Fort Spaghetti Station, where several rustic wood-paneled rooms await you. Fort Spaghetti Station claims to have the world's greatest individual Old West gun collection (valued at $1.5 million), and indeed it must. While our kids "oooh" and "aaah" over the size of the rifles and Colt pistols, the adults in our crowd reminisce when they see the 1892 Winchester rifle that Steve McQueen used in *Wanted: Dead or Alive*. All this and food too!

For lunch you can choose from many kinds of pasta with several different sauces (all served with salad, bread, and ice cream), sandwiches, salads, and even steak. For dinner, choose from pastas and steaks (all served with salad, bread, and ice cream). Children will enjoy the spaghetti with tomato or meat sauce for $4.

During the day there's hardly ever a wait; in the evening, be prepared for a 20- to 30-minute wait if you come between 6:30 and 8:30pm on weekend nights. There's free parking in the lot.

FLAKEY JAKE'S, 101 E. Katella Ave. Tel. 714/535-1446.

Cuisine: AMERICAN. **Reservations:** Not accepted. **Directions:** Take the Santa Ana Freeway (I-5) to the Katella Avenue exit.
$ Prices: $4.60–$9. MC, V.
Open: Sun–Thurs 11am–11pm, Fri–Sat 11am–midnight.
Children's Services: Children's menu, highchairs, booster seats.

If the kids are just dying for a good old-fashioned hamburger, take them to Flakey Jake's. There's no table service here, but you'll find huge hamburgers and grilled-chicken sandwiches for the adults (baked potatoes and taco salads too), and Jake's

Junior menus for the kids. Jake's Junior meals (burgers, fish sandwich, and hot dogs) include fries and a beverage with free refills for $2.50. Best of all, the food is as fresh as you'll find anywhere. The kids love the place, and they occupy themselves during the wait for food in the small video arcade.

NEWPORT BEACH & ENVIRONS

Of late, the coast from Huntington Beach to San Clemente has been called the American Riviera. That swath of beautiful sandy beach is excellent for swimming, surfing, sunbathing, and boating. In Newport there are ecological reserves, harbors, and coves waiting to be explored. Newport and its companion, Balboa Island, have been family-resort towns (albeit for the very rich) for many years. Even today, families flock to this sun-drenched area for weeks of relaxation and play.

GETTING THERE Newport Beach is just south of Los Angeles. Take the Santa Ana Freeway (I-5) or the San Diego Freeway (I-405) south to the Costa Mesa Freeway (Calif. 55) west to the Pacific Coast Highway (Calif. 1) and Newport Beach. Or follow the scenic route down the Pacific Coast Highway (Calif. 1) all the way.

INFORMATION One of the first things you'll want to do is to contact the **Newport Beach Conference and Visitor's Bureau,** 366 San Miguel Drive, Newport Beach, CA 92660 (tel. 714/675-7040).

WHAT TO SEE & DO

The main attractions of the area are the wonderful wide sandy beaches and the harbor with its yachts and sailboats. The other activities of greatest interest for families are concentrated in a small area along the shore.

BALBOA PENINSULA AND BALBOA ISLAND Balboa Peninsula creates a gentle bay where eight small islands sit, old-fashioned auto-ferries run, and children play in the warm sand. Homes on the peninsula and on Balboa Island remind you of New England. Indeed, like Cape Cod, since the 1930s Newport Beach (and Balboa in particular) has been a summer-resort town where well-to-do families rent clapboard cottages for a month at a time.

Start with the **Balboa Pier,** a 919-foot-long structure that is lined with fishermen of all ages. At the foot of the pier you'll find a nice public beach with play equipment, showers, and rest rooms. At the end of the pier is Ruby's Diner (see "Where to Eat," below, for details). To get to the pier after you're on Balboa Peninsula, go to Palm Street and turn right to the public parking area.

The **boardwalk** is a terrific place to skate or bicycle, and enchanting little Main Street offers places to stop and grab a quick snack. You can rent bikes and roller skates at **Ocean Front Wheel Works,** at 105 Main Street just before you get to the pier (tel. 714/723-6510). They rent adult bicycles, bikes with child carriers, children's bikes, and three-wheel bikes (which aren't allowed on the sidewalks), as well as beach items. Open Monday through Friday from 10am to 6pm and on Saturday and Sunday from 10am to 8pm (but times vary according to season).

On the harbor side of the peninsula (actually only a few blocks away) is the historic

Balboa Pavilion, an ornate Victorian structure that today houses a restaurant and gift shop, and is the terminus for harbor excursions, whale-watching trips, and Catalina Island transportation. It's considered the hub of Newport Harbor. This registered historic landmark was built as a bathhouse and originally served as a terminal for the electric Red Car. The pavilion was also the place where many of the big-band greats played—Benny Goodman and Count Basie among them.

At the pavilion, you can book a cruise on the double-decker *Pavilion Queen* (tel. 714/673-5245), which has regularly scheduled tours of the harbor. During the summer (June through August), tours depart at 11am, noon, and 1, 3, 4, and 5pm; during the rest of the year, they leave at noon and 1, 2, and 3pm. The 45-minute cruises cost $5 for adults and $1 for children; 90-minute cruises are $7 for adults, $1 for children. Call for details.

Davey's Locker, at Balboa Pavilion, 400 Main Street (tel. 714/673-1434), offers fishing excursions, and has all-day boat trips that go to Catalina Island. The fishing trips leave at midnight, return at 4pm, and cost $50 for adults, $34 for children (includes a bunk). There are also half-day boat trips, with fishing from Huntington Beach to south of Laguna. Whale-watching cruises go out from December through mid-March. You can rent fishing poles here and buy fishing licenses. Davey's Locker is open daily from 5am to 6pm.

The **Fun Zone** is a small area along the waterfront near the Balboa Pavilion that's specifically geared to children. Kids of all ages can spend hours here riding the ferris wheel ($1.50 per ride) and the merry-go-round ($1 per ride), with its regular-size and miniature horses perfect for very little children, as well as playing in the three video arcades. Fast-food stands dot the little strip. You can rent pedalboats or pontoons, or take one of the harbor cruises from this area as well.

The Fun Zone is where you catch the **Balboa Island Ferry** (tel. 714/673-1070). (You can also drive onto the island on Jamboree Road, but parking is atrocious on the island, so we suggest that you park in the public lot near the Balboa Pier and ferry across without your car.) This short, delightful ride transports only a few vehicles at a time across to Balboa Island, but it's a treat—one the kids will remember. Ferry service runs Monday through Friday from 6:30am to midnight and on Saturday and Sunday from 6:30am to 2am, and costs 65¢ for a car with one passenger (20¢ extra for each additional passenger), 40¢ for a bicycle, and 25¢ for pedestrians; children are 10¢.

Balboa Island is a tiny, picturesque village with homes placed so close together that windowboxes and miniature gardens replace the more usual southern California front and side lawns. Its very size makes it perfect for walking. Marine Avenue is the place to go for gifts, restaurants, and ice-cream shops. You can comfortably see the island in 45 minutes, which will give you the flavor of it while allowing you time to get back to the peninsula and the better beaches.

NEWPORT BEACH AND PIER Known as McFadden's Pier, this is where you'll see the one-of-a-kind **Dory Fishing Fleet.** Each morning at about 6am the fleet sets out to sea. Some of the fishermen may go as far as Catalina Island. At about 8am they return, set up their weighing scales on the boats, and sell their catch on the beach. It's the stronghold of a dying life-style.

The boardwalk area is vintage 1940s. The beach is just over 5 miles long, with volleyball nets, outdoor showers, and rest rooms. Pier fishing is a popular sport. (No state license is required to fish from the pier.)

You can rent a variety of items at **Baldy's Tackle,** 100 McFadden Place, at the foot of the pier (tel. 714/673-4150). In addition to renting fishing equipment (as the name suggests), Baldy's also rents beach cruisers and children's bikes, bodyboards, beach chairs, and umbrellas. Open in summer (June through August) daily from 6am to 8pm; in winter Sunday through Thursday from 7:30am to 5:30pm and on Friday and Saturday from 6am to 6pm.

UPPER NEWPORT BAY ECOLOGICAL RESERVE   For some truly wonderful outdoor experiences, you'll enjoy this 700-acre state ecological reserve, home to all kinds of wildlife and birds. Get the kids out here on bicycles or on foot, and savor the quiet, natural setting. Take Back Bay Drive to the reserve.

Newport Dunes Aquatic Park, 1131 Backbay Drive, Newport Beach (tel. 714/729-DUNE), is located on a 15-acre lagoon. After the morning clouds burn off, this is a place where kids can build sandcastles to their hearts' content and swim in the calm water. You can rent paddleboats, sailboats, windsurfers, and kayaks (lessons are available). It's equipped with a playground, café, shower, and barbecues. For your protection there are lifeguards and first-aid stations from June 15 to Labor Day. The kids love the floating whales that mark the cordoned-off children's swim areas. Admission is $5 per day per car, $20 per day per van.

OTHER AREA BEACHES AND TIDEPOOLS   The protected coves of **Corona Del Mar Marine Life Refuge** (tel. 714/644-3047) are teeming with sea life. To get to the tidepools, park your car where Poppy and Ocean Boulevard meet and walk down the asphalt pathway. You can walk on the rocks when the tide is low and help the kids spot sea urchins and other wonders. Remember to replace everything you pick up—exactly where you took it from. For tide tables, call the number above, or ask at any of the bait-and-tackle shops nearby. Tours are given by park rangers, but call ahead.

According to people in-the-know, the best beach in the area for families may be **Corona Del Mar State Beach,** better known as Big Corona, off Ocean Boulevard and Iris. The large beach is sheltered so that wave action is usually gentler than at other areas. There are barbecue pits, showers, a snack bar, and rest rooms. The beach is open daily from 6am to 10pm.

Adjacent to Huntington Pier, off the Pacific Coast Highway (Calif. 1) is **Huntington City Beach** (3 miles north of Newport). There are lifeguards, volleyball nets, and concession stands. **Huntington State Beach** is just south of there. With 3 miles of shoreline, lifeguards, snack stands (seasonal), showers, and rest rooms, it's very popular.

SURFING   Huntington Beach may be the most popular surfing beach around. In fact, some say that Huntington Beach epitomizes the ever-famous California surf scene. However, this popular sport is allowed at most beaches—with certain restrictions during the summer. Call before you go. **Huntington State Beach** (tel. 714/536-5281), **Huntington City Beach** (tel. 714/536-5281), **Newport** (tel. 714/673-3371 for surf report), **Corona Del Mar** (tel. 714/644-3047), and **Dana Point** (tel. 714/496-5794) are places to try.

BIKE PATHS   There is a wonderful bike path that extends from the north at Bolsa

Chica State Beach south along the shoreline into Newport Beach. You'll see dozens of families piling out of their cars at any of the beach parking areas along the route.

In Newport Beach, you can take the **Backbay Drive bike path** that winds through the ecological reserve. This path climbs gradually up the hill, past the Backbay, offering bicyclists the chance to see all kinds of birds.

The Anaheim Area Visitors and Convention Bureau suggests the following **bike tour** through Newport Beach and Balboa: Start at the Balboa Pier and head south to the "wedge." This picturesque stop is very popular with body surfers, and the kids will love watching them ride the waves. Double-back toward the Balboa Pavilion and take the Balboa Auto-Ferry to Balboa Island. Take any of the streets on the island. You might want to stop on Marine Avenue for a snack. Then head back on the ferry and ride north to McFadden's Pier (Newport Pier). If you get there before noon, you're likely to see the Dory Fleet selling fish. The ride is level, with wonderful views throughout the entire trip. Call the Department of Parks and Recreation for further information (tel. 714/644-3151).

In addition to **Ocean Front Wheel Works** and **Baldy's Tackle** (see above), you can rent bikes at **Pedal Pusher Bikes,** 122 23rd Street (tel. 714/675-2570), open daily from 10am to 5pm.

SHOPPING Newport Beach and nearby Costa Mesa have some wonderful shopping malls. **Fashion Island,** at Newport Center (tel. 714/721-2000), is an exclusive shopping district with more than 200 shops and services, including Neiman-Marcus, J. W. Robinson's, and I. Magnin.

Located in Costa Mesa, **South Coast Plaza** (tel. 714/435-2000) is one of the most interesting malls in southern California. With approximately 300 shops such as Nordstrom, Laura Ashley, and Ann Taylor, you know the plaza is upscale. In addition to being a beautiful mall with a stained-glass dome, there's a concierge service, valet parking, and a carousel for the kids.

A DAY TRIP OUT OF NEWPORT

You can spend all day at **Wild Rivers Waterpark,** located at 8770 Irvine Center Drive (tel. 714/768-WILD). With over 40 water rides and other attractions, Wild Rivers, a 20-acre water park, is a big hit with the kids. The park has an African theme and boasts southern California's largest man-made earth mountain, which offers 19 water rides. Wild Rivers Mountain offers white-water innertubing, super-speed rides down a slide the size of a football field, and a jet-speed ride through a dark tunnel.

Explorer's Island is designed for families. Some of the rides at Wild Rivers Mountain have been scaled down for children. The little ones in our group loved Pygmy Pond—less than a foot deep, with swings and slides. We loved the Safari River Expedition, an innertube float.

The newest attraction is Thunder Cove, which has two side-by-side wave-action pools in which you and the kids can bodyboard and surf. Rentals are available.

As with all water parks, utmost caution should be taken by the kids so that accidents are avoided.

Wild Rivers is open from mid-June through the beginning of September, daily from 10am to 8pm; mid-May to mid-June and mid-September to October, on Saturday, Sunday, and holidays from 11am to 5pm. Schedules change, so check before you go. Admission is $14.95 for adults (10 and older), $10.95 for children 3 to 9. Children 9 and under must be accompanied by an adult.

To get there, take the San Diego Freeway (I-405) to Irvine Center Drive, adjacent to the Irvine Meadows Amphitheater.

WHERE TO STAY

As you might imagine, in a city with so much wealth first-class hotels are easy to find; moderate ones are difficult.

NEWPORT BEACH MARRIOTT HOTEL AND TENNIS CLUB, 900 Newport Center Dr., at Fashion Island, Newport Beach, CA 92660. Tel. 714/640-4000, or toll free 800/228-9290. Fax 714/640-5055. 586 rms, 6 suites. A/C TV TEL **Directions:** Take the San Diego Freeway (I-405) to the Jamboree Road exit; follow the signs to the Fashion Island shopping complex at Newport Center—the hotel is opposite.

$ Rates: $139–$169 standard room single or double; $145–$165 concierge-level rooms single or double; $500–$800 suite. Children under 12 stay free in their parents' room. Older children and adults $15 per night; cribs and rollaways free. Inquire about special packages. AE, CB, DC, DISC, MC, V. **Parking:** Valet parking ($6 per day).

You can feel quite comfortable with even the grumpiest youngsters at this fine hotel. The hotel staff exudes a warmth and delight with children, while appreciating that not all guests want such a group next door. From Memorial Day to Labor Day the hotel has a free "Kids Klub" with organized activities.

The recently renovated hotel is built as a series of towers connected by covered passageways centered around a large outdoor pool and lovely flower-filled atrium courtyard. Guests are welcome to sit in the atrium when private parties are not using it. The pool areas are palm-edged gardens, nice places to sit. The main pool is free-form in shape, with a great shallow end for the kids. It has ample chaise longues as well as tables with umbrellas. The smaller pool is much quieter. This is a great place to come with the kids.

Set up on a bluff, many of the 600 rooms have a view of the golf course or ocean. Decorated in "California casual," with floral bedspreads, pale walls in peach tones and slate blues, every room has a balcony or patio, remote-control color TV with free HBO but pay movies, tub/shower combinations, and a complimentary basket of toiletries. In the evening, Ghirardelli chocolate squares will be left on your pillow to beckon sweet dreams. The rooms in the north tower are quite spacious. Some have a king-size bed and a couch, easy chair, and coffee table. Others have two double beds. All have adequate space to accommodate a crib.

Dining/Entertainment: The hotel has several restaurants. J. W.'s Sea Grill offers casual dining, open daily for breakfast, lunch, and dinner; the children's menu choices run about $3. The View Lounge on the north tower's 16th floor offers snacks and dancing for adults. Food service is available poolside. Just ask if you don't see what you want on the menu—the staff probably will be able to accommodate you.

Services: Room service (6am to 1am), concierge, children's program, babysitting, same-day and overnight laundry service, evening turn-down service.

Facilities: Two swimming pools, two whirlpools, eight lighted tennis courts, pro shop, full health club, gift shop, golf privileges at the 18-hole Newport Beach Country Club next door, two coin-operated washers and dryers.

NEWPORTER HYATT, 1107 Jamboree Rd., Newport, CA 92660. Tel. 714/729-1234, or toll free 800/233-1234. Fax 714/644-1552. 410 rms and suites. A/C MINIBAR TV TEL **Directions:** Take the Corona del Mar Freeway (72S) to the Jamboree Road exit.

$ Rates: $125–$145 single or double; $275–$395 suite. Children 12 and under stay free in their parents' room. Cribs free; rollaways $15. Ask about special packages. AE, CB, DC, DISC, MC, V. **Parking:** Valet ($6 per day), free self-parking.

This may be the quintessential southern California luxury resort hotel. Even the sunny rose-colored buildings invite you to share the good life . . . and to our surprise, you can do it with your kids!

The lobby is California design, bright and airy, with countless doors opening onto the patio inviting you to relax in the sun on 26 beautifully landscaped acres. The pool areas have patios for dining and sunning, as well as grassy slopes for playing; one pool is especially for children. In summer an activity director oversees such daily activities as volleyball and hula-hoop contests. We love to rent bikes and ride the bike path along Newport's Backbay where the wildlife sanctuary is located, or cross the street to Newport Dunes Aquatic Park where the kids can enjoy the sand and water sports. Ask the concierge for a pamphlet that lists additional children's activities. Camp Hyatt is available on weekends for ages 3 to 15. Tennis is available for a small fee. The John Wayne Tennis Club offers nursery service from 9am to noon.

The 410 guest rooms, suites, and villas are large, light, and pretty, much as you'd expect from the rambling villa-type architecture. They look out onto the golf course or pool areas. All rooms have either a king-size bed or two double beds, remote-control cable TV with free HBO and in-room pay movies, and a complimentary deluxe amenity basket. Some of the larger rooms have small sofas and coffee tables; all have game tables and chairs. All rooms feature tub/shower combinations with separate vanity areas and small refrigerator/minibars. Connecting rooms are available.

Dining/Entertainment: There is indoor/outdoor dining at the Jamboree Café. For those parents who have the energy at night to enjoy live entertainment, there is Duke's Lounge, where cocktails and appetizers are served.

Services: Airport shuttle, concierge, same-day laundry and valet, room service, baby-sitting, children's program.

Facilities: Three swimming pools and Jacuzzis, Ping-Pong, volleyball, exercise spa, tennis courts, shuffleboard, bicycle rentals, and a nine-hole par-three golf course.

BEST WESTERN BAY SHORES INN, 1800 W. Balboa Blvd., Newport Beach, CA 92663. Tel. 714/675-3463, or toll free 800/222-6675. Fax 714/675-4977. 20 rms and suites. A/C TV TEL **Directions:** Take the San Diego Freeway (I-405S) to the Harbor Boulevard/Costa Mesa exit; the inn is eight blocks from the bridge.

$ Rates: (including continental breakfast) $72–$79 single; $79–$99 double; $129–$209 suite. Children under 12 stay free in their parents' room. Additional guests over 12 $7 per night; cribs free; no rollaways. Inquire about lower off-season (October–May) rates. AE, DC, DISC, MC, V. **Parking:** Free.

Although this Best Western is nothing fancy, it's in a wonderful location, one block from the bay and a few blocks from the ocean. This plain but well-kept motor inn has small, tidy rooms. Units with two double beds are adequate for four, however, and the suites (which have full kitchens, dining rooms, and separate bedrooms) are large enough to sleep six. A number of the rooms have ocean views, and each unit has a videocassette player (there are free films in the lobby), hairdryer, and a tub/shower unit with amenity baskets of shampoo, conditioner, and even dental floss. A free newspaper is delivered to your door each day. There is a coin-operated washer/dryer on the premises; laundry soap is complimentary. No pool.

Home or Apartment Rentals

When you consider the price of rooms in Newport Beach, it's not surprising that many families simply rent homes or apartments for a week or longer. The prices are much more reasonable, and while you don't have maid service, it is an excellent alternative to consider in this pricey neighborhood.

Rental agents will match you with an accommodation that fits your needs (and, hopefully, your budget). Some typical rentals are two-bedroom oceanfront properties (ranging from $750 to $3,000 per week) and beach cottages or duplexes (ranging from $500 to $1,400 per week). Most properties are within a few blocks of the beach. If at all possible, view the property before you rent it (ask how the realtor handles that). If you're planning to be in Newport during the summer, you should begin to make your arrangements at least 6 months in advance. Be prepared to put down a refundable cleaning and breakage deposit, and to add a 9% bed tax.

Three local rental agents are **Playa Realty,** 108 McFadden Place, Newport Beach, CA 92663 (tel. 714/673-1900); **Mel Fuchs' Pavilion Realty,** 700 East Balboa Boulevard, Balboa, CA 92661 (tel. 714/675-8120); and **Burr White Realtors,** 2901 Newport Boulevard, Newport Beach, CA 92663 (tel. 714/675-4630).

Camping

Camping facilities are available at a number of beaches. **Huntington City Beach** offers RV camping (but no hookups) from mid-September through May. For reservations, contact City of Huntington Beach–Sunset Vista, P.O. Box 190, Huntington Beach, CA 92648 (tel. 714/536-5281).

Doheny State Beach, 25300 Harbor Drive, Dana Point, CA 92629 (tel. 714/496-6171), has over 100 campsites, and you can make reservations through MISTIX (tel. toll free 800/446-7275 in California).

San Clemente State Beach, 3030 Avenida Del Presidente, San Clemente, CA 92672 (tel. 714/492-3156), has sites with hookups for RVs. Make your reservations through MISTIX at the number above.

WHERE TO EAT

Expensive

REUBEN E. LEE SHOWBOAT, 151 E. Pacific Coast Hwy. (Calif. 1), Newport. Tel. 714/675-5910.

Cuisine: CONTINENTAL. **Reservations:** Accepted. **Directions:** Take the San Diego Freeway (I-405) to the Jamboree exit to Pacific Coast Highway (Calif. 1) and turn right.

$ Prices: Lunch $7–$11; dinner $11.95–$25. AE, DC, DISC, MC, V.

Open: Lunch Mon–Thurs 11:30am–4pm; dinner Sun–Thurs 4–10pm, Fri–Sat 4–11pm; brunch Sun 10am–3pm.

Children's Services: Children's menu, highchairs, booster seats.

For another innovative place to eat on the waterfront, we like the *Reuben E. Lee*. Built in 1963 to re-create a Mississippi riverboat, the *Reuben E. Lee* is 190 feet long, 52 feet wide, and is a floating restaurant that actually moves slightly on the water. This is a genuine treat for kids, who are always excited to experience something unusual—and indeed this is different! Wooden planks surround the showboat so you can view the harbor from all vantage points. The interior is done in antebellum southern decor, with hardwood floors, small-print wallpaper, and mirrors; there is a huge grand staircase that takes diners up to the top deck and dining rooms.

Comprised of seafood and prime rib specialties, the portions are large and very tasty. Dinners include soup or salad. The children's menu offers four dishes for $6: prime rib, shrimp, grilled cheese, and a cheeseburger. Everything but the prime rib is also served at lunch. Nonalcoholic creations can be made for young patrons. Tuesday through Sunday there's a piano player. Valet and self-parking are available.

VILLA NOVA, 3131 Pacific Coast Hwy. (Calif. 1), Newport. Tel. 714/642-7880.

Cuisine: ITALIAN. **Reservations:** Required Sat–Sun, recommended Mon–Fri. **Directions:** Take the San Diego Freeway (I-405) south to Calif. 55 south (becomes Newport Boulevard), to the Pacific Coast Highway (Calif. 1) and turn south.

$ Prices: Main courses $9.25–$24. AE, CB, DC, MC, V.

Open: Daily 5pm–2am.

Children's Services: Children's menu, booster seats.

This is one of our favorite places in Newport, and it's on the harbor. Villa Nova is a little Italian villa look-alike that even has a bit of honest-to-goodness history. Created to resemble the owner's ancestral home in Venice, complete with a mini-tugboat docked outside, the restaurant was originally established more than 50 years ago on the Sunset Strip in Los Angeles, where it was the watering hole for many a celebrity during the Strip's heyday. In 1967 the family moved it to Newport. Inside, wall murals continue the theme of waterfront Venetian dining.

Owner Jim Dale says that they want to help give youngsters the chance to appreciate fine dining. Indeed they must, because teens who once came to Villa Nova for prom night are now bringing their children! You'll be surprised at some of the selections for kids—scampi and (according to Dale) the kids' favorite, scaloppine piccata (veal dipped in egg-and-lemon butter). Children's plates cost $6.50 to $11. The extensive adult menu includes many different kinds of pastas (spaghetti, ravioli, fettuccine, mostaccioli, manicotti, lasagne, and on and on) plus more than a dozen veal dishes, and chicken, beef, and seafood.

Nonalcoholic drinks will be made at the bar, and baby bottles and baby food can be warmed in the kitchen. Special extras include birthday cakes, which can be either ordered or brought in; miniature chocolate sundaes, made on request; and window seats that offer a view of the restaurant's mini-tugboat. Valet parking is offered.

Moderate

CRAB COOKER, 2200 Newport Blvd., Newport. Tel. 714/673-0100.

Cuisine: SEAFOOD. **Reservations:** Not accepted. **Directions:** Take the San Diego Freeway (I-405S) to Calif. 55, to Newport Boulevard and go 1 mile past the Pacific Coast Highway.

$ Prices: $8–$19. No credit cards.

Open: Sun–Thurs 11am–9pm, Fri–Sat 11am–10pm.

Children's Services: Child's plate, highchairs, booster seats.

If your children are fish or seafood lovers, the Crab Cooker is a small hole-in-the-wall (street parking; there's no lot) you'll want to check out. The throngs of people waiting on benches outside this seafood grill should be enough to tell you that the food is good, and the prices are probably the best in all of Newport Beach. But don't expect anything fancy—Linoleum floors, heavy-duty paper plates, and plastic silverware is what you'll get here. The main dining room also houses the glassed-in grill area, where you can watch chefs cook the seafood. We usually put our name on the waiting list, buy a small bowl of the tasty clam chowder, and wander the streets enjoying the town.

A combination plate with shrimp, scallops, and choice cuts of fish broiled on a skewer is $8.95 at lunch and dinner; charcoal-broiled lobster runs between $13.50 and $18.40. The child's plate (broiled fish on a skewer) can also be ordered by adult "light eaters," and costs $4.65 for a filling meal. All plates come with potatoes or rice and coleslaw or tomatoes.

TONY ROMA'S, 2530 W. Pacific Coast Hwy. (Calif. 1), Newport. Tel. 714/642-9070.

Cuisine: BARBECUE. **Reservations:** Not accepted. **Directions:** Take the San Diego Freeway (I-405S) to Calif. 55 south, to the Pacific Coast Highway and turn south.

$ Prices: Main courses $4–$13 at lunch, $5–$14 at dinner. AE, DC, MC, V.

Open: Lunch, daily 11am–4pm; dinner, Sun–Thurs 4–10pm, Fri–Sat 4–11pm.

Children's Services: Children's menu, highchairs, booster seats.

For good food and fast service, Tony Roma's is the place. The menu is the same as at other locations—tasty barbecued ribs, chicken, and steak (as well as salads and burgers), and is a good alternative to some of the more expensive restaurants in the area. All dinners include coleslaw, beans, or potato. The children's menu offers burgers, ribs, and chicken. The manager suggests coming between 4:30 and 6:30pm for dinner for the shortest wait. They'll deliver, too, even to your hotel if it's within their delivery area. Valet parking is available.

Budget

B.J.'S CHICAGO PIZZERIA, 106 Main St., Balboa Peninsula. Tel. 714/675-7560.

Cuisine: ITALIAN. **Reservations:** Not accepted.

$ Prices: $4.25–$5.75; pizza $7.95–$14.10. AE, MC, V.

Open: Mon–Thurs 11:30am–11pm, Fri–Sat 11:30am–midnight.

Children's Services: Reduced prices, highchairs, booster seats.

This lively pizza house at the base of the Balboa Pier is a great place after a day at the beach. Basic wood tables and booths set the mood for this inexpensive eatery. There are great deep-dish pizzas, or you can choose from a selection of pastas and sandwiches as well as a large salad bar. Servers will gladly warm baby bottles and baby food in the kitchen. There is no children's menu, but they will serve a child's pasta dish for $1 less, or a mini-pizza for $3.10. Expect a long wait during peak hours, but you can order your pizza ahead of time so it will be almost ready when you sit down. Park in the nearby public lot.

RUBY'S, at the end of Balboa Pier. Tel. 714/675-7829.
   Cuisine: AMERICAN. **Reservations:** Not accepted.
$ Prices: $4–$5. AE, MC, V.
   Open: Breakfast daily 7–11am; lunch/dinner Sun–Thurs 11am–9pm, Fri–Sat 11am–10pm.
   Children's Services: Children's menu, Sassy seats, booster seats.
When you're near Balboa Pier (1½ miles south of the Newport Pier), Ruby's is a great little place to grab breakfast, lunch, or a very early dinner. You can order from a fast-food–like window outside and eat on the pier or wait for a table inside the restaurant. Either way, plan to spend time watching the fishermen reel in their catches. Ruby's is novel, fun, and small. It has four long booths and three long tables that can accommodate families. With windows all around, you feel as if you're on the water (and on clear days, you can see Catalina Island).

The chili cheeseburgers with fries are great! And the mocha malts finish off the meal perfectly. If that sounds a bit heavy for you, you might try the grilled cheese, tuna burger, or simple Rubyburger. There are also salads, chowder, and chili to choose from. The children's menu includes such favorites as mini-burgers, corn dogs, and more; they come with fries and a drink for $3. For breakfast, you can have omelets, eggs, and other breakfast specialties.

There are *no rest rooms* here—or at this end of the pier. Expect a long wait for breakfast or dinner on weekends and during the summer if you want to eat inside. There's a parking lot at the pier entrance.

LAGUNA BEACH

Some people say that Laguna Beach is the most beautiful beach town in southern California. Whether that's true or not, Laguna is unlike other nearby coastal towns. It prides itself on its artistic core, its galleries and art festivals. It is cultured with a distinctive seaside flair. This delightful upscale village is centered where Pacific Coast Highway meets Broadway. On one side you have Main Beach; on the other, little streets filled with boutiques, restaurants, and novelty stores radiate eastward toward the hills. And for blocks along the Pacific Coast Highway you'll find galleries and craft shops.

Summertime is festival time in Laguna. The world-famous **Pageant of the Masters,** the **Festival of Arts,** and the **Sawdust Festival** draw an international crowd. Laguna is essentially not a child's town, but because of the famous art festivals and the beauty of the setting, it's a place adults enjoy—and one that kids can enjoy for a few hours. The coves of Laguna Beach are well-known play areas for kids.

GETTING THERE Laguna Beach is southeast of Newport Beach, about an

11-mile drive down the Pacific Coast Highway (Calif. 1). From Los Angeles, take the Santa Ana Freeway (I-5) or the San Diego Freeway (I-410). Exit the Calif. 133 (Laguna Freeway). This will take you right to Laguna Beach.

INFORMATION For information about Laguna, contact the **Laguna Beach Chamber of Commerce,** 357 Glenneyre Street (P.O. Box 396), Laguna Beach, CA 92652 (tel. 714/494-1018); it's beneath the library.

WHAT TO SEE & DO

Centrally located **Main Beach** is said to be one of the best-planned beaches around. Indeed, it's a beach that integrates the town and the sand. Although it gets a bit too crowded for our taste, Main Beach has many attractions. There is elaborate wooden play equipment, lawn areas, showers, and volleyball nets. A lifeguard tends the beach area. The park and adjacent beach back up to some of the local shops, making it extremely convenient if you need any supplies or kiddie treats.

Heisler Park, off Jasmine Street or Myrtle Street (which intersect the Pacific Coast Highway), north of Main Beach (tel. 714/494-1018), is a large park perched on a bluff overlooking the ocean. This is a wonderful place for a picnic or barbecue lunch or dinner. There is a large grassy area, picnic tables, rest rooms, and shuffleboard nearby. Take the stairs to get down to the beach.

These same streets (Jasmine and Myrtle) will take you down to beaches with tidepools. There is **Picnic Cove,** which has a ramp, and **Diver's Cove.** Lucky children may see sea urchins, starfish, mussels, even baby octopus. And you'll find great shells. (But remember that this is a preserve, so leave everything where you found it.)

WHERE TO EAT

THE COTTAGE, 308 N. Pacific Coast Hwy. (Calif. 1). Tel. 714/494-3023.
   Cuisine: AMERICAN. **Reservations:** Recommended.
$ Prices: Breakfast $2–$8; lunch $3.25–$8; dinner $8–$12. AE, MC, V.
   Open: Daily 7am–10pm.
   Children's Services: Highchairs, booster seats.
If you want a bite to eat, stop at the Cottage, a turn-of-the-century home that was a residence until 1938, when it became a café (the current restaurant opened in 1964). Beautiful antiques grace the rooms, and there is a fabulous photographic exhibit in the waiting area. The dining areas were once living areas and are wonderfully restored with solid oak and colored leaded glass. But don't let the antiques stop you—there's a cozy, warm feeling welcoming to families.

The Cottage serves home-style food for breakfast, lunch, and dinner. Items on the breakfast menu include such favorites as buckwheat and cranberry-orange pancakes or eggs with ham, sausage, or top sirloin. The junior breakfast (bacon, eggs, and pancakes) costs $2.75. Lunch offers such dishes as lasagne and Swiss steak, and a lighter fare of salads and sandwiches. Dinners include a variety of meat dishes (braised sirloin tips, Swiss steak), poultry, and fish, as well as two chef's specials each day. Junior dinners are luncheon-size portions of selected full dinners and run $6 to $9. Dinners include soup or salad, fresh vegetables, and rolls or popovers. Highchairs and booster seats are available.

The Cottage is open 365 days a year. Reservations are recommended because the wait can be long without one. Street parking is available.

DANA POINT

Dana Point is a gem of a place to visit between Orange County and San Diego. We go there for long weekends knowing we really don't have to spend a lot of time lining up for sightseeing attractions. If we feel like it, we roam the small harbor, or make our way on foot to **Doheny State Beach.** The bicycle trail, which begins at the beach, takes you all the way to San Juan Capistrano. The **Orange County Marine Institute,** and its adjacent tidepools, can keep us occupied for hours. We haven't tried the **whale-watching trips** or **parasailing** yet, but they are available at the harbor or through the Dana Point Resort.

GETTING THERE   Dana Point is on the Pacific Coast Highway (Calif. 1) about 7 miles south of Laguna Beach. To get there direct from Los Angeles, take the Santa Ana Freeway (I-5) south to the Dana Point exit.

WHERE TO STAY & EAT

DANA POINT RESORT, 25135 Park Lantern, Dana Point, CA 92629. **Tel. 714/661-5000,** or toll free 800/533-9748. Fax 714/661-5358. 341 rms, 12 suites. A/C MINIBAR TV TEL **Directions:** Take the Santa Ana Freeway (I-5) to the Dana Point exit and turn left onto Harbor Drive; the resort is at Harbor Drive and Park Lantern.

$ Rates: $170–$290 standard room single or double; $200–$240 single or double on the concierge floor. Children under 16 stay free in their parents' room. Cribs $10; rollaways $20. Inquire about special packages. AE, CB, DC, MC, V. **Parking:** Valet or self-parking.

The Dana Point Resort sits atop a cliff overlooking the harbor in all its Cape Cod refinement. One reason we like to stay here is because the two pool areas are so large and comfortable, and are bordered by spacious lawns that the kids can play on when they tire of the pool. The resort abuts a perfect-sized emerald-green park where we fly kites and play tag. When Janey was little we'd walk to the nearby playground, which is outfitted with pint-size equipment. There are also bikes to rent through the concierge (but bring your own for kids under 6). The bike path to San Juan Capistrano is flat—coming back *up* the hill to the resort at the end of the ride is something else! Tennis buffs get match-play service, and can participate in tennis clinics and private lessons (racquet rentals are available).

Camp Cowabunga, for kids 5 to 12, offers a day program that includes lunch and costs $25, and an evening program with dinner that costs $12. Each morning your children will get a chance to decode the "secret message" slipped under your door, telling where Camp Cowabunga will meet for that day. During the school year the program is offered weekends, until June 28; then it runs daily through September 3. Be sure, though, to check ahead--there must be a minimum of three children signed up 24 hours in advance for the program to commence.

Rooms are comfortable, but not large, except for those on the concierge floor. We liked the fact that on that floor we could get a continental breakfast in the morning and snacks and soft drinks in the afternoon. Remote-control TVs, two telephones, and lounging robes are in all the rooms.

Dining/Entertainment: At Watercolors, the resort's large restaurant, Janey found her children's menu printed on a Frisbee she could keep. But she wanted a selection off the adult menu; we found the chef most accommodating each time we made a special request. Service is geared more to adult-style dining (remember when you could finish a sandwich *and* a conversation?), so warn the kids that they may have a wait. Food is served poolside.

Services: Room service (6am to 2am), twice-daily maid service, bike rentals, concierge, children's program.

Facilities: Health club, three Jacuzzis, Nautilus equipment, basketball court (balls can be rented at the hotel), a par course, jogging trails, tennis courts with lessons and equipment rentals.

7. PALM SPRINGS & THE DESERT COMMUNITIES

To sun worshippers, tennis lovers, and golf aficionados, the Palm Springs area needs no introduction. For families who have never visited before, it does.

Palm Springs has been called the "Playground of the Stars" and the "Golf Capital of the World." Although you might still see a star or two, that's not its main attraction anymore. And while this is a popular retirement spot, it is also a fun (and relaxing) place to bring the kids. The desert communities offer great weather, plenty of ways to relax for those who seek that, and lots of outdoor activities. Combine those qualities with plenty of restaurants and a casual atmosphere, and you have the consummate resort.

When people refer to "Palm Springs," that usually encompasses all the desert communities—Palm Springs, Cathedral City, Rancho Mirage, Palm Desert, Indian Wells, and La Quinta. Although the towns are set one right after the other along Calif. 111, each has its own identity.

The "season" is really October through June. The warmest fall/winter months are October and November, and March and April in the spring, when daytime temperatures average 86°. Summer, which is when family rates are popular, can be really hot, with temperatures reaching 108° in July.

Plan to spend a minimum of 2 days on your excursion from Los Angeles.

GETTING THERE Getting to Palm Springs is easy. It is 107 miles southeast of L.A., about a 2½-hour drive by car via the San Bernardino Freeway (I-10) to Calif. 111.

INFORMATION You'll want to contact the **Palm Springs Desert Resorts Convention and Visitors Bureau,** located at The Atrium, 69-930 Calif. 111, Suite 201, Rancho Mirage, CA 92270 (tel. 619/770-9000), for information on current events in the area. The office is open Monday through Friday only, from 8:30am to 5pm. You can call a 24-hour **Activity Line** (tel. 619/770-1992). Or drop by the **Palm Desert Chamber of Commerce,** 72-990 Calif. 111, at Monterey, in Palm Desert (tel. 619/346-6111). It's open Monday through Friday from 9:30am to 4:30pm and on Saturday from 11am to 4pm.

PALM SPRINGS & THE DESERT COMMUNITIES

4 km

Joshua Tree National Park

Jackson St.
Monroe St.
Indio St.
Pace Lane
Indio Hills
Madison St.
42nd Ave.
40th Ave.
Jefferson St.
La Quinta
Fan Hill
Dillion Rd.
Adams St.
Bermuda Dunes
Indio Hills
Washington St.
Washington
Indian Wells
Holeman Way
Thousand Plains Canyon Rd.
Ramon Rd.
Waring Dr.
Sky Valley
Hidden Springs
Cook Rd.
Country Club Dr.
Hot Springs Rd.
Varner Rd.
Palm Desert
Skyridge rd.
Desert Moon Dr.
Thousand Palms
Fred
Aqueduct Rd.
Monterey Ave.
Dillion Rd.
Edom Hill
Bob Hope Dr.
Rancho Mirage
Frank Sinatra Dr.
Varner Rd.
Flat Top Mountain
Date
Ramon Rd.
Palm Dr.
Mountain View Rd.
Cathedral City
Murray Hill
Palm Dr.
Autry Trail
Gene
Palm Springs Regional Airport
Canyon Dr.
E. Palm
N. Palm Springs
Indian Ave.
Garnet

SIGHTS:

Ice Capades Chalet ➊
Indian Canyons ➋
Joshua Tree National Monument ➌
The Living Desert Reserve ➍
Moorten Botanical Garden ➎
Palm Canyon & Trading Post ➏
Palm Springs Aerial Tramway ➐
Palm Springs Oasis Waterpark ➑
Palm Springs Swim Center ➒
Tahquitz Canyon ➓

ACCOMMODATIONS:

Hyatt Grand Champions Resort ❶
Marriott's Desert Springs Resort & Spa ❷
Marriott's Rancho Las Palmas Resort ❸
Oasis Villa Hotel ❹
Quality Inn ❺
The Ritz-Carlton ❻

WHAT TO SEE & DO

DESERT OFF-ROAD ADVENTURES, P.O. Box 4528, Palm Desert, CA 92261. Tel. 619/773-3187.

⭐ Kids 6 and over get a kick out of taking these tours. The Santa Rosa tour takes you 2,000 feet up into the mountains in a seven-seat Jeep. Riders learn how the Native Americans lived in the mountains, about the animals and birds native to the area, and about the terrain.

The Mystery Canyon Adventure tour runs along the San Andreas earthquake fault, California's dubious claim to fame. Intricate rock formations appear throughout the canyons and ravines. You'll get an earful of the story of the Coachella Valley.

Tours take approximately 3 hours and are led by personable, knowledgeable guides. We found the morning departure to be the best because it's cooler. Complimentary hotel pickup, and continental breakfast in the morning or beverages and snacks for the afternoon departure, are included. It's fun to bring a picnic lunch, or, with advance notice, have the Jeep company provide one. Take a hat, sunscreen, and a jacket in the winter months. No tours are given in July and August. Children under 5 are not permitted unless you arrange for a private tour (with a minimum of five people).

Prices: Rates vary seasonally and by tour. For the Santa Rosa tour, adults $84 Jan–May, $74 Oct–December; seniors and children 5 to 12 $76.

THE LIVING DESERT RESERVE, 47-900 Portola Ave., Palm Desert. Tel. 619/346-5694.

⭐ Don't miss this outdoor museum. Janey has been introduced to many new birds, animals, and insects at the wildlife park's special "critter closeup."

Allot 1 to 2 hours for this family activity, which is perfect for any age. There are numerous animal species living in naturalistic habitats—many we've never heard of! As you walk from setting to setting, you travel through botanical gardens made up of 10 desert regions. There are fascinating plants, even prehistoric species. Indian exhibits, hiking trails, an animal nursery, and a gift shop are all on the grounds. In addition to critter closeups, a weekend Discovery Room and special nature walks are featured.

Rest rooms, water fountains, and soft-drink machines are conveniently located. Although there are shaded areas throughout the grounds, you might want to bring extra drinks, hats, and sunscreen. Make a day of it and bring a picnic lunch to eat at the park's shaded picnic area.

The reserve is stroller-accessible, and there are strollers and wheelchairs available for use. Parking is free.

Admission: $6 adults, $5 seniors (62 and over), $3 children 3–15, free for children under 3.

Open: Sept 1–June 15, daily 9am–5pm (last admission at 4:30pm). **Closed:** June 16–Aug.

PALM SPRINGS AERIAL TRAMWAY, at Calif. 111 (north) and Tramway Rd., Palm Springs. Tel. 619/325-1391.

The 18-minute ride to the top of Mount San Jacinto takes you on a trip the equivalent of a drive from Sonora, Mexico, to the Arctic Circle, in terms of the flora and fauna you'll see.

Be sure to take layers of clothing with you, as the temperature drops greatly at the top. If you aren't prepared, there's a gift shop at the entrance that sells mittens, sweatshirts, hats, and other warm clothing.

Once you get to the top, you'll be in **Mount San Jacinto State Park.** If you never get on one hiking trail, you'll enjoy the immediate area outside the tram station. There's a great hill after you pass the first curve of the concrete, hand-railed path. It's an easy climb for older kids, a bit of work for the toddler set.

If you continue down the winding concrete path to the park itself, you enter 54 miles of campgrounds, hiking trails, and a ranger station. A sign at the end of the path illustrates where the three-quarter-mile self-guiding **Nature Loop Trail** begins and shows you where the ranger station is in nearby Long Valley (walking distance). Check at the station for maps and information on guided nature hikes. Camping is allowed in the wilderness with a permit, available at the ranger station. If you don't feel like hoofing it, a guided mule-back **Wilderness Trail Ride** is available during the hot summer months. The ride is 20 minutes long. Signs at the tram station will lead you to the mules.

Each tram station (coming and going) has a snack bar, cocktail lounge, gift shop, observation areas, and rest rooms. There's ample parking, with shuttle service from outlying lots. Not stroller-accessible.

A Ride 'n' Dine package is available for those who want to have dinner at the top.

Admission: Round-trip fare, $14 adults, $9 children 13 and under; round-trip fare and dinner, $18 adults, $11.50 children 13 and under.

Open: Cars run at least every half hour. During daylight savings, trams up Mon–Fri 10am–9pm, Sat–Sun 8am–9pm (last tram down at 10:45pm); the rest of the year, trams up Mon–Fri 10am–8pm, Sat–Sun 8am–8pm (last tram down at 9:45pm). During holidays the wait for a tram up can be anywhere from a half hour to 2 hours. **Closed:** The first 2 weeks in Aug.

BALLOONING

Hot-air ballooning is usually not recommended for children under 5, especially because very young children are often frightened by the loud noise of the burners used to fill the balloons. Know your child before you decide to spend this kind of money. Ballooning is an exhilarating experience, and one you'll all remember forever. But once you're up there with a group of people, you can't get away from a frightened, screaming child.

In addition to the following two companies, you might also try **Fantasy Balloon Flights** (tel. 619/568-0997, or toll free 800/GO-ABOVE) or the **American Balloon Society** (tel. 619/568-6700).

DESERT BALLOON CHARTERS, P.O. Box 2713, Palm Desert, CA 92261. Tel. 619/346-8575.

John Zimmer's company will fly you over the desert for an hour and 15 minutes. He and his crew take children over 8 years old. Make reservations for your ride, which is available October through May.

Prices: $125 adults, $19 children under 14.

SUNRISE BALLOONS, 82-201 Airport Blvd., Thermal, CA 92274. Tel. 619/346-7591, or toll free 800/548-9912.

This company, with its own balloon park between La Quinta and Indio, has been making desert flights since 1976. Pregnant women cannot fly with Sunrise, and children under 10 years old are advised not to fly.

Prices: Call for rates.

BICYCLING

If you're coming by car, you're best off bringing your own bikes, carriers, and helmets to the desert—most bicycle-rental locations don't have child carriers for rent. If you don't need the carrier, there are some small bikes for rent, but no helmets.

There are bike paths all over town, including some on hotel or condominium properties (for guest use only). The *Palm Spring Life's Desert Guide* pullout sometimes includes a **"Bicycle Touring Guide,"** which outlines paths from 3 to 14½ miles long. The **Palm Springs Recreation Department,** 401 South Pavilion Way, Palm Springs (tel. 619/323-8272), has bike-path maps.

Note: Don't let your kids ride along Calif. 111. It's much too busy, and there are many prettier places to ride.

BURNETT'S BICYCLE BARN, in the Alpha Beta Center, 429 S. Sunrise Way at Ramon Rd., Palm Springs. Tel. 619/325-7844.

Rentals include 3- and 10-speeds, tandems, trailers (to pull children), three-wheelers for two people, side-by-sides, and kids' bikes. Open Thursday through Monday from 8am to 5pm and on Tuesday from 8am to noon; closed Wednesday. Call for current rates.

CANYON BICYCLE RENTALS AND TOURS, 210 W. Sunny Dunes Rd., Palm Springs. Tel. 619/327-7688.

Rentals are by the half day, day, or week. Children's bikes are available. Open daily from 9am to 5pm. Call for rates.

MAC'S BIKE RENTALS, 700 E. Palm Canyon Dr., Palm Springs. Tel. 619/327-5721.

Mac's rents by the hour, day, week, or month, and they deliver if you rent for a minimum of a day. Children's bikes and baby trailers can be rented, and helmets are provided. Open Monday through Saturday from 9:30am to 5:30pm and on Sunday from noon to 5pm. Call for current rates.

HIKING

The entrance to the **Indian Canyons** can be found on South Palm Canyon Drive. You may not know that the Palm Springs area was originally settled by the Agua Caliente Cahuilla Indians. Much of the land in the area is still owned by Native Americans, and many hotels and homes sit on that land, their owners paying rent on 99-year leases. The Cahuillas created their communities inside five canyons: three are open to the public and one requires a permit to hike; the last, Chino, is where you'll find the Aerial Tramway. Still part of the Indian reservation, the canyons are maintained by the Agua Caliente tribe.

In **Palm Canyon** you'll find the Trading Post, which sells hiking maps, snacks, and Native American art and artifacts. There is a footpath near the post that leads down into the canyon. You can hike from this point, or just bring a picnic lunch and sit by the stream. The paths aren't too steep for young children. This canyon is known to have the most palm trees in the world and is listed on the National Register of Historic Places.

Hiking in **Andreas Canyon** is for the more adventurous. Not ready for a tough hike? Picnic there instead. There's a foot trail through the canyon and picnic tables along the way. Be sure to check at the Trading Post as to whether the grade is too steep for your kids (or yourself!).

Murray Canyon is less accessible, but if you're determined to see it, you can hike there from Andreas. If you're lucky, the children just might spot a wild pony or some mountain sheep.

Tahquitz Canyon, just west of Palm Springs, can be entered only by special permit from the Tribal Council Office, 960 East Tahquitz Way, Palm Springs (tel. 619/325-5673). This canyon is known for magnificent waterfalls. (Tahquitz has been recently under reconstruction. Call for information.)

Admission to the canyons is $3 for adults, 75¢ for children 6 to 12. If you're on horseback, it will cost you $3.50. The canyons are open September through June, daily from 8am to 5pm.

HORSEBACK RIDING

RANCH OF THE 7TH RANGE, off Calif. 111, La Quinta. Tel. 619/564-1414.

Not far from the PGA West headquarters (call for directions), horses and ponies are for rent by the hour, and a guide is required for large groups, families, and novice riders. Experienced riders can ride without a guide. Although they allow children 3 and under to ride double with a parent, we don't recommend this. The cost is $20 per person per hour, plus $20 per guide per hour (fee is split by the group). Pony leads are $6. Reservations are recommended.

SMOKETREE STABLES, 2500 Toledo Avenue, Palm Springs. Tel. 619/327-1372.

Smoketree offers hourly rentals ($15 per hour, adults or children), and all-day pack trips (call for rates). The stables are open year round. Children must be at least 5 to ride their own horses. Guides are furnished.

ICE SKATING

What a welcome relief in the middle of the summer! At **Ice Capades Chalet,** in the Palm Desert Town Center Mall, 72840 Calif. 111, Palm Desert (tel. 619/340-4412), public skating is offered daily year round at various times, day and evening (call for the schedule). For those not staying long enough to get into a class, director Nalani Philipson offers private lessons at $11 for 15 minutes, $22 for a half hour (call in advance). Skate rental is available for ages 2½ through adult ($2). Wednesday is family night, with special prices. Admission to the rink is $5.

TENNIS

If your hotel courts are tied up, there are public courts at **DeMuth Park,** 4375 Mesquite Avenue (four night-lit courts); **Ruth Hardy Park,** 700 Tamarisk Road (eight courts); and **Palm Springs High School,** 2248 Ramon Road (five courts). The **Palm Springs Tennis Center,** 1300 Baristo Road, with nine night-lit courts, is open to the public for a small fee. For more information, call 619/320-0020.

WATER SPORTS & FISHING

PALM SPRINGS OASIS WATERPARK, 1500 Gene Autry Trail, Palm Springs. Tel. 619/325-SURF.

The waterpark is just what its name says—an oasis in the middle of the desert. On a hot summer day in the desert there's no better place to be. Every age group is represented here. For your youngest ball of energy, there is "Squirt City"—small slides, giant squirt guns, and a splashy pool. There's another slide area just for toddlers, and a third for children 30 inches tall.

Whitewater River is a slow-moving innertube ride set in 3½ feet of water. Lots of youngsters ride in it alone, and lifeguards are stationed all along the 600-foot loop. There's also a family slide so junior can travel down to the 80° water with mom or dad on an innertube.

Even the young kids can surf on the 3½-foot waves in the wave pool. Surf- and bodyboards can be rented. Although lifeguards are on duty, this is a huge pool—we suggest that you accompany your young children.

All together there are seven slides—two are seven stories high, and you (not me!) travel at speeds up to 40 m.p.h. Four slides are for riders at least 48 inches tall; three others are geared for kids 40 inches and up.

Day passes to the Oasis Health Club can be purchased. It offers a private spa and fitness center with a whirlpool, aerobics, steam, sauna, and a wide array of cardiovascular and weight-training equipment. Private cabañas with food service will run you $50 on the weekend for four people.

Come early on weekends for shade or chaise longues. There are three food concession stands, lockers, changing rooms, and showers. Self-parking is $2, and valet parking is available.

Admission: $14 adults, $9.95 children 4–11, free for children under 4. Families who stay at the Oasis Villa Hotel earn several free passes (see "Where to Stay," below).

Open: Mid-Mar to May, daily 11am–6pm; June to mid-Sept, daily 11am–8pm; mid-Sept to Oct, Sat–Sun 11am–6pm.

PALM SPRINGS SWIM CENTER, in the Sunrise Plaza Center, corner of Sunrise Way and Ramon Rd., Palm Springs. Tel. 619/323-8278.

An outdoor Olympic-size pool is open to the public, with lifeguards year round. There's a diving board and separate shallow area of the pool roped off for children. Children 6 and under can take private swimming lessons, $41 for five 30-minute classes.

Admission: $3 adults (ages 13 and up), $2 children 4 to 12, free for children under 4.

Open: Daily 11am–5pm (in summer, also open for night swimming).

WHITEWATER TROUT FISHING, in Whitewater. Tel. 619/325-5570.

If you're willing to make about a 25-mile round-trip, you can catch trout to your heart's content at Whitewater (take the Whitewater exit off I-10 west). After little Peggy has caught "the big one," you can grill and eat it right there. Or the staff will clean and box your catch for no charge. Fish range from 1 to 5 pounds.

Admission: $2.50 for tackle, bait, bucket, towel, and cleaning, plus $2.55 per pound of fish caught.

Open: Tues–Sun 9am–5pm, year round.

WHERE TO STAY

RATES Unlike other situations where hotel rooms are a fixed price, you have options in the desert. Be sure to call the hotel directly and ask questions before you choose your accommodations: What's the best price I can get? Are two connecting rooms a better deal than a suite? If I come next weekend instead of this weekend, is there a better price? Is there a special family rate? Are any package deals currently available?

Also check on minimum-stay requirements. Some establishments demand a 3- or even 4-night minimum on holiday weekends.

SEASONS Hotel and condominium rates are based on three seasons. Winter rates are the highest, shoulder rates in the middle, and summer rates the lowest. To make it less complicated, we list only winter and summer rates. Although it might seem as if we've listed a disproportionate number of "Very Expensive" accommodations, note that their summer rates are often quite reasonable.

Below are the basic date cut-offs for each season. But be sure to double-check at the hotel you choose. Its season cut-off could be a few days before or after the following dates, changing the price of your room substantially.

Summer: June 1 through September 12.
Shoulder: September 13 through December 19.
Winter: December 20 through Memorial Day weekend.

HOTELS

Very Expensive

HYATT GRAND CHAMPIONS RESORT, 44-600 Indian Wells Lane, Indian Wells, CA 92210. Tel. 619/341-1000, or toll free 800/233-1234, 800/826-1112 in California. Fax 619/568-2236. 340 rms and suites. A/C MINIBAR TV TEL
Directions: Take the San Bernardino Freeway (I-10) to the Washington Street exit to Calif. 111.
$ **Rates:** Winter, $210–$290 standard parlor suite; $315 Regency Club room; $365 Penthouse suite; $725–$925 villa. Summer, $95–$155 standard parlor suite; $180 Regency Club room; $210 Penthouse suite; $350–$450 villa. A connecting room is charged at 50% of the full rate. Children under 18 stay free in their parents' room. Additional adults $25 per night; cribs and rollaways free. AE, DC, MC, V.
Parking: Valet or self-parking.

★ When it first opened, the Grand Champions had that tag of luxury and formality that kept some families away. That's not the case anymore. You *can* bring your little ones and feel comfortable in this elegant resort hotel. While the decor is decidedly European and luxurious, and the lobby is grand, the staff will treat your children with respect.

As with other Hyatt hotels around the country, this one has its own children's program called "Camp Little Champions," for kids 3 to 15. It is offered when there's a minimum of three children signing up and runs weekends during season and summer days based on need. Parents can sign their children up for the whole program or for hourly periods. Some moms and dads even accompany their tots for part or all of the day. Activities consist of volleyball, kite flying, relay races, lawn games, and croquet, all geared to the ages of the participating children. Swimming is not offered. In the hot summer months, most of the activities are indoors, for which a permanent fully equipped suite has been set aside just for the kids. The charge for the program is $25 per day, or $5 per hour, per child.

While your little ones enjoy meeting and playing with other kids, you can check out the Hyatt facilities, and sign up for spa treatments, massage, or aerobics classes, and enjoy the indoor spa, sauna, and steam room. Bicycle rentals can be arranged in the Club. There are two 18-hole championship golf courses, plus 12 tennis courts (including a sunken celebrity court and a 10,500-seat stadium for special events).

The all-suite rooms are decorated in pale, soft colors, European in feel, but not stuffy. The standard parlor suites are split-level accommodations facing the mountains, pool, or golf course. The marble bathrooms are spacious, and each one has an individual deep tub, glass-enclosed shower, and fluffy bath towels. A small serving bar and minibar are adjacent to the sleeping alcove, which is furnished with either two double beds or one king-size bed. The step-down living area contains a writing desk and sofa and chair; in some rooms the sofa pulls out into a bed. Balconies with table and chairs are comfortable. Robes, hairdryers, two telephones, full-length mirrors, remote-control TVs, and pay movies are all standard.

One step up in accommodations is the Regency Club, offering guests concierge service, complimentary continental breakfast, champagne and truffles, cocktails, and hors d'oeuvres. The rooms on this floor are also parlor suites, with prime pool views. Penthouse suites have separate bedrooms, a sitting room and 1½ baths, large terraces, stereo/cassette players, and other amenities.

The villas are one- and two-bedroom accommodations housed separately, each with a private courtyard and Jacuzzi. Every villa is decorated differently. They have wood-burning fireplaces, two-line phones, and stereo/cassette players. But best of all, they come with a 24-hour European-trained butler who fills your culinary needs!

Dining/Entertainment: Within the hotel is a fine dining room, Jasmine, open for dinner. Pianissimo is the lounge with live entertainment and a dance floor. Afternoon tea is served on the fifth floor in the Regency Club lounge ($14). Trattoria California is where you and the kids will feel the most comfortable, whether dining al fresco or indoors. It's open for breakfast, lunch, and dinner, and has a children's menu quite reasonably priced—breakfasts are $1.50 to $2; lunch and dinner, $2.50 to $3.50. Charlie's is a separate restaurant located near the Tennis Club open for lunch and dinner. Poolside food service is available.

Services: 24-hour room service, concierge, children's program, baby-sitting, laundry and valet, evening turn-down service.

Facilities: Fitness club, aerobics classes, bicycle rentals, two 18-hole championship golf courses, 12 tennis courts, four pools, two Jacuzzis, massage, sauna, and spa treatments.

MARRIOTT'S DESERT SPRINGS RESORT & SPA, 74855 Country Club Dr., Palm Desert, CA 92260. Tel. 619/341-2211, or toll free 800/228-9290. Fax 619/341-1872. 891 rms and suites. A/C MINIBAR TV TEL **Directions:** Take the San Bernardino Freeway (I-10) to the Monterey Avenue exit; the resort is between Monterey Avenue and Cook Street.

$ Rates: Winter $245–$295 standard room single or double; $285–$325 concierge floor room single or double; $450–$1,400 suite. Summer, $105–$125 standard room single or double; $125–$150 concierge floor room single or double; $250–$500 suite. Children under 18 stay free in their parents' room. Additional adults $10; cribs and rollaways free. AE, CB, DC, DISC, MC, V. **Parking:** Valet ($9 daily); free self-parking.

This is a hotel designed for activity. The sound of waterfalls flowing into the hotel's lagoon greets you first. Look up and you'll see the gigantic eight-story atrium lobby; look down and you'll see an oasis in the middle of the desert—mini-tour boats greet guests at the lagoon dock offering to take you on a boat tour of the hotel grounds or drop you off at two of the hotel restaurants.

A hospitality desk in the lobby offers information on the area, while a separate resort activities desk representative is there to tell you what's going on in-house. Special family programs are planned for Easter, Memorial Day, Labor Day, Thanksgiving, and Christmas. Year round, kids can practice at an outdoor putting green, where they'll be given clubs and balls. The children love the giant lawn chess (or checkers) outdoors. You can all learn bocce ball or lawn bowling and can join in on a volleyball game. One of the three pools is surrounded by a man-made sandy beach.

There are a variety of rooms to choose from. Rooms with two double beds, by themselves or connecting to a room with a king-size bed, are quite popular for families. And the one-bedroom suites are in high demand. The hotel offers a concierge level, where rooms include special services such as complimentary light breakfast, drinks throughout the day, and complimentary hors d'oeuvres. Children are welcome to stay on this floor, but they are not allowed in the concierge lounge.

Rooms are furnished in desert pastels and feature minibars, in-house movies that can be turned off at the desk, remote-control TVs, and patios with chairs. Rooms are good-sized, with space for a crib. The large bathrooms are designed in marble and have separate showers. There are lots of personal-care amenities and plush towels.

Note: The busiest time is summer weekends (make reservations at least 3 weeks in advance) and Memorial Day and Labor Day weekends (make reservations at least a month in advance).

Dining/Entertainment: There are 12 restaurants, lounges, and snack bars on the premises. The Mikado is a Japanese restaurant that serves teppenyaki tableside style. If you wish, they'll serve kids smaller portions. At one pool, a cafeteria-style snack bar makes it easy to have lunch at the pool without having to change clothes.

Services: Room service, concierge, hospitality desk, resort activities desk, family programs, baby-sitting, laundry and valet service.

Facilities: Shopping colonnade, three swimming pools, spa, health club, tennis, two golf courses.

MARRIOTT'S RANCHO LAS PALMAS RESORT, 41000 Bob Hope Dr.,

Rancho Mirage, CA 92270. Tel. 619/568-2727, or toll free 800/228-9290. Fax 619/568-5845. 400 rms, 8 suites. A/C MINIBAR TV TEL

$ Rates: Winter, $260–$280 standard room single or double; $460–$1,400 suite. Summer, $99–$119 standard room single or double; $250–$750 suite. AE, DISC, MC, V. **Parking:** Valet or self-parking.

The first encounter with this four-star resort at Bob Hope Drive and Ramon Road is like a step back into Old California. First you see gorgeous early California architecture framed in brilliant bougainvillea and surrounded by lush landscaping. You enter a lobby designed in the authentic decor of that era and are met by a gracious hotel staff person. You might not think this resort would be a choice for families—just honeymooners and "old" married folk—but you'll be surprised at what this Marriott has to offer.

Each holiday weekend you can expect both adult and children's activities. Based on a theme, the programs offer family Bingo, movies, aerobics, scavenger hunts, carnivals, and ice-cream socials. During the summer, children ages 6 to 12 can participate in the usual children's club activities in Kactus Kids Kamp, half days, for a nominal charge ($5). On Friday and Saturday night the Sundown Kactus Kamp is offered for kids 5 to 12 for the same $5 charge.

The rooms are not fancy, but they are certainly deluxe. Double rooms come with small sofas, some of which pull out for an extra bed, and comfortable reading chairs. There is room for a crib. Patios have a chaise longue and table. All rooms have remote-control TV (you can even check out via TV). Bathrooms are small. *Note to parents of toddlers:* When requesting ground-floor accommodations, be sure to avoid the rooms that open up to the little ponds, which are not fenced off. Parlor connectors are a good alternative to connecting rooms for families who are staying more than a weekend. The bedroom has either two double beds or one king-size bed. The parlor is furnished with a Murphy bed or sleeper sofa, a table and four chairs, a chaise longue, a dressing area, and a bathroom. By night you have two bedrooms; by day, a bedroom and a living room. Suites are spacious and elegant.

Dining/Entertainment: There are four restaurants in the hotel, but the Fountain Court is the best choice for families with young children. It offers a children's menu (crayons included) for breakfast, lunch, and dinner at quite reasonable prices. Poolside food and beverage service is available.

Services: 24-hour room service, concierge, baby-sitting, children's program, laundry and valet service.

Facilities: Three swimming pools, golf course, tennis courts (junior tennis is regularly scheduled), clubhouse.

THE RITZ-CARLTON, 68-900 Frank Sinatra Dr., Rancho Mirage, CA 92270. Tel. 619/321-8282, or toll free 800/241-3333. Fax 619/328-3167. 240 rms, 12 suites. A/C MINIBAR TV TEL

$ Rates: Winter, $275–$355 standard room; $395 Club Floor room; $625–$1,700 suite. Summer, $95–$150 standard room; $250 Club Floor room; $400–$900 suite. Children under 18 stay free in their parents' room. Additional guests $25 per night, cribs and rollaways free. Inquire about special packages. AE, CB, DC, DISC, MC, V. **Parking:** Valet.

Nestled in the foothills of the Santa Rosa Mountains at the intersection of Frank Sinatra Drive and Calif. 111 in Rancho Mirage, the Ritz is the neighbor of—and sometimes host to—a herd of rare bighorn sheep, whose protected reserve is just behind the resort. The hotel's formality might put you off at first, but you'll discover that it's a very friendly resort, with comfortable rooms and fine service.

On holiday weekends children can participate in a variety of planned events, including art projects, golf-cart rides, outdoor games, and outings at the pool. In addition to these familiar children's activities, the Ritz offers nature-focused activities such as animal exhibits, nature hunts, and guided nature walks, and will theme even snack time to that end. Parents will receive a list of possible things to do in their room and can sign the kids up in the morning. The fees depend on the activities. Children 4 to 12 are welcome, and there is a fee of $10 per child. There are also themed holiday programs. The annual Teddy Bear Tea can also be reserved during this time period. Have little Johnny and Susie bring along their favorite teddy, and treat them to hot cocoa and other snacks at this adorable little tea. The cost is $5.25 per child. Children's board games, balls, and croquet equipment are available any time of the year, and group or individual tennis lessons are offered for kids at the hotel's Tennis Club.

Although the pool area is delightful, the Tennis Club is one of the hotel's biggest draws. Tom Gorman, coach of the U.S. Davis Team and the U.S. Olympic tennis team, is the on-premises director, and two teaching pros are on staff. The club has 10 courts lit for night play and a full-service restaurant. Golf lovers aren't left out either. The Ritz-Carlton has reciprocal agreements with several courses in the area.

Accommodations in the hotel are spacious, comfortable, and traditionally decorated, and have large, luxurious bathrooms. All the room amenities you'd expect of a first-class hotel are offered, including maid service twice a day and valet service daily. Armoires contain the remote-control TV and honor bar. A comfortable reading chair and ottoman can be moved around for a view of the pool.

Rooms are classified as "minimum," "superior," or "deluxe." The difference is the view: The first offers a view of the Santa Rosa foothills; the next gives you the choice of the Santa Rosa Mountains or the valley below; and a deluxe room has the possibility of a pool, courtyard and valley, or mountain view.

If you stay on the Club Floor, a private concierge will painstakingly explain the complimentary continental breakfast, afternoon tea, hors d'oeuvres, and after-dinner treats displayed each day in the exclusive lounge.

Dining/Entertainment: The poolside restaurant is very casual, while the other hotel restaurants are "elegantly casual." The main dining room requires jackets for men. You can assume your children should dress accordingly. There is a children's menu in the more casual Café.

Services: 24-hour room service, concierge, twice-daily maid service, laundry and valet service, baby-sitting, children's program.

Facilities: Pool, spa, massage, health club, tennis club, running trail.

Expensive

DOUBLETREE RESORT PALM SPRINGS, Vista Chino at Landau Blvd. (P.O. Box 1644), Palm Springs, CA 92263. Tel. 619/322-7000, or toll free 800/528-0444. Fax 619/322-6853. 289 rms, 15 suites, 200 condos. A/C TV TEL

$ Rates: Winter, $195–$225 standard room; $235–$300 condominium. Summer, $79–$99 standard room; $110–$160 condominium. Children under 18 stay free in their parents' room. Additional adults $15; cribs and rollaways free. Ask about numerous summer specials, golf and tennis packages, and discounts for extended stays. AE, DC, MC, V. **Parking:** Valet and self-parking.

It may be off the beaten path, but many families have discovered that the Doubletree makes a good family destination. The fenced-in pool area is very large, with sloping steps at one side of the pool where all the little tykes like to play.

The Doubletree has a tennis and fitness club, in addition to three volleyball nets, 27 holes of golf, 10 tennis courts, and two indoor racquetball courts. Bike rentals can be arranged. The adventurous among you might want to explore the rest of the property, which houses condominiums (some of which the hotel rents) and 45 pools, which hotel guests are free to use. During the summer and on holidays there are supervised activities for the children. Schedules and activities vary, so call ahead.

All rooms have balconies or patios and desert or mountain views. You can get a room with a king-size bed or with two double beds and there's still room for a rollaway or a crib. Bathrooms are roomy and all have double sinks and tub/shower combinations. Each unit has a refrigerator; use of the room safe costs $5. For a bedtime snack, everyone gets a package of special chocolate-chip cookies on their first night's stay. Sunday through Thursday, checkout is extended to 6pm for no extra charge.

On the grounds are 200 one- and two-bedroom condominiums, some with dens, all available for rent. Extended-stay discounts are also applicable to condominiums.

Dining/Entertainment: Families will feel most comfortable in the open-air Promenade Café, where breakfast, lunch, and dinner are served. The children's menu covers all tastes and is reasonably priced at $2.25 or $3 for all choices. Standard coffee-shop fare is available for mom and dad. There are often specially priced menus during the summer months. As for room service, you'll have to ask for children's items—they're not on the menu. Poolside food service is open year round.

Services: Room service (6:30am to 11pm), bicycle rentals, children's program.

Facilities: Swimming pools (45 of them!), tennis and fitness club, volleyball, golf course, tennis courts, racquetball courts.

OASIS VILLA HOTEL, 4190 E. Palm Canyon Dr., Palm Springs, CA 92264. Tel. 619/328-1499, or toll free 800/247-4664, 800/543-5160 in California. Fax 619/324-8659. 110 condominiums. A/C TV TEL

$ Rates: Winter, $239 standard two-bedroom villa; $299 two-bedroom villa with a den. Summer, $129 per villa. All rates are based on four adults per unit. Children 12 and under stay free in their parents' room. Additional guests $45 per night; cribs free. Inquire about special holiday and weekly packages, plus packages including Waterpark tickets. AE, MC, V. **Parking:** Free.

Staying in a hotel-style condominium or "villa," is one way to have the best of both worlds—family-style accommodations with all the services of a full-scale hotel, and quite luxurious for the price. Each villa has two bedrooms, a private garage, its own patio with furniture and a gas barbecue, and a private washer and dryer. The kitchens are fully equipped with dishwashers, microwaves, dishes, and pots and pans. Some villas have breakfast nooks *and* dining areas. The living rooms are spacious, the decor is bright and light, and the furniture is comfortable. Ground-floor accommodations are the most convenient if you have young children.

The grounds, at the corner of East Palm Canyon Drive and Cherokee Way, are set up like a miniature suburban community—they have gates with 24-hour security. Some guests bring bikes from home and let the kids ride through the complex.

Facilities: Eight pools, Jacuzzis, five night-lit tennis courts.

Moderate

QUALITY INN, 1269 E. Palm Canyon Dr., Palm Springs, CA 92264. Tel. 619/323-2775, or toll free 800/472-4339. Fax 619/323-4234. 124 rms, 20 suites. A/C TV TEL

$ Rates: Winter, $65–$105 single or double Mon–Fri, $79–$135 Sat–Sun. Summer, $39–$65 single or double Mon–Fri, $49–$79 Sat–Sun. Children 18 and younger stay free in their parents' room. Additional adults $5 per night; cribs free; rollaways $5. AE, DISC, MC, V. **Parking:** Free.

Having gone through a recent $1-million renovation, the rooms at this hotel, at the corner of Sunrise Way and Palm Canyon Drive, are cheerful and spotless with their new white furniture and fresh bed linens and upholstery. The small deck area and pool, plus a children's wading pool and Jacuzzi, are quite popular. A barbecue and gazebo are available for guest use. Sometimes you'll see families picnicking on the 2½-acre park adjacent to the hotel.

The new family suites are very popular. There are only 24 available, so reserve one well in advance. Each one consists of two connecting rooms, one with a king-size bed, the other made into a small living room with a sleeper sofa. Each suite has two full bathrooms, two TVs, and two phones, and there is one refrigerator. Like all the hotel accommodations, the family suites have cable TV and pay movies, a small table and chairs, and a coffee maker. Double rooms have two queen-size beds, while single-bedded rooms are available with a queen- or king-size bed. Standard rooms have space for either a rollaway or a crib, but not both. A coin-operated laundry and no-smoking rooms are available.

There's no hotel restaurant, but a Carrow's (open 24 hours) and Jeremiah's (serving dinner, with nightly entertainment) are steps away and offer hotel charge privileges.

Budget

HAMPTON INN, 2000 N. Palm Canyon Dr., Palm Springs, CA 92263. Tel. 619/320-0555, or toll free 800/426-7866. Fax 619/320-2261. 96 rms. A/C TV TEL **Directions:** Take the San Bernardino Freeway (I-10) to the Palm Springs/Calif. 111 exit; the inn is on the left after about a 10-mile drive.

$ Rates: (including continental breakfast): Winter, $64–$74 single Sun–Thurs, $74–$84 Fri–Sat and hols; $69–$79 double Sun–Thurs, $79–$89 Fri–Sat and hols. Summer, $39–$49 single Sun–Thurs, $49–$59 Sat–Sun and hols; $44–$54 double Sun–Thurs, $54–$64 Fri–Sat and hols. Children 18 and under stay free in their parents' room. Third and fourth adults free; cribs free; rollaways $10. AE, CB, DC, MC, V. **Parking:** Free.

The Hampton Inn is a pleasant surprise. Located close to the Palm Springs Aerial Tramway, yet away from the hustle and bustle of downtown Palm Springs, it provides an affordable way to enjoy the desert. The heated outdoor pool and spa are fenced in. The pool area, though small, has plenty of shady areas with umbrella tables and chaise longues.

Rooms aren't huge, but they are clean and relatively new. The "king study" has a king-size bed and a sleeper sofa, plus a separate vanity, small bathroom, and full-length mirrors. All king studies have refrigerators. The standard king-bedded room comes with a recliner, and there is room for a crib. A room with two double beds affords you space for four people and room for a crib. Amenities include free local phone calls, remote-control TVs with free movie stations, radios, and same-day valet service. No-smoking and handicapped rooms are available.

There's no restaurant on the premises, but you'll be within walking distance of several family-friendly spots. In addition to the usual sweet breakfast offerings for the continental breakfast, they stock up on sugar-free cereals, breads, and juices.

TRAVELODGE, 333 E. Palm Canyon Dr., Palm Springs, CA 92264. Tel. 619/327-1211, or toll free 800/255-3050. Fax 619/320-4672. 158 rms. A/C TV TEL

$ Rates: Winter, $55–$75 single or double; summer, $35–$45 single or double. Poolside rooms $10 extra. Children under 17 stay free in their parents' room. Additional adults $10; cribs free; rollaways $10. AE, CB, DC, DISC, MC, V. **Parking:** Free.

This hotel is centrally located between North and South Palm Canyon Drive, near downtown Palm Springs, and features two heated pools, a Jacuzzi, coin-operated laundry facilities, and a small games area. Rooms are motel style (parking is close to each room), with tiny patios and sliding glass doors. A unit with two double beds still has room for a crib. There is cable TV with movie channels and instant coffee in each room. Refrigerators are available upon request at $3 per day. Most accommodations have shower stalls, so if you need to bathe a baby in a bathtub, be sure to request such a room in advance.

CONDOMINIUMS

For longer stays, the advantages to staying in a condominium or rental home are obvious: the comfort of having separate sleeping quarters, a place to cook, a washer and dryer, a living room, a private pool (in a rental home), and rates that are usually quite reasonable. Although most of these rentals do not include daily maid service, arrangements can be made separately. Some rentals are within country clubs that offer golf and tennis privileges.

If you call the following companies and state your family's needs, they'll try to locate the right accommodation. There's usually a minimum length of stay, especially for private homes. Rates vary so drastically between accommodations that they are not listed here.

FRONTIER VACATION VILLAS, 5652 Camp Walk, Long Beach, CA 90803. Tel. toll free 800/284-5527.

These condos will afford you a great location, two super pool areas, and spacious, comfortable lodgings at reasonable rates. The accommodations are located in the 102-unit Plaza Villas complex in downtown Palm Springs, within walking distance of the Convention Center and Palm Canyon Drive.

Each one- or two-bedroom unit has a dining room, large fully equipped kitchen, washer and dryer, color TV, direct-dial phones, air conditioning, and private patio. Sheets, towels, dishes, and cooking utensils are provided, but maid service isn't. The master bedroom has a king-size bed and private bathroom. The second bedroom comes with two twin-size beds, and there's a second full bathroom. The "super" two-bedroom unit is furnished with a hide-a-bed in the living room, making the unit large enough for six people. Cribs are available; no rollaways or highchairs.

Call for rates, and be sure to ask about summer, weekend, and holiday weekend packages.

THE RENTAL CONNECTION, 170 E. Palm Canyon Dr., Palm Springs, CA 92264. Tel. 619/320-7336, or toll free 800/468-3776, 800/232-3776 in California, 800/458-3776 in Canada.

The Rental Connection can provide you with condos or private homes. They'll set you up in one of more than 40 locations throughout Palm Springs. Call to find accommodations for your specific needs.

SUNRISE COMPANY RENTAL DIVISION, 76-300 Country Club Dr., Palm Desert, CA 92260. Tel. 619/345-5695.

Sunrise specializes in renting condominiums located within prestigious country clubs such as Rancho Las Palmas, The Lakes, Monterey, Palm Valley, and PGA West at La Quinta. All these clubs include tennis and golf facilities as well as pools and spas. Call for information.

WHERE TO EAT

MODERATE

GARCIA'S, 42540 Bob Hope Dr., Rancho Mirage. Tel. 619/340-5531.
   Cuisine: MEXICAN. **Reservations:** Accepted.
$ Prices: $3.25–$11.95. AE, CB, DC, MC, V.
   Open: Mon–Thurs 11am–10pm, Fri–Sat 11am–11pm; Sun brunch 10am–4pm, dinner 4–10pm. Summer hours vary on Sat–Sun.
   Children's Services: Children's menu, highchairs, booster seats.
Garcia's, at Bob Hope Drive and Calif. 111, is large, light, and airy, and serves up mild Mexican food. Adults have a full menu to choose from, which includes lots of combination plates, sampler plates, interesting house specials, and many à la carte selections, as well as some "Yankee Favorites."

Kids 12 and under can have a taco, burger, grilled cheese, mini-tacos and chimichangas, or a tortilla with melted cheese for $3 (including beverage). On the back of the menu, the kids can draw a self-portrait, which, if selected by the staff, will win them a free kids' meal. Ask about Garcia's Pablo Piñata Club. Adult portions can be split for the kids, and they'll warm baby bottles in the kitchen. Park in the lot.

LAS CASUELAS TERRAZA, 222 S. Palm Canyon Dr., Palm Springs. Tel. 619/325-2794.
   Cuisine: MEXICAN. **Reservations:** Advised.
$ Prices: Lunch $4.75–$8.75; dinner $6.50–$12. AE, MC, V.
   Open: Mon–Sat 11am–10pm, Sun 10am–10pm.
   Children's Services: Children's menu, booster seats, highchairs.
Las Casuelas, between Arenas Avenue and Ramon Road in downtown Palm Springs, is a landmark to most visitors and residents. Almost everyone has walked by its covered

outdoor, vine-covered terrace at one time or another—probably getting a spritz of the Micro Mist used to cool the patio in summer. The restaurant gets its charm and character from the small alcoves with intimate booths, high ceilings decorated with ceiling fans and piñatas, a large dining room, and of course, the terrace. The beautifully costumed servers are sensitive to children's needs, and bring crackers along with the highchairs.

At lunch or dinner, youngsters 10 and under can order a hamburger, taco, or burrito with rice for $4.25. Lunch features several varieties of quesadillas and combination plates, as well as house specials such as shrimp enchiladas, fajitas, and a burrito ranchero. There are hamburgers and salads as well. Several brunch offerings are included on the lunch menu, all featuring eggs. During dinner there are some additional choices: full dinners of steak, chicken, and machaca, all served Mexican style, which include soup, tortillas, and rice and beans. There are also *especiales del mar*—specialties of the sea—that are complete dinners. At either meal, you can treat yourselves and the kids to deep-fried ice cream, flan, or an empanada, this restaurant's version of apple pie.

Baby food and bottles can be warmed. Virgin drinks of any kind can be ordered from the full bar. Light, popular music is played each evening. Reservations are usually honored within 15 minutes (in season, it's a long wait without reservations). Park in the lot or on the street.

MARIE CALLENDER'S, 123 N. Palm Canyon Dr., Palm Springs. Tel. 619/323-7437.

Cuisine: AMERICAN. **Reservations:** Not accepted.

$ Prices: Main courses $6–$14. AE, MC, V.

Open: Sun–Thurs 8am–10pm, Fri–Sat 8am–11pm.

Children's Services: Children's menu, highchairs, booster seats.

If you're familiar with other Marie Callender's, you know they serve basic American food without frills. This turn-of-the-century–style location, next to the Fashion Plaza Mall in downtown Palm Springs, has great historic black-and-white photos of Palm Springs from the Historical Society lining its walls. In a separate dining room, named the Celebrity Room, management encourages local folks—and anyone who thinks he or she is a celebrity—to donate a picture of themselves to the collection on the wall.

Pot pies are the specialty, as is the meatloaf sandwich, old-fashioned chicken and noodles, and bread-basket stew. There are also full dinners of broiled pork chops; rainbow trout; roasted, fried, or barbecued chicken; hamburgers; and main-course-size salads. The salad-bar fixings are fresh, and the soup choices depend on the day you visit.

The children's menu (with crayons) is for kids under 12. Spaghetti, chicken fingers, ham or turkey sandwich, grilled cheese, a burger, or a trip to the salad bar can be ordered any time of day. Prices are $3.55 to $3.95. After 4pm, roast chicken, fried chicken, or barbecued ribs are added to the kids' selections, and they cost $4.75 and $4.95. Breakfasts are basic—eggs, pancakes, cereal, cinnamon French toast—and cost $2.50 to $3.50.

Save some room for dessert, because Marie Callender's is famous for its pies. The varieties start with the letter *A* and work their way to the letter *S*.

Servers will warm your baby's bottle or baby food in the kitchen, and will provide special children's drinks from the bar. Figure on a 20- to 30-minute wait on Friday and

Saturday evenings, and on Saturday and Sunday during the day. There's parking in the Fashion Plaza Mall lot.

Ask about the 38-minute movie about the history of Palm Springs shown in the upstairs theater. Admission is charged.

Two other nearby branches are in Cathedral City at 69830 Calif. 111 (tel. 619/328-0844) and in Palm Desert at the Palm Desert Town Center Mall (tel. 619/773-4743).

TGI FRIDAY'S, 72-620 El Paseo, Palm Desert. Tel. 619/568-2280.

Cuisine: INTERNATIONAL. **Reservations:** Not accepted.
$ Prices: Main courses $3.75–$13. AE, MC, V.
Open: Daily 11:30am–2am.
Children's Services: Children's menu, highchairs, boosters.

At TGI Friday's, at Calif. 111 and El Paseo, children are made to feel welcome. Distinctively dressed servers greet them with balloons and a coloring-book menu and crayons. If one of your brood is celebrating a birthday, the staff will sing special songs and provide a complimentary dessert and a bouquet of balloons.

There are Mexican, Asian, American, and Italian dishes to choose from—something for everyone. The kids' menu is quite complete. In addition to such standard favorites as hamburgers, hot dogs, and grilled cheese sandwiches, children can order pasta straws (long macaroni noodles with marinara sauce and a garlic roll), pizza bites (made of baguette bread and topped with tomato sauce, pepperoni, and mozzarella cheese), deep-fried shrimp, and a fresh-fruit and cheese platter. Most meals are served with strawberry applesauce and french fries or onion rings. Prices are $1.95 to $2.75. Brunch selections add cheesy eggs, a bacon-and-egg muffin, and stuffed French toast to the usual listings ($1.85 to $2.45).

Drinks and desserts are particularly appealing (to us, too!). No doubt you'll be as thrilled as we were when junior orders an REO Speedwagon—crumbled Oreo cookies and vanilla ice cream made into a creamy drink. We felt a little better when Andrew ordered a Banana Kong—a drink of strawberries, bananas, orange sherbet, and vanilla ice cream. Servers will split adult items for two kids and will warm baby food and bottles upon request.

Management says reservations are not necessary and that, except on rare occasions, you'll be seated immediately. Street parking.

BUDGET

LOUISE'S PANTRY, 124 S. Palm Canyon Dr., Palm Springs. Tel. 619/325-5124.

Cuisine: AMERICAN. **Reservations:** Not accepted.
$ Prices: Lunch about $4; dinner about $8. No credit cards.
Open: Daily 7am–9pm.
Children's Services: Sassy seats, boosters.

Louise's is known by everyone in Palm Springs. It's located right on the main strip, off Tahquitz Canyon, and you can't miss it because you'll see a line out the door and halfway down the block. Famous for its home-style cooking, Louise's serves chicken pot pie, fried chicken, roast beef, and baked ham, among other favorites. Lunch and dinner come with soup and salad. Pies, cakes, and sweet rolls are baked on the premises.

There's no children's menu, but servers will gladly split orders. The best time to come with restless kids is between 2:30 and 4pm. Call for summer hours. Street parking.

Another location is in Palm Desert at 44-491 Town Center Way, Suite A, across from the Palm Desert Mall (tel. 619/346-1315).

NICOLINO'S, 35325 Date Palm Dr., Cathedral City. Tel. 619/324-0411.
   Cuisine: ITALIAN. **Reservations:** Accepted only for groups of eight or more.
$ Prices: Dinner about $9. MC, V.
   Open: Mon–Thurs 11am–9pm, Fri–Sat 11am–10pm. **Closed:** July–Aug.
   Children's Services: Children's menu, highchairs, booster seats.

If your kids are tall enough to play the video games, and you're all in the mood for pizza in a super-casual setting, head for Nicolino's, on Date Palm Drive between Dinah Shore Drive and Gerald Ford Drive. If you eat in, the kids can play the video machines in the next room while you wait for your order in relative quiet. There are the usual Italian dishes for dinner, plus pizza, which comes in three sizes with several toppings. Lunch offerings include pasta, sandwiches, and Italian salads. If the kids want pasta, those under 12 can have spaghetti or ravioli with a meatball, garlic bread, and a beverage for $3.95. Bambino fried chicken is another possibility at $4.25. There is a $2.50 charge for splitting dishes. They'll warm baby bottles. Park in the restaurant lot.

NO FINER DINER, in the Lucky's Plaza Center, 35955 Date Palm Dr., Cathedral City. Tel. 619/324-7707.
   Cuisine: AMERICAN. **Reservations:** Not needed.
$ Prices: $3–$9. MC, V.
   Open: Daily; hours are seasonal, so call ahead.
   Children's Service: Boosters, Sassy seats.

Keep your eyes open for this cute little diner, tucked away in the shopping center at the corner of Date Palm Drive and Gerald Ford Drive. Once you find it, you'll be glad you did, especially for breakfast. There are many reasonably priced selections served by nice people. The requisite small jukeboxes line the counter, and soda-shop chairs sit atop red-and-white-checkered floors. Authentic 45s and LPs decorate the walls along with posters of James Dean and "American Bandstand" regulars.

Your kids might enjoy a real trip to the past—a jelly omelet for $3.50, for instance, or maybe just French toast or hotcakes. The homemade biscuits are "delish." They call their hot dogs "tube-burgers," and their chicken burgers "un-burgers." Everything else is readily identifiable. Sandwiches are simple—like fried egg, cold meatloaf, and bacon, lettuce, and tomato. Little Susie can get her peanut-butter and jelly sandwich with banana. Fried steak, roast turkey and stuffing, and deep-dish chicken pot pie are three of the "comfort food" blue-plate specials, which come with soup or salad, a potato, vegetable, and bread and butter. Fountain treats are plentiful: double-thick milkshakes, malts, egg creams, and more. Beer and wine are served.

Park in the shopping center lot.

SWENSON'S, in the Palm Desert Town Center Mall, 72840 Calif. 111, Palm Desert. Tel. 619/340-6229.
   Cuisine: AMERICAN. **Reservations:** Not accepted.
$ Prices: $1–$6.25. No credit cards.
   Open: Sun–Thurs 8am–10pm, Fri–Sat 8am–11pm. Call for summer hours.

Children's Services: Children's menu, boosters, highchairs.

Swenson's is especially fun for dessert or for a treat after skating or the movies. It also features children's meals throughout the day. The Kiddy Korner menu offers an egg or French toast with bacon or sausage ($1.50 to $1.75). At lunch, there's a $2.95 Cable Car Kid's Meal for kids 12 and under, which is served in a cable car—choice of hamburger, grilled cheese, peanut butter and jelly, or hot dog, all with fries and a ticket for a free single-dip ice cream cone. Sunday-night dinner might entice the whole family—pan-fried chicken, mashed potatoes and gravy, black-eyed peas, vegetable, soup and salad, biscuits, and apple cobbler or apple strudel ice cream. Adults pay $8; children 12 and under, $4.

INDEX

GENERAL INFORMATION

SIGHTS & ATTRACTIONS

LOS ANGELES & ENVIRONS

NOTE: An asterisk indicates an Author's Favorite

EXCURSION AREAS

ACCOMMODATIONS

LOS ANGELES

EXCURSION AREAS

KEY TO ABBREVIATIONS: *B* = Budget; *CG* = Campground; *Co* =Condominiums; *E* = Expensive; *M* = Moderately priced; *VE* = Very Expensive; *$* = Special Savings; * = an Author's Favorite

RESTAURANTS

LOS ANGELES

BY CUISINE

AMERICAN
The Burger That Ate LA, West Hollywood (*B*), 115
Carney's Express Limited, Hollywood (*B**), 115
The Daily Grill, West Hollywood (*E**), 140
Dupar's Restaurant, Hollywood (*I*), 143–4
Edie's Diner, Marina del Rey (*I$*), 137–8
Fatburger, West Hollywood (*B*), 115
Flakey Jake's, West Los Angeles (*I$*), 131–2
Hamburger Henry, Santa Monica (*I*), 139
Hard Rock Cafe, West Hollywood (*M*), 141–2
Islands, West Los Angeles (*I**), 132
Jeremiah P. Throckmorton Grille, Beverly Hills (*B*), 116
Johnny Rocket's, downtown (*B*), 116
Larry Parker's Beverly Hills Diner, Beverly Hills (*M*), 127
Lawry's The Prime Rib, Beverly Hills (*E*), 123
Ocean Park Omelette Parlor, Santa Monica (*I*), 139
The Original Pantry, downtown (*I*), 146
Pacific Dining Car, downtown (*E*), 145–6
Pantry Bake & Sandwich Shoppe, Downtown (*I*), 146
Philippe's, Downtown (*I$*), 146–7
Pink's Chili Dogs, Hollywood (*B**), 116, 118
RJ's, The Rib Joint, Beverly Hills (*E*), 123–4
Robin's, Pasadena (*M*), 148
Rose City Diner, Pasadena (*B**), 148
Rosie's Barbecue Grillery, West Los Angeles (*M*), 130–1
Souplantation, Hollywood (*I$*), 145–6
Souplantation, Pasadena (*I$*), 148
Tail O' the Pup, West Hollywood (*B*), 118
Victoria Station, Universal City (*I*), 149

BARBECUE
Tony Roma's A Place for Ribs, Universal City (*M**), 150

BISTRO
Pioneer Boulangerie, Santa Monica (*I*), 139–40

CHINESE
Fung Lum Restaurant, Universal City (*I*), 149–50
Genghis Cohen, Hollywood (*E*), 140–1
Hunan Taste, Mid-Wilshire district (*M*), 142–3
Ocean Seafood Restaurant, Downtown (*M*), 147

CONTINENTAL
Café Casino, Santa Monica (*I*), 136

Chez Melange, Redondo Beach (*E*), 132–3
Good Stuff, Hermosa Beach (*I**), 138–9

COOKIES, CANDIES & ICE CREAM
Baskin-Robbins, Hollywood, 118
Ben and Jerry's, Santa Monica, 118
Blue Chip Cookies, Century City, 118, 120
C.C. Brown's, Hollywood, 120
Double Rainbow, West Los Angeles, 120
Little John's English Toffee House, downtown, 120
Mrs. Field's Cookies, West Hollywood, 120
Penguins, Westwood Village, 120
Robin Rose, Venice, 120–1
Scoop 'M, downtown, 122
Sees, West Hollywood, 122
Stan's Donuts, Westwood, 122
Thrifty, Beverly Hills, 122

DELIS
Canter's, Hollywood (*I*), 143
Fromin's Restaurant, Santa Monica (*I*), 138
Junior's Deli, West Los Angeles (*M*), 129–30
Nate 'N Al Delicatessen, Beverly Hills (*M**), 128
Rose City Diner, Pasadena (*B**), 148

DINER FOOD
Ed Debevic's Short Orders/Deluxe, Beverly Hills (*I**), 128–9

FAST FOOD
The Burger That Ate L.A., West Hollywood (*B*), 115
Carneys Express Limited, Hollywood (*B**), 115
Fatburger, West Hollywood (*B*), 115
Jeremiah P. Throckmorton Grille, Beverly Hills (*B*), 116
Johnny Rocket's, West Hollywood (*B*), 116
La Salsa, West Los Angeles (*B*), 116
Pink's Chili Dogs, Hollywood (*B**), 116, 118
Tail O' the Pup, West Hollywood (*B*), 118
Tito's, West Los Angeles (*B*), 118

FRENCH
Cafe Casino, Santa Monica (*I*), 136

INTERNATIONAL
The Cheesecake Factory, Beverly Hills (*M*), 126
The Cheesecake Factory, Marina del Rey (*M*),

BY AREA

EXCURSION AREAS

NOW, SAVE MONEY ON ALL YOUR TRAVELS!
Join Frommer's™ Dollarwise® Travel Club

Saving money while traveling is never easy, which is why the **Dollarwise Travel Club** was formed 32 years ago to provide cost-cutting travel strategies, up-to-date travel information, and a sense of community for value-conscious travelers from all over the world.

In keeping with the money-saving concept, the annual membership fee is low—$20 for U.S. residents and $25 for residents of Canada, Mexico, and other countries—and is immediately exceeded by the value of your benefits, which include:

1. Any TWO books listed on the following pages;
2. Plus any ONE Frommer's City Guide;
3. A subscription to our quarterly newspaper, *The Dollarwise Traveler;*
4. A membership card that entitles you to purchase through the Club all Frommer's publications for 33% to 40% off their retail price.

The eight-page *Dollarwise Traveler* tells you about the latest developments in good-value travel worldwide and includes the following columns: **Hospitality Exchange** (for those offering and seeking hospitality in cities all over the world); and **Share-a-Trip** (for those looking for travel companions to share costs).

Aside from the various Frommer's Guides, the Gault Millau Guides, and the Real Guides you can also choose from our Special Editions, which include such titles as *Caribbean Hideaways* (the 100 most romantic places to stay in the Islands); and *Marilyn Wood's Wonderful Weekends* (a selection of the best mini-vacations within a 200-mile radius of New York City).

To join this Club, send the appropriate membership fee with your name and address to: Frommer's Dollarwise Travel Club, 15 Columbus Circle, New York, NY 10023. Remember to specify which single city guide and which two other guides you wish to receive in your initial package of member's benefits. Or tear out the pages, check off your choices, and send them to us with your membership fee.

FROMMER BOOKS
PRENTICE HALL TRAVEL   Date_____
15 COLUMBUS CIRCLE
NEW YORK, NY 10023

Friends: Please send me the books checked below.

FROMMER'S™ COMPREHENSIVE GUIDES
(Guides listing facilities from budget to deluxe, with emphasis on the medium-priced)

☐ Alaska	$14.95	☐ Italy	$19.00
☐ Australia	$14.95	☐ Japan & Hong Kong	$17.00
☐ Austria & Hungary	$14.95	☐ Morocco	$18.00
☐ Belgium, Holland & Luxembourg	$14.95	☐ Nepal	$18.00
☐ Bermuda & The Bahamas	$17.00	☐ New England	$17.00
☐ Brazil	$14.95	☐ New Mexico	$13.95
☐ California	$18.00	☐ New York State	$19.00
☐ Canada	$16.00	☐ Northwest	$16.95
☐ Caribbean	$17.00	☐ Puerta Vallarta (avail. Feb. '92)	$14.00
☐ Carolinas & Georgia	$17.00	☐ Portugal, Madeira & the Azores	$14.95
☐ Colorado (avail. Jan '92)	$14.00	☐ Scandinavia	$18.95
☐ Cruises (incl. Alaska, Carib, Mex, Hawaii, Panama, Canada & US)	$16.00	☐ Scotland (avail. Feb. '92)	$17.00
		☐ South Pacific	$20.00
☐ Delaware, Maryland, Pennsylvania & the New Jersey Shore (avail. Jan. '92)	$19.00	☐ Southeast Asia	$14.95
		☐ Switzerland & Liechtenstein	$19.00
☐ Egypt	$14.95	☐ Thailand	$20.00
☐ England	$17.00	☐ Virginia (avail. Feb. '92)	$14.00
☐ Florida	$17.00	☐ Virgin Islands	$13.00
☐ France	$15.95	☐ USA	$16.95
☐ Germany	$18.00		

0891492

FROMMER'S CITY GUIDES

(Pocket-size guides to sightseeing and tourist accommodations and facilities in all price ranges)

☐ Amsterdam/Holland	$8.95	☐ Minneapolis/St. Paul	$8.95
☐ Athens	$8.95	☐ Montréal/Québec City	$8.95
☐ Atlanta	$8.95	☐ New Orleans	$8.95
☐ Atlantic City/Cape May	$8.95	☐ New York	$12.00
☐ Bangkok	$12.00	☐ Orlando	$12.00
☐ Barcelona	$12.00	☐ Paris	$8.95
☐ Belgium	$7.95	☐ Philadelphia	$11.00
☐ Berlin	$10.00	☐ Rio	$8.95
☐ Boston	$8.95	☐ Rome	$8.95
☐ Cancún/Cozumel/Yucatán	$8.95	☐ Salt Lake City	$8.95
☐ Chicago	$9.95	☐ San Diego	$8.95
☐ Denver/Boulder/Colorado Springs	$8.95	☐ San Francisco	$12.00
☐ Dublin/Ireland	$10.00	☐ Santa Fe/Taos/Albuquerque	$10.95
☐ Hawaii	$12.00	☐ Seattle/Portland	$12.00
☐ Hong Kong	$7.95	☐ St. Louis/Kansas City	$9.95
☐ Las Vegas	$8.95	☐ Sydney	$8.95
☐ Lisbon/Madrid/Costa del Sol	$8.95	☐ Tampa/St. Petersburg	$8.95
☐ London	$12.00	☐ Tokyo	$8.95
☐ Los Angeles	$8.95	☐ Toronto	$8.95
☐ Mexico City/Acapulco	$8.95	☐ Vancouver/Victoria	$7.95
☐ Miami	$8.95	☐ Washington, D.C.	$12.00

FROMMER'S $-A-DAY® GUIDES

(Guides to low-cost tourist accommodations and facilities)

☐ Australia on $40 a Day	$13.95	☐ Israel on $40 a Day	$13.95
☐ Costa Rica, Guatemala & Belize on $35 a Day	$15.95	☐ Mexico on $45 a Day	$18.00
		☐ New York on $65 a Day	$15.00
☐ Eastern Europe on $25 a Day	$16.95	☐ New Zealand on $45 a Day	$16.00
☐ England on $50 a Day	$17.00	☐ Scotland & Wales on $40 a Day	$18.00
☐ Europe on $45 a Day	$19.00	☐ South America on $40 a Day	$15.95
☐ Greece on $35 a Day	$14.95	☐ Spain on $50 a Day	$15.95
☐ Hawaii on $70 a Day	$18.00	☐ Turkey on $40 a Day	$22.00
☐ India on $40 a Day	$20.00	☐ Washington, D.C., on $45 a Day	$17.00
☐ Ireland on $40 a Day	$17.00		

FROMMER'S CITY $-A-DAY GUIDES

☐ Berlin on $40 a Day	$12.00	☐ Madrid on $50 a Day (avail. Jan '92)	$13.00
☐ Copenhagen on $50 a Day	$12.00	☐ Paris on $45 a Day	$12.00
☐ London on $45 a Day	$12.00	☐ Stockholm on $50 a Day (avail. Dec. '91)	$13.00

FROMMER'S FAMILY GUIDES

☐ California with Kids	$16.95	☐ San Francisco with Kids	$17.00
☐ Los Angeles with Kids	$17.00	☐ Washington, D.C., with Kids (avail. Jan '92)	$17.00
☐ New York City with Kids (avail. Jan '92)	$18.00		

SPECIAL EDITIONS

☐ Beat the High Cost of Travel	$6.95	☐ Marilyn Wood's Wonderful Weekends (CT, DE, MA, NH, NJ, NY, PA, RI, VT)	$11.95
☐ Bed & Breakfast—N. America	$14.95		
☐ Caribbean Hideaways	$16.00	☐ Motorist's Phrase Book (Fr/Ger/Sp)	$4.95
☐ Honeymoon Destinations (US, Mex & Carib)	$14.95	☐ The New World of Travel (annual by Arthur Frommer for savvy travelers)	$16.95